Patterns in Forcible Rape

Patterns in Forcible Rape

Menachem Amir

The University of Chicago Press · Chicago and London

International Standard Book Number: 0–226–01734–6
Library of Congress Catalog Card Number: 79–140222
The University of Chicago Press, Chicago 60637
The University of Chicago Press, Ltd., London
© 1971 by The University of Chicago
All rights reserved
Published 1971
Printed in the United States of America

Contents

v

Foreword

The crime of rape reaches back into man's history as far as records take us. It is also virtually a universally proscribed act. There have been many case histories reported in the psychiatric and psychoanalytic literature. There is an abundance of anecdotal records about rape episodes, and a good bit of our fiction is laced with events leading up to and following rape.

Statistically, among all crimes, or even among all major crimes, rape is a relatively infrequent phenomenon. Only about one percent of the FBI's annual number of serious crimes are classified as forcible rape. But what is viewed as important by a society is not judged only by frequency of occurrence. The total size of the United States population, age and sex distribution, and similar sociological variables are significant for analyzing probabilities of who may commit rape and who may become victims. But there are reflected emotions of fear and a collective conscience about deterrence, retribution, and prevention in the FBI's recounting each year for us that one rape occurs in this country every seventeen minutes.

Forcible rape is judged by many as the most serious crime, after murder. Eleven states, all in the South, still retain the death penalty as the maximum penalty for rape. And perhaps the fear of being raped has a greater disparity with the reality of the probability of victimization than any other offense. Strangers on the street are raped now and then, after all, and the privacy of the home is occasionally invaded by an assaulter. The crime is not common, but the fear is genuine and based on the gravity attributed to its consequences.

A sexual assault on a victim who gives no consent, on a victim who lacks the capacity to give consent—a child or a mentally deficient—is perceived as an impediment to personal freedom, as an invasion on personal choice. The exhibitionist invades our freedom by imposing an unwanted object on our range of vision. The voyeur visually invades our privacy of conduct without consent, the pedophile invades the child's process of choice before he acquires capacity for rebuttal. The rapist engages in a much more blatant and sharp assault on our ability to reject, on our freedom of action.

Sociological study of rape has been rare and incomplete. The research and analysis in this volume by Menachem Amir represent the most thorough, rigorous, and detailed study in the literature. The author has dissected the major dimensions of the drama—the act, the offender, the victim—and has presented cross-tabulations that have previously not been available. He has subjected his statistics to standard tests of significance and has provided clarity and chiaroscuro that are new. But beyond the array of the basic data he has clothed his hard-earned statistics with an analytical perspective that reveals intellectual capacity and erudition. His bibliography alone, assiduously collected and digested, makes this work a valuable one.

Amir's study of rape is part of the increasing interest in what has become known as the phenomenological approach to crime. Among other things, this approach involves taking a specific criminal activity, examining descriptively as many parameters as possible about the character of the legal deviation, the attributes of the offender, the victim and their interrelationships, and the adjudication of the defendant. A phenomenological approach places an analytical microscope on the crime and reveals interactional ingredients. Base-line statistics are used, but much of the methodology is dependent on an intense internal analysis of the phenomenon. The sociology of the drama is only one part of the inherent multifaceted features of this approach, but it is surely the necessary beginning. Age, sex, and race do not alone make for the phenomenology nor the sociology of rape. The dimensions needed are much deeper and broader. But most importantly, perhaps, are the interlinkages, the patterns, regularities, and uniformities discovered in the analysis.

This study relies upon official statistics for most of its source material. Unreported offenses, distorted descriptions found in some police and court records, and doubts about the validity of the charges are, of course, issues that particularly affect the crime of rape. Yet, Amir is keenly sensitive to these problems and handles them with scholarly care that adds confidence to the conclusions.

No important study of rape in the future can ignore this work. For the analysis here offers sociological researchers, lawyers, psychologists, and psychiatrists a model and firmly based study upon which further sociological insights and perspectives in criminal law and administration can surely find evidence for improving knowledge and justice.

It is a special pleasure for me to see this study published. As one of Amir's professors during his doctoral studies, I was early impressed with his prodigious energy, maturing erudition, and sensitivity to the significant. I am no stranger to his work and am pleased that it will now be available to the many students of criminology here and abroad who have made inquiries about it and have had glimpses of it in less elegant form.

MARVIN E. WOLFGANG

Acknowledgments

Professor Marvin E. Wolfgang encouraged me to undertake this study, constantly lending his suggestions and insight until its completion.

Professor Thorsten Sellin, with his encouragement and suggestions, proved to be invaluable to me. My debt to Professors Wolfgang and Sellin is self-evident.

Acknowledgment must also be made for valuable advice and criticism offered by friends and colleagues too many to enumerate.

The present work could not have been started without the cooperation of the Philadelphia police in allowing me access to files and to witness and participate in investigations of rape cases.

My thanks also to Mrs. Maya Landau, who so patiently supervised the typing and the editing of this work.

Finally, this study is dedicated to my wife Delila and to my daughter Orly, who shared the joys and sadness of developing and writing this work.

M. A.

I

Introduction

1

The Nature of the Study

Purpose

To date, criminology has been concerned mainly with the perpetrators of crimes, rather than with the phenomena of the crime itself—that is, the characteristics of the crime and those human and circumstantial aspects of it which precede hypotheses and theory. It is with the "subject matter" of crime rather than with the psychology of the criminal that this work is concerned.[1] The problems involved here are, first, to find those situations which increase the likelihood that a specific type of crime will be committed and those situations in which a certain crime will be sanctioned, tolerated, or encouraged. In case of rape one must consider the existing notions about male and female sex roles when they encounter a situation charged with sexuality. Another element is the opportune situation and its definition by the offenders who may already have antisocial and sexual-aggressive attitudes which make the act possible. Such a situational approach allows gaining insight into the problem of differential behavior of predisposed persons or of those who are pulled in to committing the crime by the circumstances of the situation.

The object of any science is not only to formulate and verify theories of causation but also to construct an order among observable phenomenon. Also, explanations can be presented in other than causal form—for example, in terms of probability statement, functional relationship, and development notes which can be formulated into propositions that do not depend upon causal explanation. Thus, the second phase will be to turn

1. For a discussion of this subject matter of criminology see: Bianchi; Vold.

to the systematic study of various behavior patterns labeled as "criminal" and "delinquent."[2] This, in turn, involves forsaking attempts to create general theories to account for all criminal behavior, discarding a global conception of crime in favor of studies of specific patterns of criminal behavior and the nature of particular types of offenses, that is, the context in which the crime is committed and those involved in it. Such attempts have been made for different types of nonsexual offenses.[3] Some sexual offenses have been analyzed, but the emphasis was on the offenders rather than on their offenses.[4] On the other hand, a systematic study of forcible rape,[5] except for one short report, does not exist.[6] The existing data on the crime of rape is about the psychology of the rapist, and some of his social characteristics. There are some references to certain attributes of the offense, but it is usually dealt with as part of a survey which includes other sex offenses.

The next step is to relate distinguishing patterns of offenses with the backgrounds of the parties involved. Usually such background includes social characteristics and criminal career.

Referring to sexual offenses, Bowman claims that "no research has so far demonstrated a functional connection between specific patterns of family interpersonal relations and specific patterns of deviant sexual activities."[7] Nor have community and class factors influencing sexual offenses been adequately studied, although McCord and McCord made a first move in this direction by investigating patterns of family relationship and specific sexual deviations.

Such studies of specific patterns of criminal behavior still need further development. In the existing specific studies, we are provided with information on types of offenders and the patterns of crime they have committed. However, one must pursue the explicit, logical relation between these types of offenders, as well as between the different patterns of crimes, which will lead to a "comprehensive and formal typology from separate but specific studies."[8]

2. On the problem of labeling see: Becker, *The Other Side* and *Outsiders;* Clinard and Quinney.

3. See: Clinard and Wade; Cressey, *Other People's Money;* Lindsmith and Dunham; Redl and Wineman; Robin; E. H. Sutherland, *The Professional Thief* and *White Collar Crime;* Wolfgang, *Patterns in Criminal Homicide.*

4. For instance: *California Sexual Deviation Research;* Ellis and Brancale. Other surveys and reports will be discussed throughout the study, and a complete bibliography is given at the end of this study. For an approach similar to this study's see Mohr, "Rape and Attempted Rape" and Mohr, et al., which appeared after the completion of this work.

5. Hereafter forcible rape will be referred to simply as rape.

6. Svalastoga.

7. *California Sexual Deviation Research,* pp. 148–49.

8. Gibbons and Garrity, p. 52.

Observations which have been made on rape fall into two broad categories: clinically oriented case studies and criminologically oriented group studies.[9]

Most observations in the first category have been drawn from case-psychiatric practice and those in the second from studies of offenders from the court or from correctional institutions. These observations do not, however, have the advantage of being based on representative samples adequate in size. It is obvious, therefore, that the various assumptions about rape, its occurrence, distribution, and causes have been predominately determined by the source of the data and by the theoretical orientation of the investigators. The data is centered mainly on the offenders rather than on the nature and circumstances of their crime.[10] The primary phenomenological factors determining the concept of rape are the offenders, the victim, and the nature of the act. The personal and social characteristics of victim and offender become important since the interaction between them, the situation under which the rape occurred, may determine the nature of the act.

In this study, the main concern will be with information on social characteristics of the individuals involved in the offense and with variables surrounding the commission of the crimes. It will be observed whether there is some significant conjuncture of events prior to or during the crime. Thus, the time, place, and circumstances of the crime are of great importance, as well as the characteristics of both offenders and victims and the relationships between them.

It should be clear that a phenomenological study such as this precludes a prior hypothesis. The existence, however, of accumulated empirical data in other works allows the formulation of some proposition about the relationships among variables. The data for this study, which comes from information in police files, was approached through several rough propositions by which it was hoped that some meaningful relationships between variables might be clear. At the same time, some hypotheses to be tested were drawn up while the study proceeded, and as a result other hypotheses were provided for further research. Finally, the interpreta-

9. There are also hosts of journalistic "scare writings" which appear in waves, see: Abrahamsen, "Comment"; Bent; Cutton; F. J. Davis; A. Deutsch; "Editorial: Sex Offenses and the Public"; Harris; Hoover; Liebowitz; Schapper; Shoenfield; M. Stern; Witteles.

10. See: Abrahamsen, "102 Sex Offenders"; Apfelberg, et al.; Baker; Brancale, et al.; Collins, et al.; *The Dangerous Sex Offender;* Dunham; *Illinois Commission Report on Sex Offenders;* Krinsky and Michaele; Kupperstein; Leppman; Magnus, "Sexual Deviation Research in California"; *Massachusetts Report;* "Michigan Commission"; Mohr, "Follow-up Survey" and "Short Survey"; *New Hampshire Report; Pennsylvania Sex Offenders; Report of the Mayor's Committee; Report on the Study;* Rofer; Tappan, *The Habitual Sex Offender.*

tions given were aimed toward formulating a theory of rape to be applied and tested by further studies.

Scope of the Study

This inquiry was initiated in 1961, and its purpose was to analyze forcible rape occurring in the Philadelphia area under the jurisdiction and power of the Philadelphia police department. Data was collected on all cases of forcible rape listed by the police in the city for two years, 1958 and 1960. Thus, any generalizations to be made are limited to urban areas and to the time span of this research.

In this study several chapters have been devoted to examining the theories advanced to explain rape. Since these theories reflected partisan attitudes, mainly in the psychological discipline, they suggest a narrow individualistic attitude which can be but little affected by changes in the social structure. No attempt was made in this study, however, to assess the personalities of offenders and victims (in the light of clinical reports), for it is a mistake to relegate the discussion of rapists and their victims exclusively to the domain of psychology or psychopathology.

There is still no historical analysis of rape. One can imagine a historical survey of rape starting with the Bible, going through the Greek and Roman periods into the "dark Middle Ages," and arriving at modern times. Stories of notorious rapes of nobly born women would probably be included in this survey, along with life histories of the offenders and the situation of the offenses. Like books on the history of prostitution,[11] such a book on "the history of rape" would discuss legal and punitive measures. It is easy to see that such a book would probably be more of a cross-cultural survey than a historical study.

There are some accounts of the history of sexual research which deal with shifting ideas about sex deviations.[12] The shift is usually from a moralistic to a medical and clinical attitude. A methodological shift can be seen from isolated case studies in psychiatric periodicals and textbooks through some statistical surveys of sex offenders and sex offenses, to the beginning of specific studies of certain types of sex deviation. The present work will be neither a historical analysis nor a compilation of previous research accounts.

The phenomenon of rape has had a long and colorful history. Thus, some interesting insights into the rape situation can be gained by reading plays, novels, and short stories. This is so because such fictional sources involve force, humiliation, and degradation, and can be conceived as the utmost dramatization of the conflict and fate of the personalities involved.

11. See Sanger, for example.

12. Chall; Ehrmann, "Some Knowns and Unknowns"; Karpman, *The Sexual Offender.*

However, most of the fictional descriptions of individual cases of rape concentrate upon the dynamics of the event and the physical characteristics of the dramatis persona rather than upon cultural and social circumstances and their possible relationship to the offense. For the offender, rape is often seen as a tribute to his aggressiveness and virility, and to an omnipresent latent impulse suddenly erupting, such as in Levin's description of Leopold's act in *Compulsion*. While in Tennessee Williams', *A Streetcar Named Desire* the homosexual perspective of rape is advanced, both he, as well as Theodore Dreiser in *The Hand of the Potter* describe rape situations in which the brutish and animal nature of the human male breaks through due to the confusion which exists between hatred and destructiveness on the one hand and sexual desire on the other. William Faulkner's novel *Sanctuary* describes an unusual type of rape by an impotent criminal. In the writings of the Marquis de Sade we find a profound misogyny, and hate and destructiveness mistaken for sexual virility. In Mario Praz's work *The Romantic Agony,* a scholarly study of perverse eroticism in literature, there is a particular emphasis on sadistic and destructive feelings thought to be dominant in rape.

As for the victim, from Chaucer's "Miller's Tale," Shakespeare's "Rape of Lucrece," Balzac's *Droll Stories,* and Cervantes *Don Quixote* we can perceive the old and popular belief that it is impossible to rape a woman against her will (an opinion held also by the late Sutherland).[13] While rape may still seem to be regarded as a "fate worse than death," the fictional portrait is often of an experience not devoid of certain satisfaction, such as in John Updike's *Couples* and in William Murray's *The Americano.*

It is with regard to group rape that a more sympathetic view of the victim appears in contemporary American fiction. Such compassion is aroused toward the heroines in Hemingway's *For Whom the Bell Tolls,* or to the victim of gang rape in Nelson Algren's *Never Come Morning* and Hubert Selby's *Last Exit from Brooklyn.* In Dale Wasserman's play *Man of La Mancha* and Bunnel's movie *La Viridiana* we can see the ultimate debasement of the victim who set herself to help the needy, the poor but rough.

Other novels and plays can be cited which stress other elements in the crime of rape. In Harper Lee's *To Kill a Mockingbird* an interracial rape aroused the latent antagonistic division of the Southern town, while in Lang's *Town without Pity* we see one example of community reaction to the victim due to false accusation and the victim's social position. In Robert Traver's *Anatomy of a Murder* an alleged rape provides an op-

13. E. H. Sutherland, "The Sexual Psychopath Laws."

portunity for depiction of courtroom strategies. But enough has been said to demonstrate the value to the sociologist of literary artifacts. It would be valuable one day to have a study of "Rape in American Fiction" like that of H. Davis on homicide.

A study of the causes of rape is outside the scope of this work, because no psychological data is available about the offenders studied. However, a summary is given of the theories advanced to explain aggressive sex behavior, and this summary includes some comments on rape. From these theories were extracted those concepts which might be integrated into a sociological theory. In terms of causation, the analysis provided in this study shows only statistical averages of the situations and social characteristics of the parties involved in the rape situation. Degrees of association can be shown between the statistical results, but these can serve only as useful clues for new hypotheses and generalizations about causation, as well as about the nature of the crime itself.

The study is called "Patterns in Forcible Rape" in order to distinguish this type of rape from incest and statutory rape. The cases analyzed are only those crimes which were defined by the Philadelphia police as forcible rape and which appear in the Uniform Crime Report Code under number 211. There are, in fact, several types of peripheral problems even in the study of forced rape which can here be only briefly mentioned: The crime of rape has been dealt with extensively in the law books and law journals. They deal mostly with problems of consent, reliability of the victims' stories and corroborative evidence. In the present work, these problems will be dealt with only slightly. Once the police decide upon a case as "founded" and worthy of further legal steps, the case is brought before the grand jury or the court. The status of the case can be changed in the court when the offender pleads guilty, if a bargain on a lesser crime is made, or if a victim refuses to prosecute. These legal processes bring up interesting problems, but they will be discussed only when relevant to the main topic. There are problems, too, in the court's disposition of the case. The "mortality" rate of criminal cases from arrest to sentence is a topic in the analysis of the crime. But, again, these problems are for the most part beyond the scope of this work. Some special laws were established to deal with sex offenders. In the 1950s, a rash of "sex psychopath laws" swept the country. Pennsylvania adopted a special statute named the Barr-Walker Law. Problems dealing with the application of these laws, however, will not be considered. It is also outside the range of the present study to deal with diagnosis and treatment of rapists. However, we shall comment on this problem in the light of the available literature, in order to offer a full picture of all the aspects involved in the investigation of forced rape.

Sources and Use of Data

Throughout this study the analysis of forcible rape is made only on the basis of police data. All files containing complaints of rape were analyzed regardless of who made the actual complaint and regardless of whether or not the offender was apprehended or was known to the victim and the police. To be sure of obtaining other information which might not be in the file, information about offenders' and victims' criminal records was collected from FBI files at police headquarters.

Because it was extremely difficult to locate and gain access to court files, and because only some of the offenders appeared before the court, it was decided to rely on the information in police records. Furthermore, since our concern is to analyze the offense (in terms of the largest group of offenders possible), "rape known to the police" provides the most valid and comprehensive term to describe the phenomenon studied here, and is the best index to the volume and the nature of this offense. Other reasons, too, influenced the decision to use police data rather than court and prison statistics. First, the mortality of cases in each step in the law enforcement process means that only a selective group of cases are to be found in court records.[14] Then, too, many cases still remain on the police level and are classified as undecided because the victim or her guardian refused to prosecute the offender; the offender has not been detected, or has not yet been apprehended; the victim is unable to furnish enough information to charge and arrest the offender; the police need more evidence to corroborate the victim's story in order to issue a warrant for arrest; or because the offender was permitted to plead guilty to a lesser crime. Thus, unsolved rape or unclear cases would not normally be included in court statistics.

Data from courts provides a larger sample, dealing with all those alleged offenders whose behavior is deemed to warrant adjudication. The predominant view in the nineteenth century regarded court statistics as the most meaningful measure of crime and criminality. But it must be remembered that the arrest-conviction ratio does not remain constant. As Bonger stated, "The amount of crime actually punished . . . may not be [an] infixed or unveering ratio to the amount of crime committed."[15] Changes in conviction statistics may reflect the cultural norms held by the judges or the juries, the public opinion at that period about the specific crime,[16] or the differential administration of justice toward cer-

14. Grunhüt, "Statistics in Criminology"; Sellin, "The Basis of Crime Index"; Van Vechten.

15. *Race and Crime,* p. 34.

16. Shiver.

tain groups.[17] Also, social class, as well as race, influence the ability of the plaintiff to be adequately represented and defended.[18] Thus despite the criminologists' preference for court statistics there were early exponents of police statistics who felt that in order to render the statistics of crime of real value a register was needed of the actual offenses committed, without reference to subsequent detection and conviction.

Data supplied from prisons and other penal institutions reflect only the number of persons who have been completely processed by the criminal law and its machinery and hence indicate only that amount of criminal behavior which is, in fact, detected and punished. However, only in particular cases are rapists sent to prison. The age and race differences, the nature of the offense, and the offender's prior criminal record, partially determine whether the offender will be sent to prison. There are differences of sentencing practices between juvenile courts and adult courts, as well as between individual judges in those courts.

The outcome of all this is that prisoners are not representative of the average arrested person,[19] and one may suspect that this is especially the case with the sex offender.[20]

Because of these factors, all cases of rape known to the police were used for analysis. There are certain advantages in using this source: Police files came closer than any other available records to reflecting the actual number of rapes committed in the area under police jurisdiction; and it was found that the police play a relatively minor role in the detection and arrest of alleged sex offenders.[21] Nevertheless, by using reported rapes, we could come still closer to the actual number of rapes, including unsolved cases, and avoid the disadvantages inherent in other types of statistics.

In spite of these advantages of police statistics, one should not overlook their pitfalls. Dealing with the records of only one community limits somewhat the conclusions which are reached in this study.

The victim or her guardian may refuse to prosecute after a complaint has been made, or the victim, because of her age or her mental and emotional condition, may be unable to identify her assailant. She may also change her story, and in that case the police cannot be sure whether she is making a false accusation or whether she is afraid or has other motives

17. Sellin, "The Negro Criminal"; J. D. Turner.

18. G. B. Johnson.

19. Bates.

20. For the disadvantages of prison statistics as applied to research in sexual crimes see Ellis and Brancale, pp. 3–6.

21. Laughlin.

for not telling the truth.[22] The case, therefore, although it cannot be dismissed by the police, is designated as unclear.

Many rape cases are unsolved, and their status is unclear because the offender is still at large, or there is not sufficient evidence for issuing an arrest warrant against him. Also, he may refuse, under the order of his lawyer, to talk to the police investigator, or he may change his story or may lie. Then, too, the race, the age, the nature of the offense, and the previous criminal record of the offender may influence police decisions, especially when there is not sufficient evidence against him. Other factors in the situation may thwart the effort to obtain clear-cut cases, such as when witnesses refuse to supply information or when they will not tell the truth.

Also on the police level, those who investigate rape complaints and those who make decisions have, at most, a scant legal training. They also carry with them biases toward certain kinds of sexual behavior, especially when there are race and age differences between the offender and his victim.

It is widely assumed that the police employ different standards when dealing with certain groups of offenders. The sex offender may be subjected to more pressure to "confess" the crime,[23] or Negroes may be arrested with less evidence than is required to arrest white offenders.[24] The police may react indifferently and dismiss a case when there is a slight suspicion of false accusation made by a Negro victim, or as has been shown, when the victim is suspected of being promiscuous.[25] These factors and others were found not only to influence the number of rapes recorded in police statistics, but also to reflect the consistency and reliability of data in the files.[26]

Notwithstanding these problems, the present work is based on police statistics, because I believe that they introduce less bias than court or prison statistics, and because the class of "crimes known to the police" is the highest number of crimes reported.

The study covers the period from 1 January 1958 to 31 December 1958 and from 1 January 1960 to 31 December 1960. Several considerations led to the choosing of these two years:

1. In this period no "wave" of sex crime was apparent in the statistics nor was one "reported" by the newspapers in Philadelphia; therefore,

22. Cushing.
23. Westley.
24. Candy; Kephart.
25. Curran and Schilder.
26. *Crime Reports in Police Management.*

it was less likely that the number of rape complaints or charges of rape was influenced by pressure from the district attorney's office or from the public.

2. This period was sufficiently removed from special political and economic events. It was a few years after the Korean War and the economy was not in any major cycle which might be blamed for the existing crime rates.

3. The period was close to the 1960 census and the census data could be used as a basis for calculating rates and ratios.

4. The *Uniform Crime Reports* of 1958 made some changes in recording offenses, including the separation of forcible rape from statutory rape.

5. Another important factor was that of convenience. The records for 1958 and 1960 were still concentrated in the morals squad department, where the majority of the cases were investigated.

6. The period was divided into two separate years for the purpose of avoiding the analysis of a yearly cycle of rape. If the period of 1958–60 had been taken, any analysis would have involved either the full cycle or part of its phases. The cycle of certain crimes and their correlates is an interesting subject in itself, and it has already received attention as part of the whole phenomenon of crime and has been correlated with, for example, economic[27] and seasonal[28] cycles. An analysis of a seasonal pattern (but not of a yearly cycle) will be included in the present work according to the data collected.

7. Because the number of rape cases in 1959 was not at great variance from those in 1958 and 1960 (348 vs. 329 and 298, respectively), it was seen that the years of 1958 and 1960 are representative enough for valid analysis.

When a complaint of rape is made or a policeman is called to the scene of the crime, the investigation of the case, as in any sexual offense, is conducted by the morals squad in the Philadelphia police department. Sometimes, when the morals squad cannot conduct the investigation, it is done by the detective bureau of the area where the offense took place. In the process of collecting the data, it was found that there are differences between the morals squad and the detective units in designating the cases. It was also found that the records of the morals squad were better organized and had more data, which perhaps reflects the fact that the squad is more experienced in handling such cases.

For this study, information from each file was transcribed on a special analysis form which provides headings for the data used in the analysis.

27. Sellin, *Research Memorandum.* See also Henry and Short, chap. 3.
28. Falk, "Influence of the Seasons"; Kaplan, pp. 160–92.

Each item was categorized before coding and recording the date on IBM punch cards.

Propositions and Relationships Sought

It was formerly stated that the nature of this study precludes a priori hypotheses to be tested and confirmed. Some empirical data exists, however, which allows us to formulate some propositions about the relationships among certain variables. The main propositions and the references on which they are based can be divided into three main groups: those concerning the parties involved (and here we shall distinguish between white and nonwhite offenders and victims, as well as between juveniles and adults); those propositions concerning the nature of the act; those concerning conditions of the situation before the crime was committed and which might be considered as predisposing the rape.

PARTIES INVOLVED. On the basis of surveys made of arrested, convicted, or imprisoned rapists,[29] and on the basis of the knowledge of the nature of juvenile delinquency,[30] the offenders in this study may be expected to be concentrated around the ages of 20–24. The age of victims will not differ much from the age of the offender. However, under certain conditions, age differences between the victim and the offender will be markedly great.

RACE. In the present study, whites and Puerto Ricans are combined for comparison to the Negro group. The reason for this step is the negligible number of Puerto Rican offenders (10) as well as victims (8) in our cases. The Negro group dominates the sample of offenders and victims, especially in rapes committed by juveniles and adults. It was shown that the crime rate of Negroes exceeds that of whites for crimes against the person, such as assault and homicide.[31] It was also shown that in crimes of violence, the offender and the victim are usually of the same race and social class and reside near each other. Thus, it is as likely that Negroes will rape Negroes as it is that Negroes will kill Negroes.[32] Various surveys do not prove that the Negro is more likely to commit rape than the white, and as Guttmacher stated, "the Negro criminal is not primarily a sexual criminal."[33] However, in light of the fact that rape is also a crime involv-

29. See n. 10 above.

30. Cohen and Short, Jr., "Juvenile Delinquency."

31. Sutherland and Cressey, *Criminology* (5th ed.), pp. 138–51.

32. DePorte and Parkhurst; Wolfgang, *Patterns in Criminal Homicide,* p. 31.

33. *Sex Offenses,* pp. 59–60.

ing violence, we make this assumption of overrepresentation of Negroes in the present study.

In this work, it is assumed that, especially in matters of social class and social status, the race factor should be analyzed, for it is consistently found that rapists and their victims come mainly from lower classes or low status groups. The fact that violence in general is predominantly a lower class phenomenon justifies this assumption. It is further necessary to assume that there is symbolic relationship between sexual violence and status, from which the next step is a consideration of differential sexual striving and sexual frustrations among different social strata or status groups. Also, it involves analyzing different social and personal controls of aggressive and sexual behavior in these groups, as well as different norms of relationships between the sexes.

MODUS OPERANDI. This aspect involves the nature of the offense, that is, the way in which it was carried out, the behavior of the partners in the rape situation, the condition of the victim prior to, during, and after the assault.

It would be expected that there are more group rapes committed by juveniles on victims who are close to their own age. In cases where there are marked age differences between the offender and victim, the rape will occur either when the victim is helpless due to her intoxicated condition or when she fails to resist the commission of robbery, or the initial advances of her assailant. The victim of a rape is not as a rule treated brutally. The breaking of her "will" and the preparatory actions "without her consent" assume more the nature of duress than of force. Force may be used, however, in carrying the victim to a "safe place." Sexual humiliation and brutality are common when rape is inflicted on an intoxicated victim, or on a victim of group rape. When the rape is interracial the amount and nature of brutality and force used will be the same as in intraracial rape.

TEMPORAL PATTERNS. Rape is usually thought to be a summer, weekend, and nocturnal type of crime. During these times, social interaction is more intensive, partly because of the increased use of alcohol.

SPATIAL PATTERNS. Very few studies touch upon the site of the rape,[34] fewer still provide data about the actual place where the rape occurred.[35] Rapes are expected to be committed more in open spaces, away from police control and social observation. However, this will vary

34. Radzinowicz, *Sexual Offenses,* pp. 100–101; Svalastoga, p. 50.
35. *Report of the Mayor's Committee.*

according to season, type of rape, and special circumstances, such as presence of alcohol, offender-victim relationship, and so on.

It has already been argued that a distinction should be made between *areas of crime commission* and *areas of delinquent residence.*[36] This distinction may help to determine prior relationships between the people involved, as well as other practical and theoretical considerations. In the present work, a distinction is made between the two types of areas in hope of finding a positive correlation between the residence of offender and victim and the area in which the crime was committed. On the other hand, some exception might occur—for instance, when the crime is committed by adult offenders and a vehicle was involved to transfer the partners to and from the crime scene. This brings us to see another concept in the ecology of criminal behavior—that of the movement of the scene of the crime. This variable is often applicable in cases of rape committed by a group of adults on an intoxicated victim or by juveniles on young or retarded victims. It will occur also in cases when the victim is subjected to perverse sexual practices by her assailants.

ALCOHOL. Although it is hard to determine the role of alcohol in the rape situation, it can be assumed that when alcohol is present it will be more often in adult victims, and the chances are that they will be raped by offenders much younger than they are. It is assumed that the intoxicated victim will be more subjected to sexual humiliation and physical injuries and that there is a greater chance that she will be the victim of group rape.

PREVIOUS RECORD. The relationship between the offender's previous record and the act of rape is a crucial but complicated problem. Criminal record for what? Arrest or conviction? What type of criminal record? Offenses against property, against the person, or disorderly conduct due to alcohol? Is there any pattern in the criminal record of the rapist? Prior sexual crimes? Does the offender progress from minor sexual and non-sexual crimes to serious crimes, which involve violence? All these questions have been partially scrutinized in other studies but a clear and consistent result of the various studies does not emerge.

On the basis of previous data, few offenders are likely to be found with records of sexual crimes and still fewer with previous records of rape. A pattern of previous crimes may be difficult to detect. However, among Negroes proportionately more previous records will appear. It is natural to find more adults than juveniles with previous records, as well as more convictions among them. Among the victims, adults will have prior records with more charges of drunkenness and disorderly conduct, while

36. Morris, p. 20.

the juvenile victims will generally be charged with "promiscuity" and "bad reputation."

VICTIM-OFFENDER RELATIONSHIP. Rape, we assumed, is mainly an intraracial crime, among those living in residential proximity, who have some kind of prior relationship. This relationship may range from their being complete strangers, to their being close neighbors, to their being lovers. In many cases there is interaction beginning before the rape, assuming an atmosphere of familiarity due to mutual relationships or due to participation in common activities, such as drinking or dancing. The "Jack the Ripper" complex of a strange offender who attacks his victim and disappears will more likely occur in interracial rapes and in felony-rape situations. The previous relationship of offender and victim, the places frequented by the victim, and her behavior in general often serve to precipitate the rape itself.

STATISTICAL TECHNIQUES USED AND THE INTERPRETATION OF THE DATA. Descriptive and test statistics are used in the analysis of the data for expressing and testing suggested relations between variables. Both numerical values and percentages of frequency distributions are presented, as well as rates and ratios. Chi-square analysis was used as a test of the association between a given social characteristic and a variable of forcible rape, as well as of the correlation among the variables themselves.

Conventionally, the chi-square test is not used when the expected frequency is less than 20 percent of the observed frequency. However, whenever it was found possible to combine classes of frequencies without distorting the data, this was done, and the chi-square analysis employed.[37] The 5 percent level of significance (P) was used; thus, whenever the term "significant association" appears, it indicates that the level of P is not greater than .05.

As a measure of the degree of association, the coefficient of association (Q) was computed. The nature of the association or "the amount of proportion of change in the incidence of one attribute which is associated with the change from one to another of the categories of the other attributes"[38] is expressed in percentages.

After an association was shown to exist, possible explanations for it were given and later some were changed after additional data was analyzed. Explanations and interpretations were checked in the light of existing information on the subject in other studies. In this way, the existing accumulated knowledge was tested and confirmed; or alternative hypotheses were developed for further study.

37. See Blalock, chap. 15.
38. Hagood, p. 498.

2

General Perspectives of Forcible Rape

The Law

As a general rule, the term "forcible rape" means the carnal knowledge of a woman by a man, carried out against her will and without her consent, extorted by threat or fraudulence. Statutes may use either the wording "against her will" or "without her consent" or "by force." While for the public it seems that there is no ambiguity as to the moral nature of the offense and the moral status of the offender, the endless bickering in the court and the legal literature point to the need for authoritative resolution of disagreements, especially since it involves the moral character of the victim.

The following is a synopsis of the *Pennsylvania Criminal Law and Criminal Procedure*,[1] which is the legal basis and framework for this research and for the aforementioned problems.

> Whoever has unlawful carnal knowledge of a woman, forcibly and against her will, or whoever, being of the age of sixteen (16) years and upward, unlawfully and carnally knows and abuses any woman child under the age of sixteen (16) years with or without her consent, is guilty of rape, a felony, and on conviction, shall be sentenced to pay a fine not exceeding seven thousand dollars ($7,000), or undergo imprisonment by separate or solitary confinement at labor, or by simple imprisonment, not exceeding fifteen (15) years, or both.

1. Hoffman, "Rape," § 721.

Upon the trial of any defendant charged with the unlawful carnal knowledge and abuse of a woman child under the age of sixteen (16) years, if the jury shall find that such woman child was not of good repute, and that the carnal knowledge was with her consent, the defendant shall be acquitted of rape, and she shall be convicted of fornication.

The essential elements of rape are the use of force and the absence of consent of the woman. (Stenick v. Com., 78 Pa. 460 [1875].)

In rape, which is the unlawful carnal knowledge of a woman forcibly and against her will, and in adultery, penetration is an essential element. Force and absence of consent of the woman are necessary constituents of common law rape, but are not ingredients of adultery or fornication. (Com. v. Moon, 151 Pa. Super. 555 [1943].)

Force and absence of consent of the woman are essential elements of rape both at common law and under this section. (Com. v. Shrader, 354 Pa. 70 [1946].)

To constitute the crime of rape there must be penetration, however slight, but entrance in the labia is sufficient. (Com. v. Bower, 166 Pa. Super. 625 [1950].)

To carnally know and abuse any woman child, there must be penetration or an attempt to have intercourse. There must be at least contact of sexual organs. In this case, the proof of penetration rests solely on circumstantial evidence and is generally accepted as the law. (Com. v. Exler, 61 Pa. Super. 423 [1915].)

A male over sixteen years of age may properly be convicted both of common law and statutory rape for the same offense. (Com. v. Garybush and Fay, Pa. 47 [1949].)

Actual resistance, outcry and prompt complaint are material elements of rape. (Com. v. Moran, 97 Pa. Super. 120 [1929].)

In rape prosecution, evidence of prosecutrix should be carefully considered in determining whether she consented, and ordinarily proof of failure to make outcry and complaint tend to show consent. (Com. v. Berklowitz, 133 Pa. Super. 190 [1939].)

All who are present aiding, abetting and encouraging the ravishing are guilty of rape, although only one of the defendants may be the actual ravisher. (Com. v. Garybush and Fay, Pa., 47 [1925].)

One who stands by and does not prevent commission of rape may be convicted. (Com. v. Ford, 86 Pa. Super. 483 [1925].)

Evidence that defendant assisted companions in forcibly having intercourse with prosecutrix sustained conviction of rape regardless of whether defendant himself achieved penetration. (Com. v. Goldberg, 162 Pa. Super. 203 [1948].)

Evidence of bad reputation for chastity is admissible on rape charge as substantive evidence bearing on question of the female's consent. (Com. v. Eberhardt, 164 Pa. Super. 591 [1949].)

In prosecution for robbery and rape, Commonwealth was properly permitted to introduce evidence that defendant two days before alleged offenses had in another state made attempt at sexual intercourse with a chance acquaintance by use of considerable force and intimidation, in order to show design. (Com. v. Ranson, 164 Pa. Super. 591 [1949].)

Prompt complaint by victim to third person is admissible in evidence in rape prosecution. (Com. v. Eberhardt, 164 Pa. Super. 591 [1949].)

In rape prosecution, where there was testimony that when prosecuting witness left taproom she was seized by one of the defendants, that another struck her in the face and that she became unconscious, testimony of the witness who lived in an apartment above the taproom, said that she was awakened by hearing a woman scream and that she looked out and saw young men around a parked automobile was admissible as tending to corroborate the other testimony.

A doctor who has four years of medical training and fifteen months' experience as an intern in a hospital may properly be permitted to testify as to the facts found upon physical examination of an alleged victim of rape, even though he is not licensed to practice medicine and may not be permitted to express a professional opinion. (Com. v. Jackson, 183 D & C 200, Duph. 326 [1953].)

Man cannot be convicted of rape where he has a carnal knowledge and intercourse with another man's wife, who assents to such intercourse in belief that he is her husband because she finds him in her bed. (Com. v. Duchicz, 42 C. C. 651 [1914].)

No matter what trickery, fraud or deception is used, it is not rape if the woman consented, if she is over the age of sixteen years. Connection with a woman who is insensible or unconscious is rape. (See: Com. v. Childs, 2 Pitt. Rep. 391 [1863]; Com. v. Sollager, 3 Clark 127 [1939].)

In the case of rape, declaration of the victim made to a third person immediately following the commission of the crime are admissible in evidence on behalf of the Commonwealth. (Com. v. Laconna, 2 Lacka. 345 [1920]; Com. v. Reinhold 20 Dis. 743 [1921]; Com. v. Keller, 34 York 185 [1921].)

One acquitted of a charge of rape cannot be convicted of adultery for the same act of intercourse. (Com. v. McIlvain, Dist. 175 [1875].)

The absence of specific instruction in trial for rape that prisoner might be convicted of fornication if jury doubted guilt of the more serious charge was not ground for reversal, where no such instruction was requested. (Com. v. Moskorison, 170 Pa. Super. 332 [1952].)

Some considerations of these statutes and decisions is worthwhile to illuminate a few of the problems facing a sociological analysis of forcible rape.

The criminal code can be considered as a specification of the following method of establishing a crime: "who does it to whom? how, and under what circumstances?"[2] In order of their importance, five sets of interdependent problems can be abstracted from the legal code quoted above.[3] The following paragraphs are a short discussion of them as separate issues.

Consent and Resistance

The word "consent" connotes a self-perceived attitude, which is also understood by others: The burden of proof is on the claimant. Thus, the

2. "Rape Allegations of Force," pp. 802–3.

3. For a discussion of various court decisions annotated with cases from various legislations see: Drzazga, chap. 8; Ploscowe, *Sex and the Law,* chap. 6.

woman's behavior at the scene and her ability to relate accurately what happened and to communicate it are important to the court. The most obvious proof of nonconsent is the resistance the victim offers. However, the courts understand that consent cannot be implied by lack of resistance only, and that in each case it must be brought within the meaning of some of the conditions specified in the statutes. For example, the elements of force or fear of bodily harm are necessary conditions in the conviction for rape. Though defense lawyers and some physicians argue that it is impossible to forcibly rape a woman if she is in good health and sound mind, the law responds by specifying conditions other than the actual use of force which may have made the victim yield or submit to her assailant. Here enter notions of misrepresentation, fraud, and the sexual abuse of retarded and mentally ill women, as well as the possibilities of stupefication and intoxication of the victim. It is, therefore, important for the court to establish the fact of resistance or its absence as a sign of consent or nonconsent. Here a new set or problem arises. What is the amount, duration, and quality of resistance the woman must show in order to validate nonconsent? Or, could she show that although she was capable of physical resistance, she had to yield because of intimidation, terror, or mental conditions? Courts have taken these possibilities into account and require less evidence than was formerly needed to establish proof of resistance on the part of the woman. It is necessary only to prove that the offender actually used some pressure on her and that she in fact did not agree, and perhaps even consented in certain end stages of the assault out of fear of being maimed or killed.

Now, the immediate threat to the physical well-being of the woman, by brandishment of a weapon or verbal threat, are not the only means of coercion into submission. Threats which may be urgent in terms of the personality and social needs of the victim are known to exist; for example, the threat of loss of a job or suitor, or a threat to the well-being of relatives. Generally, the law refuses to deal with such threats as anything more than reasons for giving consent, which thereby bars conviction of rape.

An attitude such as this reflects the utilization and operational characteristics of the law. However, from a sociological point of view, it is worthwhile to distinguish between true consent where the victim could not by her nature, or the nature of the situation, give her consent, and apparent consent, where the victim may have assented in the end stage of the assault or under conditions of fraud or trickery.

Another distinction should be made for consent as mere submission to force or equivalents of force. This latter distinction is important for the second set of conditions specified in the statutes.

The Victim's Condition

The law fixes the age of legal consent to sexual intercourse so that sexual relations with a woman below the statutory age of consent is rape, whether accomplished by force or not. Also, most of the statutes specify that sexual relations with a mentally defective or insane woman, providing the man knows of her condition, is considered as forcible rape, because she has no mental capacity to consent. In either type of case, it is presumed that the woman does not know the nature and consequence of the act. The question of force (actual or its equivalent) and of consent are immaterial in these cases.

Similar considerations exist when sexual intercourse is effected with a woman stupified by drugs, if they were not taken as an aphrodisiac. Intercourse with a female intoxicated to the extent that she is "unable to resist" is considered forcible rape. This is so even though she drank voluntarily.

A distinction, however, should be made between such an intoxicated woman who is victimized by a stranger and one who was taken advantage of by her drinking partner. The latter case weakens her accusation, since by drinking she took a chance, made herself vulnerable, and also introduced an element of stimulation for the male.

Sexual intercourse with a sleeping woman is considered as forcible rape. In this situation, too, she cannot exercise her will and the act was committed against her consent.

In discussing the problems of consent, it would seem that the use of the terms "consent" and "will" is aimed at differentiating between two types of conditions. "Without her consent" usually means that the woman withheld actual approval for sexual intercourse. However, once it is specified that there might be unlawful consent, or consent given without understanding the nature and the consequences, the term "against her will" is used. It is, therefore, important to establish whether the victim consciously opposed the violation of her body. Each one of the two terms has a long history in judicial decisions, and, although it seems that there are differences between them, they are still used interchangeably.[4]

Victim's Character and Relationship to the Offender

As a rule, prior unchastity of the female is not defense against the charge of rape. Generally the character of the female need not be established as proof of alleged consent, especially when she is a child victim. Some statutes, however, make the previous chastity of the female an element in determining the crime. For example if there is no physical evidence of

4. Puttkamer.

the rape, the court must rely on the circumstances of the encounter, in which case the character of the parties and the previous relations between them are important for deciding the likelihood that the act was consensual. Hence, when it is established that the parties were previously acquainted, or perhaps had even engaged in previous sexual relations, or the assault occurred in a "dating" relationship, the assumption is that the woman cannot claim nonconsent. The court either infers a continuous state of mind, or the unlikelihood of a serious attitude of opposition.

A victim's "moral character" may be admissible as a defense in some statutes. Again, the assumption is that an unchaste female, or a female with such a reputation, is more likely than not to consent to sexual intercourse in any given instance.

From the previous discussion, a sociological factor arises in the definition of rape. It is taken for granted that force is used in rape to enable the offender to render the woman submissive; but there may be other overtures to the act which accomplish the same thing. Use of force is therefore a sufficient but not a necessary condition to the victim's justifying submission without utmost resistance. Thus, though force is a necessary component in the legal definition of rape, it is not the term "force" which should enter the sociological definition of rape, but that of "power." Once this is accepted, power relations of dominance and subordinance between the parties, as well as previous relationships between them and special situations like intoxication, can be seen in a new light.

With the recognition of various kinds of coercion and of different types of reaction on the part of the victim, the court is faced with the problem of distinguishing a true attitude of nonconsent when active opposition did not occur or ceased very quickly. A few statutes require only a degree of "good faith" resistance which makes the woman's nonconsent reasonably evident. However, most of the statutes hold that the amount of resistance must be proportional to the relative strength of the parties, the woman's condition, and the futility of continued resistance, or of offering resistance at all. These considerations bring us to another set of conditions specified in the statutes: those dealing with problems of proof, evidence, and corroboration.

Proof, Evidence, and Corroboration

Rape, as Lord Hale observed, "is an accusation easily to be made and hard to be proved, and harder to be defended by the party accused, tho never so innocent." Because of the danger that innocent men will be convicted, some statutes adopted the rule of corroboration to support rape conviction. In this area, problems arise in the use of medical evidence as original or other corroborative material.[5] Another set of problems arises over the issues of penetration and emission. Generally, any penetration, however slight, is sufficient to complete the crime (with or without the rupturing of the hymen), and emission is not essential to the commission of the crime. The rule is that completed coitus is also not essential.

In order to provide safeguards against unfounded accusation, and to help the court to gauge the credibility of the complaint, many statutes specify that no conviction can be made for rape unsupported by other evidence.[6] The victim's efforts to report the attack promptly, as well as knowledge of her character and reputation, are evidence for her complaint. Rarely does a clearly defined rule of other evidence which constitute corroboration exist in the statutes. Generally, those statutes which require corroboration either will demand it in all cases or only when the event sounds improbable, or factors of age and mental state seem to require it. In short, evidence must tend to show that the crime of rape was actually committed as claimed by the complainant and that the defendant was the one who committed it.

Who Is An Offender

The last set of conditions specified in the statutes deal with those who cannot be charged with rape, although they had sexual intercourse with a woman without her consent. Despite the fact that most rape statutes declare that anyone who forcibly has sexual intercourse with a female may be guilty of the crime of rape, "there is not a single reported case of a woman convicted as principal."[7] This is, of course, because the act requires a genital penetration. A woman, however, may be guilty of rape if she procures, counsels, or aids a man to commit rape upon another woman.

A husband cannot personally be guilty of rape on his own wife, but if he "counsels, aids or abets, assists or forces another to have sexual intercourse with her, or forces her to submit to sexual intercourse with another, he is guilty of rape."[8]

Most of the statutes also specify the legal age below which the offender cannot be conceived as capable of committing the act. Generally the age is fourteen years.

5. For the problems of medical evidence of rape see: Bronson, "Case of Rape"; "Editorial: Miscellaneous Cases of Rape"; Gilbert; Gonzales, et al.; Graves, "Clinical and Laboratory Evidence" and "Detailed Examination"; Hewitt; Hukner; Mapes; Pollak; "Rape: Physical Examination"; Rife; Simpson, 481–83; D. E. Sutherland; Tyler.

6. See discussion and summary of states' procedures in "Corroborating Charges of Rape."

7. "Rape Allegations of Force," p. 802.

8. "Problems of Consent in Forcible and Statutory Rape," p. 6.

The defense of not knowing the female's mental condition or her true age is accepted in most of the statutes.

Sociological Analysis

And so it can be seen that a discussion of the legal problems of establishing a rape charge brings to light some considerations for a sociological analysis of the crime. First, the existing law may allow easier enforcement because by its definitions it limits the situations covered by the offense; but it fails to recognize the social and cultural patterns of sexual behavior which give new dimensions to the crime. The fact that adolescents mature younger and are more sophisticated and more experienced sexually should be recognized in a differentiation, let's say, between forcible seduction and traditional common-law rape situations.[9] Second, the law certainly allows very little use of existing accumulated scientific knowledge, and the concepts it uses are devoid of sociological considerations which would do justice not only to the existing social and intellectual conditions of the community but also to the partners involved in the actual rape. Thus, the use of "power" instead of "force" has been suggested to apply to those types of dominant-submissive situations in which the partners may find themselves. Also, existing psychological knowledge can be used to differentiate between different types of consent, on behavioral and attitudinal levels. Third, omitted in the law are various patterns of victim-offender relationships, according to duration, intensity, and so on, as well as various types of situational backgrounds (before and after the encounter). Up to now, they have been used as corroborative evidence but not in the definition of the act.

The way the law has been interpreted has hindered the clear definition of rape, because the emphasis has been mainly on the social characteristics of participants, and on certain characteristics in the modus operandi (e.g., violence, fraud, duress).

The New Solution

The law's emphasis on the problem of consent in the crime of rape supposedly defends our social structure,[10] existing mortality,[11] and the male concept of sexual property rights,[12] as well as protecting the morals and security of young or incapacitated women.[13] However, the existing

9. Ploscowe, "Sex Offenses," pp. 217–25.

10. Murdock, pp. 260–61.

11. Kinsey, Pomeroy and Martin.

12. K. Davis, "Jealousy and Sexual Property," 395–405.

13. New York court decisions: People v. Marks, 146 App. Div. 11, 130 NYS 524 (1911).

laws do not seem to accomplish all these things, and they therefore need to be revised.[14]

Near the end of World War II new legislation on sexual offenses was enacted in many states in the United States. During this period the country evidenced a great concern over what appeared to be an alarming increase in the number and seriousness of sexual crimes.[15] In spite of evidence refuting the claims of a "sex crime wave."[16] and of its dangerous nature,[17] many states hastily enacted new legislation[18] to provide (in addition to the existing codes) new statutes, commonly known as "sex psychopath laws." Because of their "remedial nature," these new laws lacked validity,[19] and in many aspects they violate the traditional procedural safeguards for criminal defendants[20] and accepted conclusions of contemporary psychological knowledge.[21]

In their application to the crime of rape, these new laws retain the old notions of "force" and the old concepts and ramifications of "consent." A few parts of the old laws need to be retained, but other cons'derations as indicated above should be included in defining the nature of the act: the use of brutality; the exploitation of a young, mentally ill, or intoxicated female; and the relative age of the partners.[22]

Volume, Scope, and Trends: Problems of Measurement

The difficulties of obtaining an accurate estimate of the number of rapes actually committed in Philadelphia and elsewhere are part of the whole

14. Ploscowe, "Sex Offenses," p. 224.

15. C. Allen, *Sexual Perversions and Abnormalities;* Harris; Hoover; Witteles.

16. *California Sexual Deviations Research;* Dunham; Hirning, pp. 233–56; *Massachusetts Report; New York City Report;* Tappan, *The Habitual Sex Offender,* pp. 12–13.

17. E. H. Sutherland, "The Sexual Psychopath Laws," pp. 543–45; Tappan, *The Habitual Sex Offender,* p .14.

18. Levy.

19. Garrel.

20. See: Davidson; Hacker and Fryn; Haines, et al.; Hughes; Leonard; Mihim; "Note: Legal Disposition"; Ravenscraft; Reinhardt and Fisher; "Should Sexual Psychopaths Be Subjected to Bail?"; E. H. Sutherland, "The Sexual Psychopath Laws"; Tappan, *The Habitual Sex Offender,* pp. 26–36, "Sentences for Sex Criminals," and "The Sexual Psychopath." For a comparative view on legislation and practices concerning sexual offenses see Radzinowicz, *Sexual Offenses,* chaps. 19–23. On the Pennsylvania sex psychopath law see: DeMay; Levy; "Recent Legislation." For the most recent discussion on the application of these laws see Craig.

21. *California Sex Deviation Research,* pp. 15–59. This source also includes a synopsis of sex psychopath laws in the United States (esp. pp. 41–59). See also: Bowman and Engel, "Sex Offenses"; Ellis and Brancale, pp. 75–93; Porterfield.

22. Group for the Advancement of Psychiatry.

problem of validity and reliability—that is, do the numbers given measure what they claim and mean to measure? Do they consistently measure the same thing?

On the level of criminal statistics which we are dealing with ("crimes known to the police") the following aspects are of prime importance: (1) reportability, (2) detectability, (3) recordability, and (4) the process of organizational contingencies, such as administration of justice, prosecution, and sentencing practices which effect 1, 2, and 3, and the relation between numbers of crimes and criminals to the above four variables.[23]

Reportability

The extent of reportability of various crimes depends on factors directly related to the commission of the crime (the amount of injury done to the victim, etc.); the characteristics of the parties involved and their relationships, if there were any at all; age or race differences, the presence of witnesses, and so on; factors outside the offense, such as the values which are violated by the crime—the organized "resistence potential"[24] of the violated norms expressed in community reaction and law enforcement activities toward the crime and its perpetrators.

Thus, in compiling criminal rape statistics, reportability is a matter of stating the number, extent, and consistency of reporting the crime in the total population and in various groups in it at a given time and in various places.

It is therefore concluded that it is manifestly impossible to decide what proportion of offenses committed is not reported.[25] This unknown figure of "dark numbers"[26] or "hidden criminality" may not be a constant one.

As to the reportability of rapes, it is said that this offense is one of the types which has a high degree of reportability.[27] This results from the injury inflicted upon the victim[28] and the high social value placed on the protection of females and the defense of sexual morality. The *Uniform Crime Reports* estimated that the crime of rape is generally not reported, so that the 7,000 cases of rape (reported in 1960) probably represent slightly over 30 percent of the estimated number of nearly 20,000 cases committed in that year.[29] Bowman and Engle state that the reported cases are only 20 percent, while Haines maintains that only 5 percent are

23. Sellin, "The Basis of Crime Index" and "Significance of Records."
24. Sellin, *Culture Conflict and Crime,* pp. 34–35.
25. Radzinowicz, "English Criminal Statistics," p. 175.
26. Grunhüt, "Statistics in Criminology."
27. Short and Nye.
28. Radzinowicz, *Sexual Offenses,* pp. 250, 318–30.
29. 1960; hereinafter cited as *UCR.*

reported, which would raise the number of committed rapes, based on the *UCR* (1960) to about 140,000.[30] Karpman gives numerous quotations from various authorities, covering the years 1937 to 1951, in which different opinions are given about the extent of reported rapes.[31] Sutherland states that the difficulties in reportability arise partly because "it is impossible to determine at present, how many rapes are forcible," and how many of the reported ones are false.[32] He noted, that the *UCR* reports that approximately 50 percent of all rapes known to the police of the United States are forcible rapes.[33] He also intimates, that those who prepared the plans for the *UCR* hesitated for some time before including rape as one of the crimes to be reported. It was "due to the belief that the statistics of rape would be less reliable than any other criminal statistics,"[34] because of the problem of reportability.

Deciding when a case of rape should be reported or when it should be concealed is governed by many factors which vary with each particular case. Following is a list of those reasons assumed to be most commonly involved:

I. For reporting
   A. Characteristics of the parties
      1. Age difference—the greater the age difference between the victim and the offender the higher the rate of reportability; this depends, however, on whether the young victim tells it to guardians or other adults, or whether there are witnesses, or when (in some way) the case has become known. The opinion is that very young victims usually do not report the event.[35]
      2. Ethnic or race difference—it is argued that when the offender is nonwhite there is a greater tendency to report the crime.[36]
   B. Modus operandi variables
      1. Injury to the victim—the greater the injury, the greater the tendency to report.[37]
      2. When witnesses are present who report, they or the victim will report to avert suspicion of consent or promiscuity.[38]

30. Haines quoted in Bloch and Geis, p. 290.

31. *The Sexual Offender,* pp. 24–25.

32. E. H. Sutherland, "The Sexual Psychopath Laws," p. 545.

33. Ibid., p. 544.

34. Ibid.

35. Bender and Blau; Dunham, p. 10; *Report of the Mayor's Committee,* p. 15.

36. Sellin, "Significance of Records."

37. "Forcible and Statutory Rape."

38. Sellin, "Significance of Records"; E. H. Sutherland, "The Sexual Psychopath Laws," p. 546.

C. Community variables
   1. Morals of the community—the value it places on sexual morality.[39]
   2. When community is under the "scare" of a "wave" of sex crimes, the tendency is greater to report.
   3. "Increased protection [is] afforded by the courts and the press to victims of extortion or blackmail."[40]

II. For concealment and nonreporting
   A. Parents and other protective agencies want to prevent attention, publicity, further ordeal, and emotional injury to the young victim by the police investigation and appearance in the court.
   B. Shame, fear of blackmail, and protection of reputation.[41]
   C. The injury was negligible and the adult victim, who has already had sexual experience wants to forget the humiliation and prevent further ordeal by not appearing before the police and the court.[42]
   D. The victim refuses to be bothered and to lose time by following through on the case.
   E. The negative evaluation toward rape is frequently extended to the victim, and she is accused of active participation or provocation, or irresponsibility or carelessness.
   F. Fear of the offender.
   G. Fear of the husband or parents when the event occurs under special circumstances, for example, after drinking, association with certain males, or in violation of other leisure rules set by parents or husband.[43]
   H. The victim may extend protection to the offender when special relationships existed with him.

The list can continue almost indefinitely, but in the light of what we have seen about the reportability of rape, two statements may be made which apply to other sexual crimes. First, it is quite impossible to arrive at any reliable estimate of the actual number of the unknown instances of any sexual crime; second, it is difficult to estimate the extent to which recorded change in the number of rapes and sexual crimes involved is a genuine one or merely indicates a change in the reported instances of those crimes.[44]

39. See n. 38 above.
40. E. H. Sutherland, "The Sexual Psychopath Laws," p. 145.
41. Ibid.
42. Ploscowe, "Sex Offenses."
43. Dunham.
44. Radzinowicz, *Sexual Offenses,* pp. xiv, 518.

Detectability

This is another variable which is important in gauging the relations between committed and recorded rape. By "detectability" is meant the ability of the police force to apprehend the offender; its ability and efficiency in elucidating from the victims, witnesses, and offenders the true circumstances before, during, and after the event; the ability of police to influence the victims and witnesses to prosecute the offender and to tell the truth in the successive investigations. The efficiency of the police operation depends upon how soon the case was reported to them, which, in turn, is related to the general stand of the police in the community. Bensing concluded that in Louisville, Kentucky, the role of police was exaggerated in detection of sexual crime and that reportability is a major factor. Ferracuti, Hernandez, and Wolfgang imply that it is the policemen's education, training and experience which explain the differences between the efficiency of their recording. Whatever the degree of reportability and the extent of reporting, and whatever the efficiency and consistency of police operations, these two variables (reportability and detectability) will be reflected in police recording of the crime, and it is to this subject that attention is now given.

Recordability

By recordability we mean the accuracy of recording crimes reported to or discovered by the police; the degree of accuracy depends upon the policemen's facilities and their methods, and upon the maintenance of arrest statistics. Much criticism could be leveled against the recording of crimes by the police, but the following are the most frequent ones: (a) There is intentional misrepresentation in record keeping so that the number of crimes recorded as "known to the police" is not an accurate picture of the crime actually known to the police. This occurs because by under-reporting the police can accomplish statistically what they cannot fulfill otherwise—that is, "the obligation to protect the reputation of their cities."[45] Various studies have shown the conscious abuse of statistical records for this or other reasons.[46] (b) In time of "scare" about a sex crime wave, there is undue pressure on the police from the public and district attorney's office to "solve" cases, and as a result there is an over-recording of rape cases "clear by arrest."[47] (c) Because rape is difficult to prove, prosecutors commonly permit the defendant to plead guilty to a lesser offense,

45. Cressey, "The State of Criminal Statistics," p. 237.

46. See: "Abuses in Crime Reporting," in *Crime Records and Police Management;* D. Bell, pp. 151–75; Wolfgang, "Uniform Crime Reports," p. 716. On police discretion in recording and charging in rape in Philadelphia see, "Comment: Police Discretion."

47. Judge Nochem S. Winnet, in *The Problem of the Sex Offender.*

which results in under-recording of rape cases actually committed and known to the police.[48] (d) There is a discrepancy between police areas in recording rape cases, that is, there is no unity in recording the same fact among policemen and among different police areas—a fact which raises the possibility of inconsistency between and within police areas. (e) Because of the classifying and scoring techniques in which only the highest order of index offense is used when there are multiple offenses committed in a single criminal event, some cases of rape are lost (e.g., in murder-rape cases); some are classified rape when they should not be so classified (e.g., in incest-rape cases.)[49] (f) The number of crimes recorded as "known to the police" may represent only a proportion of the crimes actually committed in that year, because crimes do not always become known to the police during the year that they were committed.

The Administration of Organizational Contingencies

A serious problem exists in determining the numerical relationship between offenses and offenders, either for crimes as a whole or for a particular offense.[50] In the case of rape, this problem arises because, first, more than one offender may be involved in the rape case, and none or only some of the offenders may be apprehended; second, whatever the number of offenders, an offense may be "cleared by arrest" so long as at least one person is made available for prosecution; third, studies have indicated that phenomenon of "criminal case mortality"[51] or "administrative shrinkage"[52] or "process sieve"[53] in which the number of offenders is reduced in each phase in the law enforcement process.

If, in the light of the foregoing discussion, one has to be cautious in using police criminal statistics of a particular community, one must be all the more careful with the national criminal statistics as represented by the UCR.[54] Recognizing its own shortcomings in completeness, correctness, and adequacy for comparative analysis, the FBI annually prints the caveat "the FBI is not in a position to vouch for the validity of the reports received."[55]

As for studies on sexual crimes, again, UCR was stated to be inadequate

48. Newman, "Effect of Accommodation"; Shoenfield, "The Sex Criminal."

49. See the discussion in Wolfgang, "Uniform Crime Reports," pp. 721–24.

50. Van Vechten.

51. Ibid.

52. Sellin, "Significance of Records."

53. Eaton and Polk, Measuring Delinquency, pp. 1–6.

54. Wolfgang, "Uniform Crime Reports." For a new use, theoretical and practical, of "biased" police statistics see Wheeler, "Criminal Statistics."

55. UCR (1961), pp. 27–28.

and of limited value.[56] To rely on newspapers to gauge changes in the volume of rapes is to rely on misconceptions, prejudices,[57] and the pitfalls of the *UCR*. Studies on the subject indicate that: public conceptions of rape are limited to those cases where force or brutality was used, or when the victim was a child or when a white woman was attacked by a non-white offender;[58] newspapers dwell upon certain cases to arouse fear of a crime wave;[59] public opinion reflects trends in the volume of newspaper coverage and not the true volume of this type of crime[60] (thus, do newspapers tend more to mold opinion than to reflect reality?)[61]; public indignation may increase faster than the volume of rapes.

On the basis of an evaluation of the alternative sources for estimation of the volume of rape, the following conclusions can be drawn:

1. From official statistics it is impossible to know whether the number of rapes given indicates changes in the occurrence of rape or whether it represents changes in reporting or in police practices and activities.

2. The relationship between rapes committed and the number of offenders participating is also impossible to know; and like the number of actual rapes, the number of offenders remains a "dark figure," and the number of "arrested offenders" has no direct relation to the volume of reported offenses.[62]

3. It is also hard to gauge the proportion of rapes reported but not recorded.

4. The value of published criminal statistics at all levels is very small and should be taken very cautiously, but comparative study can be undertaken provided that one knows or can determine the effect of population changes and composition, the variations in legal contexts and in administration of justice, and the specific police methods and practices in detection and recording.

5. Data on the volume and trends in rapes, outside the FBI reports, is for the years 1948–53. As a reaction to the Kinsey Reports and to the sexual "crime wave" scare, some surveys were made with analyses of volume and trends. Today still, the FBI is issuing scare reports through the *UCR*. In the 1961 *UCR* one can find the use of

56. Ellis and Brancale, pp. 3–8.
57. A. N. Fox; Tappan, "Some Myths."
58. Lukas, "What are the Common Beliefs?"
59. Wyeheart.
60. Ibid.
61. F. J. Davis.
62. *California Sexual Deviation Research,* p. 95.

adjectives like "alarming" concerning a rise of 8 percent in forcible rape. This statement is made without reference to population base, using indexes and inexact numbers of "offenses cleared," "offenders found guilty," and so on.[63]

Therefore, given these conditions, the presentation of raw and comparative statistical data in this study takes the following directions:

1. Statistics are presented on the police level, that is, concerning recorded rapes. Analysis, however, will be made on those cases which are decided to be genuine rape cases. Thus, differences exist between the number of cases reported by Philadelphia police and the number we are concerned with. This is because many files could not be found, although they were registered in the central registration office in the police headquarters. Also, many cases already on the police level were classified as unfounded, yet were recorded in the central registration. It was found also that cases of attempted rape and assault with intent to ravish were given to the *UCR*. Incest cases were also recorded as rapes and included in the report to the FBI. This was done as a result of the policy of using the highest order of an index offenses for tabulation when there are multiple offenses committed in a single criminal event.

   Furthermore, the impossibility has already been noted of ascertaining the relationship between the offenses cleared by arrest and offenders cleared—arrested or known or unknown but not yet detected, found, or arrested. Hence, any analysis of offender characteristics must rely on the data at hand.

2. The *UCR* data will be used only for comparison of Philadelphia with other cities of comparable size.

3. A trend study was contemplated but was given up when it was learned that in 1958 the FBI made a major revision in classification and representation of data. Until that year the category of rape in the *UCR* included statutory rape. This is one of the reasons for the study's beginning with 1958.

4. Also avoided was any attempt to compare the volume of rape to the other types of crime, since, first, it is outside the scope of the study; second, it involves depending on *UCR* data, or at least on data not collected; and third, there is no theory to present the relationships between rape and other types of offenses as was attempted by Henry and Short in the case of homicide and suicide. Dunham and Radzinowicz proposed to show the relationships between sex crimes and other types of offenses—but no theoretical

63. *UCR* (1961), p. 2.

explanation was forwarded or resulted from the mere presentation of tabulated statistics.[64] Beattie already indicated that the tendency of one type of crime "to increase or decrease may have no relation whatever with other types of criminal behavior."[65] However, it is claimed that rape has a very low rate (around 9.9 and 3.5 per 100,000 in the United States and England, respectively) in comparison with other sexual offenses, and to criminal activity in general.[66] All this is true in the face of the trend of recorded rapes to increase every year.

Problems of Definition, Classification, and General Rates

Throughout the study, and particularly in the data collection stage, the legal basis provided by the Pennsylvania Criminal Code had to be relied upon. The term "rape" is so broadly used, and so lacking in a uniform classification and definition, that to measure its extent in a given population is almost impossible. The law distinguishes between forcible rape, statutory rape, attempt to rape, and assault with intent to ravish. Yet, often, they are lumped together in reported statistics so as to make comparative studies difficult. To the sociologist there is little significance in the distinction between, let us say, attempted rape and forcible rape. In both there are similar actions and probably identical motivation, while they differ in the success of accomplishing and terminating the act. But because the law still makes this distinction, and since often attempted rape or assault with intent to ravish are charges entered after pleading guilty and "bargaining" with the district attorney, it was found necessary to include in our sample only those cases the police recorded as rape.

Under this definition of rape, and its statutory limitations, the following figures are pertinent. In the three-year period, 1958–60 (inclusive), the central registration office of the Philadelphia police listed 1,727 rapes. For each of the three years respectively there were 556, 642, and 529 rapes which resulted in an average annual number of 575. For the two years which this study is dealing with (1958, 1960) the average annual number of rapes was 542, which indicates that the third year in the "broken cycle" was not significantly different from the two adjacent years.[67] The *Uniform Crime Reports* for 1958–60 showed that rates per 100,000 for forcible rape throughout the nation were 8.4, 8.3, 8.7, and

64. Dunham; Radzinowicz, *Sexual Offenses.* See also Bemmelen; Sievert.

65. p. 180.

66. See Wolfgang, "Volume of Sexual Offenses."

67. According to calculation there were 349 cases of rape as against 642 cases reported by the Philadelphia police.

with an annual average of rape cases of 15,000.[68] Forcible rapes for five cities over one million population were 17.2, 19.5, and 20.0, respectively. See table 1 for the numbers and rates from the 1958–60 *UCR* data for Pennsylvania.

Table 1: Rape in Pennsylvania and Philadelphia,
by Absolute Numbers and Rates

	1958 Cases	1958 Population	1959 Cases	1959 Population	1960 Cases	1960 Population
Standard metropolitan areas	839	8,793,903	955	8,729,354	962	8,813,274
Other cities	27	969,416	20	989,816	16	929,972
Rural	49	1,337,819	54	1,499,784	45	1,576,170
Total	916	11,101,179	1,029	11,219,034	1,023	11,319,366
Rate	8.2		9.2		9.0	
Philadelphia	643	4,190,757	735	4,289,194	619	4,342,897
Rate	15.8		17.6		16.5	

Source: adapted from *UCR* (1958–60), p. 2.
Rates are per 100,000 in this table and hereafter.

In order to compare the city of Philadelphia with other cities of equivalent population, an attempt was made to secure information from annual police reports of such cities. Only partial success was achieved in getting such reports, but those which were obtained revealed the differences between what was reported by the police annual statistics, and those numbers and rates reported for the same cities by the *UCR*. The annual police statistics from several cities with population over one million were compared in absolute numbers and percentage differences to the *UCR* for the same year. Table 2 shows the results of this comparison.

One explanation can be offered for these differences; the *UCR* gives the numbers for the Standard Metropolitan Area complexes,[69] which includes each city plus its neighboring townships and suburbs, while the annual police statistics pertain to population within the city limits only.[70]

68. *UCR* (1959), p. 4; (1960), p. 2.

69. For a full definition of SMA, see U.S. Bureau of Census, 1950, pp. xxxi–xxxiii.

70. Von Hentig already pointed to differences between the *UCR* figures and his own percentage of rapists found guilty. The *UCR* figure was 56 percent versus his of 25.7 (see *Crime*, p. 56).

Table 2: Rape Cases in Annual Police Statistics Compared with Reported
Forcible Rapes in the *UCR*, by Absolute Numbers and Percentage
Differences

	1958	Annual Police Report	Per-cent Diff.	1959	Annual Police Report	Per-cent Diff.	1960	Annual Police Report	Per-cent Diff.
	UCR			UCR			UCR		
Atlanta	129	101	21.7	96	80	16.6	77	44	42.8
Baltimore	132	96	27.3	162	121	25.3	146	108	26.03
Buffalo	40	16	60.0	35	11	68.5	28	10	64.2
Chicago	643	532	17.2	676	587	13.3	997	880	11.7
Dallas	74	40	45.9	58	49	15.5	63	53	15.9
Kansas City	72	41	43.05	65	30	53.9	61	40	34.4
Los Angeles	1,934	1,028	46.9	1,931	1,036	46.9	1,920	1,022	46.7
Miami	52	46	11.5	89	40	55.05	63	45	28.5
New York City	1,040	1,115	−7.2	856	1,247	−45.6	893	910	−1.8
Washington, D.C.	159	71	55.3	168	73	56.5	202	115	43.06
Philadelphia	643	556	13.5	735	642	12.8	619	529	14.7

Source: adapted from *UCR* (1958–60), pp. 53–57; and from the annual police reports for
each city.

On the basis of the *UCR,* the rates and the mean annual rates per
100,000 were computed for cities with over one million population. Table
3 demonstrates the results.

According to *UCR* (tables 1 and 3), Philadelphia rape rates (15.8,
17.6, 16.5), and the annual mean rates (16.06), compare unfavorably to
communities throughout the nation as well as to its own region and state.
By rank, Philadelphia is leading the nation in annual mean rates, after
Los Angeles (29.07), but standing before such cities as St. Louis (16.03),
Houston (13.06), Detroit (12.8), and Chicago (12.8).

Sellin has said that crime rates should at least be computed on the
basis of the population capable of committing crimes, that is, the *potential*
offenders. "The rates for rape should only be computed on the basis of the

Table 3: Rape Rates and Mean Annual Rates per 100,000 Population

Source	1958 No.	Rate	1959 No.	Rate	1960 No.	Rate	Mean Annual Rate	Popula-tion Base 1960
Uniform Crime Reports	643	15.8	735	17.6	619	16.5	16.06	4,342,897
Philadelphia *Annual*								
Police Report	556	77.25	642	89.20	529	73.50	78.31	719,704[a]
Three-year study	348	48.35	349	48.49	298	41.54	46.12	719,704
Study, 1958 and 1960	348	48.35	...	...	298	41.54	42.44	719,704

a. Total number of male population age 14 and over.

male population . . .; it would be advisable to compute rates on the population above the age of ten or twelve years."[71]

Hence, on the basis of Philadelphia's 1960 census[72] and the number of rapes given by the police in its annual report, specific rates were calculated for the total male population in the age group 10–60 years and over.[73] For each of the three years (1958, 1959, 1960) the specific rates per 100,000 were 72.25, 89.20, 73.50, with the mean annual rate of 78.31.

When calculated according to the number of cases in this study, the rates were 48.35, 48.49, 41.54, with a mean annual rate per 100,000 of 46.12. Although these specific rates vary from those calculated on the basis of the police statistics, it is the latter rates which serve as a framework for this study, for it is possible to come closer to a reliable general comparative study with police records of several cities. Rates based only on the samples gathered for this study are too particular for such effort, but they should nevertheless be kept in mind.

In absolute numbers and in rates of rapes, there were no significant changes in Philadelphia during 1958–60, which again makes it possible to study the two nonsuccessive years, especially since the population of the city was only slightly changed.

The failure of other statistics to distinguish between single and multiple offenders rape events (where the offense occurs between two or more victims and offenders) makes it impossible to use any comparative statistics in this study. However, in the analysis, a distinction is made between the criminal event and offenders and victims involved.

In the present study there were 646 cases of rape (348 in 1958, 298 in 1960). There were 1,292 known offenders, of which 845 were apprehended. It should be noted that the fact of multiple offenders increases the number of cases and makes the rates greater when computed on the basis of offenders, rather than on cases or victims involved.

Thus, in the subsequent discussion 646 victims and 1,292 offenders are analyzed and only for the years 1958 and 1960. The differences between the numbers in the present study and those numbers given by the police arises from the fact that many files registered in the central office were not found. Also, many files already defined as "unfounded complaint" were recorded, as well as cases of indecent assault with intent to ravish; all of these were excluded.[74]

71. Sellin, "Significance of Records," p. 500.

72. U.S. Bureau of Census, *U.S. Census of Population (1960)*, vol. 3, chap. 42, p. c.(1) 40(d) Pa.

73. Number of males age 10–60 was 719,704.

74. It is not my purpose to criticize the content of police files or the methods used in recording information. However, it is regrettable that so much

In this study, the cases of rape are counted according to the number of victims involved, since this procedure was used by the police. However, there can be a further breakdown of rape situations according to the number of offenders involved. By taking into account the number of offenders, one may distinguish three types of rape situations: single rape—when the encounter is between one offender and one victim; pair rape—when two offenders assault one victim; and group rape—when three or more rape one female.[75]

We are dealing, therefore, with 370 cases of single rape, 105 cases of pair rape, and 171 cases of group rape. We have more offenders than victims, a circumstance that is explained by the fact of pair and group types of rape.

Sexual crimes recorded by the Philadelphia police are classified under four headings:[76]

1. *unfounded*—investigation revealed the crime was not attempted;
2. those *disposed* when the offender in single rape or part, or all the offenders in pair or group rape were apprehended and the police have sufficient information to institute criminal proceedings—400 cases (62 percent);
3. those *active* when the offender was caught and the police felt that he was responsible for the crime, but no action or criminal proceedings were begun—either the victim refuses to prosecute or more and other offenders are sought, and so on—68 cases (10.5 percent);
4. those *inactive* cases, when the offender is not known and the case rests for more clues to his identity, but the police no longer are intensively looking for him—110 cases (17.1 percent).[77]

Basically, there are only two legal statutes for the cases: "cleared" and "uncleared." The classification of the legal status of the crime "is not identical with the one which distinguishes between detected and undetected . . . offenders."[78] These units of classification are different. However, a detected offender is not necessarily one who is apprehended. Such

---

information was missing, misfiled, and so on, making it more difficult to conduct the present study.

75. A further breakdown is according to the number of victims involved. In the sample, only in 6 cases did an offender rape more than one victim. All these cases involved small girls, who were sisters assaulted by an adult neighbor. The police recorded the incidents separately—that is, as 12 cases of rape. Because of the small number no special analysis was made of this group of cases.

76. Letter from Inspector Duran, Central Police Record Division, Philadelphia Police Department, 21 June 1963.

77. There is no information available on the status of two cases.

78. Radzinowicz, *Sexual Offenses,* p. 218.

is the case, for instance, when there is still insufficient evidence for criminal proceedings to be taken against the apprehended or known offender.

Thus, the data on the incidence of detected and undetected offenders reveals that of 1,292 offenders, 845 were apprehended, while 447 were, at the time of the study, still undetected. Of this last group, 407 suspected offenders were unknown to the victims, who could give only information about their color and make some guess about their age; and 40 had disappeared, but the police know their former addresses, as well as other items furnished by the victims who know them.

Analysis of the victim's account of the event and her behavior after it reveals one of the reasons for the victim's failure to describe the offenders and of the police's difficulty in apprehending them. In 186 of the cases, two to twenty-four hours elapsed between the end of the crime and the victim's report to the police, and in 10 percent of the cases, the report was made between one day and a week after the rape. Only in 45 percent of the cases was the crime promptly reported (about 30 minutes after), and in 14 percent (90 cases) a police patrol car discovered the crime, or a call was made by someone who had discovered the victim at the place of the event, or the offenders were found in flagrante delicto. Also, victims gave inconsistent stories, were intoxicated hours after the rape (7 percent) or refused to give further information and to cooperate. An analysis of reasons given by the victims for their failure to report the attack promptly shows that in 52 (8 percent) of the cases, the reason was fear of the offender who threatened them; fifty victims were afraid of their parents, guardians, or husbands. In three percent of the cases, report was made only after fear of pregnancy arose. Parents' hesitation led to a late report in 57 cases (9 percent). It is obvious that in such circumstances, the detection and apprehension of the offender is difficult, and an accurate picture of the offender and the circumstances of the crime is almost impossible.

II

The Victim and the Offender in the Rape Situation

3

Race Differences

The Philadelphia Data

Whatever the reasons underlying differences in race distribution of rape in a distinct racial population, an outstanding feature of the comparison of such distribution is the extent to which Negroes exceed whites as victims and as offenders, both in absolute numbers and in proportion to their representation in the total population of Philadelphia.

In 1960 the "potential"[1] population which can be involved in rape constituted approximately 26 percent of Philadelphia's total population,[2] and contributed 96 percent of all rape cases.

Table 4 presents the actual picture of rape by race of all victims and offenders involved.[3] We note that of 646 victims, 80 percent were Negro and that of 1,292 offenders, 82 percent belong to the Negro group. Testing the difference in proportionate distributions of Negroes and whites, either as victims or offenders, reveals that there is a *significant* association between race and forcible rape.

Table 5 presents the incidence of racial distribution of victims and offenders in each case of rape. It appears that rape cases in which both the offender and the victim are Negro exceed proportionately all other combinations of race differences of the participants in the rape event.

1. The concept of "potential" population includes females of all ages and males from age 10 onward.

2. Philadephia City Planning Commission, p. 1, table 1.

3. Hereafter, unless stated otherwise, every table presents data for the years 1958 and 1960.

Table 4: Victims and Offenders, by Race, Philadelphia, 1958 and 1960

	Victim		Offender		Total	
	No.	%	No.	%	No.	%
Negro	520	80.5	1,066	82.5	1,586	81.8
White	126	19.5	226	17.5	352	18.2
Total	646	100.0	1,292	100.0	1,938	100.0

In 646 rape events, 77 percent involved a Negro victim and a Negro offender, while in 18 percent of the cases the victim and offender were white. The situations in which the offender was a Negro and the victim white, and those in which the Negro victim was raped by a white offender constitute 3 and 4 percent of the total, respectively.

Table 6 presents the rate of involvement in rape per 100,000 persons according to the race of both victims and offenders. Two series of rates could be presented; the first calculated on the basis of the total population, the second as an accurate representation, utilizes the concept of the "potential" population.

It appears that Negroes (offenders and victims) have *significantly* higher rates than whites (offenders and victims). The frequencies of involvement in rape are more stable within racial groups, than between the races, and they are *significantly* greater between the races whatever the race of the participants, that is, they are greater for both Negro offenders and victims. For instance, calculating the rate of involvement in rape on the basis of the total female population, the rate for Negro victims (50) is four times the white rate (12). If we adjust the base figures and calculate the rate of Negro victimization on the basis of the Negro female population, and the rate of white victims on the basis of the white female population, the Negro rate is 185, while the white is 17. The potentiality of the Negro female to become a victim of rape is almost twelve times greater than that of the white female. Similarly, among offenders the Negro male rate (148) is almost five times greater than the rate for white offenders (31), on the basis of total male population of both races. However, if the rate is computed on the basis of male population in each racial group, the rate for Negro offenders is 591, which is twelve times greater than the rate for white males (49).

Table 5: Victims and Offenders by Race of Participants

	Offender/Victim				
	Negro/Negro	White/White	Negro/White	White/Negro	Total
Number	497	105	21	23	646
Percentage	76.9	16.3	3.3	3.6	100.0

Further, the Negro offender group, on the basis of total population of both races, has a rate of participation (148) which is only three times greater than the rate for Negro victims (50) based on the total female population of both races. When compared to the specific rates on the basis of potential race population the Negro male rate (591) is three times greater than the rate for Negro victims (85). In the white group, the rate of white male offenders (31), on the basis of total male population is almost three times greater than the rate for white victims (12). When compared to specific rates based on the "potential" race population, the white male offender rate (42) remains almost three times greater than the rate for white victims (17).

Table 6: Rates per 100,000 Population, Victims and Offenders, by Race

	Rate			
	Total Population		"Potential" Population	
	Rate	No.[a]	Rate	No.
Victim				
White	12.10	1,041,467	16.58	759,893
Negro	49.92	1,041,467	184.68	281,893
Offender				
White	31.40	719,704	41.90	539,414
Negro	148.12	719,704	591.25	180,290

a. Based on Philadelphia City Planning Commission, *Philadelphia Population by Race, 1960–1961.*

It would seem then that the generalization regarding the significance of racial differences in involvement in rape holds true for interracial differences, as well as for intraracial rapes. Not only are there differences when racial involvement is calculated on the basis of total population, but these differences are accentuated when rates of involvement are calculated on the basis of the potential group which "offers" participants for the crime of rape.

As a general conclusion it can be stated that the Negro rates rise approximately 300 percent for both offenders and victims, while maintaining the same relative ratio to each other. Whites' rates for offenders and victims rise about 30 percent while maintaining a stable ratio to each other.

Race Differences Noted in Other Studies and Reports

That Negroes are involved in crime to a degree that is disproportionate to their representation in the population can be seen from the 1960 *Uniform Crime Reports*.[4] Although Negroes constitute approximately 10.5

4. P. 95, table 20. For a general discussion on the problems of Negroes and crimes see: Savitz; Wolfgang, *Crime and Race.*

percent of the total national population, 30 percent of all arrests for all crimes in 2,446 cities over 25,000 in population were Negroes. Their arrest rate per 100,000 for Part I offenses was 30.5. Negroes comprise 53 percent of all persons arrested for forcible rape, which is five times greater than their proportionate representation in the nation's total population.

It is unfortunate that the *Annual Reports* of the Police Department of Philadelphia[5] do not give statistical data on rape. Therefore, any generalization based on arrest record on the disproportionate share of Negroes in any major crimes is made only on the basis of Negroes' share in crime rates in other similar cities. For rape rates, we have to rely on our study alone.

An analysis of rape rates by race is made only in some surveys based on court and prison samples which include the race of the offenders.[6] In spite of the incomparability of these data, we shall review the studies, keeping in mind that for the Negroes, involvement in crime increases at each step in the law enforcement process—that is to say, that the further from the act of crime the greater the excess of Negro over white rates.[7] Of the other perspectives, the following will be reviewed: arrest reports on the basis of the *Uniform Crime Reports;* court data; prison statistics; regional and community comparisons.

Most studies using *UCR* as a basis for their conclusions tend to demonstrate the high rate of Negro involvement in crime, especially in crimes against the person. It is, therefore, no wonder that these reports conclude that Negroes engage in rape to a greater extent than whites. Such a view was mentioned as early as 1904.[8] After that time, computations to find Negro rates of involvement in crimes against the person, and their excess rates over whites depends on the year of the *UCR.* It is regrettable that crime rates and arrest rates computed from the *UCR* do not permit insight into race differentials of the offender and victims involved, as well as race differentials between and within the group.

Even taking into consideration the fact of "race prejudice in the administration of justice,"[9] Negro rape rates taken from the *UCR* exceed those of whites. Such were the findings of Taft in 1927, Von Hentig in 1930, Johnson in 1941, Bonger in 1943, Vold in 1952, Korn and McCorkle in 1950–56, and Sellin in 1959.[10] McKeown studied arrest rates for spe-

5. City of Philadelphia.

6. For a general discussion on the involvement of Negroes in sex offenses see Savitz and Lief.

7. Sellin, "The Negro Criminal."

8. Work.

9. Sellin, "Race Prejudice."

10. Bonger, *Race and Crime;* G. B. Johnson; Korn and McCorkle, pp. 232–36; Sellin, "Crime and Delinquency"; Taft, *Criminology,* pp. 133–34; Vold, "Extent and Trends"; Von Hentig, "The Criminality of the Negro."

cified crimes, in 1930, in 55 cities of 100,000–250,000 population and in 36 cities with over 250,000. Correlating the rates with the percentage of Negro population in those cities, he concluded that for rape and non-negligent manslaughter, there was a relationship between the proportion of Negroes in the community and their higher rates for those crimes. The coefficient for rape, however, varies from one year to another and from one class of city to another and justifies no conclusion regarding the association between Negro population and crime rates. Sutherland and Cressey found Negro arrest rates to be three times higher than their proportionate representation in the population, but relatively low for rape.[11] Douglass points to the need to see crime rates within the racial groups compared with similar rates within the communities concerned. On the basis of *UCR* of 1957, he observed the excess of Negro arrests and convictions for violent crimes including rape.

It has been shown that Negro rape rates are higher only in the South; Reuther showed that in 1910, Negroes accounted for 66 percent of all rapes in the South and only 13 percent of all rapes in the North.[12] Others point out the fact that rates are usually compiled on cities' populations with no allowance given to rural rates.[13]

Only two published reports based on police *Annual Reports,* have appeared. J. B. Williams reported that in 1945 Negroes in Washington, D.C., comprised 34 percent of the population while contributing 90 percent of all rapes. G. G. Brown, in his report on Philadelphia, observed that Negro arrest rates for rape were five times higher than those for white. Negroes were involved in 42 percent of all rapes in that city in 1947.

The high Negro rates for rape were also verified by some court and prison statistics.[14]

From these diverse sources, with all their theoretical and methodological deficiencies, it appears that Negroes do have a higher proportion of involvement as offenders in rape, a proportion higher than their share in the population. However, no such generalization can be made about victims. Unfortunately, racial differentiation among victims and offenders has not been adequately analyzed for the crime of rape.

Along with studies which confirm the belief of excessive Negro criminality and of their involvement in rape, there are other empirically supported as well as unsupported opinions which suggest that the Negro rate is somewhat lower for rape than the white rate. Such were the findings of

11. E. H. Sutherland and Cressey, *Criminology* (5th ed.), p. 146. See also Kinsey, Pomeroy, and Martin, p. 393.

12. See also Chamberlain.

13. Korn and McCorkle, p. 233; Sellin, "Crime and Delinquency."

14. Apfelberg, et al.; *California Sexual Deviation Research,* (1952) pp. 12–17 and (1954) p. 120; Fox and Volakakis; Frumkin; Glueck, Jr., *New York Final Report,* p. 94, table A–4; J. B. Williams.

Hoffer's early examination of Virginia jail population, as well as Reid's in the Western Penitentiary in 1924 and data for New Jersey in 1931.[15] Doshay, on the basis of New York City Child Court files for the years 1928–43, found that of the 256 juvenile sex offenders, Negroes comprised 10.5 percent of the offender group.[16] Their percentage for aggressive sex crimes which includes rape was 7.2, less than among the white subjects. The *Report of the Mayor's Committee for the Study of Sex Offenders* revealed that of 418 cases of rape, 85 percent of the convicted rapists were white.[17] Negroes comprised only a little more than 1 percent of this group. The percentage of Negroes in the population at that time (1930–34) was 10.7 percent. Candy, on the basis of prison statistics, proved that in 1946 the Negro prisoners for rape were only slightly higher in number than whites.[18] He continued to state that those Negro rapists who were convicted, were convicted for attacking white victims, while a Negro who raped a Negro female usually drew a light sentence. Gillin, in his famous study *The Wisconsin Prisoner* observed that Negroes comprise only 1.6 percent of all imprisoned sex offenders; in the total group examined, 1,106 were white (96 percent) and 219 were Negroes, while their proportion in the population at that time was 4 percent.[19] Ruskin found only 17 Negroes among the 123 cases of psychiatric patients who committed sex offenses; they were also negligibly represented in the small group of 5 cases of rape (11 percent).

Psychiatrists who have written about sex offenders have tended to generalize, on the basis of "case studies," or some superficial survey that, "the participation of Negroes in rape is somewhat lower than their participation in other offenses,"[20] but it would seem that Negroes are less-often referred to the clinic. Taft suggested that although the Negro offender was punished far more often for rape than was his white counterpart, his relative arrest rates for this crime were not excessive as compared with other offenses.[21] The reason for this, he maintained, was that Negroes were not charged with rape if the victim was a Negro too. Surveying police reports in southern and western cities, as well as in some cities in the northern part of the country, has revealed to us the validity of the first part of Taft's statement about the excessive involvement in the offense of rape by the Negro.

15. *The Negro in New Jersey.*
16. P. 82.
17. P. 81.
18. Pp. 274–75.
19. P. 224.
20. Abrahamsen, *The Psychology of Crime,* p. 157. See also: Bromberg, *Crime and the Mind,* p. 85; Guttmacher, pp. 59–60.
21. *Criminology,* pp. 134–35.

In terms of regional and community comparisons, we can assume that rape rates in the Southern States are higher than in other parts of the country.[22] This can be simply interpreted by the fact that there is a large number of Negroes in these states or that rape rates for the white group in those Southern States are higher than in the North.

On the basis of the *UCR* for the years 1958–60, the mean annual rates for rape were computed and were found to be 8.2 per 100,000 for South Atlantic States; 6.9 for East South Central; 9.2 for West Central; and 3.8 for the New England States. It seems that the rates decline with the decline of Negro population in the region. Now, on the assumption that Negroes constitute the majority of rural residents in the South, the rape rate for the same year was computed again on the basis of the *UCR*, but this time for the rural areas in these regions. The following is revealed: 4.0 per 100,000 for the South Atlantic States; 2.8 for the East South Central; 5.1 for the West South Central; and 1.4 for the New England States. Contrasts between the regions again correspond to variations in the Negro population, but the differences between the two sets of rates with no substantial differences in the rate of decrease also indicate that the whites in the South contribute a larger share to the rates, so that the rates for the southern and western states are higher than those for New England. When compared, however, to the Middle States with the Negro population almost wholly urban, all these other regions score lower (7.5 per 100,000), while for the rural areas with their relatively large Negro population, the rate for the Middle Atlantic Region was 0.03.[23] (See table 7.)

It is, therefore, fair to conclude that regional rates "mask" the contribution of whites as well as of Negroes to rape rates, and for that reason it is necessary to compare the rape rate to the proportion of the racial group in specific communities.

Two alternatives present themselves. One consists of looking for the

Table 7: Rates per 100,000 by National Region

	Mean Annual Rates for the States	Rural Areas Rates	Rate Differences	Percentage Differences
South Atlantic	8.2	4.0	4.2	50
East South Central	6.4	2.8	4.1	45
West Central	9.2	5.1	4.1	50
New England	3.8	1.4	2.4	60

22. Wolfgang, *Crime and Race,* pp. 43–44.
23. Delaware, Maryland, New Jersey, New York, Pennsylvania.

racial differentiation in the light of the proportion of races in the regions' or communities' general population; the other is to compare the rape rates per 100,000 for Negroes or whites in one region or community with the rate for the same groups in other areas. The aim of each approach is to identify that group which shows disproportionately higher rates within the context of a given environment which includes the other racial group. Thus, the "tendency" of Negroes to be more involved in rape will be seen in the framework of their proportionate representation in the total population of the area under examination, and in the proportion of Negro involvement in all rapes. The communities' norms and the operation of general social and law-enforcement factors are other variables in the framework.

4

Age Patterns

"How safe is your daughter?" asks J. Edgar Hoover. How safe is any female, of whatever age, from being raped? Do offenders of specific age groups set age limits in selecting their victims? In short, has forcible rape a fortuitous nature with regard to age? In the analysis of the data, age patterns with respect to both victims and offenders emerge and are supported by the number of surveys which deal with this problem.

Analysis of the persons involved in the rape is made by five-year age classifications and is given first by annual rate per 100,000 population of specified age groups. Because females at almost any age level have been known to be raped (the age range in the present study is from one year to 68 years) the classification for victims is, therefore, from birth to 60 years and over. For males, the age of legal responsibility for rape is 16 years.[1] However, I have decided to start the age classification for offenders from the age of 10. Our sample includes 47 cases in which the age of the offender is between 10 and 15.

Age Patterns

The data (Table 8) shows that the majority of both offenders and victims come from the same age groups (ages 15–24). However, victims tend to be younger than their assailants. The highest rate for offenders is 796.8 (ages 15–19), and their second highest 566.4 (20–24). Among victims in general, the highest rate is 232.2 (ages 15–19), and their second highest 158.4 (10–14). Victims as a group are, therefore, between five and ten

1. *Pennsylvania Criminal Law and Criminal Procedure.* Commonwealth v. Corybush Faz, C. J. 49 (1949).

years younger than the offenders. The same conclusion is arrived at when frequency distributions are analyzed among 646 victims and 1,292 offenders (table 8). Both offenders and victims tend to come from the same age groups (ages 15–24), but a wider range is covered for "critical" age groups. Thus, only 14 percent of all offenders are 30 years of age or older compared to 33 percent for all victims. Finally, the median age for all offenders is 23.0 years compared to 19.6 years for victims.

Table 8: Rates per 100,000 Population and Percentages of Victims and Offenders by Race and Age

	Both Races			Negro			White		
	No.	%	Rate	Rate	No.	%	Rate	No.	%
Victim Age									
0–10	51	7.9	27.6	57.8	38	7.3	10.9	13	10.3
10–14	123	19.9	158.4	448.8	109	21.0	26.2	14	11.1
15–19	161	24.9	232.3	641.9	121	23.3	79.3	40	31.7
20–24	87	13.5	133.4	384.7	74	14.2	28.5	13	10.3
25–29	68	10.5	110.1	274.8	57	11.0	26.8	11	8.7
30–34	50	7.7	74.2	200.1	45	8.6	11.1	5	4.0
35–39	44	6.8	59.8	155.6	35	6.7	17.6	9	7.1
40–44	21	3.3	28.5	88.6	17	3.3	7.3	4	3.2
45–49	18	2.8	25.1	87.9	15	2.9	5.4	3	2.4
50–54	9	1.4	1.6	21.6	3	0.6	11.6	6	4.8
55–59	1	0.2	7.5	8.0	1	0.2	...	....	...
60–over	13	2.0	62.0	19.6	5	1.0	5.4	8	6.3
Total	...	...	...	184.68	520	100.0	16.58	126	100.0
Offender Age									
10–14	47	3.6	59.0	163.9	39	3.6	14.3	8	3.5
15–19	521	40.3	796.8	2,655.6	442	41.5	162.1	79	34.9
20–24	332	25.6	566.4	1,798.3	262	24.5	158.9	70	30.9
25–29	207	16.0	340.0	1,055.5	179	16.0	63.7	28	12.4
30–34	98	7.7	153.5	431.1	81	7.6	37.2	17	7.9
35–39	37	2.8	55.5	156.9	31	3.0	12.8	6	2.6
40–44	21	1.6	32.6	72.5	12	1.0	18.8	9	3.9
45–49	8	0.6	12.5	47.5	7	0.7	2.0	1	0.4
50–54	11	0.8	18.7	40.5	5	0.4	12.9	6	2.9
55–59	5	0.3	9.3	43.4	5	0.4	...	...	...
60–over	5	0.3	5.9	20.4	3	0.2	2.8	2	0.8
Total	...	...	179.52	591.25	1,060	100.0	41.9	226	100.0

When age differences are broken down further by race, other patterns emerge (table 8). Both Negro and white offenders show a tendency for committing forcible rape in the age groups 15–19 and 20–24. This is true when rates are calculated on the basis of the total male population of both races, or when computed from the specific age level within each racial group. Regardless of the population basis, the rates for Negroes in these "top risk" age groups are higher than those for whites. The rate among Negro offenders for ages 15–19 is 2,655.6. For the age level 20–24, the rate is 1,798.3. The two highest rates for the white offenders are 162.1 for the age group 15–19 and 159 for 20–24. Comparison of the lowest age-specific rates for the Negro and white offenders, again show the greater involvement of Negroes in forcible rape. This is true in every age group. The lowest rate for Negro offenders (20.4), in the age category of 60 and over, is still seven times greater than that of the white offenders (2.8). A *significant* difference is, therefore, found in age-specific rates between Negro and white offenders, regardless of the basis for rate computations.

The age pattern for victims is somewhat different from that of the offenders. Their age covers a wider range for the "critical" age group. Although the highest rates for Negro and white victims are in the same age range as offenders (15–29), the second highest rate for Negro and white victims is 10–14, while for the offenders it is for ages 20–24. High proportions of both Negro and white victims are victimized between the ages of 15 to 19, and 10 to 14, while the third "top risk" age grouping is 20–24. This is so when the rates are calculated on the basis of the total female population of both races, or when they are computed for the age-specific group within each racial category. However, regardless of the population base, the rates for Negro victims in these "top risk" age groups, are higher than the rates for white victims.

Among Negro victims the concentration of the two highest rates is between the ages of 10 to 24. Their highest rate (642) is for the ages 15–19, and the second highest rate (449) is for the ages 10–14. The highest rate for the white victims was 79, and the second highest rate (29) is in the age group of 20–24; almost the same rate (26) was found for the ages 10–14. This does not mean, however, that white victims are younger than Negro victims. On the contrary, the second highest rate for the Negro victims is in the same age level (10–14). These results only indicate that victims of both races also tend to be younger than their assailants (but, again, they are more widely spread over the age range); that Negro victims are liable to victimization more often and that their highest rates occur at the same age level as white victims, in every age group (excluding victims between 50 to 54 years of age). The lowest rate for Negro victims (8) in the age category 55 years and over, is four times greater than the lowest rate for white victims. It is clear, therefore, that *significant* differences exist in the rate of victimization between the rates by age groups.

By comparing victims and offenders from each racial group, we see that Negro victims and Negro offenders yield the highest rate in the same age group (ages 15–19). The second highest rate for Negro victims (449) is for the ages 10–21 years, and for Negro offenders it is for the ages 20–24.

The same holds true for white offenders and victims. Furthermore, the same is true for the Negro offender and the white victim. The highest rate for the latter group (79) is in the age level 15–19. For the white offender, and for victims of both races, the same pattern prevails. The highest rate for the white offenders (162) is at the age of 15–19, and the highest rates for the white and Negro victim are concentrated at the same age level.

Another pattern emerges when we compare age-specific rates for victims by race (see table 9). The average rate difference between the races is about 5 times greater for the Negro victim on the basis of intrarace population. The rate for Negro victims (age 50–54) is two to eighteen times greater than the white victim rate (age 30–34), and the average difference in rate is 11.

The Negro offender rate is from three (age 40–44) to forty-three times greater than the white offender rate (age 55–59). The average rate difference is 15. It should be noted that in the age group 50–54 the rate of the white victims is higher (1.5) than that of the Negroes, and in the age group 55–59 there are no white offenders at all.

Table 9: Average Rate Differences between the Races

	Rates from Total Population of Both Races, Age Specification	Rates, Intraracial Own-Age Specific
Victim	4.4	11
Offender	4.4	14.6

The highest age-specific rate for all victims and offenders of any race is approximately four times as high as the rate for all persons in these same respective categories. For example, the highest age-specific rate for all offenders regardless of race is 797 (ages 15–19), while the overall rate for offenders of all ages is 180. The highest age-specific rates for Negro offenders is 2,655 (ages 15–19), and the rate for Negro offenders of all ages is 591. Table 10 reveals this pattern for offenders.

Table 10: Rates of Rape, Offender and Victim, by Race

	Both Races		Negro		White	
	Offender	Victim	Offender	Victim	Offender	Victim
Five-year age group with highest rate	796.8	232.3	2,655.6	641.9	162.1	79.3
Rate for all ages	179.52	62.02	591.25	184.68	41.90	16.58

Rates are per 100,000.

The same pattern is seen among victims too. The highest age-specific rate for all victims, regardless of race, is 232 (ages 15–19), while the rate for victims in all ages is 62. Again the highest rate for Negro victims is 642 (ages 15–19), whereas the rate for all Negro victims is 185. For white victims the highest rate is 79 (ages 15–19), while the rate for white victims of all ages is 17. Thus, this same rate differential between the rate for the age group having the highest rate and the rate for all ages roughly applies to both victims and offenders, both to gross race categories and to specific race age groups.

It appears, therefore, that knowledge of the highest rate for any race group by five-year age categories makes possible a good estimate of the general rate for all ages of these same groups. Similarly, knowledge of the general rate allows us to estimate with considerable accuracy the highest five-year age-specific rates.

As noted previously victims are of the same general age as the offenders (15–24) but tend to be somewhat younger than their assailants in interracial events. Table 11, showing the median ages for each race group, makes this statement clearer.

Table 11: Median Age of Offenders and Victims by Race

| | Median Age | | |
	Offender	Victim	Difference
Both races	21.6	19.6	2.6
Negro	21.0	19.7	1.3
White	22.2	19.7	2.5

In examining our sample for the age distribution of offenders for given victim age cohorts (table 12), we find that the higher the age of the offender the more likely it is that the victim would be from a younger age group. Furthermore, over age 30, the statistical chance that one will be the victim of an older offender becomes greater. Only 14 percent of all offenders are 30 years of age or older, compared to 29 percent of all victims.

When the cases are broken down into offender, victim, race, and their relative age difference, some nuances appear. Table 13 shows the relative age differences according to victim-offender race in the rape events.

It may be noted that in 64 percent of the cases studied offender and victim were of the same age cohort. This pattern holds true even if we consider racial patterns. Thus, 66 percent of Negro offenders attacked Negro victims of their own age (not more than ±5 years). Similarly, in 62 percent of the cases involving only whites, the victims and offenders were of the same age (not more than ±5 years). If we consider those cases in which there was an age discrepancy, there is some racial variation, though this is not great. Thus, the 34 percent of the cases involving only Negroes in which the victims were either more than ten years older or more than ten years younger than their assailants are divided equally; 17 percent of the victims were "much younger," and 17 percent of the victims were "much older" than their assailants. Of the 38 percent of the cases involving only whites in which there was a marked age discrepancy, 23 percent involved victims who were ten or more years younger than their assailants while 15 percent involved victims who were much older than their assailants.

Table 12: Offender-Victim Age Disparity

| Offender Age | Age Disparity | | | | | | | |
| | Victim Younger (−10 years) | | Both Same Age (±5 years) | | Victim Older (+10 years) | | Total | |
	No.	%	No.	%	No.	%	No.	%
10–14	13	27.6	34	72.3	...	...	47	3.6
15–19	33	6.3	424	81.4	64	12.3	521	40.4
20–24	58	17.5	184	55.4	90	27.1	332	25.6
25–29	36	17.4	116	56.0	55	26.6	207	16.1
30–34	34	34.7	52	53.1	12	12.2	98	7.7
35–39	27	73.0	9	24.3	1	2.7	37	2.8
40–44	16	76.2	3	14.3	2	9.5	21	1.7
45–49	5	62.5	3	37.5	...	...	8	0.7
50–54	8	72.7	...	...	3	27.3	11	0.8
55–59	5	100.0	...	...	...	...	5	0.3
60–over	5	100.0	...	...	...	...	5	0.3
Total	240	18.6	825	63.8	227	17.6	1,292	100.0

For interracial rape, this picture changes. In cases of Negro attacks on whites, 44 percent of the cases involved victims who were at least ten years older than their assailants, while only 29 percent of the cases involved victims who were at least ten years younger than their assailants; 27 percent of the cases involved victims of the same age as their assailants. In cases of white attacks upon Negroes, in 55 percent of the cases the victim was of the same age cohort as the offender. In 31 percent of the cases the Negro victim was "much younger," while in only 14 percent of the cases she was "much older." These findings apparently indicate that, in general, offenders and their victims tend to be drawn from similar age cohorts. However, in cases of interracial rape, it appears that Negroes tend to attack older victims while whites tend to attack younger victims.

Table 13: Victim-Offender Age Disparity by Race

| | Offender/Victim | | | | | | | | | |
| | Negro/Negro | | White/White | | Negro/White | | White/Negro | | Total | |
	No.	%	No.	%	No.	%	No.	%	No.	%
Victim much younger (−10 years)	174	17.0	45	22.8	12	29.3	9	31.0	240	18.6
Both same age (±5 years)	676	66.0	122	61.9	11	26.8	16	55.2	825	63.8
Victim much older (+10 years)	175	17.0	30	15.3	18	43.9	4	13.8	227	17.6
Total	1,025	100.00 (79.3)	197	100.0 (15.2)	41	100.0 (3.2)	29	100.0 (2.2)	1,292	100.0

In the light of this distinction it would be interesting to consider the circumstances under which intraracial rapes occur.

Age Differences in Other Studies and Reports

The literature on rape describing age distributions of offenders, reveals results similar to those found in the present study. However, differences appear regarding the relative ages of offenders and victims. The reasons may be explained by differences in the samples; by the use of total population, rather than age-specific groups as points of reference; by the surveying of selective groups, such as convicted, hospitalized, or imprisoned offenders; by the use of different age classifications; or by the use of different descriptive statistics.

Few surveys give age-race distributions of offenders, and even fewer deal with victims' age; information about offender-victim race-age distribution is almost nonexistent.

It is accepted by criminologists that one of the conspicuous trends in crime during the past three decades has been the increasing involvement of youth.

According to the UCR (1960),[2] in 25 percent of 6,886 arrests for forcible rape, the offenders were between the ages of 20 to 24; 31.4 percent were in the age group 15–19; and 15.5 percent of the offenders were 25 to 29 years of age. It seems that from the age of 25 on there is a decline in the number of arrests for rape, the peak ages being 20–24. Under age 25, according to the same reports, can be found about 20 percent of the of-

2. P. 92, table 17.

fenders: this was the case in all *UCR* data for the years which the present study covers (1958, 1960).

A survey of the Philadelphia police *Annual Reports* for the same years, shows the highest frequency of rapists' ages was 15–24, with 23 as the median age. A tendency for the number of cases to decline appears at the age level 30–34. Other studies have shown the age of rapists to range from 19–30 with the medians around 25.[3] Other studies show that the medians of rapists is somewhat younger, ranging from 16 to 20.[4]

Very few sources are available with which to compare the present study's data regarding age-race distribution of offenders. A study in Detroit concluded that because Negroes in the population were, on the average, younger in age than whites, they tended to commit more crime —including rape.[5] Tappan, on the basis of his survey on sex offenders recorded by the New Jersey state police (1930–39), found almost no differences between the ages of white and Negro rapists.[6] His findings, at a crude classification of age levels, were: among whites, 30 percent were under 12 years of age, 63 percent were minors, and 37 percent were adults. Among Negroes, 20 percent were under the age of 12, 69 percent were minors, and 31 percent were adults. Thus, the differences between the ages are very slight.

Von Hentig suggested that standardization of age differences of the white and Negro groups would substantially reduce the Negro crime rate at all age levels.[7] Indeed, this was found in Pennsylvania by Bates for crime rates, as well as by Sheldon and Spirer. Nevertheless, these researchers did not tackle the problem of how standardization would affect the age rate of specific crimes committed by Negroes.

On the basis of the "sex ratio" theory advanced by Von Hentig, there might be a reason to believe that the upset of the balance between the sexes will lead to more rapes.[8] From the presumption of a surplus of males in ages 18–25 years, it can be further inferred, that victims and offenders will be of the same age—with victims, however, somewhat older or younger, to compensate for this imbalance. Studies have disproved this

3. Apfelberg, et al., p. 763; *California Sexual Deviation Research* (1952), pp. 12–17 and (1954) chap. 2; Collins, p. 3; *The Dangerous Sex Offender*, p. 7; Fitch, 19–20; Frosch and Bromberg; Gillin, *The Wisconsin Prisoner*, pp. 212–13; Glueck, Jr., *New York Final Report*, p. 94; Guttmacher, p. 61; Svalastoga, p. 50.

4. Radzinowicz, *Sexual Offenses*, p. 114; *Report of the Mayor's Committee*, p. 76; *Report on the Study*, pp. 65–95; Ruskin, p. 956; Stürup, pp. 1–19.

5. *The Negro in Detroit.*

6. *The Habitual Sex Offender*, p. 20.

7. "The Criminality of the Negro."

8. "The Sex Ratio."

theory,[9] suggesting as a critical factor the surplus of bachelors among young males in the critical ages 18–24. As far as the Negroes are concerned, there is ample evidence,[10] that whatever the sex ratio is in their group, the young Negro males have ample opportunities for pre- and extra-marital sexual relations which may eliminate the necessity to resort to rape for sexual outlet.[11]

Turning our attention to victims' age, only meager data is available. A California study shows, that among 124 victims (in San Francisco), 46 percent were in the age 14–17 and 38 percent were under 14 years of age.[12] The range of victim ages was 18–38. Regarding the age difference between offenders and victims (frequently used to measure the seriousness of the offense), 50 percent of the cases showed a difference of 17 or more years, and in 25 percent the victims were 30 or more years older than the offender. However, most of the young offenders were involved with victims of their own age (14–17), while older offenders with victims of 4 to 10 years of age. An earlier report from California shows that the offenders and victims were in the same age levels, the most extreme case was that of a 24-year-old who raped an 18-year-old-victim.[13] Dunham also found that victims were in the same age levels as their assailants (ages 20–24).[14] A Pennsylvania study indicated that paroled sex offenders were involved with victims who were: in 12 percent of the cases 1 to 11 years old; 24 percent of the victims were between 11 to 15 years old; in 12 percent of the cases the victims were between the ages of 16 to 20; and in 21 percent they were 21 years and over. A survey in Minneapolis found the mean age of victims to be 16.7,[15] but the *Report of the Mayor's Committee* shows that girls under 10 years of age were also victims.[16] Another New York report found that of 39 rapists, in seven cases, girls under 10 years of age were victims of older offenders.[17] In the remaining cases, the victims were in the same age level or slightly younger than the offender. Abrahamsen, generalized the results of this study, saying that, "rapists tried to avoid women of their own age," therefore, ". . . a great discrepancy in age, . . . usually existed between rapists and their victims."[18] This

9. Svalastoga, p. 48. The data pertains to European studies; see also his notes 5 and 6.

10. A. J. Reiss, "Sex Offenses," p. 313.

11. Childers; Dollard, pp. 293–96; Frazier, "Sex Morality among Negroes."

12. *California Sexual Deviation Research* (1954), chap. 5.

13. Ibid. (1952), chap. 3.

14. Dunham, chap. 6.

15. Collins, et al., p. 6, table 3.

16. *Report of the Mayor's Committee,* pp. 76–77.

17. *Report on the Study,* pp. 63–65.

18. *The Psychology of Crime,* p. 166.

generalization is not borne out after a careful reading of all cases reported in this study. In another New York study, by Glueck, it was found that 40 percent of the victims were between 12 to 30 years of age and 50 percent between 31 to 45.[19] In ten percent of the cases, the victims were between 10 to 17 years of age. Radzinowicz reported that in 78 percent of the assault cases (which we understood to include rape), the victims were under 14 years of age; in 34 percent they were under 8 years, and in 48 percent they were between the ages of 14 to 18.[20] Another breakdown shows the following: ages 8–13, 27 percent; 14–15, 39 percent; 16–20, 14 percent, and 21 years and over accounted for 7 percent. The most dangerous age for victimization was, therefore, 15–19.

Stürup, observed 16 rapists for the effects of castration upon their social adjustment.[21] He found that in almost all cases offenders and victims were of the same age group.

Svalastoga found a similar age range of victims (8–77 years), with 77 percent of the victims between the ages of 10 to 24. In 50 percent of the cases, victims were between 15 to 19 years of age.[22] Finally, Gillin, in his famous study of Wisconsin prisoners, found victims of rape to be (in the majority of cases) above 10 years of age.[23]

19. *New York Final Report,* table (p. 24), p. 295.
20. *Sexual Offenses,* p. 28.
21. Stürup, pp. 10–12.
22. Svalastoga, p. 52.
23. *The Wisconsin Prisoner,* pp. 128–31.

5

Marital Status, Employment, and Occupation

The general impression obtained from the literature on sexual offenses is that since forcible rape is committed particularly by youthful offenders, the majority of rapists are unmarried. It is further claimed that for the youthful offenders the possibility of a disturbed sex ratio is a factor in the explanation of rape.[1] Others have suggested that a sex ratio imbalance among unmarried adults in the peak marital propensity period makes them resort to rape because finding a legitimate sexual outlet is a difficult problem.[2] Other factors (such as physical, social, or emotional disabilities) making it difficult to secure sexual partners may also be involved; but the nature of this study does not lend itself to the pursuit of this latter problem.

The marital status of offenders and victims was analyzed in order to see what patterns emerge and to check upon the sex-ratio-imbalance theory. Analysis of marital status patterns in forcible rape is made in table 14. Rates are computed on the basis of the United States Census.[3]

From table 14 it appears that, in general, victims are "dependent," that is, below the age of marriage; and offenders are more often "single," that is, above the age of marriage but unmarried. Victims and offenders of both races have almost the same rates for marriage status. Race differences do exist in other marital-status categories.

Among victims, the highest rates exist for the dependent group (92.0);

1. Von Hentig, "The Criminality of the Negro," pp. 622–80.
2. Svalastoga, p. 48.
3. United States Bureau of Census, 1960, p. c.(1) 40B, Pa. table P–2.

the second highest rate is for the single group (74). Offenders, on the other hand, show the highest rate in the single class (270), with the second highest rate in the dependent group (109). Again, these statistics coincide with the fact that offenders are somewhat older than their victims but there are also many who are of the same age level as their victims.

When marital-status categories are broken down further by race, it appears that Negro offenders have higher rates than white offenders in the single status (841). Their second highest rate is in the dependent

Table 14: Rates per 100,000 Population, Victims and Offenders, by Marital Status

Marital Status	Negro	White	Both Races
Victim			
Single	299.1	27.1	74.3
Married	111.4	7.0	33.2
Separated	57.8	22.7	45.5
Divorced	18.7	14.9	16.0
Widowed	11.0	7.8	8.5
Dependent	188.9	19.7	92.0
Offender			
Single	841.3	91.4	270.1
Married	...	95.7	7.7
Separated	27.5	10.7	20.9
Divorced	35.9	...	8.2
Widowed	34.6	...	8.7
Dependent	360.2	16.5	109.5

category (368), and it is 23 times higher than for the white dependent group (16).

A *significant* difference is found in the single and dependent status specific rates between Negro and white offenders.

Victims are more concentrated in the dependent status group: 43 percent, compared to 17 percent of the offenders. The reason for this fact is that victims tend to be younger than offenders. However, victims are more evenly distributed over the marital status structure; therefore, for the married, separated, divorced, and widow statuses, victims have higher rates than offenders. This finding coincides not only with the fact that victims have a broader age range than the offenders, but also with the fact that adult and middle-age group victims are attacked by younger offenders.

For the Negro female population, 299 are single and 189 are dependent. The same is true of the white victim, but Negro rates are consistently higher than those of the white victims at each marital status category. A *significant* difference in rates of dependent and single marital status categories is found between the relative rates of Negro and white victims. This finding is accounted for by the greater involvement of Negro victims in the crime of rape and by the fact that they are on the average younger than white victims.

Note on the Demographic Explanation of Forcible Rape

A demographic explanation for rape has been proposed by Von Hentig, who argues that a disturbed sex ratio for unmarried persons aged 15–49 years, which leads toward the direction of male surplus, creates a problem of securing sexual partners.[4] Svalastoga reports on some European studies on rape which were conducted under this assumption of overall disturbed sex ratios or imbalance where the proportion of young males in the marriage propensity age exceeds that of female.[5] He tested this hypothesis in his study on forcible rape in Denmark, and found that the regions with the highest positive departures from a sex-ratio equilibrium (rural communities) have the highest relative-age incidence.[6] However, he also found great differences in the frequency of forcible rape in regions having roughly the same sex ratio. He explains this result in terms of differentiated availability of other kinds of sexual outlet, such as prostitution. The only study available about relationships between prostitution and sex crime refutes this explanation.[7]

I attempted to test the hypothesis of the disequilibrium sex ratio, using Philadelphia census statistics. First tested is the assumption of a disturbed ratio among unattached persons, and then the assumption of imbalanced sex ratios in the marriage propensity age.

According to the demographic structure of Philadelphia, 60 percent of the female population age 16 and above is married (table 15); however, if we consider the categories of single, divorced, and widowed, for the total age range, almost an equal number are maritally unattached (45 percent). If we add the dependent victims, the percentage of maritally unattached females is 81 percent of all females up to 60 years of age.

The same picture emerges for each racial group. Of Philadelphia Negro females, 60 percent are married, as compared to 59 percent of the white females. However, the maritally unattached Negro females comprise 51 percent (without the dependent group), and 86 with dependent group included. The percentages for the white female group are 43 and

4. "The Sex Ratio."
5. Svalastoga, p. 48.
6. Ibid., p. 51.
7. Kinsie, "Sex Crimes and the Prostitution Racket."

76.5 percent, respectively. Both female groups have the same proportion of dependents, but the Negro female population has a higher proportion of maritally unattached persons due to high proportions in the separated category: 12 percent versus 2 percent in the white group.

For the Philadelphia male population, the same observation is valid. Of the total male population of both races age 16 and above, 65 percent are married. However, if we consider the total age structure and the marital status categories of unattached, then 54 percent of the total male population belong to the latter category. This includes the dependent group; without this group the percentage is lowered to 38.

Table 15: Percentage of Population and of Victims in Rape by Race and Marital Status

Victim	Percentage of Females in Marital Categories in Total Population			Number and Percentage of Marital Status in the Present Study					
	Both Races	Negro	White	Negro		White		Total	
				No.	%	No.	%	No.	%
Single	23.2	22.4	23.4	131	25.2	38	30.2	169	26.27
Married	59.8	61.0	59.0	133	25.6	25	19.8	158	24.5
Separated	4.7	12.4	2.2	14	2.7	3	2.4	17	2.6
Divorced	2.4	2.7	2.2	1	0.2	2	1.6	3	0.5
Widowed	14.6	13.9	15.0	3	0.6	7	5.6	10	1.5
Dependent	35.9	34.2	33.4	228	43.8	50	39.7	278	43.0
				(518)		(49)		(267)	
No information	...	...	...	10	1.9	1	0.8	11	1.7
Total	100.0	100.0	100.0	520	100.0	126	100.0	646	100.
					(80.5)		(19.5)		

According to race breakdown, a predominant number of white and Negro males are married: 65 and 55 percent, respectively. Again, Negroes have somewhat higher proportions of maritally unattached persons: 53 percent when computed with the dependent group, 40 percent without it. The white male group included 50 percent unattached computed with the dependent group and 34 percent without it.

When this demographic data is compared with the figures obtained in the study, the picture drastically changes. Of the victim group, only 24 percent are married, and the proportion of unattached is 74 percent with the dependent group, and 31 percent without it; 43 percent are dependent. According to race breakdown, 72 percent of Negro females are un-attached, as opposed to 79 percent of white females; these figures include the dependent group. Without the latter, the proportion is 29 and 40 percent, respectively. Negro victims have a higher proportion of the dependent status (44 percent Negro; 40 percent white), although more white victims are single, 30 percent, against 25 percent of Negro victims. Negro victims were found generally to be younger than white victims.

As with the male group, the proportion of unattached persons in the study is much higher than that in the total population: 84 percent including the dependent group and 68 percent without it, compared to 54 and 38 percent, respectively, in the total population. A race breakdown reveals more of this tendency; 91 percent of the Negro offenders are unattached (the dependent group included), as compared to 52 percent in the total population. Without the dependent group, the proportions are 65 and 40 percent, respectively. This fact is due mainly to a low proportion of married Negro men in the study: 16 percent, against 65 percent in

Table 16: Percentage of Population and of Offenders in Rape by Race and Marital Status

Offender	Percentage of Males in Marital Categories in Total Population			Number and Percentage of Marital Status in the Present Study					
				Negro		White		Total	
	Both Races	Negro	White	No.	%	No.	%	No.	%
Single	28.3	24.3	28.3	400	63.3	139	76.0	539	66.1
Married	65.1	64.8	65.2	104	16.4	27	14.8	131	16.1
Separated	3.4	8.7	1.7	4	0.6	1	0.5	5	0.6
Divorced	1.7	1.7	0.6	1	0.2	...	...	1	0.1
Dependent	15.8	13.0	15.2	170	26.9	15	8.2	185	16.6
				(63.2)	(77.5)	(183)	(22.5)		
No information	...	...	...	434	...	43	...	...	...
Total	100.0	100.0	100.0	1,066	100.0	226	100.0	1,292	100.0

the total Negro population in Philadelphia. As with the white offenders, 84 percent are unattached (the dependent group included), as opposed to 50 percent in the total white, male group in Philadelphia. Without the dependent group the figures are 76.5 and 34 percent, respectively. Again, this percent is due to a low proportion of married offenders. Examination of sex differences in the total population shows that there is slight predominance of married males (65 percent) over married females (60 percent). On the other hand, the proportion of unattached females in the population is larger than that of males. With the dependent group included, the percentage of unattached females is 81 percent, compared to 54 percent of males. Without the latter group, the proportion is 45 percent of unattached females against 38 percent of unattached males. The reason for this difference is in the higher percentages of victims (15 percent) and dependent females (36 percent) in comparison to the male group (5 and 16 percent, respectively).

A breakdown according to race shows similar patterns. Negro females have higher proportions of dependent persons (43 percent) as opposed to 34 percent dependent in the Negro male population. The proportion of married, however, is found to be similar; 61 percent of Negro females in Philadelphia were married, compared to 65 percent of males. Also, the percentage of widows and separated Negro females is much higher than that of Negro males. Therefore, there are 86 percent unattached Negro females (dependent group included), as opposed to 53 percent of Negro males. Without the dependent group the proportion is 40 and 34 percent, respectively. Among the white population, females also exceed males in the unattached status category: 76 percent against 50 percent, the dependent group included, and 43 percent as opposed to 34 percent when the latter group is excluded. When this demographic data is compared to the figures obtained in this study, the results are as follows: there are many more single males than females (66 percent versus 26 percent), but the percentage of dependent victims is much higher (43 percent) than dependent offenders. However, the offenders' group shows higher proportions of unattached persons than the victims' group with or without the dependent group: 84 percent against 74 percent with the dependent group; 68 percent against 31 percent, when the latter group is excluded. The explanation for this result is the higher proportion of single males. Also, this outcome of the study completely differs from that obtained from the census data, where the proportion of unattached females was higher for both races and for each racial group. Imbalance of marital unattachment in the community thus cannot explain the propensity of males to rape, especially since it may mask race differences.

A breakdown according to race, however, shows the same pattern. Offenders of both races have higher proportions of unattachment than victims, with or without the dependent group. Table 17 clearly illustrates this and the previously discussed race patterns.

To further test the hypotheses of the sex ratio theory examine table 18, which shows the sex ratio balance reversed, both for the total population and for each racial group. As has been demonstrated, in the most critical ages (15–19), the sex ratio is in favor of the males. Especially in the Negro group, there is an excess of females in every age level. For the white group, the balance tips a little, the highest sex ratio being the age level 25–29 with 107 males for every 100 females. In this study, then, the age-sex ratio hypothesis is not proved as an explanation for forcible rape.

Von Hentig,[8] in his discussion on the sex ratio, comments on the com-

8. "The Sex Ratio," p. 448.

Table 17: Proportion of Unattached Persons, Victims and Offenders in
Rape, by Race and Sex Differences in Philadelphia
Total Population (In Percent)

	In Total Popu- lation of Both Races		In Total Popu- lation within Each Racial Group		In the Study	
	Females	Males	Females	Males	Victim	Offender
Negro						
With dependent	...	...	85.6	52.9	72.5	91.5
Without dependent	...	...	51.4	39.9	28.7	64.6
White						
With dependent	...	...	76.5	49.6	79.5	84.31
Without dependent	...	...	42.8	34.4	39.8	76.5
Total						
With dependent	81.1	54.1	...	...	74.3	84.3
Without dependent	45.2	38.3	...	...	31.3	67.7

putation of the ratio, stating that a refined sex ratio is that which excluded those who were never married. According to this suggestion, the marital status ratio is computed with and without the dependent group (table 19). Here is found in the single group 108 males to every 100 females, a predominance common to both racial groups, but not large enough to produce "structural strains" which may lead to the attempts to secure

Table 18: Sex Ratio among Total Population of Both Races, and of the
Negro and White Groups, Ages 14 to 60 and Over,
Philadelphia, 1960

	In Total Population of Both Races	In the White Group in the Population	In the Negro Group in the Total Population
10–14	102.5	104.6	97.9
15–19	94.4	96.7	88.2
20–24	89.9	96.8	75.7
25–29	98.6	107.1	81.7
30–34	94.7	100.3	83.5
35–39	90.5	91.8	87.8
40–44	87.6	88.1	86.2
45–49	88.6	89.4	86.3
50–54	89.5	89.7	89.1
55–59	89.9	89.1	93.1
60–over	49.1	49.6	57.9
Total	87.0	89.3	82.6

Source: Sex ratio was calculated on the basis of United States Bureau of the Census, *United States Census of Population*, 1960, pp. 40, 243.

sexual gratification by force. In each of the separate unattached categories—separated, divorced, and widowed—the imbalance is reversed,
that is, there is an excess of females over males. This applies to the total
population and to each racial group within it.

Table 19: Marital Status Ratio among Total Population of Both Races, and
of Negro and White Groups, Philadelphia, 1960

Marital Status	Total Population of Both Races	White	Negro
Single	108.7	108.7	108.5
Married	96.9	94.4	91.0
Separated	63.8	70.9	60.0
Divorced	64.0	21.6	53.2
Widowed	29.4	28.7	31.9
Dependent	32.9	35.7	27.0
Ratio of the Unattached			
Without the dependent group	75.9	73.2	74.7
With the dependent group	53.8	48.0	55.6

Source: Based on United States Bureau of the Census, *United States Census of Population, 1960.*

A ratio of the total unattached category fails also to indicate an upset
of the normal sex-marital status ratio. On the basis of this evidence, it
seems that the sex-ratio theory, significant as it is when applied to the
present study, is not proven. This conclusion finally can be seen in the
comparison between the sex ratio rape rates and the number of rapists
(table 20).

Table 20: Comparison of the Sex Ratio and Rape Rates by Race,
Philadelphia, 1960

	Sex Ratio among Married Persons (10–60 years)	Forcible Rape Rates	Number of Rapists
Total population	69.1	44.94	1,292
White	70.9	41.90	226
Negro	64.0	591.25	1,066

Again the inconsistency is obvious and does not lend itself to demographic arguments as an explanation for forcible rape.

Marital Status and Forcible Rape Noted in Other Studies

The Philadelphia police and the *UCR* do not report on the distribution of offenders among the various categories of marital status. Although such data is supposed to be recorded in the files as standard procedure, the amount of "no information" in the rape files is very great. Hence, the information on marital status of offenders is confined to surveys and studies of offenders incarcerated or held in custody for treatment. Most studies have shown that offenders in general are unmarried—either single, divorced or widowed, depending on the sample.[9]

Employment and Occupation

The *UCR*, as well as *Annual Reports* of the Philadelphia police, do not use standard classifications in listing and recording the occupations of those involved in crime. The occupation of a victim or offender is generally not reported with the same care given to other aspects of the crime that have more bearing on police work. For this reason, the Philadelphia police department (and for that matter, any police bureau), in its recording, confuses levels of employment and skill, the nature of offenders' or victims' occupations (industrial, laborer, etc.), and the fact of unemployment. This absence of standard recording of occupation makes any attempt to use occupational status for the analysis of forcible rape a hazardous venture. However, the large number of Negroes involved in forcible rape, as well as their heavy concentration in the lower part of the occupational hierarchy, warrants some remarks on the relationship between occupation, race, and forcible rape.

Even if agreement can be reached on the criteria for placing individuals in occupational and class position, it is still impossible to make a general statement about the association between occupation and victimization. We can suggest, first, that victims come from mixed occupational backgrounds and, second, that certain women run a greater risk of being victimized because of their occupation (e.g., nurses, waitresses). However, since housewives, students, laborers and professionals are known to have been sexually attacked, it indicates that, generally, sexual victimization is not occupationally bound. But, because occupation is associated with social class, it can be plausible to conclude that the risk of lower-class women in low-status and low-income occupations is greater than

9. See: Apfelberg, et al., p. 764; Bender, p. 515; *California Sexual Deviation Research* (1954), p. 11; Dunham, p. 16, table 14; Fitch, p. 22; Gillin, *Wisconsin Prisoner*, p. 232, table 38; Glueck, Jr., *New York Final Report*, p. 252; *Report of the Mayor's Committee*, p. 87; Ruskin, p. 953; Radzinowicz, *Sexual Offenses*, pp. 115–17; Svalastoga, p. 50; Tappan, *Crime, Justice and Correction*, p. 197; *Wisconsin Experience*, p. 30.

that of middle-class women. Again race and residence are intervening variables in the association between occupation, social class, and sexual victimization.

It can be contended that if the social-class variable were controlled, the Negro rate would not be as high as the white rate. On the basis of other studies on the occupational status of offenders in forcible rape it is safe to assert, as is also true for homicide and other violent offenses, "that 90 to 95 percent of the adult offenders of either race are in the lower end of the occupational scale or from the category of salaried workers down through the unemployed."[10] In contrast, victims are composed also of the higher class. The question is raised then as to the possibility of substantial numbers of middle-class rapists who are not apprehended or that offenses against middle-class women are committed primarily by lower-class men. It is this latter situation which seems more plausible. As we shall see later, rape is also ecologically bound, and thus it is presumed that lower-class women are more likely to be a victim of rape by a lower-class offender.

Table 21 shows the distribution of employed and unemployed detected offenders in the occupational hierarchy.

We observe that 90 percent of offenders of both races belong to the lower part of the occupational scale (from skilled laborers down to the retired and the unemployed.)[11] Of the Negro offenders, 92 percent are unemployed. Negro offenders also comprise 74 percent of the total group of unemployed offenders. Altogether, 92 percent of the Negro offenders are at the lower end of the occupational scale, in contrast to 50 percent of the white offenders.

According to the census report of 1960,[12] white males were classified occupationally as follows: 74 percent of all skilled laborers; 72 percent of the semi-skilled; and 37 percent of the unskilled laborers. Unemployed white males constituted 14 percent of all white males age 16 and over in the labor force in Philadelphia, or about 5 percent of the total unemployed at this time.

For the sake of rate computation, the categories of professional, proprietors, clerical, and sales are eliminated, and it is assumed that all forcible rapes were committed by the lower occupational group of of-

10. Wolfgang, *Patterns,* p. 37.

11. This group does not include students and those serving in the armed forces. However, we have included the "no information" cases, assuming they are concentrated in the low end of the occupational scale. Bias, if any, occurs for the upper end of the scale. Without the "no information" cases, the percentage is still above 50.

12. U.S. Bureau of Census (1960), p. c.(1) 40D, p. 509, table 109; p. 749, table 122.

fenders. This assumption introduces a bias against whites, since their proportion in the higher occupational status is greater than that of Negroes. However, it still amounts to a small proportion—a fact which makes the assumption plausible.

In the light of the assumption that all the white offenders (226) were members of these lower occupational groups, the rate of forcible rape for white offenders in these groups is 74 per 100,000. This figure is twice as high as the rate (42) based on all white males in Philadelphia from age 14 and over in all occupations.

Table 21: Offenders in Rape by Race and Occupation

| | White | | Negro | | Total | |
	No.	%	No.	%	No.	%
Professional technical and kindred	1	0.4	0	0	1	0.1
Clerical and kindred	3	1.3	2	0.2	5	0.4
Managerical proprietors	1	0.4	1	0.1	2	0.2
Services	12	5.3	4	0.4	16	1.2
Laborer, skilled	8	3.5	2	0.2	10	0.8
Laborer, unskilled	41	18.1	407	38.2	448	34.7
Student	30	13.3	66	6.2	96	7.4
Armed forces	3	1.3	10	0.9	13	1.0
Retired	3	1.3	2	0.2	5	0.4
Unemployed (except student)	60	26.6	177	16.1	237	18.2
No information	64	28.3	395	37.2	459	35.6
Total	226	100.0	1,066	100.0	1,292	100.0

Note: Rates—"low occupation status," 73.8 (white) and 348.3 (Negro); "without the skilled category," 115.0 (white) and 542.8 (Negro).

According to the same census report, among the employed male population in Philadelphia, Negroes comprised 26 percent of all the skilled laborers; 28 percent of the semi-skilled and 63 percent of the unskilled. Unemployed Negroes constituted 35 percent of all Negro males over 16, or about 11 percent of the total unemployed male population. Again, in line with the above assumption that all 1,066 Negro offenders were stationed in the low occupational group, the rate of forcible rape is 348.3 per 100,000. This rate is almost twice as high as the rate (148.12) computed on the basis of the Negro male population in Philadelphia in all ages and occupations.

Previously, the rate for Negro offenders was shown to be four times greater than that for the white offenders; the new set of rates, however, based on the occupational groups as a population unit, is again about four times greater than that for white offenders. When the same type of analysis is made after eliminating skilled workers from the population base (thus retaining the assumption that rape offenders were members of only the semi-skilled, unskilled, and unemployed categories), the rate for Negro offenders is 543, or about five times as great as that of the white offenders (115). It is easy to see, therefore, that a crude control for the occupation variable produces little change in the differential rates between the offender's race, and that the rate for Negroes in forcible rape still exceeds that for the whites. This fact of differential rates for social classes has been demonstrated already for other types of crime,[13] and it will likely exist in further attempts to control other indexes of social class. The effect of educational level on sexual victimization is not yet specified, and it may be associated with other intervening variables such as social class, residency, or occupation. Since the choice of the victim does not depend on education, it can be assumed that women of all educational levels can be victimized.

There is no information on the educational achievement of offenders, because such information is not recorded in the police files. However, on the basis of other studies,[14] and because 13 percent of the white offenders and 6 percent of the Negro offenders in the present study are students, and on the assumption that low economic status is connected with low educational attainment, it can be stated that, if the educational variable is held constant, little change will occur in the differential rates between the races, with Negroes' rates exceeding that for whites.

Employment and Occupation Noted in Other Studies

Both the clinical case studies and the surveys of selected groups of offenders in custody demonstrate the fact that most rapists are to be found in the lower-end of the occupational and general status scale. This generalization remains true in spite of the variety of methods by which the information was assembled and presented.[15] Some investigators use level of employment skill as a measure, others the nature of employment, while still others present data on general socioeconomic status. Whatever the method or material used, rapists emerge as socially unprivileged in their occupation, their education, and their social status.

13. Moses; Wolfgang, *Patterns,* p. 38–39.

14. Bonger, *Criminality,* pp. 616–18; *California Sexual Deviation Research* (1954), chap. 5; *Dangerous Sex Offender,* p. 38, table III–5; Gillin, *Wisconsin Prisoner,* p. 225, table 24; Glueck, Jr., *New York Final Report,* p. 87, table H–6; *Report of the Mayor's Committee,* pp. 85–86; *Wisconsin Experience,* table 5.

15. Bonger, *Criminality,* pp. 616–18; *California Sex Deviation Research* (1954), p. 11; *Dangerous Sex Offender,* pp. 8–9; *Fitch,* p. 28; Gillin, *Wisconsin Prisoner,* p. 232; Glueck, Jr., *New York Final Report,* p. 190, tables K–7, K–8; Le Maire, reported in Svalastoga, p. 11; Radzinowicz, *Sexual Offenses,* pp. 126–27; *Report of the Mayor's Committee,* pp. 86–87; Svalastoga, p. 51.

It has already been shown that there is a relationship between low economic status and crime.[16] We can only speculate whether or not low occupational status or low income bear directly on the offenders being rapists. The issue is not the fact of crime but the kind of crime, or how economic status is connected with sexual crimes and with forcible rape. A further question is the relationship between the particular occupation or level of skill with rape. Even if one agrees with Vold that economic explanations of crime tend to be more scientific since they lend themselves better to statistics and quantitative evidence,[17] no proof is yet given, because the relation of economic status and criminality is indefinite and not so simple and unilateral as it is sometimes believed to be. Thorough research is hindered by looseness in the use of terms like "occupation" and "status," in police records. Furthermore, how, if at all, can we relate factors like financial needs and stress to rape? The assumption that poverty prevents rapists from marriage or from patronizing prostitutes and that they therefore resort to rape, is only a conjecture. There is no data on these points. It should be remembered, however, that many of the offenders in the present analysis are students and others are married. Also, we have already presented the opinions that lower class males have more access to women for sexual outlet, which makes the presumption about the direct relationship between rape and economic status a doubtful and tenuous one.

16. Wooton, *Social Science,* pp. 95–113.
17. *Theoretical Criminology,* p. 181.

6

Temporal Patterns

Historically, in charting temporal patterns, the major concern has been the relationship of crime to seasons,[1] temperature, and, on a few occasions, to other elements of weather phenomena. This concern may have originated in the nineteenth-century studies of this topic and especially in Quetelet's "thermic law of delinquency."[2] One may even begin with M. DeGuerry who, like Quetelet, found a relationship between regional variations and crime against the person and property crimes, which are due to variations in climatological conditions, specifically expressed in terms of warm and cold weather. Thus, Quetelet, and later, Mayo-Smith,[3] found that crimes against the person, especially those involving violence, are more prevalent in warm weather, while in the winter months, property crimes are more prevalent. These studies,[4] in spite of their methodological shortcomings and theoretical weakness,[5] prepared the way for examining the possible relationship between seasonal and other temporal variations of forcible rape.

1. DeQuiros, p. 10.

2. Cited in Pamelee, *Criminology*, p. 45.

3. *Statistics and Sociology*, pp. 271–72.

4. For a survey of this literature, especially on the seasonal aspect, see: T. Cohen, "Geography of Crime"; Aschaffenburg, pp. 16–30; G. J. Falk.

5. See Tarde's early criticism on climatological theories, *Penal Philosophy*, pp. 297–318; Barnes and Teeters, *New Horizons in Criminology*, pp. 142–44; Kaplan, "The Geography of Crime"; Sutherland and Cressey, *Criminology* (5th ed.), pp. 97–98.

By Month and Season: The Philadelphia Data

According to table 22, the combined two years of our study show an upward rise in the incidence of rape, beginning in the month of June and running to the end of September, with 42 percent of all the cases for the year occurring in this period. July is the summit month, accounting for 12 percent of all the cases of forcible rape.

Table 22: Monthly Distribution of Rapes by Race of Victim

| | Negro | | White | | Total | |
	No.	%	No.	%	No.	%
January	39	7.5	13	10.4	52	8.0
February	25	4.8	6	4.8	31	4.8
March	33	6.3	12	9.6	45	7.0
April	37	7.1	6	4.8	43	6.7
May	48	9.2	6	4.8	54	8.4
June	53	10.2	10	88.0	63	9.8
July	57	11.0	22	17.6	79	12.2
August	59	11.3	11	8.8	70	10.8
September	50	9.0	11	8.8	61	9.4
October	45	9.6	11	8.8	56	8.7
November	42	7.9	4	3.2	46	7.1
December	32	6.2	14	11.2	46	7.1
Total	520	100.0	126	100.0	646	100.0

However, on the basis of theoretically expected equitable distribution of rapes for each of the twelve months, the observed frequencies do not differ to such a degree of statistical significance to exclude chance and other variables as responsible for the variation. Dividing the year into four quarters, we note that more forcible rapes occurred during the hot months of May, June, July, and August (41 percent), followed closely by the relatively warm spring and autumn months of March, April, September, and October (32 percent); and that the lowest frequency is in the winter months of January, February, November, and December (20 percent). Thus, there is a slight but insignificant association between season and number of rapes.

More Negro than white females (table 22) are victimized during almost any given month of the year, but the proportion of Negroes is higher in the summer months, July and August being the peak months (11 percent each). July is the highest month for white victims, which account for a third of the number of incidents of rape in this peak month. The number of Negro victims varies less than the number of white victims, although white victims show an increase toward the summer months with July the summit month (17 percent).

Charting the monthly variations of offenders (table 23) shows a similar pattern to that of the victims. Again, summer months have the highest involvement of offenders, but a greater proportion of Negro offenders are involved in the crime in any given month. For the offender group as a whole and for the Negro group in particular, the monthly distribution of forcible rape appears to be more stable than that observed for the victim group as a whole and for each of the racial groups within. However, the number of white offenders increases suddenly in July, which has a three times greater incidence of the crime (21 percent) than, for example, the preceding month (8 percent); the same is true for white vic-

Table 23: Monthly Distribution of Rapes by Race of Offender

	Negro		White		Total	
	No.	%	No.	%	No.	%
January	99	9.3	27	11.9	126	9.7
February	65	6.3	5	2.2	70	5.4
March	74	6.9	12	5.3	86	6.6
April	78	7.3	17	7.5	95	7.4
May	106	9.9	14	6.2	120	9.1
June	99	9.3	19	8.4	118	9.1
July	120	11.2	47	20.7	167	12.8
August	107	9.9	24	10.6	131	10.1
September	107	9.9	21	9.4	128	9.8
October	87	8.3	17	7.5	104	8.1
November	76	7.2	7	3.1	83	6.4
December	48	4.5	16	7.2	64	4.9
Total	1,066	100.0	226	100.0	1,292	100.0

tims. July, therefore is the highest month for both Negro and white victims and offenders. Nevertheless, since in the majority of cases (95 percent) rape is an intraracial affair, with 79 percent of the rapes being committed by Negro offenders upon Negro victims, it appears that Negro rapes vary somewhat less frequently than white forcible rapes. The number of rapes among Negroes (table 23) gradually builds up from a February low of 25 rapes to an August high of 59, then starts to decline, but still maintains a relatively stable number (an average of 40 rapes) throughout the last four months. The highest incidence is almost twice as great as the lowest incidence. White rapes, on the other hand, show a consistent increase in the summer months, and the July high of 22 rapes is more than three times greater than the November low of 4 cases. Variations such as these, with no significant or positive association noted, make it necessary to reject a hypothesis which suggests a relationship between monthly or seasonal changes and variations in forcible rape.

The seasonal pattern of multiple rapes (where more than one offender assails one victim) provides a stronger case, though not a conclusive one, for relating forcible rape to seasons. In table 24 we observe the tendency of pair-rape and group-rape to increase during the summer months and to decline unevenly during the autumn and winter months. Of 105 cases of pair-rape, 55 cases (52 percent) occurred during the summer months.

Table 24: Monthly Distribution of Rapes by Type of Rape

	SR		PR		GR		Total	
	No.	%	No.	%	No.	%	No.	%
January	23	6.2	7	6.7	22	12.8	52	8.0
February	18	4.9	4	3.8	9	5.2	31	4.8
March	28	7.6	7	6.7	10	5.8	45	7.0
April	26	7.0	8	7.6	9	5.2	43	6.7
May	37	8.6	7	6.7	15	8.8	54	8.4
June	33	8.9	11	10.5	19	11.1	63	9.8
July	45	12.2	13	12.4	21	12.3	79	12.2
August	42	11.3	11	10.5	17	9.9	70	10.8
September	32	8.6	13	12.4	16	9.3	61	9.4
October	33	8.9	7	6.7	16	9.3	56	8.7
November	26	7.0	10	9.5	10	5.8	46	7.1
December	28	7.6	8	7.6	10	5.8	46	7.1
Total	370	57.3	105	16.2	171	76.5	646	100.0

However, the monthly distribution is marked by the greater incidence of single-rapes in each month; this fact suggests that although there might be an association between seasonal pattern and forcible rape involving more than one offender, the dominant type of rape (single rape, 57 percent) with the irregularities observed before, does not allow for accepting the hypothesis that there is a seasonal pattern to the crime.

Months and Seasons Noted in Other Studies and Reports

As far back as the beginning of this century (and the beginning of scientific criminology), it was found that in Europe sexual crimes occur most frequently in the warm months of the year and least often in the cold season from November to January. Such was the finding of Aschaffenburg who gives German statistics for 1883–84 and finds the months of April to September as the peak period, with July the summit month.[6] That the general influence of heat on sexual life also influences sexual criminality is a claim he attempts to prove by calculating the days of conceptions from a study of cohorts' birthdays.[7]

6. *Crime,* pp. 11–29.

7. Ibid., p .20.

Bonger, on the basis of English and French statistics, finds that rape on adult women increases from the spring season, achieves its peak in the summer months, and sustains a minimum frequency in the winter. In both countries, he finds that the peak is from May to September with June being the summit month.[8]

The monthly movement, argues Bonger, does not tell us much about the etiology of rape. Even the presence of greater temptations to rape and the greater opportunity of committing it in the summer, along with the frequency of offenders being caught in flagrante delicto, do not explain much. The spring temperature, he maintains, affects the sexual life in general and not sexual criminality alone (as is shown by the incidence of days of conception).[9] He believes that the economic conditions of the working classes which mainly contribute to these crimes should be the factors of explanation.[10] Ferri, in his *Criminal Sociology,* and in a paper by Aschaffenburg,[11] shows that sex crimes in France during the years 1817–69 had a constancy of frequency in the maximum and minimum months. He also detected a pattern in which adult female rape increases from April through July, the latter being the peak month. Rapes of young girls increase from May, with August as the high month. Like Aschaffenburg and Bonger, Ferri also upholds Havelock Ellis's opinion that sexual excitability increases in the summer months.[12] He also believes that the season multiplies the opportunities for the crime, since summer allows more social intercourse.[13] Ferri maintains, however, that economic conditions should also be considered as factors in the etiology.[14]

Garofalo states that it seems to be fully proved that "high temperatures exercise an indirect influence upon the evil passion," and especially if we consider the fact that "in the same century, the maximum number of crimes against the person occurs in the warm months."[15] Later, he proposes to measure the influence of climate on specific individuals and on social life in general.[16]

Lombroso, on the basis of statistical figures in England, France, and

8. *Criminality and Economic Conditions,* p. 613.

9. Ibid.

10. Ibid., p. 616.

11. Aschaffenburg, pp. 17–20.

12. Ferri, *Criminal Sociology,* pp. 210–11; Ellis, *Studies in the Psychology of Sex,* vol. 1, pt. 1, p. 150.

13. See also Aschaffenburg, p. 25.

14. *Criminal Sociology,* p. 211.

15. *Criminology,* p. 118.

16. Ibid., p. 120.

Italy, shows that forcible rape is most prevalent in the warm weather season, from June to September, and also, that the crime of rape increases in the "hot years."[17] Tarde views the causal relationship between season and forcible rape as connected with the intervening influence of urban life.[18] Forcible rape he believes, is a result of city living; of overcrowded conditions; of mobility and of intensive social contact. However, rape is more frequent in warm weather with conditions of city life serving as a catalyst in providing opportunities and temptations.

Falk in "The Influence of the Seasons on the Crime Rate" summarizes the European studies and comes to the conclusion that, as far as the data of the eighteenth and nineteenth centuries is concerned, forcible rape in France, Germany, and Italy does occur more in the warm regions and achieves maximum frequency in the summer.[19] In one of the more recent surveys of this problem, Von Hentig also detects a seasonal pattern in Europe.[20] He maintains that in moderate climates the curve of monthly crimes shows two summits: one stretches between the end of November and the end of January, and it stands for crimes against property: "Then there is another peak in the spring and early summer. At this time the crimes of violence and sex crimes reach a maximum; they rise again, but less vehemently in September or October."[21]

Von Hentig, however, maintains that each country has its own summit month: June in Italy and France; July in Germany and England. He reports on rapes in the United States according to *UCR*.[22] Although he agrees with the summer-pattern of rape, he finds the specific summit months varying. Thus, in 1940 the maximum number of rapes was in October; in 1941, in September; in 1942, in August; and in 1943 the maximum number of rapes was in June. According to his calculation, rape in Denver for every year over a five-year period culminated in July.

In another recent survey on this problem, Radzinowicz finds that in England 35.1 percent of all sexual crimes, including forcible rape, occur in the summer months (June through August); 24.5 percent in the spring (March through May); and 23.0 in the autumn.[23] He notes also that in the summer months more young victims are involved. Svalastoga states

17. *Crime,* pp. 4–11, 211.

18. *Penal Philosophy,* pp. 303–4, 355.

19. Falk, p. 211.

20. *The Criminal and His Victim,* p. 349.

21. Ibid.

22. Ibid., n. 21. A summer pattern in these years in the United States is confirmed also by Gillin, *Criminology and Penology,* pp. 72–75.

23. *Sexual Offenses,* p. 102.

that there is evidence to support Quetelet's "Thermic Law of Crime" inasmuch as in his study the four lowest figures for forcible rape occur during December through March.[24]

The *UCR* for 1960 show that for urban areas in general, as for Philadelphia, August is a high month (26.6 percent), while March and February are the low months (19.0 and 20.3 percent, respectively).[25] A chart given in the same annual report presents the variations from the annual average of forcible rape for 1955–60.[26] It demonstrates the existence of a marked monthly pattern in the variation of crime against the person and forcible rape. According to the annual report: "There is no month without crime, but certain crimes occur more frequently in their season. Crimes against the person, most notably, aggravated assault and forcible rape, reach their peaks in the warmer or summer months of the year."[27] With the year into quarters, the report further reveals that the daily average number of forcible rapes known to the police is 23.0, but the July-September quarter has a daily average of 26.2. The lowest daily average of 19.9 is in the January-March quarter. The same pattern is revealed in reports as early as 1935–40, and again in the 1954–59 reports.

Nevertheless, not all the reports in this country reveal distributions that follow the exact pattern usually reported for the nation, or that reported for Philadelphia. There are exceptions and differences in locations. In the monthly patterns of some cities in the United States, some variations are to be found, although the high months of forcible rape are still in the summer months.

Thus, the association between season and forcible rape does exist, but it is not a strong and consistent one. Some variations have been noted previously.[28] Also, in most of the studies, the relationship between season and rape is not specified.[29] There are intervening social variables, like alcohol and extensive social intercourse, but these factors should be taken as elements in the situation rather than as having a primary causal significance. Thus, in the words of Von Hentig, "It's no natural crime curve, which monthly variations reveal, but something changed by human minds and social institutions."[30]

24. Svalastoga, p. 49.
25. *UCR* (1960), p. 87, table II.
26. Ibid., p. 6.
27. Ibid., p. 4.
28. Kaplan, "Geography," p. 77.
29. Sutherland, *Criminology* (4th ed.), p. 82.
30. *The Criminal and His Victim,* p. 361.

By Days: The Philadelphia Data

A daily pattern of forcible rape is definitely discernible from the data collected in Philadelphia. There is a *significant* association between forcible rape and the days of the week when the offense occurs. From table 25 a pattern may be noted; the high frequency of forcible rape is on Saturday (24 percent), and the relatively low frequency is on Monday (8 percent). Three times as many forcible rapes occur on the day of highest frequency as occur on the day of lowest frequency. Friday and Sunday claim 14 and 16 percent, respectively—or half that of Saturday. There is neither a build-up to the Saturday high nor a gradual decline to the Monday low, for frequency during the remaining days of the week is relatively constant.

Table 25: Daily Distribution of Rapes by Race of Victim

	Negro		White		Total	
	No.	%	No.	%	No.	%
Monday	47	9.0	12	9.6	59	8.4
Tuesday	53	10.1	18	14.3	71	10.2
Wednesday	50	9.6	21	16.6	71	10.2
Thursday	63	12.0	12	9.6	75	10.7
Friday	78	15.0	17	13.4	95	14.0
Saturday	145	27.8	25	19.9	170	24.4
Sunday	84	16.5	21	16.6	105	16.0
Total	520	100.0	126	100.0	646	100.0

Of the high number of 170 victims on Saturday, Negroes constitute 145, or 85 percent. Moreover, because the Negro male is the largest contributor to the high frequency of forcible rape, it is he who produces a high frequency on Saturday (122, or 73 percent). Of 520 Negro victims, 28 percent were raped on Saturday. They comprise 85 percent of all females who were victimized on Saturday, but are only 24 percent of the total group of 646 victims. The white victim shares less in the Saturday rapes; white females make up 15 percent of those raped on Saturday and account for 20 percent of all the white victims, or 4 percent of all victims. White males make up 27 percent of those who rape on Saturday, and account for 4 percent of all 1,292 offenders. Negroes were victimized more than white females on any day of the week, with no special variation noted between Negro and white rapes during the days of the week. The number of Negro rapes is on the average three times greater than that for whites on every day of the week.

On the basis of a theoretical equal distribution of forcible rape for each day of the week, the observed frequencies for white and Negro victims and offenders do not differ to such a degree of statistical significance that chance and other variables could be eliminated as responsible for their distribution. Thus, a dominant pattern is discernible in rapes committed on Saturday, but as far as a race pattern is concerned, the equal frequencies observed for each racial group do not allow for accepting the hypothesis that there are daily patterns of the crime among the racial groups involved.

"Among the folkway in Philadelphia and probably in most American and European cities too, weekends are considered a special conjecture of time. It starts Friday evening about 8:00 P.M. and ends Sunday night."[31] Because of this fact, and because of the number of rapes which were committed at this time, it is logical and worthwhile to use Friday, Saturday, and Sunday combined as the basis for comparison of the incidence of forcible rape during weekends. Table 26 serves this purpose.

Table 26: Weekend Distribution of Rapes by Race of Victim

| | Negro | | White | | Total | |
	No.	%	No.	%	No.	%
Friday	57	19.9	12	20.6	69	20.1
Saturday	145	50.7	25	43.2	170	49.4
Sunday	84	29.4	21	36.2	105	30.5
Total	286	100.0	58	100.0	344	100.0

In Philadelphia, 69 rapes, or 95 percent of all forcible rapes which are recorded for Friday, took place between 8:00 P.M. Friday and Saturday morning. Also, 344 rapes, or 53 percent of all forcible rapes, occurred during the weekend, beginning Friday evening and ending Sunday midnight. Negro victims comprise 83 percent of all victims who were assailed during the weekend, or 35 percent of all Negro victims in the studies. White victims comprise 17 percent of all victims who were raped during the weekend, or 46 percent of all white victims in the study. The weekend pattern shows again that Saturday has the highest frequency for the whole victim group (49 percent). The same is also correct for the Negro group. It comprises 85 percent of the total Saturday rapes and contributes 51 percent to the weekend rape of the Negro victims. Of the white victims who were attacked on weekends, almost half (43 percent) were assailed on Saturday.

31. Wolfgang, *Patterns,* p. 112, and see his note on other studies on the weekday pattern.

Days Noted in Other Studies and Reports

In almost all other studies, the distribution of forcible rape by days is similar to the pattern found in Philadelphia. However, no other studies include an analysis by race. Thus, any similarity is taken on the basis of total cases. These other studies and reports enable us to distinguish between the days of maximum incidence, the day of lowest frequency, and the parts of the week which are low or high for rapes.

On the American scene we do not yet have any study comparable to the present one. However, a check of the Philadelphia police *Annual Reports* (1960), reveals a pattern (for some cities in the United States) similar to that found in ours, but with some variations. For example, in Columbus, Ohio, Saturday is the highest incidence day (25 percent) with Sunday following (18 percent). Weekend rapes, including Friday, constitute 58 percent of the cases. Washington, D.C., (1960) reports that 22 percent of the forcible rapes occur on Saturday. The second highest risk day is, however, Monday (20 percent). Weekend forcible rapes contribute 57 percent of the total cases.

Bonger reports that in Europe most of the crimes of violence, including rape, are committed on Saturday and Sunday, and are related to the consumption of alcohol on these days.[32] Falk, who summarizes the early European studies, finds that for Italy, France, and Germany, weekends, and especially Saturdays, are high-incidence days.[33]

Von Hentig maintains that crimes of violence and serious sex crimes culminate on Saturday and Sunday.[34] He, however, warns against placing an absolute reliance on figures obtained in such data. He says that often "the hour . . . is not established with absolute safety." Thus, some Saturday rapes really take place on Sunday. Later he adds that this Saturday-night criminality is "obviously caused by alcoholic and other excesses."[35]

More recent data is available on the Scandinavian countries. LeMaire, as reported in Svalastoga, finds forcible rape in Denmark to be mainly a week-end event; and Svalastoga, in his own study, indicates, however, that forcible rapes have higher than average incidence on Saturday through Monday as well as on Wednesday.[36] Verkko in Finland finds violent crimes against the person to be more prevalent on weekends.[37]

32. *Criminality*, p. 604.
33. "Influence of the Seasons."
34. *The Criminal and His Victim*, p. 392.
35. Ibid., p. 375.
36. Svalastoga, p. 49.
37. *Homicide and Suicide in Finland*, p. 82.

There the prevalence is connected with the consumption of alcohol on these days.

By Hours: The Philadelphia Data—

Distribution of forcible rape by hours of the day (table 27) has been tabulated for quarter periods, or in four six-hour divisions.[38] The observed distribution was found to be statistically *significant*. The most perilous hours are between 8:00 P.M. and 2:00 A.M., when almost half of all cases of rape (49 percent) occur. The second most ill-fated period, 2:00 A.M. to 8:00 A.M. has less than half (or 22 percent) as many rapes as the first period. The period between 2:00 P.M. and 8:00 P.M. ranks third (21 percent) and has almost the same proportion as the second. The least dangerous period, between 8:00 A.M. and 2:00 P.M. (8 percent) has only

Table 27: Distribution of Rapes by Six-Hour Periods of the Day and by Race of Victims

	Negro		White		Total	
	No.	%	No.	%	No.	%
2:00 A.M.– 7:59 A.M.	116	22.3	25	19.9	141	21.8
8:00 A.M.– 1:59 P.M.	42	8.1	10	7.9	52	8.0
2:00 P.M.– 7:59 P.M.	110	21.2	28	22.2	138	21.4
8:00 P.M.– 1:59 A.M.	252	48.4	63	50.0	315	48.8
Total	520	100.0	126	100.0	646	100.0

one-sixth the number of forcible rapes that occur during the highest period. Although only half of all forcible rapes occur between 8:00 P.M. and 2:00 A.M., a large proportion of the victims are Negro (81 percent); almost half of all the Negro victims (48 percent) are raped in this time period, along with exactly 50 percent of the total white group .

We should recognize the fact that the six-hour division of the day and the disjunction of the week by days are arbitrary delineations. They fail to take account of the fact that the set of events, such as drinking to-

38. Philadelphia police record the time on their forms, according to Daylight Savings Time, which begins in Philadelphia at 2:00 A.M. on the last Sunday in April and ends 2:00 A.M. the last Sunday in September each year. Since the population in its activities followed the same temporal sequence during Daylight Savings as during Standard Time, it was decided to use the former in this study.

gether, dating, and so on, which ultimately leads to the crime, has started before the recorded hour or day; "from this point of view, and in terms of personal social inter-relationships, the early morning hours are merely an extension of the preceding day."[39] Thus, the 141 rapes which occur between 2:00 A.M. and 8:00 A.M. may be added to the 315 rapes which are committed between 8:00 P.M. and 2:00 A.M., which makes a total of 456 forcible rapes (71 percent), occurring during this dangerous time span.

The combination of leisure hours and evenings on weekends intensifies the opportunities for personal contact, thus explaining the fact that the weekend hours are the most dangerous. From table 28 we observe that out of 95 rapes committed on Friday, 53 took place between 8:00 P.M. and 1:59 A.M. The events during this period comprise 95 percent of all

Table 28: Distribution of Rapes by Weekends and Six-Hour
        Periods of the Day

	Friday		Saturday		Sunday		Total	
	No.	%	No.	%	No.	%	No.	%
2:00 A.M.– 7:59 A.M.	12	17.4	47	27.6	40	38.1	99	28.8
8:00 A.M.– 1:50 P.M.	...	...	5	2.9	8	7.6	13	3.8
2:00 P.M.– 7:59 P.M.	4	5.8	30	17.7	15	14.3	49	14.2
8:00 P.M.– 1:59 A.M.	53	76.8	88	51.8	42	40.0	183	53.2
Total	69	100.0	170	100.0	105	100.0	344	100.0

rapes perpetrated on this day, while 53 rapes (87 percent) fall within the four hours between 8:00 P.M. and midnight—a period which claims the highest toll in each day of the weekend, or 53 percent of all weekend forcible rapes. From Monday morning to 8:00 P.M. Friday, there were 320 forcible rapes, but between 8:00 P.M. Friday and midnight Sunday, there were more rapes (344). Thus, on the average, 53 percent of all rapes occur during the shorter time span of 52 hours, while 47 percent occur during a period of 116 hours.

Hours Noted in Other Studies and Reports

As with daily patterns, the studies and reports of forcible rape by hours do not provide a detailed analysis by race. Comparisons with the present study must be made on the basis of total cases. However, in other studies,

39. Wolfgang, *Patterns*, p. 109.

the distribution of forcible rape by hours is similar to the pattern for Philadelphia.

Falk, in summarizing the early European studies, concludes that most of them indicate that rape is prevalent in the late evening hours, the peak being the two hours before midnight.[40] He attributes this fact to the consumption of alcohol in the evening, especially on weekends.

Le Maire, in his study of forcible rape in Denmark, finds the nightly period between midnight and 8:00 A.M. to be the "high risk" time, especially on Saturday and Sunday.[41] Svalastoga, who studied all forcible rapes brought before the court in Denmark (146 in 1958), shows the critical hours to be between midnight and 2:00 A.M. Two-thirds of the cases in his sample occurred between 10.00 P.M. and 4:00 A.M.[42]

Verkko, in another study of a Scandinavian country (Finland), finds that crimes against the person (including rape) occur mainly in the late evening hours.[43] He also attributes this fact to alcohol consumption.

Radzinowicz, in his study of England, finds, however, that 35 percent of sex offenses (including rape) occur between 1:00 P.M. and 6:00 P.M. and another 30 percent between 6:00 P.M. and 10:00 P.M.[44] He concludes that summer nights are the "risky" ones.

Moving from the European scene to the United States, Glueck, in his study on sexual offenses in New York City (June 1952 to June 1955), indicates (using different time divisions) that 80 percent of rapes occur between 10.00 P.M. and 7:00 A.M., while the second most crucial period is between 12:00 P.M. and 6:00 P.M. (13 percent).[45]

Police *Annual Reports* (1960) show that for Columbus, Ohio, the highest incidence of forcible rape (50 percent) occurs between the hours of 8:00 P.M. and 2:00 A.M., while in Washington, D.C., 30 percent of the cases occur at the same time. The *Dallas Texas Annual Police Reports* (1960) shows 60 percent of the cases during the same initial time period; Kansas City, too, reports 44.5 percent of their crime during the hours of 8:00 P.M. and 2:00 A.M. In all of these cities the second highest incidence occurs in the period between 2:00 A.M. and 8:00 A.M.

We can, therefore, conclude that forcible rape is preponderantly a nocturnal crime; and that it tends to be a weekend, midnight, and summer occurrence.

40. "Influence of the Seasons."
41. Reported in Svalastoga, p. 49.
42. Svalastoga, p. 49.
43. Verkko, p. 82.
44. Radzinowicz, "English Criminal Statistics," p. 101.
45. Glueck, Jr., *New York Final Report,* p. 293.

7

Spatial Patterns

It is beyond the scope of this study to delve into the host of problems involved in the ecology of crime. Questions about the importance of whatever is defined as a "criminal area";[1] the problem of indexing crime in these areas;[2] or the merit of the "criminal area" concept at all—issues like these are still argued in the criminological literature.[3] The victimological problems involve the two variables of territoriality and accessibility, therefore: Are victims more likely to be attacked in certain locations than others? What role does the location of initial meeting play in the opportunity the offender will have to commit the offense in the same or a different place. From the literature on this subject, one can derive some concepts which may shed light on the data at hand. The concentration of the crime of rape in certain city areas will be dealt with briefly here, but without entering into a description of these areas. In considering spatial patterns as related to forcible rape, we are interested in the relationships between the persons involved in the crime and the spatial variables, between the areas of their residence and the locations where the crime took place, and in the specific place in the residence where the rape occurred.

Offenders or would-be offenders have a tendency to cling to those areas of the city which they conceive of as their secure territory. The institution of the "turf" is one of the more salient manifestations of this tendency.

1. Jonassen.
2. S. M. Robison.
3. Mays.

But even where it does not exist, offenders tend to restrict their territory to those areas where they can function inconspicuously in what they feel secure. Also, the knowledge of the terrain assures fast and efficient escape.

Easy access from areas of criminal habituation also increase the potential for criminal activity. To the extent that crimes are opportunistic in nature and not planned in advance, offenders will move their place of residence or hangout to other places to commit their offense.

In terms of spatial characteristics certain women have a higher chance of becoming a victim of crime than others. A drunken woman on a deserted street at 2:00 A.M. is much more prone to be attacked by a stranger, or temporary drinking acquaintance, than a middle-class wife driving a car. Furthermore, the presence of victim, or the likelihood of finding one in a given place at a given time is closely related to victim's behavior, age, race, her relationship with the offender, as well as the motivation of both her and her potential assailant.

Terence Morris argues for establishing a distinction between area for crime commission and area of delinquent residence.[4] Shaw and McKay, he maintains, have dealt with only the latter. Lind provides some further concepts for analyzing the variety of relationships between area of residence and area of crime. First, there is the "delinquency triangle": although most petty crimes against property are committed by members of the same racial group, the more serious the crime becomes, the greater is the association with out-groups.[5] Second, there is the "neighborhood triangle," in which "the house of two or more offenders and the place of offense are located in the same neighborhood."[6] And third, he names the "mobility triangle of delinquency," a situation where "the houses of two or more offenders lie within the same local community, while the place of offense is situated outside."[7] Boggs in a similar vein reconceptualizes crime occurrence in terms of environmental opportunities relevant to each of twelve index crime categories. On the basis of factor-analytic tests of these crime-specific occurrence rates and the corresponding criminal-offender rates, he differentiates between neighborhoods according to their appropriation for different kinds of crime. Also differentiated are those neighborhoods where offenders live and those where they commit the offenses.[8]

Lind deals with crimes against property and his analysis applies to the distinction between predisposing factors in the area of residence (which

4. *The Criminal Area,* p. 20.

5. Lind, p. 218.

6. Ibid.

7. Ibid.

8. Boggs. See also Schmid, "Urban Crime Areas."

create the potentiality for delinquency) and conditions precipitating the offense which are not necessarily the same area.[9] He also maintains the distinction between localized and nonlocalized crime.

Without reference to areas of residence, such a distinction can be inferred from many studies, but actually most of them deal with the gradient theory of crime.[10] Lottier, for instance, claims to prove a gradient theory of crime against the person. However, this theory was shattered by Lander.

The Ecology of Forcible Rape

The inner city of Philadelphia is predominately black, and the white paranoia takes the form of inner-city blacks invading the white sections to pillage and rape.

No assumption can be made concerning contact between victims and offenders prior to the crime in these areas, but as we shall see later, a sizable proportion of victims knew the offender as neighbors or acquaintances before the offense.

The Philadelphia police department in a summary report (1960), ranked its districts according to the number of Part I offenses committed in them.[11] This report is compared to the figures of the number of rapes committed by whites and Negroes within these districts. Another comparison is that of rank by rate per 100,000 population and by racial groups, obtained from census-tract statistics, matched with population groups within the boundaries of Philadelphia police districts[12] (table 29).

The data reveal an agreement of figures between those districts which rank high in offenses against the person and those showing the greatest proportion of rape. Both of these figures are supported by the rate per 100,000 population for rape as obtained from the census tract; the latter source obviously presents a better index, or ranking device. It is evident that in certain areas there is a definite correlation and concentration of crime against the person and rape.

A more accurate picture may be drawn by ranking these figures by rates (table 30). The rates were calculated on the basis of racial groups within each census tract of the six leading districts. These six areas have a combined population of 442,694 inhabitants—304,311 Negroes and 138,383 whites. Although the combined population comprises 22.6 per-

9. See also: Morris, chap. 8; Reckless, *The Crime Problem,* p. 55; Taft, "Testing."

10. Hayner; Lottier; Schmid, *Social Saga of Two Cities,* pp. 334–41.

11. "Summary of Monthly Part I Offenses, 1960," *The Annual Philadelphia Police Report,* 1961.

12. Philadelphia City Planning Commission.

Table 29: Rank by Police and Census Districts by Offenses against the Person and Forcible Rape

Police District	Rank of District by Police according to Part I Offenses[a]	Rank of Police District for Forcible Rape	Rank of Census Tracts Matched with Police Districts	Cases in District in the Study No.	%
1	20	20	19	2	.3
2	22	21	20	11	.2
3	7	14	14	12	1.9
4	14	17	7	6	.9
5	23	19	17	3	.5
6	4	6	3	41	.3
7	21	18	18	4	.6
8	5	7	6	33	5.1
12	15	11	10	23	3.6
14	12	13	12	17	2.6
15	16	15	14	11	1.7
16	8	4	4	46	7.1
17	3	3	5	51	7.9
18	11	10	9	26	4.0
19	10	8	11	31	4.8
22	1	1	2	128	19.8
23	2	22	1	88	13.6
24	19	18	16	4	.6
25	13	16	15	9	1.4
26	6	5	8	42	6.5
29	10	15	11	11	1.7
35	17	17	21	6	.9
39	9	9	8	29	4.5
90[b]	18	12	...	22	3.4

a. This category includes: murder, manslaughter, forcible rape, robbery, and aggravated assault.
b. District number 90 is the city park.

Table 30: Rank of Police Districts, Rapes, by Rate of Race Groups

Police District	General Rank	Rate	Negro Rank	Rate	Percentage of Negroes in Area
23	1	147.9	3	135.86	87.9
22	2	131.7	1	169.86	93.9
6	3	114.0	2	163.73	54.3
16	4	85.4	5	89.85	84.3
17	5	60.7	4	92.06	60.7
26	6	34.36	6	64.44	36.82

cent of the total Philadelphia population, 57.5 percent of the Negroes in the city and 15.2 percent of the white inhabitants live here.

The table indicates that when the ecological factor is held constant, there is a relationship between race and rape. The proportions of rapes are higher in those six police districts and census tracts where Negroes are concentrated. These areas contribute 61.3 percent of all rape cases with a mean rate of 164 per 100,000 population, which is almost three times greater than the rate for the whole city (42.4).

Area of Criminal Residence and Area of Crime Commission

In the previous discussion of the ecology of crime, three variables were kept in sight: the residence of the offender; the residence of the victim; and the place where the offense was committed. Data has accordingly been collected on these variables by comparing on a map the offender's address, the victim's address, and the place where the crime took place. The following combinations are possible: offender lives in the area of offense but not in the area of victim's residence; offender lives in victim's vicinity, but the crime was committed elsewhere, that is, outside the victim's and offender's vicinity; offender lives in vicinity of the victim and of the offense; offender does not live in the vicinity of the victim or of the offense.

The term "vicinity of crime" denotes an area of five city blocks. It is assumed that this area is small enough to allow offenders or victims at least to see each other and perhaps even for the offender to have some specific knowledge of the victim's "reputation." It is sufficient here to point out that in 19 percent of the cases the victim stated in the police interrogation that the offender was a neighbor, and in 10 percent she knew him to be "generally from the neighborhood." It should be noted that for adolescents, distance is less a barrier to sociability than for adults.

A superficial look at table 31 reveals that in 82 percent of known cases, offender and victim live in the same neighborhood or vicinity, while in 68 percent a neighborhood triangle occurred, that is, offenders lived in the vicinity of the victims and offense.

It may be observed that in 26 percent of the cases (or in 16 percent of the total offender groups) the offenders live both outside the area of victim's residence and the scene of the offense. Also, in 3 percent of the rape events (or in 2.4 percent of the offenders group) the site of the crime was in the area of the offender's residence but not that of the victim. A kind of *mobility triangle* exists here, which takes into account the victim's residence area as well as the area where the offense took place and the residence of the offender. This fact may partly explain the intra-racial and intraclass patterns of rape. This is so because racial and class phenomena are considered ecologically bound. Indeed, such explanation is supported by observing the results obtained by breakdown of residence and crime area by specified racial groups of offenders and victims. Of 606 offenders who lived both in the vicinity of their victims and near the place of the crime, 92 percent are Negroes who assailed Negro victims. Or, among the 704 Negro offenders who raped Negro victims, 79 percent show this pattern of *delinquency triangle*. In the *crime mobility triangle* pattern, of 36 offenders who lived in the victim's vicinity but committed the crime outside the boundaries of their residence, 64 percent were Negro offenders who raped Negro victims. In the *residence mobility triangle,* 52 percent of the Negro offenders lived in the area of offense but not in the area of their Negro victims.

Table 31: Area of Residence and Crime, Offender and Victim, in Rape Events, by Race

Offender/ Victim	Offender Lives in Area of Offense Only Not Victim's Residence		Offender Lives in Victim's Vicinity But Rape Committed Elsewhere		Offender Lives in Vicinity of Victim and Offense		Offender Lives Not in Vicinity of Victim or Offense		No Infor- mation[a]		Total
	No.	%	No.	%	No.	%	No.	%	No.	%	
Negro/Negro	16	51.6	23	63.8	557	91.9	328	50.9	321	78.9	1,025 (704)
White/White	14	45.2	13	36.2	38	6.2	74	34.9	58	14.3	197 (139)
Negro/White	...	...	...	...	8	1.3	13	6.2	20	4.4	41 (21)
White/Negro	1	3.2	...	...	3	0.49	17	8.0	8	1.9	29 (21)
Total	31	100.0	36	100.0	606	100.0	212	100.0	407	100.0	1,292 (885)

Note: The figures in parentheses refer to the known cases.
a. Since in 163 rape events no information exists about offender's residence, the follow-ing discussion pertains to 74.74 percent of the cases. It also entails 407 unknown offenders or 68.5 percent of the 1,292 offenders.

Among offenders who raped white victims, a delinquency triangle exists in 27 percent of the total white offenders; a crime mobility triangle in 36 percent of the white offender group; and a residence mobility tri-angle in 45 percent.

In the interracial rape events, the proportions of each of these triangles in relation to the total is very small. No cases of a crime mobility or an area mobility triangle exists in cases of Negro offenders and white victims. In the cases of white offender and Negro victim we found no crime mobil-ity triangle and only one case of residence mobility, that is, the offender lives in the area of crime but not of the victim's residence. It appears that forcible rape is an intrarace, ecologically bound offense. It was found to be *significantly* so in the rape events where Negro offenders rape Negro victims and, indeed, in all rape cases in general.

In our analysis of age patterns it was found that offenders and victims were in the majority of cases in the teen-age and adolescent period. We can now claim that they were also neighbors. From table 32 it can be seen that of 825 offenders, 79 percent were of the same age as their victims and lived in the victim's vicinity. A delinquent triangle existed in 69 percent of the cases involving offenders who were of the same age as their victims, a relation which was found to be statistically *significant*.

Table 32: Area of Residence and Crime, Offenders and Victims, in Rapes, Victim Age Disparity

	Offender Lives in Area of Offense Not Area of Victim's Residence		Offender Lives in Victim's Vicinity But Rape Elsewhere		Offender Lives in Vicinity of Victim and Offense		Offender Lives Not in Vicinity of Victim and Offense		No Information		Total	
	No.	%	No.	%	No.	%	No.	%	No.	%	No.	%
Victim much younger (−10 yrs.)	9	29.0	3	8.3	145	23.9	35	16.5	48	28.0	240 (192)	18.6 (21.7)
Both same age (±5 yrs.)	17	54.8	3	86.1	383	63.2	124	58.5	270	32.7	825 (555)	63.8 (62.7)
Victim much older (+10 yrs.)	5	16.2	2	5.6	78	12.9	53	25.0	89	29.3	227 (138)	17.6 (15.6)
Total	31	100.0	8	100.0	606	100.0	212	100.0	407	100.0	1,292 (885)	100.0

Note: The figures in parentheses are the known cases.

When offender and victim were of different ages (table 32) again a delinquent triangle pattern dominated. In 77 percent of the cases when a victim was at least ten years younger than the offender, they lived in the same neighborhood; in 76 percent of the cases the offender not only lived in the same neighborhood as the victim but the offense also occurred within this area. In the cases where the victim was at least ten years older than her assailant, the former pattern occurred in 58 percent of the cases, and the latter (delinquency triangle pattern) was observed in 56 percent of the cases. A *significant* relationship was also found to exist between offenders' specific age level of 15 to 24 years and a crime triangle, as well as between victims' specific age level of 8 to 10 years and the crime triangle pattern.

Areas of Crime and Area of Residence Noted in Other Studies and Reports

Finding whether the residence of the offender is close to that of his victim is an important element in police interrogation. Some of the theoretical considerations accorded to this subject in the literature on the ecology of sex offenses have already been reviewed. It was seen that the analysis of sex offenses and rape usually ignore the relationship of the area of the crime to the area of the offender's residence.

Eralason, in a special note "on sex offenses as related to the residence of the offender," summarizes a survey made in Chicago (between January 1938 and June 1946), where "87 percent of all sex offenders committed their offenses within the neighborhood where they were residing."[13]

Crook on the basis of a study of delinquents in Chicago (1900–31) found that sexual offenses were ecologically bound between juveniles who were of the same ethnic origin.[14] In rape the social and sexual prejudices were not dissolved, and victims and offenders tend to be from the same neighborhood and same social background. Promiscuous girls and boys patronizing prostitutes were not bothered by such prejudices and both left the neighborhood for their sexual escapades. (A further calculation reveals that the white groups in these areas have higher rates than those in other police districts with an average rate of 50.8, a fact which may support a class rather than a racial explanation for the crime.)

Radzinowicz, in his characterization of the relationship between offenders and victims, mentioned that 22 percent of all sexual offenders (including rape) were living in the neighborhood of the victim.[15]

White studied the distance between the residence of felons and the location of the offense. He found that for 492 felonies the mean distance from offender's residence to place of offense was 1.66 miles. For all crimes against the person the distance was 0.85 miles; for rape (11 cases), it was 1.52 miles, and for assault it was 0.91 miles. For crime against property the distance was 1.72 miles. He concluded that "crimes against the person are crimes against neighbors."[16]

13. Eralason, 339–40.

14. Crook, "Cultural Marginality" and "Sexual Delinquency." See also Lindsey and Evans, pp. 66–67.

15. Radzinowicz, *Sexual Offenses,* p. 96.

16. "The Relation of Felonies," p. 511.

Different results are presented in two recent studies. Boggs, in St. Louis, found no relationship between rape and certain neighborhoods where mainly Negroes reside. Rape, he found, has no ecological and social concentration.[17] Schmid came to the same conclusion, and classified rape as "a typical crime factor."[18]

Sutherland and Cressey state, in regard to crime, that "within the city the places of crime are, generally, close to the residence of the criminals. This is characteristic of crimes against the person, for the offenders and the victims are usually of the same race, of the same economic class, and they are also from the same neighborhood."[19]

17. "Urban Crime Patterns," p. 907.
18. *Social Saga of Two Cities,* p. 598.
19. *Criminology* (5th ed.), p. 48.

8

Alcohol

The relationship between alcohol and sex crimes has long been asserted.[1]
It is therefore the aim of this chapter to determine whether there is, in
fact, any direct or indirect relationship between alcohol and forcible
rape, and whether the manner in which the crime is committed (violence
and sexual humiliation) is associated with alcohol and any temporal or
spatial factors in rape events.

Some Theoretical and Legal Considerations

"The true influence of alcohol on crime," maintains Aschaffenburg, "can
be ascertained only when crime is a direct consequence of the consumption of alcohol."[2] A direct relationship is assumed to exist if those involved in the offense were under the influence of alcohol when the crime
was committed.[3] Even then, the role that alcohol plays in the crime is
hard to assess. First, not all offenders are apprehended. Second, those
arrested may deny their indulgence in alcohol prior to the crime, while
others may overstate it in order to escape punishment;[4] the latter will
exploit the legal possibilities such as extenuating circumstances and
temporary nonculpability due to alcohol consumption.

1. For crimes against the person see, for example, A. Fink, *Causes and
Crime,* chap. 4 "Alcohol and Drugs," pp. 76–98; also, Wolfgang, *Patterns,*
chap. 7 "Alcohol and Violence," pp. 134–67.

2. *Crime and Its Repression,* pp. 75–76.

3. Hurwitz, p. 277.

4. Banay; "Alcohol and Crime," pp. 146–47; N. W. East, p. 192; Guttmacher, p. 70.

In criminal law the presence of alcohol in the offender is considered one of the extenuating circumstances of nonculpability insofar as the drinking person temporarily does not know the nature of what he is doing and cannot distinguish between right and wrong. While the law may sometimes allow being under the influence of alcohol to offset the assessment of specific intent, it does not free persons from responsibility when they voluntarily engage in behavior which has a foreseeable dangerous consequence.[5] Thus, the Model Penal Code expresses recognition of the elements of the victim's drinking in suggesting that when a woman loses capacity to control her own behavior by voluntary use of intoxicants or drugs, any resulting intercourse cannot be charged as rape.[6]

Even when the direct relationship between alcohol and the crime appears to exist, the nature of the causal nexus is very complex. Alcohol may be one of many factors involved in a given crime and varies in importance from being a minor consideration to a central causal factor. The role of alcohol in traffic offenses is relatively easily determined; but in a crime such as rape, although alcohol may not involve the offender, it may be a criminogenic factor.

Hurwitz, following Aschaffenburg, suggested that when one approaches the study of alcohol and sex crimes, a differentiation should be made between a *direct* relationship (or "acutic" relationship in Aschaffenburg's terminology) and an *indirect* relationship ("chronic").[7] For instance, an indirect relationship is one in which alcohol influences the general behavior and personality of the offender, as in the case where the offender is a chronic alcoholic; but at the time of the particular offense, was not under the influence of alcohol. Likewise, an indirect relationship is one in which alcohol is present in the victim rather than in the offender, or the case of victim and offender participating in a drinking party with both, or at least the offender, abstaining from alcohol. Here the effect of alcohol is on the total situation rather than the offending act itself. In determining whether there is any relationship between alcohol and rape, this study separately measures the significance of the frequency of victim drinking immediately prior to the rape and offender drinking immediately prior to the rape, as well as their occurring together. Most of the previous studies have focused on the presence of alcohol in the offender. The presence of alcohol in the victim has been virtually neglected; and the presence of alcohol in both offender and victim, as far as is known by the author, has not been studied before.

5. On the problem of alcohol as an element in criminal responsibility see: Drzazga, p. 66; Hall, "Intoxication"; Thompson, "Legal Aspects"; Wichsler.

6. See *Model Penal Code,* 207.4, comment at pp. 248–49.

7. Hurwitz, p. 289; Aschaffenburg, pp. 74–75; see also Tarde, p. 89.

The Philadelphia Data

There is very little information in criminal statistics about intoxication at the time of the offense. Such information can be obtained through the statements of convicted persons—hardly a reliable source of information —but the most often used in the United States.[8] Another source of data exists in the police case files. The police do not, however, record and test the amount of alcohol consumed by either the offender or the victim. There is, thus, no way of accounting for the presence of alcohol in offenders apprehended after a lapse of time, or in a victim tested some time after the crime.[9]

For each case of forcible rape in Philadelphia, the police investigated the victim, the offender (if apprehended), and witnesses to determine whether those involved in the offense were drinking prior to the commission of the crime. Also, an observation was made by the police as to whether either the offender or the victim were intoxicated during the investigation. Within these limitations it was possible to determine from the police case files whether those involved in the offense had been drinking directly before the rape. Unless the presence of alcohol is specifically mentioned in the case file, the absence of alcohol is assumed. Therefore, if there is recorded bias in any direction, it is in favor of the absence of alcohol.

The results in table 33 are clear-cut. Alcohol played no role in the commission of the offense in 429 (66 percent) of the 646 forcible rapes. In these cases, police secured no evidence, or did not record that either the victim or the offender had been drinking prior to the crime (at least during the day of the rape). Since the drinking habits of those involved were not known, no assumptions could be made regarding the possible indirect relationship of alcohol. Of the 646 forcible rapes, alcohol was present in the victim in only 62 (10 percent) of the cases. In 3 percent of the cases, alcohol was present in the offender only; in 21 percent, alcohol was present in both victim and offender.

For measuring the association of alcohol and forcible rape, the categories involving the presence of alcohol are combined. Thus, reference to "the presence of alcohol in the rape situation" means that either the victim or the offender, or both, had been drinking immediately prior to

8. Hurwitz (pp. 210–13) gives some data to show the contradictions obtained when such a method is used. See also: Ellis and Brancale, pp. 56–67; *Report on the Study,* pp. 21–22.

9. There are several studies in which actual tests of alcohol in the victim and/or offender have been made, including: Adler; *California Sexual Deviation Research* (1954), chap. 8; Frosch and Bromberg, p. 768; Glueck, Jr., *New York Final Report,* p. 306; Radzinowicz, *Sexual Offenses,* p. 99; Shupe, pp. 661–64.

the crime. This combination tells us that in 34 percent of the total number of cases, alcohol was present in at least one of the persons directly involved in each rape. Of these 217 cases in which alcohol was present in the rape situation, 63 percent showed alcohol present in both the victim and the offender, an association which reached *significance*.

Table 33: Rape and the Presence of Alcohol by Race of Offender and Victim in Rape Events

	Negro/Negro		White/White		Negro/White		White/Negro		Total	
	No.	%	No.	%	No.	%	No.	%	No.	%
Alcohol in both	98	19.7	28	26.6	4	14.8	6	35.3	136	21.1
In victim only	53	10.7	3	2.8	2	7.4	4	29.4	62	9.6
In offender only	16	3.2	3	2.8	...	...	...	...	19	2.9
Total alcohol present	167	33.6	34	32.2	6	22.2	10	64.7	217	33.6
Total alcohol absent	330	66.4	71	67.8	21	77.8	7	35.3	429	66.4
Total	497	100.0	105	100.0	27	100.0	17	100.0	646	100.0

Offender/Victim

In addition to the separation of alcohol present in victim and/or offender, the factor of race was included in the analysis, which increased the number of combinations considerably. The following facts on presence of alcohol and race emerge and reach the level of *statistical significance:*[10]

1. *Race of the offender.* Alcohol was present in the rape situation in 42 percent of the cases where a white person was the offender, but in 24 percent of the cases where a Negro was an offender.
2. *Race of the victim.* Alcohol was present in the rape situation in 26 percent of the cases where a white person was the victim, but in 20 percent of the cases where a Negro was the victim.
3. *In offender only, in both offender and victim, and race of the offender.* Alcohol was present in 30 percent of the white offenders and present in 22 percent of the Negro offenders.

10. It should be remembered that there were 646 multiple defendants, in addition to the principal offenders who were involved as two or more offenders in one rape. Therefore, even if only one of the offenders had been drinking prior to the crime, in cases where two or more raped one victim, alcohol was considered to have been present in the rape situation.

4. *In offender only, in both offender and victim, and race of the victim.* Alcohol was present in 28 percent of the white victims and present in 23 percent of the Negro victims.

5. *In victim only and race of the victim.* Alcohol was present in 11 percent of the Negro victims and present in 4 percent of the white victims.

A certain pattern emerges from these seemingly confusing associations. First, when alcohol is present in both offender and victim, it is the white victims and white offenders who are involved more frequently. When alcohol is present in the victim only, the victims are usually Negro.

If the critical factor of alcohol is its presence in both offender and victim, it is pertinent to ask whether race is associated with the presence of alcohol in either one or both of the persons involved in the same rape event (table 33).

Alcohol was found to be present in the rape situation in 34 percent of the 602 intraracial rape cases and present in 36 percent of the 44 cases of interracial rape events. After investigating the various relationships between alcohol and the race of the participants in each rape event, the following facts emerge and reach the level of *significance:*

1. *Intraracial events.* Alcohol was present in the rape situation (in the victim, offender, or both) in 27 percent of the white intraracial rape events and in 20 percent of the Negro intraracial rape events.

2. *In the offender only, in both offender and victim, and intraracial events.* Alcohol was present in 29 percent of white intraracial events, but in 23 percent of Negro intraracial rape events.

3. *In the victim only and intraracial events.* Alcohol was present in 11 percent of white intraracial events and 3 percent of Negro intraracial events.

4. *In the victim only or in the offender only.* In these cases it was the Negro offender and victim who were most often involved.[11]

Alcohol played a role in the rape situation more often when both offender and victim were involved in drinking. This means that the relational aspect of drinking, rather than alcohol itself is of utmost importance in exploiting the role of alcohol in forcible rape.

One way to estimate this relational aspect is to examine the presence of alcohol in the victim only, and in the offender only. We find (table 33) that when alcohol was present in the rape situation, in only 10 percent of the 646 forcible rape events the victim alone consumed alcohol. A breakdown by race shows that alcohol was present in 11 percent of the 520

11. The numbers in the cells of the fourfold tables for interracial events are too small; and since we dealt with dichotomous data, no adjacent categories could be combined. Thus, use of the test was not possible. Therefore, the comparison between intra- and interracial rape events is missing.

Negro victims compared to 1 percent in the white victims, an association which reaches *significance*.

Another measure of the relational aspect is to consider the presence of alcohol in the offender only. In terms of rape events, alcohol was present in the offender only in 19 cases or 3 percent of the total cases of 646 rapes (table 33). Moreover, in terms of the offender group (table 34), alcohol was present in the offender only in six percent of the total 1,292 offenders.

Table 34: Rape and the Presence of Alcohol by Race of Offender

	Negro		White		Total	
	No.	%	No.	%	No.	%
Alcohol in both	190	17.8	82	36.4	272	21.0
	(74.6)		(86.4)		(77.7)	
In offender only	65	6.1	13	5.7	78	6.1
	(25.4)		(13.6)		(22.3)	
Total alcohol present	255	23.9	95	42.1	350	27.1
	(100.0)		(100.0)		(100.0)	
Alcohol absent	811	76.1	131	57.9	942	72.9
Total	1,066	100.0	226	100.0	1,292	100.0

A breakdown by race shows that alcohol was present in offenders only in 14 percent of the white offender group, and in 25 percent of the Negro offender group. This result also points to the association between the presence of alcohol in the Negro offender and the crime of rape, and it also supports our assumption about the importance of the relational aspect in the drinking situation.

It should be remembered, as Wolfgang pointed out,[12] that associations between race and the presence of alcohol, or for that matter any other variable, should not be taken as causal connections. Neither can associations tell us the chances of becoming a rapist or of being a victim in such a crime while drinking, relative to the chances of the same phenomenon occurring while not drinking. This suggests that when inferences are made as to the presence of alcohol as a cause of rape, the special circumstances in which drinking was taking place prior to the offense must be taken into account.

The statistical results given above furnish no answers to the larger questions raised by the differences between the races in drinking and the committing of forcible rape. For such an answer we need to know the drinking pattern for each rape and sex group, the attitudes of men in these groups toward drunken women, or toward women who are drinking with men, and so on. Then, we must compare this data with a representa-

12. *Patterns*, p. 139.

tive sample of persons involved in the crime of rape. For instance, Negro men and women engage in more drinking, and the women may join the men without this being considered a sign of "bad reputation."[13] Therefore, it seems that it is the lone Negro woman who is more likely to be victimized by the very fact of her solitary drinking or by her state of drunkenness.

The white woman also appears to be more vulnerable to rape when she is drunk or is drinking with men. It may be that by drinking in public places with strangers the white woman defines herself as "prey" to her drinking companions. This would possibly explain the larger incidence of white women who are found to have been drinking with their assailants,[14] as well as the greater involvement of white women in rapes characterized by sexual humiliation.

Wolfgang has argued for the collection of data on the relative amount of time spent drinking, where it is done, with whom, and under what conditions.[15] Since drinking is a more common type of behavior than rape, the former activity should be more adequately described for the general population as well as by the variables of race, sex, age, and other social attributes in order to better appreciate the unique situation when drinking leads to rape.

Alcohol and Modus Operandi

Planning

Because planned and explosive rapes have in common the fact that it is partially the victim's behavior which leads to the rape event, it seems logical to inquire whether the presence of alcohol in either the victim, offender, or both, makes for different degrees of planning in committing the offense. It is easier to conquer a drinking female, but when the victim is drinking with the offender in a public place, he must plan either to remove her from the location of their drinking or otherwise manipulate the situation and the victim. Therefore, it was assumed that when alcohol was present in the rape situation, more planning would take place, especially when the victim was drinking.

The first part of the assumption was borne out and the association between degrees of planning and the presence of alcohol in the rape situation was found to be *significant*. In planned rape, alcohol was present in one or both parties in 23 percent of the cases; in partially planned rape in 16 percent of the cases and in explosive rape, 19 percent. When degrees

13. See Glazer, p. 183.

14. They are usually of her own race. In only two cases was a white woman drinking with a Negro male.

15. *Patterns,* pp. 139–41.

of planning were each tested as to association with alcohol in both victim and offender, *significant* association was found only between planning and the presence of alcohol. However, in the situations in which the victim was the only one who consumed alcohol, 30 percent of the cases involved planning or partial planning, and in 6 percent it was an explosive event. Thus, when alcohol is present in the victim only, alcohol appears to be important.

Violence

Because the presence of alcohol has been found to be associated with crimes of violence,[16] we assumed that an association exists between the presence of alcohol and greater degrees of violence in the rape situation. By combining the alcohol data and the evidence of physical violence, various relationships were tested and only one was found to be *significant*. There was an association between the use of violence against the victim and the presence of alcohol in the offender only. In all the cases where alcohol was present in the offender only, force was used upon the victim in the rape situation.

In the relationship between different degrees of violence and the presence of alcohol, it was found that a *significant* association exists between the presence of alcohol in the offender only and the infliction of brutal beating upon the victim. In terms of race, it was the drinking Negro victim who was involved more often in violent rape. For the white group, however, among nonviolent offenders the proportion of those who had not been drinking is higher than the proportion of those who had been drinking. A *significant* association was not found after testing all of the other combinations of degrees of violence and race of the victim and the presence of alcohol in one or both parties. It appears that, although alcohol and physical violence are associated, it holds only when the offender is a drinking Negro.

Sexual Humiliation

Does the presence of alcohol lead to further victimization or abuse of the victim in these cases? To answer this question we attempted to determine whether any relationships existed between alcohol and sexual humiliation practices, in general, and some in particular. We can assume, for instance, that because sexual capabilities are diminished by drinking the offender resorted to fellatio or cunnilingus in order to awaken his sexual desire and potency. Or, we can assume that the victim who is drinking is passive enough to become an object which allows the offender to seek further sexual satisfaction.

16. Ibid., p. 165.

Indeed, a *significant* association was found between the presence of alcohol and the occurrence of sexual humiliation in the rape situation. Sexual humiliation occurred in 44 percent of the cases where alcohol was also a factor, in 26 percent where it was absent, and in only 30 percent of the cases where alcohol was present but sexual humiliation was not involved. In the relationship between the presence of alcohol and types of sexual humiliation committed, only one association was found to be significant—the presence of alcohol in the offender only and subjection of the victim to fellatio. In all cases it was committed by Negro offenders.

It can be assumed that weekends have a disproportionately high number of forcible rapes partly because of the greater consumption of alcohol during this period. This assumption was borne out (table 35). A *significant* association was found between weekend forcible rapes and the

Table 35: Presence of Alcohol during Rape Events by Days of the Week

	Alcohol Present in Both		Alcohol Present in Victim Only		Alcohol Present in Offender Only		Total Alcohol Present		Total Alcohol Absent		Grand Total	
	No.	%	No.	%	No.	%	No.	%	No.	%	No.	%
Weekdays												
Monday	10	16.9	3	5.1	2	3.4	15	25.4	44	74.6	59	100.0
Tuesday	13	18.3	8	11.3	1	1.3	22	30.9	49	69.1	71	100.0
Wednesday	10	14.1	7	9.8	1	1.4	18	25.3	53	74.7	71	100.0
Thursday	18	24.0	3	4.0	2	2.6	23	30.6	52	69.4	75	100.0
Friday	18	18.9	9	9.5	4	4.2	31	32.6	64	67.4	95	100.0
Saturday	36	21.2	25	14.7	5	2.9	66	38.8	104	61.2	170	100.0
Sunday	31	24.5	7	6.7	4	6.6	42	42.8	63	57.2	105	100.0
Total	136	21.0	62	9.7	19	2.9	217	33.6	429	66.4	646	100.0
Weekends												
Friday	13	18.8	8	11.6	4	5.8	25	36.2	44	63.8	69	100.0
Saturday	36	21.1	25	14.5	5	2.9	66	38.5	104	61.5	170	100.0
Sunday	31	29.5	7	6.7	4	3.8	42	40.0	63	60.0	105	100.0
Total	80	23.3	40	11.6	13	3.7	133	38.6	211	61.4	344	100.0

presence of alcohol (in either the victim, offender, or both). Alcohol was present in 40 percent of 344 rapes committed on Friday, Saturday and Sunday, but in only 28 percent of 302 rapes committed between Monday and Thursday. The incidence of forcible rape in general is highest on Saturday and lowest on Monday, while the incidence with alcohol present is the second highest on the former day (39 percent), and the lowest on the latter (25 percent).[17] Many factors contribute to the association

17. Almost identical results were found by Wolfgang in his study on homicide (ibid., p. 142), which suggests the relationship between alcohol and violent crime in general.

between weekend consumption of alcohol and the proportion of forcible rape at this time. Again, we are in complete accord with Wolfgang who stated some of these factors such as greater leisure time on weekends, with more consumption of alcohol and social interaction, possibly because of more purchase of liquor due to Friday being payday.[18]

Alcohol Noted in Other Studies

There is a considerable amount of contradiction and inconsistency to be found in the studies on sex crimes involving alcohol in the rape situation. Few studies can be compared with the present one, mainly because the sources of data are different. In most studies, the proportion of sex crimes involving alcohol is higher than that found in Philadelphia, while for rape cases it is lower.

Many theoretical problems are inherent in the relation between alcohol and rape, or for that matter, any crime. The most important distinction is that of differentiating between the direct (or acutic) and indirect (or chronic) relationships. In the present study we were interested in the former, that is, those situations in which alcohol was present immediately before the crime. Some studies maintain that rape is a result of acute rather than chronic drinking.[19] Other studies have shown that chronic alcoholics have also committed rape,[20] while still others have found that alcoholics tend to commit fewer crimes of this type,[21] since heavy and continuous drinking diminishes sexual desire and sexual power.[22]

The question of the causal nexus between alcohol and violent crimes in general, and sex crimes and rape in particular, is still debated. A *significant* association between homicide and alcohol was found by Wolfgang,[23] and the association between alcohol and sex crimes is almost an acceptable premise in the traditional criminological literature.[24] Other questions still remain about the actual numerical relation between alcohol and different classes of sex crimes;[25] the type of alcoholic which the offender is (chronic or acutic); his personal susceptibility to alcohol and

18. Ibid.

19. Sullivan.

20. Apfelberg, et al., p. 865; Glueck, Jr., *New York Final Report* p. 289; Healy and Bronner, *Delinquents and Criminals,* pp. 98–100, 120–28, 137–48, 173.

21. Pittman and Gordon, p. 46.

22. Mawrer, p. 557.

23. *Patterns,* chap. 8, see references there.

24. Aschaffenburg, pp. 74–75; Bonger, *Criminality* chap. 8. For a summary of this literature see Adler, pp. 310–26.

25. Howard.

general mental makeup.[26] Finally, the nature of the relation between alcohol and rape is still unclear. Psychoanalysts assume the existence of sexual factors which are at the root of alcoholism as well as the cause of sexual crimes. Thus, alcohol only precipitates existent sexual perversions, latent incestuous wishes, and rages against the mother, or diverts sexuality to other needs, such as aggression, which may explain the aggression and sexual humiliation which appear together in the act of forcible rape.[27] Others see the influence of alcohol as destroying sexual and aggressive inhibitions and sublimations and, thus, by becoming a solvent of the super ego, eliciting criminality in general, and sexual deviation in particular.[28]

Alcohol, so it is said, excites sexual desires[29] and makes the person less conscious of the consequences of his action.[30] These explanations have been criticized insofar as they overlook social factors such as population density,[31] class and economic factors,[32] or general cultural influences.[33] They also overlook, for particular cases, the problem of the amount of alcohol consumed, and the problem of determining this.[34]

Seliger suggested that a situational explanation be found for the relation between alcohol and crime. The relationship, he maintains, exists in the fact that the crime is planned in a place where alcohol is sold. There the offender, drunk or not, looks for accomplices, and there he will encounter his victim. In the light of these points, the effect of alcohol on the psyche of the offender becomes less relevant.

This review of the studies on alcohol and rape, supports our statement concerning the considerable amount of contradiction and inconsistency among the studies on rape in which alcohol is involved. Not only are the sources of data different, all the studies deal only with the presence of alcohol in the offender, but none of them discuss rapists specifically nor has any of them analyzed the presence of alcohol among victims of forcible rape.[35]

26. Rottman; Rowe.

27. Griffith, "Alcohol and Sex"; Mawrer.

28. Abraham, "Relationship"; Abrahamsen, *The Psychology of Crime,* p. 141; Beacon; Glueck, Jr., *New York Final Report,* p. 85; Guttmacher, p. 70; Lukas, "Alcohol and Crime"; Piatrowsky and Abrahamsen; Wenger.

29. Garofalo, p. 117; Wilson and Pescore, p. 182.

30. Banay, "Alcohol and Crime"; Taft, *Criminology,* p. 28.

31. Aschaffenburg, p. 115.

32. Bonger, *Criminality,* chap. 8.

33. Banay, "Cultural Influences in Alcoholism."

34. Piatrowsky and Abrahamsen.

35. Beacon (p. 10) saw this problem as very much neglected; and both Bonger (*Criminality,* p. 352) and Healy (p. 267) mentioned this aspect, maintaining that the prospective victim is sometimes encouraged to drink alcohol to lower her level of behavior.

Bonger uses statistics from a few European nations which indicate that the percentage of forcible rapes committed while the offender was drunk ranges from 7 percent to as high as 50 percent, or between one-tenth to one-half of the rapes studied were committed while the offender was drunk.[36] Bonger used national statistics, but data from selected groups of sex offenders also yields an inconsistent pattern. Thus, some studies indicate that the incidences of the presence of alcohol among rapists are very low, ranging from zero to about 25 percent;[37] Volmer, found that in none of the apprehended rapists in Berkeley, California, during 1930–32 was alcohol present ($N = 10$).[38] The same result was found by Winkler et al. among sex offenders committed to psychiatric hospitals in Chicago (1951–52). Ellis and Brancale found that for their sample of 300 sex offenders referred to the New Jersey Diagnostic Center, alcohol played some role in 32 percent of the cases; but among the eight rapists in the sample, it was present only among 3 offenders.[39] Alcohol, they concluded, is not an important factor in sex crimes. Such a low proportion of the presence of alcohol was found also in the California study;[40] among 37 young rapists only five were under the influence of alcohol when they committed the crime. Gillin found that "drink played a part directly in the crime of only 15 percent of all its sex offenders but indirectly in most of the other cases, through association with drinking companions."[41]

A higher percentage of alcohol involvement in the crime of rape was found in some studies, with the percentages ranging from 25 to 70 percent. Thus, Frosch and Bromberg found that of 136 rapists, 24 percent were under the influence of alcohol when committing the crime.[42]

A higher proportion of alcohol present in the offender was found in two other reports. A study of 102 sex offenders at Sing-Sing Prison revealed that in over 50 percent of the cases, alcohol was involved.[43] The investigators maintained that the drinking offender was more likely to be apprehended and, therefore, he is over represented in the sample.

Glueck in his study finds that 20 percent of the rapists consumed

36. *Criminality,* 619–20.

37. Le Maire (in Svalastoga, p. 49) also found that among the 104 rapists in Denmark (1929–32), "only [in] 22 percent of the cases alcohol was considered as a dominant factor."

38. A. Volmer in Adler, p. 322.

39. *Psychology of Sex Offenders,* pp. 65–66.

40. *California Sexual Deviation Research* (1954), chap. 8.

41. *The Wisconsin Prisoner,* p. 129.

42. Frosch and Bromberg, p. 768.

43. *Report on the Study,* pp. 21–27.

alcohol before the offense to the level that their judgment and perceptive abilities were disturbed or completely lost.[44]

Shupe, who attempted to determine the exact degree of alcohol in felonious offenders when they committed their crime, found that in 55 percent of the rapists ($N = 42$) no alcohol was present. He concluded that "rape is a crime of sober passion as well as a crime of alcohol passion."[45] Finally, Grisbey who investigated the relation between crime and alcohol among 351 inmates at Raiford Prison, also sought to determine the differences between the races as to the problem of alcohol and crime. He found no differences between Negro and white sex offenders in drinking habits or drinking at the time of the offense. Another of his conclusions, which is supported by others, is that the occasional drinker rather than the habitual or chronic drinker tends to commit sex offenses.[46]

A few investigators have observed a connection between the presence of alcohol and temporal patterns of sex crimes and rape. Thus, forcible rape is said to be more prevalent in the summer months due to greater sociability and greater consumption of alcohol.[47] Other researchers looked for the relation between alcohol, days of the week, and the crime of rape. It was found that weekends and especially Saturdays are the peak days for alcohol consumption and the incidences of rape. Aschaffenburg attributed the greater involvement of alcohol on the weekend to the fact that Friday is payday.[48] This may explain the greater amount of alcohol consumption on Saturday, and the high incidences of rape. The same connection is suggested by Kinberg, and Lombroso.[49]

44. *New York Final Report,* p. 306.

45. "Alcohol and Crime," p. 664.

46. See also: Aschaffenburg, pp. 74–75; Glueck, Jr., *New York Final Report,* p. 280.

47. Sutherland and Cressey, *Criminology* (4th ed.), p. 82; Lombroso, pp. 91–92; Healy, p. 23.

48. Aschaffenburg, pp. 75–76.

49. Kinberg, p. 118; Lombroso, p. 91.

9

Previous Record

Recidivism, operationally defined as the number of arrests, convictions, or commitments for past offenses of a given offender, became important to sex crime research, to the legal discussion of sex crimes, and to penal administration in the 1940s and 1950s. At that time, the recidivism of sex offenders was connected with the growing concern about sex psychopaths, and with numerous sex crime legislation enacted or prepared in the United States.[1]

Criminologists and penologists have contended that the compulsive sex offender, who commits mainly minor offenses, is more likely to be a recidivist. Thus, Tappan saw the erroneous view "that sex offenders are usually recidivists," as second among ten "fallacies concerning the sex offender."[2]

From many case studies, surveys, and reports the impression is gained that the person who commits rape is usually a first offender, especially as far as sexual crimes are concerned—all this provided he is not a pathologically compulsive person.

Conflicting generalizations made about recidivism among sex offenders are accounted for by the fact that measurements of recidivism have been made on the basis of different types of previous records. This has resulted in the formation of uneven groups in terms of their recorded criminal past. These general statements of facts about recidivism, which also pro-

1. E. H. Sutherland, "Diffusion."
2. Tappan, *The Habitual Sex Offender,* p. 14.

109

vide a source for further hypotheses, are thus unwarranted. As a basis for determining penal policy, they are questionable.[3]

A sexual offender may have any or all of the following in his recorded criminal past: an arrest, or police record; convictions or court record; a commitment, that is, a prison or hospital record. It follows that the phenomenon of "case mortality," that is, a decrease in the proportion of offenders with criminal records, will be noted as one moves from the use of arrest data to commitment data.[4] It is therefore a matter of conjecture whether all three types of records will appear in the offender's file.

It may be contended that conviction or commitment records, rather than police records, should be used to gauge the proportion of recidivists among offenders, because in many instances the offense which was recorded by the police upon arrest may later be discovered to be unfounded and the offender unjustifiably termed a "criminal."[5] However, more serious objections are leveled against the use of conviction records, most of which apply also to the use of commitment records.

Because of the limitations of data based on the records of convicted or committed offenders, scholars have suggested, with or without explicit analysis of the various factors which biased such records, the use of arrest records to partly overcome the disadvantages of using conviction and commitment records.[6] I concur with them that arrest records are better suited for the analysis of recidivism among those who are involved in the crime of forcible rape. Some of these reasons are positive, and others are negative in that they negate the advantages of the use of conviction and commitment records:

Since arrest is the nearest step of the penal administration to the crime, the law of "case mortality" operates less here.

Fingerprints of the offender and the victim are more likely to be taken and to be available in the community where the offense occurs, and the fingerprints are easy to obtain through the services of the FBI. It allows knowing the initial charge for which the fingerprints were taken.

A previous arrest record is more likely to be present in the file of the offender who has in the past committed a crime and was brought to trial. Even if the sentence was not recorded, it is clear that in order to be brought to trial at least the offense must be known to the police who arrested him and who probably have recorded it.

The absence of a conviction record is not evidence that the crime was

3. See, for example, *Report on the Study,* pp. 9–47.

4. Sellin, "The Basis of Crime Index," p. 346; Van Vechten.

5. This problem was hotly debated about white-collar crimes; see, for example, Tappan, "Who is the Criminal?"

6. For historical exposition of the problem see Sellin and Wolfgang, pp. 17–44.

not committed. Arrest records indicate that such behavior did occur, but for some reason the offenders did not face a trial.

Also, the "vicissitudes of arrest from one period of time to another, and from one community to another, are probably less than those connected with court and sentencing procedures."[7]

Arrest records can be used for comparative studies on success of different penal experiences of offenders, as well as in assessing progression, graduation, or changes in criminal career. To gain insight about the beginning of such a career, "arrest records are more valid than other types of available records."[8]

The time element involved is another variable of importance. This is so "since delay in prosecution and the protracted length of some cases," or the discovery or admission in a particular year of past offenses "may cause a prosecution or conviction to be recorded in a given year for an offense committed in some previous year."[9] In contrast, the occurrence of the crime, its reporting, and the recording of the arrest are more likely to coincide, thus making arrest records a better basis for measuring characteristics of offenders.

The Philadelphia Data

In the present study, the criminal records of offenders and victims were investigated on the basis of what was recorded about them in the offense files. For many, only previous arrest was recorded with no further data about the disposition of the charges for which they were arrested. Thus, only arrest records were of interest to us. To be sure that all previous arrests would be at our disposal, offenders and victims were searched for in the FBI files where arrests were recorded (if fingerprints were made for past charges). It was thus possible to secure information on arrests made outside the Philadelphia police jurisdiction.

Offenses are classified according to: property offenses; crimes against the person; public disorders; drug use; sexual crimes. The last type is further divided between sexual offenses, other than rape and previous rape charges. Another division made is between juvenile and adult previous offenses.

Rapists in Philadelphia reveal (table 36), surprisingly, a relatively high proportion of previous arrest records. Victims also show such records, although the proportion of those having previous records is not as high as that of their assailants.

7. Wolfgang, *Patterns,* p. 173.
8. Ibid.
9. Sellin and Wolfgang, p. 31.

Of 1,292 offenders, 637 (or 49 percent) had a previous arrest record, while 51 percent of them were first offenders. Of 646 victims, 124 (or 19 percent) had previous arrest records. Contrary to past impressions, table 36 reveals that there is almost no difference between the races in the percentages of offenders and victims with previous arrest records. Fifty percent of Negro offenders compared to 46 percent of white offenders had a previous record; 20 percent of Negro victims and 17 percent of white victims had a record. In both races the difference for offender and victim groups amounts to less than 5 percent.

Table 36: Previous Arrest Record of Victims and Offenders in Rapes by Race

	Negro		White		Total	
	No.	%	No.	%	No.	%
Victims						
Record	103	19.9	21	16.7	124	19.2
No record	417	80.1	105	83.3	522	80.8
Total	520	100.0	126	100.0	646	100.0
Offenders						
Record	532	49.9	105	46.4	627	49.3
No record	534	50.1	121	53.6	655	50.7
Total	1,066	100.0	226	100.0	1,292	100.0

Among the 637 offenders with a previous police record, 217 had a record of one offense only; 198 of two offenses; 45, of three offenses; and 75 of four or more offenses (table 37).

The table also reveals that if white offenders had a *significantly* higher proportion of one previous offense, Negro offenders had a *significantly* higher proportion for two offenses or more.

Table 37: Number of Offenses for which Offenders had been Arrested Prior to Present Offense of Rape and Mean Number of Arrests by Race

	Negro		White		Total	
	No.	%	No.	%	No.	%
One	249	46.8	68	61.8	317	49.7
Two	176	33.1	22	20.9	198	31.2
Three	39	7.4	6	3.7	45	7.2
Four	29	5.4	4	3.8	33	5.2
Five	26	4.9	2	1.9	28	4.4
Six to ten	13	2.4	1	0.9	14	2.2
Total	532	100.0	105	100.0	637	100.0
Mean	2.0		1.5		1.9	

It has been seen that while rapists are found in all age groups, most of them, however, were adolescents and adults between 15 to 29 years of age. It appears (table 38) that the proportion of offenders previously arrested is higher in this same age group than would be thought from their representation in the total group of offenders. In the main age group, between 15 to 29, about one-half in each year of age had been previously arrested. The same proportion is revealed in the age groups 10–14 and 40–45, and the highest proportion (60 percent) is in the age group 55–59.

Table 38: Age of Offenders with Previous Arrest Record

| | 10–14 | | 15–19 | | 20–24 | | 25–29 | | 30–34 | | 35–39 | |
	No.	%	No.	%	No.	%	No.	%	No.	%	No.	%
Record	23	43.9	209	40.2	156	47.0	114	55.1	74	75.6	31	83.8
No record	24	51.1	312	59.8	176	53.0	43	44.9	24	24.4	6	16.2
Total	47	100.0	521	100.0	332	100.0	207	100.0	98	100.0	37	100.0

| | 40–44 | | 45–49 | | 50–54 | | 55–59 | | 60–over | | Total | |
	No.	%	No.	%	No.	%	No.	%	No.	%	No.	%
Record	11	52.4	6	75.0	8	72.8	2	40.0	3	60.0	367	49.3
No record	10	47.6	2	25.0	3	27.2	3	60.0	2	40.0	655	50.7
Total	21	100.0	8	100.0	11	100.0	5	100.0	5	100.0	1,292	100.0

When the age span is divided into its major groups according to points of sharp rise or decline in the total group of offenders, the following is observed (table 39): It is reasonable to assume that the older the offender, all other things being equal, the more chances he has to commit offenses and be arrested for them.[10] Such are the results observed above. Offenders in the age group 30–40 years and 40 and over were arrested in higher proportion than those under the age of 30. Of 1,107 offenders under 30 years of age, 502 (45 percent) had a record, and of 185 offenders age 30 and over, 135 (73 percent) had a record.

A further examination of the records of those who had previously been arrested shows that of the 637 offenders, 336 (53 percent) had a prior record as juveniles (persons under 18 years of age), while 301 (47 percent) had a record as juveniles and as adults. The persistency of violating the law is noted here, although no analysis was made of the intensity of such behavior.

We shall turn now to the question of the type of offense committed by those offenders (and victims) who had a previous police record. Since

10. For the problem of the first offender who is a "latecomer to crime," see Cormier et al., "The Latecomer to Crime."

Table 39: Age Differences of Offenders with Previous Arrest Record
according to Ten-Year Age Divisions

	Young Offender and Adolescents (under 20)		Young Adult (21–30)		Adults (30–40)		Older Offenders (40–over)		Total	
	No.	%	No.	%	No.	%	No.	%	No.	%
Record	232	44.4	270	51.9	105	77.8	30	60.0	367	49.3
No record	336	55.6	269	48.1	30	22.2	20	40.0	655	50.7
Total	568	100.0	539	100.0	135	100.0	50	100.0	1,292	100.0

rape is a behavior combined of aggression and sexual activity, it may be assumed that when an offender had a prior record, it was likely to consist of offenses against the person or of prior rape. However, criminological literature indicates that it is crimes against property and against public order which characterize the criminal past of rapists.

Table 40 summarizes the data about the type of previous offenses committed by the offenders. Each category of offense is computed from the total number of persons having at least one offense of these types on their arrest record. Only 80 offenders, 12.5 percent of those with arrest record, had been arrested for only one type of offense. The distribution of such cases among the different types of offenses is as follows: Only 33, or 12.3 percent of the 267 offenders who had an arrest record of offenses against property, had no record of other crimes. Only 26, or 20 percent of the 130 offenders who had an arrest record of offenses against the person, had no record of another crime. Only 21, or 14 percent of the 147 offenders

Table 40: Type of Previous Arrest Record by Race of Offenders in Rape

	Negro		White		Total	
	No.	%	No.	%	No.	%
Against property	218	41.0	49	46.7	267	41.9
Against the person	113	21.2	17	16.2	130	20.4
Public disorder	120	22.6	27	25.7	147	23.1
Drug use and/or possession	11	2.1	2	1.9	13	2.0
Sex-offenses (except forcible rape)	18	3.4	4	3.8	22	3.5
Forcible rape	52	9.8	6	5.7	58	9.1
Total	532	100.0	105	100.0	637	100.0

who had an arrest record for public disorder, had no record for another crime. None of those arrested for drug use or possession of drugs had a "clean" record. Of those with an arrest record for sex offenses (other than rape), 17 out of 77 had a record of crime against the person. Of 58 offenders who had an arrest record of rape, 24 (or 41 percent) also had an arrest record of crime against the person.

Table 40 reveals the following about the type of offenses which are on the arrest records of offenders:

1. Of 637 offenders with previous arrest records, 42 percent had a record of at least one or more offenses against property only, 20 percent against a person only, and 23 percent against public order only. Two percent had an arrest record of use or possession of drugs, 4 percent of sexual offenses other than rape, and 9 percent of forcible rape.

2. Negro offenders had a higher arrest record than white offenders for offenses against the person (21 percent and 16 percent, respectively), and for rape (10 percent and 6 percent, respectively). White offenders had a higher arrest record for offenses against property (47 percent and 41 percent, respectively) and for public disorder (26 percent and 23 percent, respectively).

An attempt was made to ascertain the continuity and persistence of offenses from juvenile to adult age. Table 41 reveals that the highest proportion for continuity was in offenses against property, and the second highest proportion was for offenses against the person.

Table 41: Type of Previous Arrest Record by Legal Age of Offenders

	As Juvenile		As Adult		Total	
	No.	%	No.	%	No.	%
Against Property	150 (56.2)	44.6	117 (43.8)	38.8	267	41.9
Against the person	78 (60.0)	23.2	52 (40.0)	17.2	130	20.4
Public disorder	84 (57.2)	25.0	63 (42.8)	20.9	147	23.1
Drugs	4 (30.7)	1.2	9 (69.3)	3.1	13	2.0
Sex-crimes (except forcible rape)	13 (50.1)	3.9	9 (40.9)	3.1	22	3.4
Forcible rape	7 (12.1)	2.1	51 (87.9)	16.9	58	9.2
Total	336	100.0	301	100.0	637	100.0

If each offense is examined separately, it is seen that a continuation from a juvenile to an adult criminal career exists in all types of crime. However, for use or possession of drugs and for an arrest record for rape, more adults are first-timers than for any other type of offense. For instance, of those who had an arrest record of rape, only 12 percent had been charged for this offense as juveniles, while over 50 percent in each type of offense (except drugs) had been arrested as juveniles. Thus, a *significant* association was found between a record of arrest for forcible rape alone or rape combined with other sex offenses and the onset of a criminal career.

Looking for persistence in criminal careers among the sexual recidivists, I found that 9 offenders with an arrest record for sex offenses (other than forcible rape) started to commit sex offenses as adults. Of these 9 offenders, 6 had an arrest record of one offense, 2 a record of two offenses and 1 a record of three offenses.

We saw that 17 out of 22 offenders who had arrest records of sex offenses also had a record of crime against the person, and of these 17, 13 were juveniles against whom offenses against the person were recorded. Further, all the juveniles who committed rape also had an arrest record of crime against the person. These last two results indicate that the clue for the explanation of forcible rape may be sought in the tendency toward violent behavior of which rape is only one aspect.

Of 646 victims, 124 (or 19 percent) had an arrest record and there was no *significant* difference in percentages between Negro and white victims. Such is the case when the races are compared according to type of offense. A somewhat larger difference appears for juvenile misconduct, where 24 percent of 21 white victims with an arrest record had been previously arrested for juvenile misconduct, as compared to 17 percent of the Negro victims who had a previous record.

Comparing arrest records of victims and offenders, it appears (tables 39 and 42) that offenders with a record committed four times as many offenses against property than did victims (42 percent compared to 10 percent, respectively). The proportion of crimes against the person is twice as great for offenders as for victims. However, while 3.5 percent of offenders with an arrest record had such a record for sex offenses (except forcible rape), 38 percent of the victims had an arrest record for sexual misconduct (promiscuity, prostitution, etc.). If we include the juvenile misconduct category, which often has a sexual connotation, this then may throw further light on the role of the victim in the rape situation.

It is possible to assume that the role of the sexually deviated female victim is expressed not only in the immediate rape situation, but also as it is reflected in the victim's past record for sexual conduct and those sexual elements included in her arrest record for juvenile misconduct.

Table 42: Victims of Rape with a Previous Arrest Record, by Race and
Type of Offenses

	Negro		White		Total	
	No.	%	No.	%	No.	%
Against property	10	9.7	2	9.5	12	9.7
Against the person	11	10.7	2	9.5	13	10.5
Public disorder	23	22.3	5	23.8	28	22.6
Drugs use and/or possession	1	1.0	...	...	1	0.8
Sexual misconduct (including prostitution)	40	38.8	7	33.3	47	37.9
Juvenile misconduct	18	17.5	5	23.8	23	18.5
Total previous criminal record	103	19.9	21	16.7	124	19.2
Total no criminal record	417	80.1	105	83.3	522	80.8
Total	520	100.0	126	100.0	646	100.0

This proposition can be augmented if we consider another type of
"record"—that is, the victim's "bad reputation." In the interrogation
after the rape event, offenders' witnesses and other persons sometimes
referred to the victim as having a "bad reputation" (without specifying
it), or noted that the victim was known to be promiscuous. The victim, if
she was below the age of eighteen, was asked if she had sexual experience
before the offense. Also, every victim was asked if she had sex relations
with the offender before the rape and if she was raped before and did not
prosecute her assailant(s). The data gathered about this aspect of bad
reputation reveal the following (table 43):

Of 646 victims, 128 (or 20 percent) had a bad reputation, with Negro
victims having *significantly* higher proportion of promiscuity and white
victims a higher proportion of being previously raped but not prosecuting the offender(s).

When the relationship between bad reputation and previous arrest
record (table 44) was tested, it was found that a *significant* association
existed between the two. Of 128 victims with bad reputations, only 9
percent had a previous arrest record, while of 518 victims with no such
reputation, less than 1 percent have an arrest record. By reversing the
perspectives, it may be noted that of 124 victims with an arrest record,
117 (or 94 percent) had a bad reputation. Hence, if a victim's arrest
record may have any bearing on her chances of being victimized, even
more so may be the case when she has a reputation of being promiscuous,

Table 43: Reputations of Victims of Rape with a Previous Arrest Record

	Bad Reputation		No Information		Total	
	No.	%	No.	%	No.	%
Against property	12	10.3	. . .	. . .	12	9.7
Against the person	10	8.5	3	42.8	13	10.5
Public disorder	27	23.1	1	14.3	28	22.6
Drug use and/or possession	. . .	. . .	1	14.3	1	0.8
Sexual misconduct	46	39.3	1	14.3	47	37.9
Juvenile misconduct	22	18.8	1	14.3	23	18.5
Total arrest record	117	8.6	7	0.3	124	19.2
Total no arrest record	11	91.4	511	99.7	522	80.8
Total	128	100.0	518	100.0	646	100.0

Table 44: Reputation of Victims of Rape by Race

	Negro		White		Total	
	No.	%	No.	%	No.	%
Known as promiscuous or having bad reputation	48	48.5	12	41.4	60	47.6
Had sex relations before with the offender	19	19.2	6	20.7	25	19.5
Had sex relations before (victim under 18 years of age)	24	24.2	7	24.2	31	24.2
Raped before but did not prosecute	8	8.1	4	13.7	12	8.7
Total bad reputation	99 (77.3)	19.1	29 (22.7)	23.0	128	19.8
Total no information about reputation	421 (81.3)	80.9	97 (18.7)	77.0	518	80.2
Total	520	100.0	126	100.0	646	100.0

sexually experienced in spite of her age, having sex relations with her future offender, or known to have been raped but reluctant to bring her assailant(s) to court. This conclusion is supported, partly, by the fact that 39 percent of the victims who had bad reputations had a criminal arrest record for sexual misconduct, or of 47 victims who had an arrest record for the latter group of offenses, 99 percent had a bad reputation. Further, of those victims who had bad reputations (117), 23 percent had an arrest record for public disorder (drunkenness, keeping a disorderly house, etc.), and 19 percent had a record of juvenile misconduct. Of those who do not enjoy such a reputation, only 14 percent had records for each of the three offenses just mentioned.

Previous Arrest Records Noted in Other Studies

Karpman gives various statements made about the recidivism of sex offenders.[11] The majority, he reports, find that the sex offender is not a serious recidivist; he is less likely than other felons to have a police record. The criminal careers of those who were previous offenders were generally short and nonsexual. Of those who repeated their sex crime, most were mentally abnormal. As for the rapists, they were found to be first offenders[12] who committed the crime incidentally as a prologue or epilogue to another crime,[13] or under the influence of alcohol. The rapist who repeats his crime is likely to be the pedophiliac[14] or the mentally sick,[15] mainly suffering from compulsion.[16] Later, in his topical synopsis on the problem of sex offenders, Karpman ponders the disagreement about the sex offender's recidivism.[17] In his answer he fails to see that these various and contradictory opinions are derived from the use of different sources of data.

It can be stated from the outset that literature analyzing the recidivism of rapists only in terms of their previous arrest record is meager, and there is none at all for victims of rape. Ploscowe, to gauge the rate of recidivism among rapists, uses the records of persons arrested compared to FBI fingerprint records. For the year 1949 he found that only 44.8 percent of those charged with "other sex offenses" had previous fingerprint records.[18] E. H. Sutherland also used the FBI reports and found that of 1,443 males

11. *The Sexual Offender,* pp. 276–78.

12. Bowling, "The Sex Offender," 11–16.

13. C. Allen, "Treatment."

14. Pollens, p. 33.

15. Hartwell, p. 172.

16. J. M. Reinhardt, "The Gentle Sex Murderer."

17. *The Sexual Offender,* p. 608.

18. *Sex and the Law,* p. 203.

arrested in 1937 for rape, only 5.3 percent had previous convictions of rape, a much lower rate of recidivism than the average for all other crimes that year.[19]

Tappan exposed two fallacies regarding the recidivism of sex offenders: first, that sex offenders are usually recidivists; and second, that the sex offender progresses to more serious types of sex crime. For the first fallacy, he states that "serious sex offenders have one of the lowest rates as 'repeaters' of all types of crimes. . . . Most of them get in trouble only once. . . ; those who recidivate [sic] are characteristically minor offenders . . . rather than criminals of serious menace."[20] Concerning the second fallacy, that of progression to more serious crime, he states that "it is the consensus of opinion among psychiatrists, confirmed by crime statistics, that sex deviates persist in the type of behavior in which they have discovered satisfaction . . . progression from minor to major sex crimes is exceptional though an individual may engage at any given time in a variety of forms of sex outlet." Further on in his report,[21] he attempts to prove these statements on the basis of FBI records and of the *Report of the Mayor's Committee*.[22] He finds from the *UCR* for 1930–39 that "as to the percentage of persons arrested who had prior criminal records of any kind . . . rape usually occupies the eighteenth to twentieth place . . . in the list of twenty-five types of offenses."[23] Like the others, he does not deal with nonsexual offenses which a sex offender may repeat.[24]

Some studies avoid using the *UCR* and confine themselves to the study of police records of a particular community. The rates of recidivism are given for the total group of sex offenders, and for some types of offenses, but neither age nor race of offenders and victims is used for further analysis of recidivism.

Dunham found that, among the alleged sex offenders investigated by Detroit police in 1949, only 33 percent of the total group had a previous police record of rape. However, 46.5 percent had a previous police record.[25]

Kupperstein made an analysis of sex offenses committed in Philadelphia during 1962. Among the 3,648 sex offenders she investigated

19. *The Sexual Psychopath Laws,* p. 549.

20. *The Habitual Sex Offender,* p. 14.

21. Ibid., pp. 22–24.

22. The same report is used as a reference for Ploscowe and for E. H. Sutherland. It will be discussed separately.

23. *The Habitual Sex Offender,* p. 22.

24. Ibid., p. 14.

25. Dunham, pp. 14–15.

there were 523 rapists. With Paul J. Gemert, Chairman of the Pennsylvania Board of Parole, she concurs that "the only rate of recidivism lower than that for sex offenses is the rate for criminal homicide."[26] If, however, the convicted offenders in her sample are used to gauge their recidivism rates, the picture is completely altered. From her data it can be learned that 65 percent of the convicted offenders had been previously arrested and the same percentage had been previously convicted. Moreover, a correlation exists between the number of prior convictions and the type of sentence imposed. Thus, "68 percent of all those with at least two prior convictions were imprisoned while 64 percent of the offenders with zero or only one prior conviction received noninstitutional sentences."[27]

The *Report of the Mayor's Committee for the Study of Sex Offenses,* has often been used as a reference for the opinion that "first offenders commit most sex crimes . . . usually for other than sex offenses."[28] From its statistics, the report concluded that although most offenders charged with sex felonies are without prior police record, the recidivist offender leads in abduction and forcible rape. The former group shows 54 percent of recidivists and the latter 52 percent. Among the rapists, only 39 (or 14 percent) had a previous record of sex crime as against 176 (or 86 percent) with records for nonsex crime exclusively.[29] This result, said the committee, indicates that rapists are not abnormal persons, nor are their crimes abnormalities but only an offshoot of their criminal propensities. Rape is frequently just incidental, committed with another type of crime, or because of the influence of alcohol, or as a part of gang activity, which "more than once brought them into conflict with the law for other than sexual offenses."[30]

In tracing the career of sex offenders, the report found that they are not careerists in crime, at least not the majority of them, and certainly not the vicious rapist. Of 40 offenders, whose records were traced from 1939 back to 1930, 31 were convicted of the same type of sex offense which caused their 1930 arrest. Only 6 of these 31 persons were rapists.[31] The conclusion of the committee was that "the recommendation that all sex offenders be segregated for life is completely unrealistic and unwise

26. Kupperstein, pp. 34–35. In Gemert's sample of 133 sex offenders, 97 (or 73 percent) were recidivists. Among them 39 (or 29 percent) were arrested for nonsexual crimes; 14 (10 percent) were arrested for sexual offenses and 44 (33 percent) had a mixed record of arrests.

27. Kupperstein, pp. 67–69.

28. *Report of the Mayor's Committee,* p. 89, and see pp. 89–95.

29. Ibid., p. 91.

30. Ibid., p. 92.

31. Ibid., p. 93–95.

... the creation of a separate specialized institution devoted solely to sex offenders is not warranted."[32]

Of studies conducted abroad, only three are of any use for comparative purposes. Svalastoga, in his study of 141 rapists coming before the court in Denmark in the years 1946 through 1958, found that "only 33 percent had no previous criminal record, while 22 percent had received two or more prison sentences prior to the rape."[33] Stürup, in his study of sex offenders charged by the court of Denmark in the years 1929 through 1939, found that of 94 rapists only 22.3 percent had previous records. In the latter group, 81 percent of them were, in his terms, homologous repeaters; that is, they repeated the same offense.[34]

Radzinowicz provides us with the most detailed study of criminal records of sex offenders. He analyzes recidivism for offenders convicted for the first time for a sex crime and the patterns of recidivism among repeaters.[35] Although his study is concerned only with convicted offenders (and it is often impossible to separate the rapists from the whole group of offenders), it is presented here because of its detailed analysis. Radzinowicz found that among convicted rapists (37 percent of them under 21 years of age), 91 percent were first sexual offenders. However, 45.5 percent had only a previous nonsexual conviction in their past. Of the whole group of heterosexual offenders (509), at least 55.5 percent had in their past one additional self-admitted, but not recorded, sex offense; 34.5 percent had 2 to 4 offenses and 10 percent had 5 or more additional, but not recorded, sexual offenses.

Through analyzing prior convictions for nonsexual offenses, it is shown that of those first sex offenders charged with carnal knowledge offenses,[36] 35 percent had one previous conviction for a nonsexual offense, 40 percent had 2 to 4 such convictions, and 25 percent had 4 or more previous nonsexual offenses. For the whole heterosexual class of offenders, the main type of these previous nonsexual offenses is against property. Only 2 percent had a record of crime against the person only, and only 9 percent in all committed such offenses.

Finally, an analysis is made of the interval between first convictions for nonsexual offenses and first convictions for sexual offenses. For 3 in 4 it was at least three years, and for 1 in 3 at least nine years.

32. Ibid., p. 95.

33. "Rape and Social Structure," p. 50.

34. "Sexual Offenders," pp. 3–4.

35. *Sexual Offenses,* pp. 136–79.

36. This group of 40 offenders includes 10 convicted rapists and 12 who were convicted for assault with intent to rape.

Radzinowicz makes that same detailed analysis of sexual recidivists.[37] Of the rapists in this group only 2 had records of previous sex offenses. The proportion of offenders with more than one previous conviction for a sexual offense was the lowest in the carnal knowledge group (1 percent). In order to see the persistencies in recidivism, analysis is made of the nature of the previous offense and the number of previous convictions for sexual and nonsexual offenses. Fifty-four percent of the recidivists had been previously convicted of sexual offenses identical with the present one, and 30 percent had previous convictions for different offenses within the same class and 14 percent in a different class. One conclusion arrived at is that there is no indication "that these offenders progressed from the less serious to the more serious offenses."[38]

The age of heterosexual recidivists when first convicted for sexual offense was in 34 percent of the cases under 21, and in 50 percent under 40. As to the interval between convictions for sexual offenses for the heterosexual group, in 30 percent it was between 1 and 3 years and in 45 percent it was 3 to 10 years. In 10 percent it was less than 1 year and in 15 percent it was 10 years or over.

An examination of the records of the heterosexual recidivist shows that in this group a larger proportion had previous convictions for nonsexual offenses than the first-time sexual offenders: 52 and 27 percent respectively. Further, the first group had a larger number of such nonsexual offenses than did the corresponding proportion among first sex offenders. Also, the vast majority of the sexual recidivists committed offenses against property, particularly larceny and breaking and entering.

A further analysis is made by Radzinowicz of the persistent sex offenders, that is, those who had three or more previous convictions of sexual offenses. Neither was there here any indication of progression from less serious to more serious sexual offenses, especially for the rapist. The conviction for sexual offenses of the persistent offender was frequently spread over long periods; 6 in 10 had at least one interval of not less than 5 years. However, it was found that the proportion of persistent sexual offenders who had "mixed" records of sexual and nonsexual offenses was higher than for exclusively sexual recidivists: 22 and 13 percent respectively.

We have dwelt lengthily on Radzinowicz's study since no American study has come close to its detail. More fruitful than his findings are the aspects of recidivism he analyzes: persistency, homology, progression, and interval between offenses.

37. *Sexual Offenses,* pp. 156–79.
38. Ibid., p. 161.

Two American studies are of interest to us, though they are not based on the records of arrested offenders, Doshay's follow-up study and Glueck's report on incarcerated sex offenders.[39] Doshay conducted a follow-up study on the criminal career of 256 juvenile sex offenders who were studied and treated at the New York City Children Court's Clinic between June 1928 and June 1934.[40] A six-year period elapsed between the child's last treatment and the conclusion of the follow-up study. In this study the rapists are indistinguishable from the offenders, but, again, this kind of pioneering study merits attention. The juveniles under study were divided into two groups: primary group—those whose offenses were only sexual; mixed group—148 juveniles who in addition to their sexual crimes were engaged in other types of delinquency. At the end of the follow-up period, there was not a single instance of known sex violations in adult life of the primary group. Only 3 in this group were charged during the follow-up period with nonsexual offenses. In the mixed group, 8 adults committed sex violations and 33 were charged subsequently as adults with nonsexual crimes.[41]

The Mayor's Committee conducted a similar study, where 555 sex offenders (including rapists) convicted in 1930 were followed for 12 years.

It was found that after this period only one-third (34 percent) were arrested again by the police. Of this group of recidivists 40 (or 21 percent) were charged with sexual offenses, none of them with rape. It also meant that 93 percent of the 555 offenders swerved away from sex crime and that, generally speaking, "sex crime is not an habitual behavior with the majority of sex offenders."[42]

Glueck has detailed his analysis with variables not found in Radzino-wicz's study.[43] Also, the convicted rapists are easy to separate from the other types of imprisoned sex offenders who were the subject of Glueck's study. It was found that 49 percent of the whole group of sexual offenders had a record of nonsexual offenses, especially property offenses and disorderly conduct, usually committed under the influence of alcohol. Further, 51 percent of them committed second crimes which were homologous, that is, they committed the same offense and did not progress to more serious ones. For the rapists, from their records and their own admission, it was observed that 20 percent were first offenders who did not have any record whatsoever. Another 20 percent committed minor

39. Glueck, Jr., *New York Final Report*, pp. 87–89.
40. *Boy Sex Offender*, p. 3.
41. Ibid., p. 92.
42. *Report of the Mayor's Committee*, p. 93, and see pp. 93–95.
43. Glueck, Jr., *New York Final Report*, pp. 286–92.

nonsexual crimes, and 47 percent committed 3 or more nonsexual offenses. In 33 percent of the rapist group the pattern of their nonsexual offenses is episodic (several offenses repeated in a short space of time); while a sporadic (committed from time to time) and chronic (offenses committed whenever opportunity occurred) pattern prevails in 25 percent of the rapist group. Isolated nonsexual offenses occurred in 13 percent of the rapist group.

In 17 percent of the cases the rapists committed their first nonsexual offense when under 18 years of age; in 40 percent, between the ages of 18 to 24 years; and in 30 percent, between 25 to 34 years of age. These proportions are not much different from the age of their first arrest for nonsexual offenses; 17 percent were arrested under 18; 37 percent, between the ages of 18 to 24; 37 percent, between 25 to 34; and 37 percent, from 35 years of age and over. The median number of arrests is 2.1, with 40 percent having been arrested 3 or more times. Their records for sexual offenses show that 50 percent admitted one offense, 23 percent two offenses, and 27 percent three or more offenses, for which they were not arrested. The pattern of their previous sexual offenses seems mainly isolated (57 percent), while in 27 percent it is sporadic, in seven percent episodic, and in only 13 percent chronic.

Charting the rapists' primary pattern(s) of nonsexual offenses (according to their descriptions rather than the plea or jury finding), it is observed that 43 percent committed property offenses and the same proportion were arrested for disorderly conduct; 15 percent had a record of assault and robbery, and five percent of gambling. No definite pattern was found in 72 percent of the cases. Violence occurred in 61 percent of the nonsexual offenses, and it was severe only in 17 percent of these cases.

The age for the first arrest for sex offenses was later than for nonsexual offenses. Thus, 17 percent were arrested while they were under 18 years of age; 37 percent, between 18 to 24, and the same proportion between 25 to 34 years of age. In 10 percent the age of their first arrest for sex offense was at 34 years of age and over. The median number of arrests for sex offenses is 1.4, with 53 percent of the rapists having one arrest record for sex offenses and 30 percent having 3 or more arrest records for past sexual offenses.

Eighty-seven percent of the rapists had committed rape before, while the rest committed different sex offenses. Seventeen percent of them committed minor offenses, and 3 percent had a past record of incest. Compared to the nonsexual patterns, the rapists committed their sexual offenses with the use of more violence (90 percent), with severe violence occurring in 30 percent of the cases.

III

The Rape Situation
and Modus Operandi

10

Modus Operandi

Rape is a unique kind of social act. As a social act it implies an interaction between two or more persons who share the same situation. However, to be considered truly social, an act must imply intent, reciprocity,
stability, and mutual orientation.[1] The apparent lack of these characteristics gives rape some of its special features. Its uniqueness is anchored in
the attempt to enforce some reciprocity and mutual sexual orientation.
The female, as rape is legally defined, does not reciprocate; that is, she
frustrates the attempt of the male to establish with her a sexual orientation. She does not consent to the male intention of forcing the complementary role upon her.

When a court decides that the attacker succeeded in the attempt to
enforce reciprocity, the act can no longer be designated as rape. Rape,
therefore, can be seen as an attempt by the male to create, through the
use of various means of force and duress, sexual relationship with a
female, in order to achieve sexual and other kinds of gratification.[2] The
act is defined as a crime due to the mode of the act, that is, the female's
self-determination and consent is violated by the use of force or duress.
The aggressive aspect of this crime is what arouses public indignation,
and further derives from the fact that the sexual self-determination of
the victim is violated.

So far we have been concerned with some personal and social char-

1. See Weber, *Theory,* p. 82.

2. The symbolic meaning of rape, other than sexual gratification, will be
discussed in chap. 18.

acteristics of offenders and victims which give a background to the crime. The separation between the criminal situation and the participants' personalities is arbitrary but analytical. Also, the crime really cannot be abstracted from the rape situation itself, that is, "from the constellation of circumstances existing immediately at and around the commission and preparation of the criminal act."[3] All these elements that we have considered, form a complex in which personality elements determine the situation, its definition and its outcome—for example, the manner in which the offense will be committed.

Our general assumptions are that there are constant pressures for sexual gratification and experience among all males and that some aggression is an expected part of the male role in sexual encounters. However, there are race and class differences for such gratification—for instance, in the alternatives available for sexual partners (the accessibility to prostitutes, the availability of promiscuous women, and the social approval of using them). There are also class and subcultural differences in the legitimation given to coercion and manipulations used in securing the cooperation of females for sexual relations.

The Perspective of the Individual and the Situation

The analyses of the modus operandi of rape is made here as an interaction and developmental process which involves the conjunction of both the offender and situation variables in determining the course and the special characteristics of the offense. The would-be offender approaches the rape event with some intent of achieving sexual gratification. He possesses certain personal and social characteristics which may influence his choice in securing a victim and his definition of the situation appropriate for perpetrating the offense. While his personal traits become stimulants for the crime, the situation serves to release some personality predispositions. Some of these predispositions may be deep-seated and pathological; others temporary—for example, when he is under the influence of alcohol or when he interprets the behavior of the females as sexually suggestive.

The course of action which the offender will take to "eroticize" the situation and to enlist the would-be victim's cooperation and consent will depend not only on the intensity of his sexual desires, but also on outside social and cultural elements which are incorporated into his personality. The choice for forceful action may be in line with that of his peer groups or with a broader sociocultural framework which shows him how to deal with a reluctant woman, or to define such action so as to solve masculine,[4] as well as status problems.[5] Also, the would-be offender may already

3. Hurwitz, p. 359.
4. See Miller, "Lower Class Culture."
5. Bloch and Niederhoffer, pp. 74–82.

have acquired or will create for the particular event some rationalization which will either serve as motive,[6] or will help him to come to terms with guilt and moral decisions.[7] His membership group may have imbued him with certain perceptions which will help him to reject the use of prostitutes or to see what is defined as rape only as a way to "make" a girl.[8]

These decisions and rationalizations imply, partly, the existence of a group which supports such explanations of the act to make it tolerable to the offender and others, and which either makes conventional means for sexual satisfaction inferior or nonapplicable to the particular concrete situation.

The existence or the absence of such factors may determine the manner by which the offense will be committed. For instance, the offender's immediate creation of rationalization may make the rape an explosive event rather than a planned occurrence, or it may determine how much force, brutality, and sexual humiliation the victim will suffer before, during, or after the act of rape.

A Note on Motives

Crime is always goal directed, without a motive it does not exist. Motives can appear as unconscious and the offender may not clearly be aware of it. Motive, however, is not the same as intent, though they are frequently confused. Intent, or *mens rea*, reflects the ability to deliberate, to comprehend one's own act and the reasons for committing it. Thus, it does or does not exist, depending on the mental state of the offender. The motivation is the reason for the goal-directed action or conduct. It always exists. Interest and motive may be quite different in the same criminal act. While in homicide motive rests more upon the intention of the offenders than their psychological state, such is not the case in rape. Rape has many motives but only one intent. The dominant motive for sexual offense is usually a strong sexual emotion, except in the case of felony rape when the rape comes after the commission of the property offense.

The would-be offender approaches the rape event with many motives but with one intent. He is making judgments and choices as to either how to enlist the would-be victim's consent, or how to subdue her quickly and make the situation safe for the commission of the rape. He is ego-involved in the situation.[9] This involvement is, however, temporary if he intends to commit the rape first through seduction. However, it is to be considered rape because seduction failed and reciprocity was not established in his relationship with the victim. The nature of the offender's

6. C. W. Mills.
7. Sykes and Matza.
8. Whyte.
9. Sherif and Cantril, p. 117.

ego-involvement is determined by the motives he has and the tensions they generate to which he responds.

In sociology, determining motivation is a frustrating task. First, what in the motivation belongs to the immediate social situation, what to the larger social system, and what to the offender's personality system? Second, is motive the "reason" given by the offender for the act, the "motive" assumed by psychiatrists, or the cause which may be neither of these two, but a situational element which has led to the offense? The question, "why did you do this?" has little meaning in police investigations, except as it is relevant to convicting the offender. Third, motive in terms of purpose of the act may not be recalled accurately, if at all, and the offender's verbal statement may not reflect the motive adequately. Thus, it is possible to infer the motive only from observed concrete behavior. If, as psychiatrists claim, the motive as a reflection of the "cause" can be elucidated only by psychological or psychiatric investigation, this is again beyond the realm of necessary police investigation, and thus beyond the purpose of the present study. Fourth, the same type of behavior can arise from different motivations. This dilemma is reflected in the multitude of "reasons," among them unconscious ones, given by psychiatrists for the phenomenon of rape. Because they disagree as to the type and content of the offenders' motives, their underlying needs, and the intensity of their demands, psychiatrists cannot agree on an explanation for a particular case of rape. Thus, although motives and other personality factors are important to the extent that they influence the commission of the particular offense, we cannot know directly what the motives were. We can only assume their existence and influence and look for clues from the situation which may have precipitated these factors and in which rape generally occurs.

Psychological motivation means, usually, a psychic emotional state which leads to an act. Sociological theory has developed its own notion of motivation, as part of the sociological role theory. There, motivation means that process by which a person "symbolically defines a problematic situation as calling for a performance of a particular act with anticipated consummation."[10] Here, motivation is seen as intellectual constructs or rationalization which defines situations and organizes acts in particular situations, the use of which can be examined empirically.[11] Motives are therefore more than specifications of the situation in which let us say, rape occurred, but they are not explanations of the offense given by the offender, victim, or police. They are social facts arising from group-

10. Cressey, "Role Theory," pp. 443–68. See also A. K. Cohen, *Deviance and Control,* chaps. 5, 6.

11. Cressey, *Other People's Money,* chap. 4; C. W. Mills. On the problem of elucidating "motives" for a crime see Bohannan, pp. 248–52.

culture social status, and situational factors, interpreted by the offenders and translated into actions.[12]

These considerations explain why social characteristics of offenders seem more important than the elucidation of their motives. We have seen how race, age, economic background, and marital status influence the amount of involvement in the crime of rape. Hence, when the rape situation and the modus operandi are discussed, these same characteristics must be further employed in describing the kinds of behavior they bring about in the situational context.

The Social Situation

In its discourse on the determination of "responsibility" and of conjecture of events which preceded the offense, the law has emphasized the "situation" as an aspect of crime. The situational aspect is connected in the law with the "rule of legal impossibility," that is, when certain external conditions of the act are absent, it is considered legally impossible to commit the crime.[13] In rape, such external conditions are important to resolve the questions of "consent," "use of force," and so on. The law, however, treats the offender and his victim as object and subject, while, from a sociopsychological point of view, the relationship between them might be much more complex than the law is able to analyze.

Psychology also emphasizes situational aspects which were later taken over by sociologists. The theoretical development was from Hull's "cognitive map" to the "Gestalt" school with its nominalism of meaningful situations in which "insight" reorganizes the perceptual field.[14] From here, social psychologists, especially Kurt Lewin contributed the importance of situational approach to the understanding of social behavior. Sociologists then, "relationize" behavior in terms of environmental cues and rewards,[15] the situational approach finally being systematized under the theory of problem-solving over time and of behavior as the property of the social system.[16]

Psychologists today emphasize the inadequacy of any approach to personality without due regard for the determination of behavior by situational factors.[17] With them, sociologists, like Parsons, use interaction as one facet in the social situation. It serves not as a theory or

---

12. See Hartung, pp. 63–64.

13. Hall, *General Principles,* pp. 117–29.

14. See Kohler.

15. Thomas.

16. Parsons and Bales, chap. 3. See also A. K. Cohen, *Deviance and Control,* chaps, 7, 8.

17. Murphy, pp. 867–68, 891.

explanation, but rather as a condition, among others, of an inquiry about how factors in the situation work together.

In criminology, it is assumed that offenders are not a special sort of people and that there are differences in the personalities of offenders. It is therefore deduced that criminal behavior can be activated by different people with different motives, or by the same motives which have led other people to other types of behavior. Also, that anybody under a given situation might offend. To understand the crime it is more fruitful then to look for those aspects in the same situation which are deemed uncommon to different would-be offenders. Korn and McCorkle stated this point, saying that "the problem of explaining *what* a person does and *how he does it* is not solved by understanding *why* he does it or what kind of a person he is."[18]

For criminological theory, the situational aspect is of prime importance for the following reasons: it might shed light on the problem of why a person's traits and attitudes will produce crime in one situation and not in another;[19] it may be considered as the causal nexus for the crime, allowing it to occur due to some factors in it which will either trigger the criminal act in a predisposed person or will furnish temptations, opportunities, and positive encouragement to the would-be offender so as to neutralize his control and inhibitions and to set him explosively against his victim in the criminal event; it may serve to determine whether there is a definite pattern of sequence, a conjuncture of events which are present when rape occurs.[20]

The situational aspects gained attention with the studies of particular types of crime, rather than with studies of criminals. One such group of studies deals with crimes which do not involve direct victims, mainly concentrating on professional property offenses.[21] Another group deals with crime against persons. Until now, only criminal homicide and robbery has been studied with attention given to situation-induced events.[22]

The Objective Criminal Situation

The situation is not only an occasion for the release of emotions rooted in the personality of the offender, but in many cases, it should be viewed "as the actual or primary explanation of a criminal act for which one will

18. *Criminology and Penology*, p. 242.

19. Clinard, "Criminological Research"; Cressey, "Role Theory," p. 12; Reckless, *The Crime Problem*, p. 80; Cohen, *Deviance and Control*, pp. 41–47.

20. Margaret Mead said that in relations between the sexes situational aspects rather than personality factors are the most important (*Male and Female*, pp. 213–20).

21. M. Cameron; Clinard and Wade; Cressey, "Role Theory"; Lemert; Maurer; Polsky; Sutherland, *The Professional Thief*.

22. Bohannan; Mohr, et al., *Pedophilia and Exhibitionism;* Wolfgang, *Patterns*. On robbery see: Einstader; Normandeau; Syvrud.

look in vain for a deeper cause."[23] A person's "tendency" for rape is not a sufficient explanation of the genesis of the act. There must be role models and social and normative support for the act, as well as opportunities to commit the crime.[24] Moreover, the situation must contain elements which will be interpreted by the would-be offender as situations worthy of pursuing, planning, and developing, since they offer a good chance for achieving his aims. Thus, the knowledge of and the relationship with the victim, her behavior, and the particular place of their meeting may either offer an immediate opportunity or be interpreted as opportune for further action to be taken by the offender. The situation can be classified, then, as chosen and planned, or unchosen, as when immediate chance opportunities present themselves to the offender.

Other important elements in the situation are those which the offender manipulates in order to neutralize the effects of social control and observability. He may do this by consuming alcohol, by creating compromising relations with the victim, or by physically isolating her. True, the intended victim may vulnerably present herself, allowing the would-be offender to interpret her behavior as a future "consent." But what should be remembered is that there is no such thing as nonculpable rape. There are conditions which may turn the event into something else in which the offender is not charged with rape. Thus, we see that our immediate problem is how to classify situational factors. We work in an ad hoc way, using the data as they appear in the police files, and the analysis discloses the patterns of the rape situations.

Phases of the Modus Operandi

To summarize, we aim to analyze processes and characteristics of the rape situation. We are interested in the modus operandi as a sequence and conjecture of events which enter into the perpetration of forcible rape.[25] This sequence involves the interplay of offender and victim, and other situational factors, which, in the end, set the stage for the crime.

The nature of this study does not lend itself to genetic analysis. The source of information, and the method of data collection precluded the investigation of underlying motivations responsible for defining certain situations as criminogenic. However, we consider the situation as part of the offender's motivation because it is connected with his assessment and selection of place, victim, and the manner by which the offense is carried

23. Hurwitz, p. 359.

24. Cohen, Lindesmith, and Schuessler, pp. 31–35.

25. Cressey attempted this in his *Other People's Money* (pp. 11–12) with a further refinement to discover those situations in which trust violation was absent. For a study which was set as a model for mine, see Wolfgang's *Patterns in Criminal Homicide,* esp. chap. 5. See also the discussion in chap. 1 and its references, this volume.

Fig. 1. Modus operandi of forcible rape

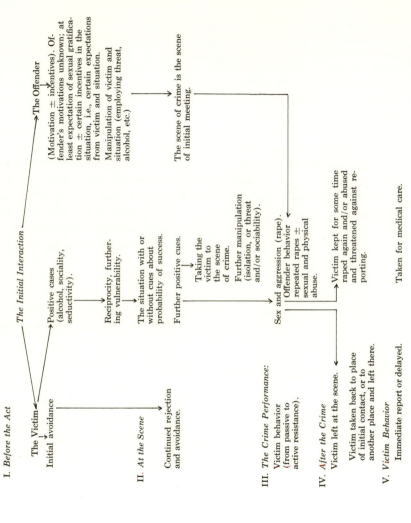

out. In analyzing situations, abstracting them for a moment from personality factors, we tend to "homogenize" the group of persons under study—otherwise we are returning to the individual "casework" or clinical approach. Actually, we already have the appearance of some groupings such as those created by social and legal definition of the age and race of rapists and their victims. Thus, we have already "homogenized" our subjects, and the situational aspects will be seen in terms of these groups.

The modus operandi will be described on the basis of victims' accounts. The following sequence of phases is constructed:

I. *The initial interaction and the meeting ground.* This phase includes the place of initial meeting between the offender(s) and his (their) victims. The scene of the crime may be that of the initial meeting place. If the crime is to be committed elsewhere, a "moving of the crime scene" will occur. The offender or offenders may have set their minds on committing this act, thus planning it, or, the act may be an explosive one, a situation-induced event. The manipulation of the victim by various degrees of coercion and force begins in the initial meeting.

II. *At the scene.* At the scene of rape, the victim may continue to resist the offender who, as a response, will try to render her submission by more violent means. Alternatively, the victim may continue giving the offender encouraging cues, or she may already be frightened and subdued.

III. *The crime.* The offender rapes the victim. He may inflict on her more physical abuse and/or subject her to sexual humiliation in the form of perverted sexual acts.

IV. *After the crime.* The victim may be left at the scene or she is kept for some time, raped, and abused again, or she may be taken to another place and left there (a further moving of the crime scene). Later, the victim either immediately reports the event herself, or confronts someone else who summons the police.

It is possible that a particular person may enter the first or the second phase, but withdraw from concluding his action and completing the full cycle. It would be interesting to know about those who start upon a rape and do not finish the crime but this is not within the scope of this study. In short, the following description (see fig. 1) applies to those who went through all the stages.

Phase I: The Initial Interaction

Meeting Places

The temporal and ecological patterns associated with rape provided a general framework for the analysis of the modus operandi of the crime.

Within this framework, we shall follow the phases suggested above. The particular place where the victim met her assailant and where the crime took place, does not cause the offense, and the offender may not have chosen one place in preference to another. But these locations, just as the motive, or the way victims were subdued, vary in frequency and may play an important role in the circumstances associated with the offense. The specific locations of initial meetings are also important in establishing the flow of events leading to the crime and understanding the behavior of both offender and victim. Moreover, these specific "locales" are variables in the offender's general assessment of risk in committing the offense, or its place and modus operandi.

An analysis of the place of initial interaction may lend support or refute the notion that the rapist attacks his victim in deserted places, streets, or fields, where the victim is unable to see or know the offender before her victimization.[26]

Earlier designations of the place where the victim first encountered her assailant, such as "open spaces"[27] or "indoor places"[28] are too general and overlook the consideration of the "movement of crime scene."

Offender and victim may make an initial contact within or outside their residence area or the area where the crime is committed. The place of meeting and initial interaction can be seen by the would-be offender as a favorable "signal," and can instill in him some "ideas" about the possibility of having the would-be victim accept his suggestions and advances for sexual relations, or of subjecting her by force to such relations. The circumstances of the initial interaction allows the offender to assess the risks which he takes by forcing his intentions upon the woman. He must also decide whether or not he can do it at the same place or whether he must arrange a situation which will offer more security in executing his plan.

THE PHILADELPHIA DATA. Table 45 shows the race of victim and offender according to the place where they initially met each other. The spatial categorization is based on the police files.

In terms of total cases, the most dangerous meeting places are the streets (48 percent, if we include the categories of "waiting for transportation" or "in front of a bar"). But, almost equal proportions are observed if we distingush between those places which allow or encourage the development of acquaintance between victim and offender, and those which do not. Combining the spatial categories for the first group (victim's home or place of sojourn, offender's home, party or picnic, and

26. Frankel; Reinhardt, "The Sex Killer."
27. Radzinowicz, *Sexual Offenses* p. 100.
28. Svalastoga, p. 49.

bar), we observe that 49 percent of the rape events start in such places. In one-third of these cases the victim met the offender at her home or the place where she was temporarily staying. In 7 and 8 percent, respectively, it was in the offender's home or a bar. Thus, the image of an offender lurking in the dark waiting for his victim is, at least in the present study, unsupported. It is true, however, that the dangerous place is not only the participants' places, but also the street. In 52 percent of the cases the victim met the offender in an open space which offered little chance for some initially sustained acquaintance; on the street while walking or waiting for transportation (42 percent), in front of a bar (3 percent), or in the park (1 percent).

Table 45: Initial Meeting Place by Race of Offender and Victim in Rape Events

Where Victim Met Offender	Offender/Victim									
	Negro/Negro		White/White		Negro/White		White/Negro		Total	
	No.	%	No.	%	No.	%	No.	%	No.	%
At her place or home	126	25.4	28	26.6	11	40.7	6	35.3	171	26.4
Where victim stayed, not home or party	46	9.3	4	3.8	2	7.4	...	...	52	8.2
At offender's home	30	6.0	11	10.4	2	7.4	...	...	43	6.7
On the street walking	222	44.7	33	31.4	8	29.7	7	41.8	270	41.8
In a bar	37	7.4	10	9.5	2	7.5	1	5.8	50	7.8
At a party or picnic	10	2.0	6	5.8	...	...	1	5.8	17	2.6
In the park	4	0.8	1	0.9	...	...	...	...	5	0.7
In front of a bar	14	2.8	6	5.8	1	3.7	1	5.8	22	3.4
On the street waiting for car or bus	8	1.6	6	5.8	1	3.7	1	5.8	16	2.4
Total	497	100.0	105	100.0	27	100.0	17	100.0	646	100.0

These results hold for intraracial rape events. Among intraracial Negro rapes, 50 percent of the victims met the offender in places which allow the development of acquaintance, while the same thing happened in 56 percent of white intraracial rapes. For both groups, in about 40 percent of the cases, the initial meeting occurs in places where the offender or the victim were staying temporarily (as visitors, etc.); in half of the cases it was at the residence of the victim or where she was staying at that time.

For interracial cases, when the offender is Negro and the victim white, the meeting ground occurs in the victim's place and in all of these cases the event was that of a felony rape. The second most dangerous meeting place is the street (30 percent). For the cases where the offender is white and the victim Negro, the street is the most dangerous meeting place (41 percent), followed by the victims' place (35 percent).

Crime in the street evokes, among other things, images of rape. Reality does not consort with this myth. However, from the data thus far presented it should not be understood that it is necessarily more dangerous for a female to go to the residence of a male than to let him come to her residence. Before such a conclusion can be drawn we would need to know the total number of times during the period of the study that females in the population who went to the residences of males were raped. Only then might we be able to estimate the relative danger of offender's place. If, as seems more likely, females more frequently go to males' residence than the reverse, the larger proportion of the former than the latter which end in rape may be a statistical artifact.

The Planning of the Offense

In the courts, "planning" of the crime is of utmost importance as part of the problem of *mens rea*. However, very little attention is given in criminological research to the preparation of the crime in its earliest stage of perpetration. A scale constructed with a planned offense at one end, with different degrees of planning in the middle, and with explosive unplanned features at the other end, is an interesting aspect in studying crimes.

Before the rape, the offender may either have set his mind on having sexual relations with whatever female he may encounter, or he may have a particular woman in mind. He will look for either a favorable situation for the deed or will create one. Once he finds the would-be victim, he will prepare and develop further the situation to suit his intentions, or the situation may be already "chosen for him"—that is, it comes to him in the form of a drunken or seemingly "friendly" female, or one who does not reject his early actions to "eroticize" the situation. Obviously, there are other nuances between these two situations; the ready-made or the prepared one.[29] Yet, the end result is that the offender will make some plan to "secure" the victim with different degrees of manipulation of the situation or the victim. In other cases ,the rape will

29. Hurwitz, pp. 363–64.

be an explosive act since the behavior of the victim and other factors in their initial encounter will lead the offender to "make" her immediately and forcefully to submit to him. The former situation may occur when the "potential" victim agrees to share a drink or a ride with her future assailant, who is a stranger, while the other situation may be a case in which robbery or burglary also becomes a rape event. The offender may find the victim so immobilized, that on the spur of the moment he will decide to possess her too. This subject of felony-rape events will be analyzed later.

Only one report deals with the problem of planning of sexual crime. In Bernard Glueck's study, the act of rape is also analyzed from the perspective of planning. Planned and unplanned rape events are considered with the purpose of establishing "the guilt felt by the offender, and the resulting need for punishment through getting caught."[30] Thus, the fact that 60 percent of the rapes reported in the study were of an immediate impulse, with no planning, is taken by Glueck as one evidence "of the mixed motivation of the offender."[31] It may also reflect that the offense was committed under the influence of alcohol.[32] Glueck, also relates that theft or snatching occurred in 20 percent of the cases of rape, but there is no way to establish which came first, the felony or the rape.[33]

From surveying other case studies and reports, one can elucidate the aspect of planning, especially when group rape is described. Nevertheless, since no systematic effort has been made to tackle this problem, no further attempt will be made to present the existing scanty data.[34]

THE PHILADELPHIA DATA. Rape events have been divided into three degrees of planning: planned; partially planned; and explosive. The verbatim description of the event by the victim and offender guided us in making these distinctions, while the terms were borrowed from Glueck's study.[35] Planned rape means that the place was arranged, elaborate enticement was employed, or the victim was deliberately sought and a plan was made to coerce her into sexual relations in the place of the initial meeting, or elsewhere. In partially planned rape, vague plans were made hastily, after the offender had encountered the victim and the situation seemed ripe for the offense. In explosive rapes, no previous idea of

30. Glueck, Jr., *New York Final Report,* p. 46.

31. Ibid., p. 294.

32. Ibid., p. 46.

33. Ibid., p. 300.

34. See "Case Description of Serious Juvenile Sex Offender," in *California Sexual Deviation Research* (1954), p. 123.

35. Glueck, Jr., *New York Final Report,* p. 94.

committing the crime prevailed, but opportunities (place of meeting, victim's behavior, etc.) created the impulse, or the offender's judgment was impaired, usually by the consumption of alcohol before the event.

These classifications may be analytically sound, but they are hard to distinguish in a concrete situation. What they mean in reality is that there are differences between "chosen" and "unchosen" situations. The first category includes those situations in which an offender has predispositions to commit the offense, due to general criminal propensities or the encouragement of peers. In the "unchosen" situation, whatever the nature of the offender's deep hesitation to commit the act, it is likely to occur when he is under the influence of alcohol, or when the elements in the situation (e.g., victim's condition and behavior) make it opportune to commit the crime.

In table 46 the planning of the crime is seen in conjunction with the initial meeting place. We find that of 646 rape events, 71 percent are planned rapes; 11 percent are partially planned; and in 16 percent of the cases the offense is an explosive event. In comparison to explosive and partially planned rapes, planned rape occurred in a variety of places

Table 46: The Planning of Rapes at the Initial Meeting Place

	Victim's Place or Home		Where Victim Stayed (not her home or party)		Offender's Home		On the Street Walking		In a Bar	
	No.	%	No.	%	No.	%	No.	%	No.	%
Planned	111	64.9	38	73.1	34	79.2	191	70.9	38	76.0
Partially planned	3	1.8	3	5.8	1	2.3	52	19.2	5	10.0
Explosive	54	31.5	10	19.2	6	13.9	22	8.1	5	10.0
No information	3	1.8	1	1.9	2	4.6	5	1.8	2	4.0
Total	171	100.0	52	100.0	43	100.0	270	100.0	50	100.0

	Party or Picnic		Park		In front of a Bar		In the Street Waiting for a Cab or Bus		Total	
	No.	%	No.	%	No.	%	No.	%	No.	%
Planned	15	88.3	4	80.0	16	72.7	10	62.2	457	70.7
Partially planned	...	...	1	20.0	5	22.8	3	18.9	73	11.4
Explosive	2	11.7	...	...	1	4.5	3	18.9	103	15.9
No information	...	...	...	...	...	...	...	...	13	2.0
Total	17	100.0	5	100.0	22	100.0	16	100.0	646	100.0

with a slight tendency toward those places which allow initial familiarity and encourage the development of acquaintanceship between the parties.

The assumption can be made that when offender and victim meet in either of their residences, no elaborate plans have to be made by the offender, once he decides to subject the woman to his sexual demands. Thus, from the point of view of planning, the rape will be either vaguely thought out, or will be an explosive event. Indeed, such are the results observed. A *significant* association is found between partially planned and explosive rapes and place of meeting. For instance, 27 percent of the explosive rapes occurred when the meeting place was at the residence of one of the participants. Those cases where the meeting ground is other than one of the participants' residences comprise only 9 percent of the explosive rapes. When planned and partially planned cases are combined, again we see that it is the explosive rape which makes the relationship between planning and place of meeting a *significant* one.

In examining the relation between the planning of the offense and the type of rape according to the number of offenders (table 47), it is assumed that, other things being equal, in the situation of group rape or pair rape, planning is vital because at least, a secure place must be found. When found, precaution must be taken to eliminate immediate detection while the offense takes place. In such cases of multiple rape, also, the victim has to be sought out and agreed upon.

Table 47: The Planning of Rape, by Type of Rape

	SR		PR		GR		Total	
	No.	%	No.	%	No.	%	No.	%
Planned	216	58.4	87	82.8	154	90.0	457	70.8
Partially planned	51	13.8	10	9.6	12	7.1	73	11.3
Explosive	93	25.1	6	5.7	4	2.3	103	15.9
No information	10	2.7	2	1.9	1	0.6	13	2.0
Total	370	100.0	105	100.0	171	100.0	646	100.0

Indeed, a *significant* association is found between types of planning and types of rape (table 47). While 25 percent of single rapes are of an explosive nature, such is the case only in 6 percent of pair rapes and in 2 percent of group rapes. To look at it differently, of all explosive rape events 90 percent are single rapes, while explosive pair-rape events and group events constitute 6 percent and 4 percent, respectively.

Strictly planned events constitute 90 percent of group rape, 83 percent of pair rape, and 58 percent of single rape. Actually, we can, therefore, say that although planned rapes are characteristic of all rape events, they are mostly connected with pair and group types of rape while explosive rapes are *significantly* associated with the single type of rape.

Phase II: At the Scene

Whatever the victim does at the initial interaction—whether she gives the offender some positive cues through her behavior or rejects him—the offender must proceed in his manipulation of the situation. Otherwise no rape occurs. If the scene of the crime is that of the initial meeting, he will attempt to secure her submission by the same type of "reasoning" he used before, or he will change it to use more physical coercion. If the scene of the crime is to be elsewhere, he will try to take her there, applying intimidation on the way and at the scene of the crime. What occurs is a "moving the scene of crime" from the place of abduction to the place of rape. This fact of "movement" becomes, later, an important matter in the court, for establishing the nature and course of events leading to the crime.

Place of Rape

This factor consists of those places which are outside the residences of the persons involved, and those places in their residences—the bedroom, kitchen, living room, and so on.

Units of analysis used in the present discussion include the following: auto and auto in the park[36]; open spaces—school yard, alley, field, vacant railroad lots, parks, or public restrooms; indoors—other than participants' residences (vacant houses, housing projects, etc.); indoors—inside participants' places (victim's residence, places where the victim stayed temporarily and which was not her home, offender's residence or where he stayed temporarily). Although there might be some problem of precise categorization of these places, most places are sufficiently clear so that no doubt arises regarding where the rape occurred.

The following analysis (table 48) is based on the frequency distribution of total victims and does not measure the chances of being raped in one place rather than another, relative to the amount of time a victim spends in these places. The latter fact probably varies by race, time of day, day of week, and so on.

Table 48 reveals that there is a *significant* association between the place where the crime occurred and the race of both victim and offender.

In terms of total cases the most dangerous place is indoors, at a par-

36. The fact that 86 cases of rape (13 percent of all cases) were committed in cars and another 10 cases (15 percent) occurred in parked cars, in parks, leads to the inclusion of a special category—"auto." Also, an auto is a "closed" space on the one hand, and "open" on the other. Hence, to eliminate the confusion it was treated separately.

ticipant's residence, where 56 percent of all victims were raped. The distribution according to race of victims and offenders who are involved in indoor rapes shows that 59 percent of Negro intraracial rapes occurred indoors as compared to 46 percent of intraracial white rapes. Viewing it differently, this means, also, that of 195 victims who were raped at their place of residence, 77 percent were Negroes and 23 percent white; of 113 victims who were raped at the offender's place, 95 percent were Negroes and 5 percent white; and finally, of 52 cases where rape occurred at the place where the victims stayed temporarily, 75 percent of the victims were Negroes and 5 percent white. Combining the two categories of indoor places, 67 percent of the forcible rapes are thus indoor affairs, and not, as it is believed, mainly dark-alley, dead-end-street encounters. This conclusion holds true for intraracial rape, but less so for interracial events.

Table 48: Place of Rape by Offender-Victim Race in Rape Events

	Offender/Victim									
	Negro/ Negro		White/ White		Negro/ White		White/ Negro		Total	
	No.	%	No.	%	No.	%	No.	%	No.	%
Auto	45	9.1	40	38.1	4	14.8	7	41.2	96	14.9
Open spaces	98	19.6	4	8.6	6	22.2	3	17.6	115	17.8
Indoors—outside participant's place of residence	65	13.1	8	7.6	1	3.7	1	5.9	75	11.6
Indoors— participant's residence	290	58.4	48	45.7	16	59.3	6	35.3	360	55.7
Total	497	100.0	105	100.0	27	100.0	17	100.0	646	100.0

References have been made to the phenomenon of moving the crime scene, an aspect of the offense that can be examined by the relationship between the place of initial meeting between the victims and offenders and the location where the crime takes place. Testing the association, two facts become apparent from table 49; first, when the meeting place was indoors, so were the rapes, with the offender's place as the most dangerous. When the meeting place was at the offender's residence, in all the cases the offense took place there. When the meeting place was at the victim's residence, in 88 percent of the cases they were attacked there. The relationship between the place of rape and the meeting at the participants' location is, therefore, found to be *significant*. Second, in many cases involving an outside meeting place, the victim was taken to another

Table 49: Place of Rape by Place of Initial Meeting

Place of Rape	At Her Place		Where She Stayed		At Offender's Place		Place of Initial Meetings In the Street Walking		In a Bar		At a Party or Picnic		In the Park		In the Street In Front of a Bar		Waiting for a Car or Bus		Total	
	No.	%	No.	%	No.	%	No.	%	No.	%	No.	%	No.	%	No.	%	No.	%	No.	%
Auto	16	9.4	2	3.8	...	...	40	14.8	18	36.0	2	11.8	1	20.0	7	31.8	10	62.5	96	14.9
Open spaces	3	1.8	2	3.8	...	...	93	34.5	8	16.0	1	5.9	...	...	6	27.3	2	12.5	115	17.8
Indoors—outside participant's place of res.	2	1.2	7	13.6	...	...	50	18.5	2	4.0	5	29.4	4	80.0	4	18.2	1	6.2	75	11.6
Indoors—participant's residence	150	87.6	41	78.8	43	100.0	87	32.2	22	32.2	9	32.9	...	...	5	22.7	3	18.8	360	55.7
Total	171	100.0	52	100.0	43	100.0	270	100.0	50	100.0	17	100.0	5	100.0	22	100.0	16	100.0	646	100.0

place and was assaulted there—for instance, when the victim met the offender in her residence or at a place where she temporarily stayed.

It should be pointed out that the automobile, which has already established itself as a vehicle of crime commission, is revealed also from our findings as a place of crime.[37] In 96 cases, or in 15 percent of all rapes, the act was committed in a car. However, it was found that the automobile is more the white offender's vehicle of crime than the Negro offender's, probably because of economic differences. Thirty-eight percent of white intraracial rape events occur in a car, while the auto was the place of rape in 9 percent and 4 percent of the respective situations. But when they met on the street, in a bar room or in front of a bar, the rape occurred in an auto in 15 percent, 36 percent, and 31 percent of the cases, respectively. Moreover, 63 percent of these instances in which the victim was waiting for a car or bus on the street and accepted a ride from the offender led to an automobile rape. In order to look more closely at the phenomenon of "moving the scene of crime" we have divided the meeting place and the location of the crime into two groups; "participant places" (residence or place of sojourn) and the "outside" (all other places), and again we seek the relationship between these two places (see table 50).

Table 50: Place of Occurrence of Rapes by Place Where Victim Met the Offenders, Philadelphia

| | Meeting Place | | | | | |
| | Participants' Places | | Outside Places | | Total | |
Place of Rape	No.	%	No.	%	No.	%
Participants' places	234	88.0	126	33.1	360	55.7
Outside places	32	12.0	254	66.9	286	44.3
Total	266	100.0	380	100.0	646	100.0

First, when the meeting place was in one of the participant places, the rape occurred in the same place (88 percent); but when the meeting occurred outside, in only 33 percent of the cases did the rape occur in one of the participant places. Thus, a *significant* association exists between the place of rape and the place of initial meeting. Second, the table shows that "moving of the crime scene" is mainly connected with outdoor rapes; among those who met their assaulters on the outside, more were raped indoors than those who met their offenders "indoors" but were raped "outdoors"!

37. On the sexual meaning of the car see Noskit, pp. 204–16.

This "moving of the crime scene" and transferring of the victim are partly a function of looking for a safer place and affording time to seduce or further coerce the victim into submission. Such is also the conclusion arrived at, from the observation that when the place of initial meeting was a place where other people were around, at a party or in the park, the rape occurred in an automobile in 30 percent and 80 percent of the cases respectively.

Does the place of rape have any relation to force and brutality used against the victim?

A *significant* association is discerned between the place of rape and the use of force (table 51). In terms of total numbers, force was mainly

Table 51: Use of Force in Rape Events by the Place of Rape

	Absence		Presence		Total	
	No.	%	No.	%	No.	%
Auto	6	6.2	90	16.4	96	14.9
Open spaces	7	7.3	108	19.6	115	17.8
Indoors—outside participant's residence	9	9.4	66	12.0	75	11.6
Indoors—inside participant's residence	74	77.1	286	52.0	360	55.7
Total	96	100.0	550	100.0	646	100.0

given for the result seen in cases where the rape was committed indoors but outside the participants' residence; the same proportions of use of force and its absence are revealed in the latter situation.

However, victims of open-space rape and automobile rape have their share of beatings. In these places, in 20 percent of the cases, force was used against the victim. In 43 percent of these cases the victim was beaten brutally and was also choked. The obvious explanation is that the street affords little security to execute the crime; the offender must overcome the used in indoor places, especially the participants' places, where 52 percent of the victims were in various degrees physically abused, including that of brutal beating. These results seem puzzling because being in his or her place, gives less reason for the offender to use force upon the victim. He is in a relatively safe place for committing the crime. However, if she screams, or fights, she may be heard, with the hope of help from neighbors. Thus, in this situation force and brutality are used by the offender as intimidating measures to prevent such reaction. The same reasoning is victim immediately to prevent her from arousing the attention of passers-by. Again, force is used here as intimidating measure.

Place of Rape as Noted in Other Studies and Reports

Already by the 1890s, an assertion was made that "any expert could confirm the statement that incomparable greater number of sexual crimes are committed outdoors than in the home."[38] Furthermore, from the findings of Aschaffenburg, Bonger, Ferri and others, concerning the seasonal (mainly summer) pattern of rapes, the same statement seems true.

Only a few studies on sex offenses have some reference about the places where the crime of rape occurred. In the California study, on the subject of dealing with types of juvenile sex offenses and characteristics of juvenile offenders, it was found that about 43 percent of the episodes of sex crimes occurred in the delinquent's own home, companion's home, in a hotel or motel room.[39] In 16 percent, a public beach or park was the scene of the sex act. There is no way to tell the distribution in terms of age or race and types of sexual crimes.

Glueck, in his report, has a different classification of places according to their "safety" in the terms of apprehensibility, as judged by the offender.[40] He found that among 123 rapists, 50 percent committed the act in dangerous circumstances, that is, in a place which other people passed frequently, in the home with family members present or expected to return, or in any public place during hours of occupancy. In another 23 percent of the cases, the events took place in "safe" places—safe from interruption or discovery. In 30 percent, the offense was committed in an "unusual place," that is, one that affords minimum privacy or that would seem eminently unsuitable.

From the *Report of the Mayor's Committee for the Study of Sex Offenses* it is impossible to separate rapes from other types of sexual offenses.[41] However, this study shows that the streets were the scene of 3 percent of the total cases of sexual crimes. Offenders' and victims' residences were the places of 34 percent and 11 percent, respectively. In 26 percent of the cases, the crimes were committed in a building other than the offender's or the victim's residence; parks were the scene of 4 percent of the cases; and 8 percent were committed in autos. Locations like hallways, cellars, stores, and so on, were the places in which 14 percent of these crimes were committed. The automobile was found to be the scene of the crimes in 8 percent of the cases.

38. Aschaffenburg, p. 25.
39. *California Sexual Deviation Research* (1945), chaps. 7, 8.
40. Glueck, Jr., *New York Final Report,* pp. 100–101.
41. *Report of the Mayor's Committee,* pp. 69–70.

Radzinowicz found that the more serious offenses (including forcible rape) occurred, mainly, in open places: parks, fields, country lanes, footpaths and vacant houses.[42] The crimes occurred at the victims' or the offenders' homes in 10 percent of these cases; and 12 percent were committed in other buildings (air raid shelters, school buildings, camp sites, church halls, garages, garden sheds, etc.). Radzinowicz summarizes his findings by stating that places where the offense occurred "were frequently but not invariably the places where the victim encountered the offender."[43] Later, he remarks that "it seems, however, that it was more the circumstance of encounter than the gravity of the offenses which determined the place where the offenses occurred. Occasionally the offender and victim travelled some distance together before the offense occurred."[44] However, he does not enlarge upon this point.

Svalastoga maintains "that rape in most cases is an open-air event. In 48 percent of the cases ($N = 141$), the crime occurred in isolated places outdoors, and in 24 percent it was also an outdoor open-air event but in a densely populated area."[45] It should be remembered that the last two studies are nationwide, and therefore include references to rural locations like "isolated" places, footpaths, and so on. This fact and the absence of analysis by age, race, and other attributes, make it difficult to compare with the present study.

Phase III: The Crime
Means and Methods Used

Rape is a deviant act, not because of the sexual act per se, but rather in the mode of the act, which implies aggression, whereby the sexual factor supplies the motive.[46] However, although it is taken for granted that rape involves the use of physical force to render the victim submissive, rapists differ in the amount and kind of violence they display in the rape event. As we shall see, other overtures to the act may accomplish the same end. Violence can include anything from forced or coreced seduction to the inflicting of blows which will cause the death of the victim. Therefore, we have differentiated between physical and nonphysical forms of violence. It is contended that the use of physical force is a sufficient, but not a necessary condition to allow, for instance, the victim to prove in the court her submission without utmost resistance.

The term "force" in forcible rape is a legal concept, and in the common

42. Radzinowicz, *Sexual Offenses* pp. 100–101.
43. Ibid., p. 101.
44. Ibid., p. 111.
45. Svalastoga, p. 49.
46. Alexander and Staub, pp. 128–38; Bak; Karpman, "Felonious Assault."

law it is a dominant factor in proving or disproving litigation for rape. In many legal codes, without proof of force, no conviction can be sustained. It is therefore an issue for arduous and controversial argument about problems such as what kind of actions can be legally termed force, or if force is only the act used to overcome the victim or aimed to subdue her resistance. The law does recognize factors like the victim's age, her mental condition, or situational dimensions (the presence of alcohol in the victim, etc.), which must enter into the definition of force. The law, therefore, also acknowledges different degrees and kinds of force, or its absence in the rape situation.

According to *Purdon's Pennsylvania Statutes,* forcible rape is "the unlawful carnal knowledge of a woman forcefully and against her will. . . ."[47] Some legal codes contain the phrase "without her consent" in the definition of rape. Force and the absence of consent on the part of the woman are necessary conditions of common-law rape. It is the term "without consent" which indicates that the law concedes to nonphysical aspects of rendering the victim into submission.[48] It is also a recognition of situational factors in which final submission to a greater force is not equivalent to consent, and a sign that further resistance, or any resistance at all, was deemed futile by the victim. She assented rather than consented.[49]

The definition of forcible rape, contains the use of force. However, some further questions arise whether or not it is used in all the stages of the offense, along with the question of what action can be legally and sociologically termed "force."

We assume, that in the initial meeting, the offender manipulates the victim, the situation, or both. Studies and surveys on rape do not tell us in what phase of the crime, or in the process of committing it, the use of force begins. For instance, the offender may seduce or coerce the victim to go with him somewhere, and only in this stage of initial encounter he will use force. If rape is committed at the scene of the initial meeting, the offender might not try to seduce his victim or solicit her consent, but will use extreme kinds of force against her to subdue her instantly. Thus, force is used either at the outset of the offender's encounter with his victim to place her where he feels safe, or later, depending, among other things, on her original condition and her behavior when meeting the offender or afterwards.

Whatever the origin and function of physical violence in the rape

47. "Rape," title 17, pp. 210, 472.

48. See "Rape Allegation of Force," pp. 802–3.

49. It is this assenting behavior which was picked up in the popular belief that maintains that a woman cannot be raped, even by the use of force.

situation, the term will be used here to mean any kind of physical and bodily interference with the victim either to overcome her initially, or to bring her resistance to naught. We are aware that determining the degrees of violence or force used, and the kind of force used, cannot serve as a sole criterion. The resistance of the victim, the emotional condition that existed in the party's encounter, to enumerate but two factors, are also important but are not constantly recorded in the files.

Nonphysical Force

For analytic purposes, the manipulation of the victim, with or without the use of violence, was divided into two kinds: the first involved the use of nonphysical violence or force, and direct bodily constraint against the victim was not used. The second division pertains to the use of physical violence or force of various degrees and kinds before, during and after the rape situation. It is true that physical force might have been used in the initial encounter, too, and we could argue that verbal coercion and intimidation with a weapon are no less an expression of aggression than the actual beating of the victim. However, we shall examine the problem of nonphysical and physical force separately because of its theoretical and practical legal importance.

THE PHILADELPHIA DATA. On the basis of police interrogations, the data on nonphysical force has been grouped as follows:
1. *Tempting.* The victim is offered money or a ride; the offender tries to arouse interest by verbal or nonverbal means. This method is used especially against young victims.
2. *Coercion.* The victim is threatened with bodily harm, or other kinds of verbal violence are employed by the offender.
3. *Intimidation.* Physical gestures and verbal threats are used.
4. *Intimidation with a weapon or an object.* Threats are reinforced with a weapon or other physical object (a stick, stone, etc.).

From table 52 we observe that in terms of total cases the more aggressive forms of duress (i.e., the two forms of intimidation) occurred in 62 percent of the cases. Combined with verbal coercion, nonphysical aggression was used in the majority of cases (87 percent). However, when relating to the race of the offender and the victim in the rape event and the nonphysical violence involved, the association was not found to be *significant.* Yet, intimidation with and without a weapon was displayed more in the cases where the offender and victim were Negroes (65 percent, as against 49 percent in white intraracial events). The popular belief that interracial rape events is more aggressive is not borne out, at least the differences are not statistically *significant.*

For instance, intimidation with a weapon occurred in 22 percent of those cases in which the offender was a Negro and the victim white, and in 18 percent vice versa. Negro offenders, however, showed more verbal violence and resorted to more aggressive types of duress in coercing the victim into submission. In 82 percent of the cases where intimidation was used, Negro offenders were involved. The proportions in cases where a weapon was used are 93 and 11 percent, respectively. These results also mean that Negro victims were more violently threatened, and were under more verbal and gestural duress than white victims.

Table 52: Nonphysical Violence Used in Rape by Race of Offender and Victim in Rape Events

| | Offender/Victim | | | | | | | | | |
| | Negro/ Negro | | White/ White | | Negro/ White | | White/ Negro | | Total | |
	No.	%	No.	%	No.	%	No.	%	No.	%
Tempting	55	11.1	16	15.2	1	3.7	3	17.6	75	11.6
Coercion	114	22.9	36	34.3	9	33.3	2	11.8	161	24.9
Intimidation	208	41.9	39	37.2	11	40.8	8	47.1	266	41.2
Intimidation with a weapon	115	23.1	12	11.4	6	22.2	3	17.6	136	21.1
No information	5	1.0	2	1.9	...	...	1	5.9	8	1.2
Total	497	100.0	105	100.0	27	100.0	17	100.0	646	100.0

When analyzing the association between the use of nonphysical violence and the age disparity between victims and offenders, the association was found to be *significant* (table 53). Whenever the offender and victim were of the same age level (not more than ±5 years), there was more display of nonphysical verbal aggression. However, no differences are displayed for the two forms of intimidation. Thus intimidation with a weapon occurred in 20 percent when the parties were of the same age, as compared to 18 percent when the victim was much younger, and 30 percent when she was much older than her assailant.

The cases where the initial stages of rape involve the display of verbal violence and gestural aggression, pertaining to the Negro offender and to situations where both parties are Negro are in line with the findings about the greater expression of hostility and aggression either expected of or permitted by Negro males in our culture.[50] As far as age is concerned, somewhat more verbal aggression and gestural violence is displayed in cases where the victim and offender were of the same age, although it was expected to be more. We found, however, that it is in the

50. Kvaraceus and Miller, vol. 2, chap. 9.

age group 15–19 years that victims encounter more verbal violence and duress. For instance, in 26 percent of the cases where intimidation occurred and in 23 percent of the cases where weapons were used, the victim was in this age group. The second highest proportion occurred in the age group 0–10 years and the third in 20–25 years of age.

The Use of Physical Force

On the basis of police files and the victims' accounts incorporated therein, the following classification of the use of "force" was made: roughness—holding, pushing; beating—nonbrutal (slapping) and brutal (slugging, kicking, beating by fists repeatedly, etc.); choking, or gagging, etc.

Table 53: Nonphysical Force Used in Rape Events, by Offender's and Victim's Age Disparity

	Victim Much Younger (−10 yrs.)		Both Same Age (±5 yrs.)		Victim Much Older (+10 yrs.)		Total	
	No.	%	No.	%	No.	%	No.	%
Tempting	26	15.2	47	12.8	2	1.9	75	11.6
Coercion	37	21.6	89	24.3	35	32.4	161	24.9
Intimidation	75	43.9	153	41.7	38	35.2	266	41.2
Intimidation with weapons	30	17.5	74	20.2	32	24.6	136	21.1
No information	3	1.7	4	1.1	1	0.9	8	1.2
Total	171	100.0	367	100.0	108	100.0	646	100.0

This classification may be subjected to criticism because the term "brutal" may be differently assessed by the observer and the victim. Also, the other division employed in table 54, of violence used before, during, and after the rape, is sometimes difficult to determine exactly. We have decided upon each case by reviewing carefully the story of the victim and other corroborative evidence available.

For the purpose of testing associations between the use of physical force in rape situations and race of victim and offender, all categories of force have been combined into one (table 54).

In 550, or 85 percent of 646 forcible rapes, force was used in the rape situation. A *significant* association exists between the use of force and the race of the offender and victim in the rape event. In 433, or 87 percent, of

497 Negro intraracial rapes, force was used. In 81, or 77 percent of white intraracial rapes, force was used—a difference which was found to be statistically *significant*.

Looking for the role of race in the use of violence, we add to the above cases those in which the offender was Negro and the victim white. In these cases, when force was used, in 83 percent it was by a Negro offender, and in 81 percent a Negro victim was involved. However, for interracial events, it was when the offender was Negro and his victim white that force was used more frequently (85 percent) than when the offender was white and the victim Negro (77 percent).

Table 54: Forms and Degree of Physical Force Used in Rape Events, by Race of Victim and Offender

	Offender/Victim									
	Negro/ Negro		White/ White		Negro/ White		White/ Negro		Total	
	No.	%	No.	%	No.	%	No.	%	No.	%
Roughness	148	29.8	28	26.7	4	14.8	4	23.5	184	28.5
Beaten not brutally before rape	110	22.6	24	22.9	4	14.8	3	17.6	141	21.8
Beaten not brutally during and after rape	15	3.0	2	1.9	2	7.4	...	...	19	2.9
Beaten brutally before rape	52	10.5	10	9.5	6	22.3	1	5.9	69	10.6
Beaten brutally during and after rape	53	10.7	4	3.8	4	14.8	2	11.9	63	9.8
Choked	55	11.5	13	13.5	3	11.1	3	17.6	74	11.5
No use of force	64	12.9	24	22.9	4	14.8	4	23.5	96	14.9
Total use of force	433	87.1	81	77.1	23	85.2	13	76.5	550	85.1
Total	497	100.0	105	100.0	27	100.0	17	100.0	646	100.0

In almost one-third of the cases (29 percent) the force used was in the form of roughness. In one-quarter of the cases the victim was beaten non-brutally during the rape situation. In one-fifth of the cases (20.5 percent) the victim was brutally beaten by the offender, and in 12 percent of the cases, the victim was choked by her assailant.

Analyses of the varying degrees of force used indicate that among the cases where force was involved: a *significant* association exists between brutal handling of the victim (brutality and choking) and the race of the offender in the rape event. Negro offenders displayed such behavior in 32 percent of all such intraracial events as compared to 17 percent among white intraracial events; the same holds true for interracial events, where the Negro offenders were more brutal to their white victims than the white offenders to their Negro victims (48 percent and 35 percent, respectively).

Again, it is in the events which involve Negro offenders and victims where *significantly* more violence occurred (brutality and choking), but not in the cases of roughness and nonbrutal beatings.

When the use or the absence of violence is charted against the age disparity between offenders and victims, a *significant* association is discernible (table 55).

Table 55: Use of Physical Force in Rape Events by Victim-Offender Age Disparity

	Victim Much Younger (−10 yrs.)		Both Same Age (±5 yrs.)		Victim Much Older (+10 yrs.)		Total	
	No.	%	No.	%	No.	%	No.	%
Absence	50	29.2	39	10.6	7	6.5	96	14.9
Presence	121	79.8	328	89.4	101	93.5	550	85.1
Total	171	100.0	367	100.0	108	100.0	646	100.0

In almost 90 percent of the cases where victim and offender were of the same age level, the rape event involved the use of force. Among the cases where there were gross differences (in at least ± 10 years) between offenders and victims, force was used in 94 percent of the situations where the offender was at least 10 years younger and in only 71 percent when he was at least 10 years older than his victim. The assumption that the greater aggressiveness of youth which leads to more violence displayed in rape situations is, thus, confirmed.

It should be noted that a *significant* association was found between type of rape and degree of violence in the rape situation. Most excessive degrees of violence occurred in group rape, with single rape showing the least violence in the rape situation. When pair rapes and group rapes were combined, again a *significant* association was discerned between multiplicity of offenders and violence in the rape situation. This means that the smaller the number of offenders, the less likely that violence will occur.

Finally, we noticed that the most excessive degrees of violence during the rape situation were more likely to occur outdoors than at the victims' or offenders' home or place. Brutal beating was the lot of the victim before the rape in 51 percent of the cases, and in 40 percent she received brutal, severe beating during and after the rape. These results compare to 30 percent and 36 percent, respectively, when the rape took place indoors in one of the parties' places.

However, in those indoor cases that involved brutality the place was most often the victim's home. In 28 percent of the cases of brutal beating before rape, and in 30 percent of the cases of brutal beating before and after rape, the rape occurred in her home. The same proportion is noticed for choking. It is hard to explain these results; a factor like victim's resistance, to mention but one, may partially account for them.

FORCE AND BRUTALITY NOTED IN OTHER STUDIES. Only two studies discuss differential degrees of force and they lack information as to race and age of victim and offender.[51] Glueck in his New York Study attempts in his classification of degrees of violence to prove the thesis that sex offenders are passive persons; thus, there is a greater likelihood that the frequency of violence in rape cases will be very low. Mixing in his classification nonphysical aggression with physical violence, he finds that brutality was used in only 20 percent of the cases while coercion (verbal) was employed in 17 percent; threat by weapon was used in 43 percent of the cases and minimal use of physical force in 57 percent of the cases. Tempting was used in 10 percent of the cases, and in 3 percent the victim was murdered.[52]

Svalastoga classifies the use of force in his study, according to types of bodily interference with the victims' attempts to resist and call for help. He constructs a scale of degrees of violence in which each category includes the former ones. Thus, the highest level of kicking and beating (21 percent) includes the following former levels: general interference with body movement (35 percent); interference with vocalization (24 percent); and interference with respiration (20 percent). With one single exception no weapon or object was used, and in no case did the violence result in the death of the victim.[53] Ellis and Brancale, in their study of sex offenders, use the fact of violence to disprove the notion that sex offenders are generally dangerous, and that it is the extent of force and brutality which determines the dangerousness of the defendant. Among their very small sample of rapists ($N = 8$) they found that all used force or duress. They argue that the force involved in these cases was of a most

51. Marces used the factor analysis method to study the relationship between aggression and crime and found aggression specifically related to rape.

52. *New York Final Report,* p. 298. *California Sexual Deviation Research* (1954, p. 116) also found that only 20 percent of the youths charged with rape used force or threats.

53. Svalastoga, pp. 49–50.

questionable nature "since many of the women who charged their sex consort with rape apparently first acquiesced voluntarily and then later preferred charges against their partner."[54] No data is given to prove this argument.

Sexual Humiliation

Though forcible rape is generally understood to involve sexual intercourse with an unwilling female, Radzinowicz rightly contends that "sometimes several forms of sexual misbehavior took place against the same victim."[55] In his study, he relates that in these cases the victims have been classified according to the offense which the police or the courts considered as the most serious.

The psychological and psychiatric case studies abound with descriptions of cases of rape where sexual perversion was practiced upon the victims. These descriptions come to prove the theory that the rapist is undersexed, impotent, or the rape is only one expression of his sexual maladjustment and abnormality.[56]

The only specific analysis regarding such sexual humiliation has been made by Glueck[57] The analysis of this aspect was made to demonstrate "the disturbed and at times chaotic patterns of sexual adaptation of the offenders . . . and would seem to confirm the formulation about the fear of approaching an adult female for the purpose of sexual gratification."[58] Although no data on age or racial differences are given in this study, it is observed that sodomy was practiced in the rape situation in 3 percent of the cases; fellatio in 23 percent, and cunnilingus in 23 percent. It was also found that in 7 percent of the cases the offender masturbated. No such behavior was reported in our data.[59]

The following pages present the analyses of these and other forms of sexual humiliation which were practiced along with the forced sexual intercourse. We believe that in some cases, especially when the victim is sexually inexperienced but also for the experienced one, it is this aspect of the offense which is considered psychologically as well as physically more damaging and humiliating than merely the unconsented intercourse.

THE PHILADELPHIA DATA. On the basis of victim and offender statements made to the police, the following classification of sexual

54. Ellis and Brancale, p. 32, and see p. 33.
55. Radzinowicz, *Sexual Offenses,* p. 97.
56. See, for example, DeRiver, chap. 4.
57. Glueck, Jr., *New York Final Report,* p. 209.
58. Ibid., pp. 47–48.
59. Ibid., p. 299.

humiliation was made: fellatio; cunnilingus; fellatio and cunnilingus; pederasty; use of prophylactics; repeated intercourse.

The first four divisions are deviate sexual practices as defined in the literature on sexual pathology.[60] The fifth category is included because it is believed that by using a prophylactic, the offender attempts to transform a forced erotic encounter into a regular "affair," or a love relationship; or he views this relationship as dangerous to himself (fear of V.D.), with no insight to the true meaning of the whole situation. The sixth category, that of repeated intercourse, is included for it entails longer captivity of the victim by the offender, and more physical abuse—besides that of further sexual shock, especially to a sexually inexperienced victim or one who was shielded hitherto from these practices.

For the sake of finding a relationship between sexual humiliation and race of the participants, all categories of the former were combined. Table 56 reveals that sexual humilation exists only in a little more than one-quarter of the rape events (27 percent). Sexual humiliation, thus, is

Table 56: Sexual Humiliation in Rape Events by Race of Victim and Offender

| | Offender/Victim | | | | | | | | | |
| | Negro/ Negro | | White/ White | | Negro/ White | | White/ Negro | | Total | |
	No.	%	No.	%	No.	%	No.	%	No.	%
Fellatio	37	30.1	17	47.2	2	22.2	4	80.0	60	34.7
Cunnilingus	6	4.9	2	5.6	2	22.2	...	...	10	5.8
Fellatio and cunnilingus	8	6.5	2	5.6	1	11.1	...	...	11	6.3
Pederasty	6	4.9	5	13.9	...	...	...	...	11	6.3
Offender used prophylactic	7	5.7	...	...	...	...	...	...	7	4.0
Repeated intercourse	59	48.6	10	27.8	4	44.1	1	20.0	74	42.8
Total presence	123	24.7	36	34.3	9	33.3	5	29.4	173	26.8
Total absence	374	75.3	69	65.7	12	66.9	12	70.6	473	73.2
Total	497	100.0	105	100.0	27	100.0	17	100.0	646	100.0

not an important feature in rape events. But if we observe those rape events in which sexual humiliation does occur, we find that a *significant* association exists between such behavior and the race of the offender and his victim in the rape event.

60. For a definition and some aspects of these types of sexual behavior see Karpman, *The Sexual Offender,* chap. 2.

Of 105 white intraracial rape events, sexual humiliation was present in the rape situation in 34 percent, but in only 25 percent of Negro intraracial rape events.

Analyses of the various kinds of sexual humiliation indicate that among the cases where such behavior occurred: in over one-third of the cases (35 percent) fellatio was enforced on the victim; in 6 percent cunnilingus was used; in another 6 percent both fellatio and cunnilingus were used; in another 6 percent pederasty was displayed; in 4 percent the offender used a prophylactic; and in 43 percent the offender forced the victim to more than one sexual intercourse. It is the cases which involve Negro offenders and victims, where some of these patterns of behavior are more clearly discerned, while for others, like fellatio and pederasty, it is the white offender who inflicted more of these kinds of humiliations upon his victim.

Yet, if we separate offenders from victims, we observe that proportionately it is more the white victims who have suffered sexual humiliation from their assailants: 34 percent compared to 25 percent of Negro victims, a difference which reaches a level of statistical *significance.* This result holds true for fellatio, cunnilingus, and pederasty.

What tentative interpretation can be given to these results, especially to the behavior pattern of fellatious cunnillingus, and the subjection of victim to repeated intercourse? Fellatio and cunnilingus are considered a titillating sexual foreplay to arouse sexual desires. The former especially in the male, the latter also in the female. Also, both practices are considered special forms for sexual satisfaction for males, especially fellatio, and have the aura of European, sophisticated style. It was alluded that these practices entered into the American sexual repertoire after World War II as part of the process of sexual sophistication which swept the country.[61] Thus, in a rape event in which one takes the liberty to violate the sexual self-determination of another person, once the latter has been rendered into submission, it is easy and tempting for the former to play the sensual libertine. Also, these are not the acts of an "impotent," which the psychiatric school so emphatically suggests. First, in the present study, these sexual practices come together with sexual intercourse and second, the proportion of repeated intercourse among these cases also eliminates such a claim. If there are some homosexual tendencies among the rapists (in our study 6 percent committed pederasty on their victim), we have to caution against any such interpretation without a knowledge of these people.

When the association between sexual humiliation and type of rape is

61. See: Ditzion; A. Ellis, *The American Sexual Tragedy;* Lerner, chaps. 8, 9.

tested, it is found that they are *significantly* associated with multiplicity in the rape situation. Sexual humiliation was displayed in 34 percent of the group-rape events and in 27 percent of pair-rape events, while it was displayed in 23 percent of single-rape events.

In terms of varying types of sexual humiliation, when we combined pair rape with group rape, the proportion of these practices from the total cases is higher in multiple-offender rapes than in single rapes.

Testing the association between sexual humiliation and the place of rape, it is observed that sexual humiliation was *significantly* associated with indoor places, such as at the participant's home. In terms of total cases when sexual humiliation occurred, in 61 percent it took place at the victim's or offender's residence or place of sojourn. If we include the automobile, the proportion is higher by 15 percent.

Finally, the association between sexual humiliation and the presence of alcohol in the rape situation is found to be *significant*. When sexual humiliation occurred, in 44 percent of the rape events, alcohol was present in the rape situation. When alcohol was absent, in 70 percent of the cases, sexual humiliation was absent too. It was when alcohol was present in the offender or in both offender and victim that sexual humiliation was found to be *significantly* associated, with fellatio as the particular deviated sex practice.

Victim Behavior

A statement was made to the effect that a woman can resist rape "because of the almost inexpugnable position she occupies on account of the topography of the sexual organs in the female body. . . ."[62] On the other hand, various conditions, psychological and social in nature, may make rape possible. Among these are: the disproportion in physical strength between victim and attacker; the victims' being in an unconscious condition due to age, drunkenness, and so on; the element of surprise which overcomes or neutralizes victim resistance; a threat which paralyzes or subdues initial resistance by the victim; fatalistic feeling and fear of bodily harm from blows and beating rather than fear of intercourse; and the unconscious desire of the victim for, or apathy to, sexual relations with a stranger.[63]

Moreover, although people tend to view rape as an act which befalls the victim without any cooperation, or reciprocal action on her part, unlike in other cases (especially offenses against property and many others besides), in sexual offenses the victim may not be free from all complicity to the act and "sometimes the so-called victim is a consenting

62. Mendelson, p. 231.
63. See discussion on this point in chap. 14, this volume.

party. . . ."[64] To this aspect, we turn our attention now; the victim's behavior during the rape situation.

LEGAL AND THEORETICAL BACKGROUND. Statutes may define forcible rape with such phrases as "against her will" or "by force" or "without her consent." These words have been used sometimes synonymously and sometimes separately and thus produced endless controversy in the court because sexual intercourse can be deemed as rape only "if it was against the will of the woman, which is manifested by the struggle that she put up against the penetration of her person."[65] Nonconsent is therefore an essential in the crime of forcible rape. However, no doubt every consent involves a submission, but it by no means follows that a mere submission involves consent.

In some cases the question of consent is hardly an issue. Such are the cases where a weapon is used by the rapist, or when the victim had to yield to a sudden attack or to an overpowering force of one or more attackers. Also, there are other situations in which the law does not demand from the victim a proof of resistance to the act. These are events where there is a presumption of nonconsent such as when the victim is fraudulently taken or she was drunk, or in abeyance or absence of cognitive faculties due to sleep, or when the rape is committed on an insane or mentally deficient female, where the victim is under age or when sexual intercourse is obtained by fraud.[66] However, in many cases, such as when the offender is not a stranger to the victim, or when he is much older than she or of a different class or race, or when some tête-à-tête relationship is established between the parties, the crucial problem is to establish the victim's resistance to the sexual act.

In all cases of rape, but especially those where there might be a suspicion of complicity, a crucial question is the amount of resistance which is expected from the woman to accept her complaint of rape. Many elements enter the question of consent and resistance. Suppose the victim's moral character is admissible as an evidence, can it be reasoned and accepted that an "immoral" female is more likely to have consented? or suppose there is evidence of prior consent, can we assume she consented this time too? Furthermore, can physical resistance be the sole criterion for nonconsent? Shall we rely solely on the victim's story, which might be different from the one she tells her parents or others? Or, what about the drinking woman who cannot resist to her utmost because the alcohol has

64. Radzinowicz, *Sexual Offenses,* p. 83.

65. Ploscowe, *Sex and the Law,* p. 160.

66. For a more detailed discussion, see: "Complaints about Rape"; Drzazga, chap. 8; "Forcible and Statutory Rape," pp. 55–62; Ploscowe, *Sex and the Law,* chap. 6; Puttkammer; Roeburt, pp. 40–53.

reduced her capability for such show of resistance? Also, while "against her will" or "without consent" may hinge on conscious and overt behavior, it is possible to assume that while the overt behavior may seem resistant, the mental attitude might be one of consent. Perhaps the resistance is merely feigned to satisfy the cultural definition of the female role in the love game; or, with some women, aggression and resistance are internal needs in the sexual encounter, either to increase gratification[67] or to deal with guilt problems which may arise after the behavior.[68]

The old law demanded from the victim a high degree of resistance. This was based on medicolegal reasons[69] and on the (cynical) belief that a healthy woman cannot be raped by one man, if full penetration is to be effected.[70] More and more it was recognized that a rigid application of the "utmost-force" ruling would eliminate a large number of unjust convictions, but it would also allow for injustice on the other side.[71] Such is the decision of the court in the case of Connecticut v. Exposito, where it maintained: ". . . to make the crime hinge on the uttermost exertion the woman was physically capable of making would be a reproach to the law as well as to common sense."[72]

A growing number of statutes are now ready to recognize that the amount of resistance depends on the relative age and strength of the parties, the circumstances of the attack, and the futility of continued resistance. Thus, only "good faith" resistance is required.[73] No criterion for the amount of resistance is laid down. However, it should be remembered that there is no explicit provision in the law for ambivalence, and if the victim does not show a definite amount of negative behavior, her behavior will be evaluated as consent.[74]

Other changes in legal views are observed. Although the medical opinion claims that rape is impossible if full penetration and emission of semen are necessary, legal decisions have been made to the effect that rape is completed with the slightest penetration, and emission is not

67. S. Freud, *New Introductory Lectures,* p. 58.

68. Alexander, *Fundamentals of Psychoanalysis,* p. 58.

69. Tyler, p. 76.

70. *Don Quixote* and Balzac's *Droll Stories* are but two examples. See also E. H. Sutherland, "The Sexual Psychopath Laws," p. 544.

71. Puttkammer.

72. Reported in Ploscowe, *Sex and the Law,* p. 161.

73. Ibid.

74. A presumption of consent may be also shown by the victim's prior behavior ("reputation") or subsequent conduct (e.g., when and to whom the complaint was made), see: *Pennsylvania Law Encyclopedia;* Commonwealth v. Goodman, 126–A 2d. 763 18a Pa. Super. 205 (1956); "Comment: Police Discretion."

necessary to complete the rape.[75] Furthermore, there is now a readiness to recognize stages of resistance, that the first resistance dissolves at some point, and it is not a sign of consent but of the futility of further resistance. One may say that the victim assents or yields rather than consents.[76] It may, however, happen that the victim first consents and later regrets her decision and cries "rape." Also there is readiness to take cognizance of different psychological reactions to fear and panic. Terror and force can prevent a woman from resisting at all; she may be paralyzed (the fright-and-flight reaction).

Such considerations affect the conceptions of "force." From the present study it is observed that rape can also be committed without the use of physical violence. The court recognizes different kinds of manipulation of the victim and the situation to render the victim into submission by preventing her from resisting or reducing her resistance to naught.[77] Threat by weapon, use of verbal gestures, intimidation and other types of duress are used by offenders on their victims. Thus, physical force is a condition, but not a necessary one, in overcoming the victim.[78] It is possible, then, to maintain that there is a difference between the legal terms "against her will" and "without her consent," the latter meaning without resistance, a proof for it. It means also taking situational elements into consideration when actual physical resistance was not displayed.[79]

So much for the legal framework of victim behavior during the rape event. To let the problem rest there, however, would limit the study to convicted cases of rape, that is, the court level sample of cases. Because we deal with the problem of modus operandi seen partly as a sequence of steps, we are bound to discuss the problem of victim behavior as a part of this whole sequence. We assume, for instance, that the victim's behavior in the rape situation is influenced by some of the variables we have analyzed before. Also, her behavior may have some bearing upon the "treatment" she will receive from her assailant. For instance, the more she attempts to resist the more she will be beaten.

Constantly we call ourselves to check upon some notions or theories advanced on different aspects of the crime. Thus statements were made to the effect that the very resistance of a woman is what the man is seeking in the normal sexual relationship,[80] and in the rape situation he wants

75. Drzazga, chap. 8.

76. "Assault with Intent to Rape." See also the rulings in Drzazga: Allison v. State Ark. (1942); People v. Flores, Calif. (1944).

77. Arada.

78. "Rape Allegations of Force," p. 802.

79. The Bible has already recognized this difference—Deut. 22: 23–27.

80. Abrahamsen, *The Mind*, pp. 118–49; Bowman; Gardner, "The Aggressive Destructive Impulse."

to assert his authority and be gratified by his conquest rather than by the sexual act itself.[81] The victim's resistance, in these instances, serves to enhance the provocation which the offender feels toward her, and she will therefore be subject to more physical brutality and sexual humiliation.[82] We are unable to know the psychological motivation of the offender, but again we can see if a relationship exists between the victim's behavior in the rape situation and degrees of violence, and the sexual humiliation she is subjected to during the rape situation.[83]

Victim behavior before the offense, at the outset of the process which led to her victimization, creates a situation in which neither the offender nor the victim can predict its outcome. Victim behavior is then seen as an important factor in the contingencies of actions which may escalate toward the completion of the event, or they may fizzle away into abortiveness. Furthermore, the victim by her behavior, actively or passively may contribute to the erotization of the situation and may influence his judgment and choices as how to subdue her resistance and make the situation safe for the commission of the offense. The victim by her behavior, then, helps the offender to define the situation, to facilitate the execution of his intentions and anticipation of their consummation.

Victim behavior during the offense, especially of minors, in terms of its degree of consent or resistance may reduce the criminal responsibility of the offender and nullify the severity of the punishment.

Victim behavior may also turn her from a seemingly innocent partner to a subject, sometimes for punitive but most often a target for treatment activities. It is therefore found important to ascertain in the pre-sentence investigation, victim's behavior prior, while and after the offense, in order to discover factors which mitigate or aggravate the offense for the offender and the victim.

THE PHILADELPHIA DATA. The complexity surrounding the victim's story about her behavior in the rape situation has already been pointed out in the discussion of the legal problems involved. The fact that we are dealing with cases in police files compels us to retain all cases which might have been dismissed by the court, when the victim's cooperation or "consent" would be decided there. Our sample, however, includes all the cases which the police found worthwhile to pursue in the court (when the offender was found) or to investigate further if the alleged offender was still at large.

81. Jenkins; Karpman, "Felonious Assault."

82. Dunham, p. 38.

83. For an attempt to assess such relationships see Elliasberg, "The Acute Psychosexual Situation."

The police did not accept the victims' stories at face value. Some victims changed their stories, and the police attempted to verify conflicting stories or to validate an unchanged one. It is the last recorded report in each case which was accepted by us for analysis. In cases where the victim changed her story (41 cases), we have made our own decision by checking the offenders' story and other evidence in the file. The same procedure was taken when parents or guardians refused to cooperate completely with the police or to follow up the charge previously made by them (10 cases).

The data on victims' behavior have been grouped as follows (table 57): submission—verbal protest, expression of reluctance only, young victim (under 10 years), or intoxicated victim; resistance—victim screaming and/or attempting to escape; fight—victim putting up a strong fight, throwing things, kicking, and so on.

Table 57: Victim's Behavior and Race of Offender and Victim in Rape

	Offender/Victim									
	Negro/Negro		White/White		Negro/White		White/Negro		Total	
	No.	%	No.	%	No.	%	No.	%	No.	%
Submissive	270	54.5	60	57.1	16	59.3	9	52.0	355	55.0
Resist	136	27.2	26	24.8	6	22.2	5	29.5	173	26.7
Fight	89	17.9	19	18.1	5	18.5	3	17.6	116	18.0
No information	2	0.4	...	...	...	...	...	...	2	0.3
Total	497	100.0	105	100.0	27	100.0	17	100.0	646	100.0

In 355 (or 55 percent) of the 646 forcible rapes the victim displayed only submissive, unwilling kinds of behavior in the situation. These cases, which include young or intoxicated victims, should not be taken as indicating consenting behavior. It is up to the court to prove such behavior, but it was not obvious from the files.[84]

In 173 (or 27 percent) of the cases the victim resisted the offender before and during the rape, and in 116 (or 18 percent) of the 646 rapes, the victim put up a strong fight against her assailant.

These findings point to the possible naïveté in expecting all women to fight for their sexual self-determination. It also refutes the belief that fighting women cannot be raped. But if any significance should be at-

84. This group includes 8 cases where the victim consented, under threat or intimidation, to one offender in a pair or group rape. In all these cases it was found that she was forced to have sexual intercourse with the other offender(s).

tached to these results, we have to look for their distribution in groups based on race and degrees of violence inflicted on the victim.

No statistically *significant* association is discernible between the behavior of the victim in the rape situation and the race of offender and victim. The distribution of the various degrees of resistance among Negro and white victims is almost equal in each type of resistance. It holds for intraracial and interracial events as well as to some age differences between intraracial and interracial rape events. The highest proportion of submission (59 percent) is in the cases where the victim was white and the offender Negro. It includes almost all the cases of felony rape where the victim was also older than her attacker.

The greater strength of youth leads to the assumption that, all things being equal, females in the adolescent and young-adult age are more resistant in the rape situation. To test this assumption (table 58) victims' ages were divided into the following: 10–14 years of age; 15–30 years; 30 and up.

Table 58: Victim's Behavior in Forcible Rape by Victim's Age

	10–14		15–30		30–Over		Total	
	No.	%	No.	%	No.	%	No.	%
Submissive	114	65.8	161	50.9	80	51.3	355	55.0
Resist	34	19.5	90	28.5	49	31.4	173	26.7
Fight	25	14.3	64	70.3	27	17.3	116	18.0
No information	1	0.4	1	0.3	...	...	2	0.3
Total	174	100.0	316	100.0	156	100.0	646	100.0

To determine whether age was associated with the degree of resistance, each type of behavior and grouping relative to this type of resistance were made and tested. The following associations emerged to the level of statistical *significance:*

1. *Between submissive behavior and age.* The younger the age, the more submissive is the victim's behavior. Thus, in the age group between 10 to 14, in 66 percent of the cases submissiveness characterizes victim's behavior as compared to 51 percent in the ages 15–30 and from 30 years of age and over.

2. *Between resistance and age of the victim.* While 31 percent of the victims in the age of 30 and over show resistance to the attack, such was only the case (19 percent) in the ages 10–14.

3. *Between resistance and fighting categories combined and age of the victim.* When resistance and fighting categories were combined, a *significant* association was found between this combination and age.

We can, therefore, state that the higher the age of the victim, the more resistance she displayed in the rape situation. The adolescent and young adult female fought more, although neither significantly more than the 30-year-old-or-more victim, nor more than the young victim (20 percent, 17 percent, and 14 percent, respectively).

It is not the victim's age alone which influenced her behavior during the attack. The age disparity between the offender and his victim may be a decisive factor, as well as the place where she was raped and the degrees and kind of force, to which she was subjected. To the first aspect we shall turn now. (table 59).

Table 59: Victim's Behavior in Rape Events by Victim-Offender Age Disparity

	Victim Much Younger (−10 yrs.)		Both Same Age (±5 yrs.)		Victim Much Older (+10 yrs.)		Total	
	No.	%	No.	%	No.	%	No.	%
Submissive	118	69.0	178	48.5	59	54.6	355	55.0
Resist	30	17.54	110	29.97	33	30.6	176	26.7
Fight	23	13.46	77	21.0	16	14.8	116	18.0
No information	...	...	2	0.53	...	...	2	0.3
Total	171	100.0	367	100.0	108	100.0	646	100.0

When the victim was much younger than the offender, as expected, she showed *significantly* more submissiveness than the victim who was in the same age level as her assailant (69 and 48 percent, respectively). Older victims attacked by much younger offenders also showed a high proportion of submissive behavior (55 percent). Victims who belong to the same age group as their assailants showed a *significantly* higher proportion of resistance; in 21 percent they were fighting the offender as compared to 13 percent when the victim was much younger and 15 percent when she was much older than the offender.

When the victim first faces the offender, the way he approaches her (tempting, intimidating her, etc.) may determine how she will behave in terms of her resistance to him. She may decide upon the futility of resisting or fighting for fear of being beaten. It may be, therefore, that it is not so much the actual force used in the rape that will determine her subsequent behavior and resistance to her assailant, as the very beginning overtures that the offender uses.

In table 60 is analyzed the relationship between the nonphysical means used by the offender upon the victim at the onset of the crime, and the type of resistance, if any, shown by the victim.

A *significant* association is discerned between victim's behavior and the type of nonphysical violence she encountered at the onset of the attack. The victims showed submissiveness in 71 percent of the cases when they were intimidated, while only 10 percent of them fought the offender in such situations. It seems that when confronted with a threat to her life or physical well-being, the victim was not willing to resist or fight.

Table 60: Victim's Behavior in Rape Situations by Nonphysical Force Used by the Offender

	Tempting		Coercion		Intimida-tion		Intimida-tion with Weapon or Object		No Infor-mation		Total	
	No.	%	No.	%	No.	%	No.	%	No.	%	No.	%
Submis-sive	27	36.0	81	50.3	145	54.5	97	71.3	5	62.5	335	55.0
Resist	23	30.7	57	35.4	67	25.2	26	19.1	...	...	173	26.7
Fight	25	33.3	23	14.3	53	19.9	13	9.6	2	25.0	116	18.0
No infor-mation	...	...	...	...	1	0.4	...	...	1	12.5	2	0.3
Total	75	100.0	161	100.0	266	100.0	136	100.0	8	100.0	646	100.0

When testing the association between each type of behavior and the nonphysical means used against the victim, we observed that the higher the degree of nonphysical violence, the lower the degree of resistance the victim showed in the rape event. Thus, submissive behavior was displayed by the victim in 60 percent of the cases when both forms of intimidation were combined. In such situations, the victims resisted only in over 23 percent of the cases and actively fought in 14 percent of the cases. The same held true for the situation in which coercion was used against the victim. In 50 percent of the cases she was submissive; in 35 percent she displayed resistance; and only in 14 percent did she fight her assailant.

A similar pattern is observed when turning to the relationship between the victim's behavior and physical violence employed by the offender, but only for submissive kinds of behavior. A *significant* association is discernible. In 93 percent of the cases where force was not used on the victim, she was submissive, displaying the same kind of behavior in 49 percent when force was used. However, since force was not used on young victims, we found such victims did not resist, which partly explains this pattern.

A further test revealed a deviation from the generalization. A reversed pattern is observed when degrees of violence are taken into consideration. Thus, the higher the degree of violence, the higher is the degree of re-

Table 61: Victim Behavior and the Use of Physical Force in Rape Situations

	Roughness		Beaten Not Brutally Before Rape		Beaten Not Brutally During and After Rape		Beaten Brutally Before Rape		Beaten Brutally During and After Rape		Choked		Total Use of Force		No Use of Force		Grand Total	
	No.	%	No.	%	No.	%	No.	%	No.	%	No.	%	No.	%	No.	%	No.	%
Submissive	112	60.8	65	46.1	6	31.6	24	34.8	18	28.6	41	55.4	266	48.4	89	92.7	355	55.0
Resist	45	24.4	41	29.1	8	42.1	29	42.0	27	42.8	18	24.0	168	30.5	5	5.2	173	26.7
Fight	26	14.3	35	29.8	5	26.3	16	23.2	17	27.0	15	21.6	114	29.7	2	2.1	116	18.0
No Information	1	0.5	...	...	...	...	...	...	1	1.0	...	...	2	0.4	...	...	2	0.3
Total	184	100.0	141	100.0	19	100.0	69	100.0	63	100.0	74	100.0	550	100.0	96	100.0	646	100.0

sistance behavior. First, the higher the degree of resistance, the higher was the proportion of violence displayed. Thus resistance was the type of behavior the victim showed in 45 percent of the cases when force was not used, but in 31 percent when force was used. The victim put up a fight in 30 percent of the cases when force was used, and in 2 percent when force was not a factor. For a possible explanation the kinds of physical force used and their timing in the rape situation were examined.

Indeed, from table 58 it is seen that the more severe the physical violence the victim was subjected to, the more intensive was her fighting. Thus, resistance ensued in 24 percent of the cases when roughness was used; in 31 percent when the victim was beaten not brutally; and in 43 percent when she was beaten brutally. The same is revealed in the situations where the victim showed a fighting resistance to the offender.

Interesting, however, are the results which indicate that resistance did not stop at the onset of this attack; it continued during the attack. In many cases it began in the middle, possibly after the victim overcame her initial shock or when she realized what the offender was up to. Hence, while the victim resisted the offender in 24 percent of the cases when being beaten nonbrutally before the actual act of rape, in 29 percent of the cases resistance followed when nonbrutal beating was used by the offender during the rape act or later. For fighting victims, the proportions were 24 and 26 percent, respectively. Age and race differences between offender and victim, as well as other characteristics and circumstances of the situation, may explain it. From the legal point of view, when the case comes before the court, a new dimension is introduced. It is not only the beginning of resistance (whatever its intensity) and its cessation which are usually important in the court, but also the reverse cycle of nonresistance or different degrees of resistance in different stages of the rape situation.

Would the place of rape make any difference in the victim's behavior? The various combinations made to gauge the relationship indicate that a *significant* association exists between the place of rape and victim behavior. However, the association found points to one direction: there was a *significant* association between submissive behavior and rape which occurred in the participant's home. This was true especially in the cases when the rape occurred in the offender's place or in felony cases.

Victims, however, did resist the offender when the rape occurred outside the participant's place, especially when the offense occurred in an automobile or in closed places other than outside the participants' places. This is connected, as we shall see later, with the fact that more pair and gang rapes occurred there.

It can be assumed that when alcohol is present in the victim or in both the offender and the victim, she is less able to resist the offender (table 62).

The following association between alcohol in the rape situation and the type of victim behavior reached the level of *significance:*

1. *Between submissive behavior and the absence of alcohol.* Victim submissive behavior occurred in 46 percent when alcohol was present in the rape situation and in 59 percent when alcohol was absent.
2. *Between resistant behavior and the presence of alcohol.* The victim resisted the offender in 34 percent of the events when alcohol was present in the rape situation, but in only 23 percent when alcohol was absent.
3. *Between submissive behavior and the presence of alcohol in the victim only.* The victim was submissive in 45 percent of the events when she was drinking alone, resisted in 40 percent of such situations, and fought in only 14 percent of the cases when alcohol was present in her alone.

Table 62: Victim's Behavior by the Presence of Alcohol in Rape Situations

	In Offender and Victim		In Victim Only		In Offender Only		Total Present		Total Absent		Grand Total	
	No.	%	No.	%	No.	%	No.	%	No.	%	No.	%
Sub-missive	64	47.0	28	45.16	9	47.36	101	46.54	254	59.2	355	55.0
Resist	43	31.6	25	40.32	5	26.32	73	33.64	100	23.3	173	26.7
Fight	29	21.4	9	14.52	5	26.32	43	19.82	73	17.0	116	18.0
No infor-mation	...	...	...	...	...	...	...	...	2	0.5	2	0.3
Total	136	100.0	62	100.0	19	100.0	217	100.0	429	100.0	646	100.0

4. *Between the presence of alcohol in both offender and victim and submissive behavior.* The victim was submissive in 47 percent of the cases when alcohol was present in both her and the offender, showed resistance in 32 percent in such situations, and fought the offender in 21 percent when both she and the offender consumed alcohol prior to her victimization.

Alcohol, it seems, does play a role in determining the resistance the victim will display in the rape situation. The presence of alcohol may diminish the intensity of the resistance which the victim will show against her attacker.

VICTIM BEHAVIOR NOTED IN OTHER STUDIES AND RE-PORTS. In rape situations the issue of victim-behavior determines what constitutes "consent" and what constitutes "force."[85] Surveys, studies, and case reports on sexual crimes, when they touched upon the subject,

85. Luckman; Machtinger; Monahan; Peto; Schultz; Trankel.

have limited themselves to describing the personality make-up of the "participant," mainly a cooperative child victim and they tend to confuse behavior prior and during the offense. Also, in these reports the victim's behavior during the offense serves as one index of her relationship to the offender. In almost all of these reports no distinction is made between the different sexual offenses in which the victims are involved. Hence, it is impossible to gauge the difference between victims' behavior in rape situations and, let us say, in an exhibitionistic encounter. Furthermore, the kinds of behavior in general and degrees of resistance (if any) which the victim displays during the event are almost invariably limited to the distinction between "participant" and "nonparticipant" coerced or passive or accidental victim on the basis of their role in initiating, maintaining or rejecting sexual relations, rather than between different degrees of resistance.

Psychoanalytic theory maintains that women have some masochistic tendencies,[86] as well as an inclination to submit themselves to forceful sexual relationships.[87] Therefore, psychologists find it not surprising that in actual rape situations many women will submit without any genuine resistance. Specific case studies and surveys on victims were conducted and it was found that, contrary to popular belief, and to victims' and parents' accounts, the child or adolescent victim showed complicity in the criminal sexual situation if not active participation. In many cases it was revealed that the victims subtly encouraged their victimization.[88] In this type of victim her neurotic behavior, due to adverse family situations, led to her "acting out" either in the form of sexual promiscuity or in unconscious behavior which brought her unguarded victimization.[89] Other reports emphasized the negative general social conditions of the victim's family (immigration, poverty, lower class living, etc.) to explain, especially, the adolescent girl's search for excitement, adventure, and so on. Her resulting actions made her vulnerable to be sexually victimized.[90]

Some studies touched upon special situations in which the victim encountered aggressive sexual behavior including rape. The victim entered into a compromising relationship with the offender, such as dating[91] or

---

86. H. Deutsch, vol. 1, p. 251.

87. Abraham, "The Experience of Sexual Traumas"; Fenichel, p. 331; S. Freud, "Three Essays."

88. See Gebhard et al., p. 54; also *California Sexual Deviation Research* (1954), p. 61.

89. Bender and Blau; Halleck; Meyers, pp. 157–60; Schultz; Weisse.

90. Abbott; Goldberg; Reckless, *The Crime Problem,* pp. 17–19; Thomas. In these, as well as in psychiatrically oriented studies, it is almost impossible to separate the rape cases from other types of sex offenses.

91. See, for instance, Kanin.

drinking situations. Rape in such situations is most likely, and the resistance of the victim is taken merely as an expected, reluctant reaction to sexual advances.[92]

Reports which contain some discussion on victims' behavior classify the victims into participant and nonparticipant or accidental victims. The first group show less, or token, resistance to their assailants and usually a certain acquaintanceship is established between them. Sometimes, however, a continuous and intensive relationship exists between them.[93] The accidental victim will show the most resistance to the offender who is usually older than she, a stranger, or one who attacks her more violently.[94] Frequently, this accidental victim cooperates unintentionally, from carelessness with the offender,[95] either by ignorance or through provocative behavior,[96] or initial acquiescence.[97]

We have found no study on rape which attempts to scale degrees or intensity of resistance to the act. The closest we come to such ventures is Glueck's study in New York.[98] With the exception of Glueck, no one looks for the distribution of participant and accidental victim, among those studying different sex crimes. Glueck classifies victims and finds that in rape cases 23 percent of the victims were rated seductive; 10 percent were cooperative; 23 percent showed submissive, unwilling behavior (verbal protest and other gestures or reluctance); and 57 percent put up resistance (in the form of screaming, struggling, etc.).[99]

It seems that "victimology," if it is to emerge as an important aspect in criminology, would gain much from what we have discussed above as the modus operandi of victim behavior, a dimension which is presently crudely analyzed and psychiatrically biased. Curiously, such is the situation in spite of the fact that sexual crimes are so much victim-oriented, and so much entangled with the problems of victim's relationship to the offender—the victim precipitating the crime, or displaying (different) degrees of complicity and resistance.

92. Ehrmann, "Premarital Sex Relations."

93. Kanin.

94. See Weisse and his bibliography on this typology. See also Gagnon; *Wisconsin's Experience* (in this report, of 33 victims of forcible rape, 28 were accidental victims showing some sort of resistance; however, the kind and degree of resistance was not stated).

95. Schultz.

96. *California Sexual Deviation Research* (1954), chap. 5; Glueck, Jr., *New York Final Report*, p. 296.

97. Ellis and Brancale, pp. 32–33.

98. Glueck, Jr., *New York Final Report*, p. 296, table 27.

99. Ibid., p. 296.

Phase IV: After the Crime

Viewing the offense as a sequence of events or in terms of stages, means that the offense does not terminate with the offender finishing the act. The involvement of the victim does not end there. Some victims are kept for some time by the offender(s), raped or beaten again, sometimes left at the scene of the crime, or taken back to the place of initial contact or to another place. Then, it is up to the victim to report her ordeal to the police, family, or others immediately; or for some reason, she may delay it. She may need medical attention and then start a new role as a citizen-victim who must prove her claim as a victim by enduring certain rituals (some of them rituals of degradation) in being medically checked and in being compelled to tell her story to the police, family, and the court. We shall consider this factor in the following pages.

Captivity

It is believed that the rape is quickly executed and the offender immediately disappears. In different situations—group rapes, felony rapes, rape committed in the offender's home, or rape committed by someone close to the victim—it was found that the victim was kept by the offender at the scene of the crime after the forced sexual intercourse was completed. Captivity is observed in 58 cases, or 9 percent of the total 646 forcible rapes. In 20 percent of these 58 cases the victim was beaten again by the offender. The span of time she was kept in captivity (after the last forceful intercourse) ranges from half an hour to 4 hours or more.[100]

From offenders' confessions it was learned that several reasons led to such behavior on the part of the offender: to cool off the victim or to hold her, in gang rape for further rape, which, however, was not committed. In 4 cases the offender was drunk and fell asleep, and the victim did not move until he left.

Another phenomenon which occurred after the rape was the return of the victim by the offender to the place from which she was taken (21 cases) or to her home (5 cases). In 5 cases she was driven to a remote place and left there.

In almost the majority of these cases (24) the automobile was the scene of rape; and interestingly enough, in 7 cases (all involving group rape) the offender who took the victim back "apologized" for the event although actually asking her not to report the offense or him to the police.

As we shall see later, not all victims immediately reported the case to the police. Among these cases, 20 went or were brought to the hospital before reporting.

100. The time was given by the victim, who could only estimate it, and measured by us from the time the rape was committed, or in cases of repeated intercourse from the last act.

It is impossible for us to deal with the medical conditions and evidence of the victim because while the study was conducted, the police stopped taking all rape victims to the hospital emergency wards, while in many cases the victims or parents refused to go there.

The following statistics are, however, illuminating:

Victim came alone to the hospital before reporting	3
Victim brought to hospital before reporting	17
Victim came alone after reporting	15
Victim brought after reporting	315
Victim went to private physican before reporting	13
Victim or parents refused treatment	29
Total	392

Not only was referral to medical treatment inconsistent and then stopped altogether, but medical reports were missing in the file for many of the cases who did enter the hospital. The following is what the reports specify in this file of 207 cases:

External injuries only (bruise, cuts, etc.)	24
Internal (vaginal) signs	75
Semen evidence only	33
Semen plus internal signs (internal ruptures, etc.)	30
Semen plus external signs (scars, etc)	45

As to the severity of injuries,[101] 9 victims were in the hospital at the time of the study; 1 victim died after the rape due to brutal beating.[102] Among the victims who were taken to the hospital, some remained a few hours and were discharged. From this point, if the police had not been investigating the crime before, the investigation of the case starts. Thus, the process of administration of justice begins.[103]

Medical Proof and Evidence

When the victim is ready to complain about the offense, some serious problems arise of medical evidence, testimony, false accusation, and corroboration.

Medical evidence of the offense serves as original or corroborative ma-

101. The psychological effect of the offense cannot be evaluated. On the psychological effect of sexual trauma (mainly studied for children), see: Bender and Blau and the follow-up report, Bender and Grugett. See also Landis; Wile. All of these studies, and others, assign a secondary role to sexual trauma as a cause for later disturbed behavior. On the other hand, Klein assumes a major disturbance occurring in subsequent psychosexual development; see also Gagnon.

102. The victim, 62 years old, was raped by two offenders who confessed.

103. For analysis of postrape problems in the administration of criminal justice and problems of effect of crime on the victim, see Amir.

terial. In cases involving bodily harm, defloration or penetration, the medical problems are relatively simple, although it may incur further humiliation to the victim, and may contribute to the reluctance of victims or their parents to report the offense and by this, avoid medical check and treatment in a public hospital or clinic. In many cases, the medical proof is the most important corroborative data, when a child victim gives changed, confused, or vague stories.

11

Felony Rape

We have previously referred to the felony-rape cases dealing with those situations in which a Negro offender attacks a white victim or in which the offender is at least ten years younger than his victim. To this group of cases we shall now direct further attention.

"Felony rape" indicates a rape which occurs while the offender is engaging in some other felony (mainly burglary or robbery). Unlike the felony-murder situation, felony rape is dealt with neither in the common law nor in the Pennsylvania Penal Code.[1] Thus, while problems of strict liability, and of differentiation between intention, recklessness, and negligence are important in felony-murder cases,[2] they are irrelevant in the felony-rape situations. The rape is not conceived of as emanating from the felony and, hence, both are dealt with separately as individual offenses rather than as necessarily connected to one another. For each offense, therefore, there is a presumption of different criminal intent, and different consequences ensue.[3] The prosecution can either charge the offender with the crime of rape only, for which he will incur more severe punishment, or he may include the lesser offense (the felony) but, again, only as a separate and exclusive offense.

1. For the felony-murder rule see: Perkins; Wolfgang, *Patterns,* pp. 238–40.

2. Hall, *General Principles,* pp. 232–35, 454–60.

3. For a summary of the legal elements in the case of rape see *Pennsylvania Law Encyclopedia,* vol. 31, pp. 129–49. This source includes all the relevant cases of rape in the legal history of Pennsylvania.

Some Theoretical Comments

Only the psychiatric school has dealt with the felony rape, and it is concerned mainly with the motivational aspects of this phenomenon. One approach in this school maintains that rape is sometimes committed by a person "who, paradoxically enough, is apparently not a true sex offender. He is the aggressive criminal who is out to pillage and rob."[4] Rape in this case is only incidental, an epilogue to another crime.[5] Another approach, more psychoanalytically oriented, contends that even the felony which preceded the rape is sexually motivated and provides a sexual, albeit deviated, gratification.[6] This latter approach is ready, in the extreme, to see every predatory offense, especially burglary and robbery, as a sex substitute, that is, it is sexually motivated and, thus, a symbolic sex act.[7] A suggestion has been made to broaden the concept of sex crimes to include "any criminal act in which some type of sexual satisfaction is the motivating force of the crime."[8] Interesting as it may be, the panoply of theoretical and methodological problems which such ventures contain does not allow their inclusion in the present study.

Another problem connected with the felony-rape is determining whether the rape or the felony is primary in a given situation. Can we say that the robbery is but a latent rape or that the offender had in mind both an attack on the victim's sexual self-determination and on her property? Or is it that he intended only one of these offenses, the other being committed accidentally? Neither of these questions can be answered in the present study, if at all. We include, however, the analysis of felony rape because it is a special type of rape, while legally and criminologically it has been overlooked.

The Philadelphia Data

In 26 cases, or in 4 percent of the 646 rape cases, a felony was committed in addition to the rape.[9] These cases involved 20 cases of single rape, 3

4. Guttmacher, p. 50.

5. Hirning, pp. 233–56. Also F. A. Allen.

6. Foxe; Hulbert; Roche.

7. Abrahamsen, *The Psychology of Crime,* p. 153; Bromberg, *Crime and the Mind,* chap. 4; Karpman, "Felonious Assault"; Rubinstein; Slovenko, pp. 609–27.

8. Thompson, "Electroshock," p. 534.

9. It should be clear that we are dealing with the cases in which rape followed burglary or robbery—that is, they are explosive rapes. In 37 cases the victim was robbed or her place was ransacked after the rape.

cases of pair rape, and 3 cases of group rape. Thus, felony rape involved 35 offenders, or 35 victim-offender relationships.[10]

In 16 cases (67 percent) of the 26 cases of felony rape, both offender and victim were Negroes, and 3 cases both were white. Interracial events occurred in 7 cases, and in 6 of them the offender was a Negro and his victim white. Thus, felony rape in these 26 cases involved 17 Negro and 9 white women. The number of white offenders who were engaged in felony rape was 4, and all of them participated in single-rape events. Negro offenders, then, were involved in 89 percent of the felony-rape cases. The representation of offenders and victims in felony rape according to their race is therefore similar to the proportion in the total number of rape cases.

Among the 35 felony-rape offenders, 3 were in the age group between 15 to 19 years; 17 were 20–24; 12 were 25–30; and 3 were between 30 to 35 years. In most cases the victim was younger than the offender; in 3 cases the victim was much younger (-10 years) than her assailant; in 6 cases victim and offender were of the same age group (± 5 years), and in 17 cases the victim was much older than the offender ($+10$ years).

Table 63: Offender-Victim Age in Felony-Rape Cases

	14–19	20–24	25–29	30–34	35–39	40–44	45–49	50–54	55–59	60	Over
Offender	3	17	2	3	...	...	...	...	...	...	25
Victim	...	2	2	1	2	2	4	4	4	5	26

Only in 3 of these cases of felony rape was the use of alcohol involved. In 2 cases the victims were drinking alone (at their homes), and in 1 case the offender admitted that he was drinking before committing the felony which led to the second crime—the rape.

Of the felony-rape offenders, 19 (or 54 percent) had a previous arrest record. Examination of the record shows the offender in felony rape to be no more recidivistic than the offender in rape generally. The greater proportion of youth involved in felony rapes may partly account for this fact. One might assume that felony-rape offenders would be more likely to have a police record, especially for offenses against property, because the primary "motive" for the offense seems to have been burglarizing and robbing the victim. This assumption is disproven by the fact that only 2 among the 19 offenders who had a previous arrest record had been arrested for property offenses, while 11 of the 19 had a record of offenses

10. The number of 35 victim-offender relationships is arrived at by adding 3 cases of group rape involving 3 offenders each plus 6 offenders in 3 pair rape events and 20 in single rape.

against the person; of these latter, only 4 had been arrested for rape and 2 for sex offenses other than rape. In order to test the hypothesis that age, or any other factor, had something to do with the fact that the total group of offenders and the felony-rape offenders had similar records, we would need a larger group than the present one, holding these factors constant.

In turning to the modus operandi characteristic of felony-rape events, it was found that in 12 of the 13 cases where the victim was intimidated, a weapon was used. This fact is understandable if the first motive in the event was burglary or robbery. When surveying the degree of force used, we found that in 6 cases no force was used, while in 4 cases the victim was beaten brutally before the rape; in another 4 cases she was beaten brutally during and after the rape; and in 7 cases she was choked. Beating (including nonbrutal beating) was claimed by the victim in 12 cases, and in 1 case the victim was handled "roughly."

Sexual humiliation was practiced on the victim in 22 cases, or 84 percent of the 26 felony rapes. One-third of all the cases where cunnilingus was enforced on the victim occurred in felony-rape events, and the same statistic holds when cunnilingus and fellatio were both practiced. The helplessness of the victim and the fact that all felony-rapes were committed in the victim's home may explain these results.

Table 64: Sexual Humiliation in Felony-Rape Cases

	Fellatio		Cunni-lingus		Fellatio and Cun-nilingus		Pederasty		Repeated Inter-course		Total	
	No	%	No.	%	No.	%	No.	%	No.	%	No.	%
Felony-rape cases	7	19.6	3	23.1	4	26.7	2	15.4	6	7.5	22	11.2
Total group	66	90.4	10	76.9	11	73.3	11	84.6	74	92.5	173	88.8
Total	73	100.0	13	100.0	15	100.0	13	100.0	80	100.0	195	100.0

We found that 20 (or 77 percent) of felony-rape victims were submissive or did not resist the attack upon them. In 4 cases they showed resistance, and only in 2 cases did the victims actually fight their assailants. Finally, in all but one case of felony rape, the offender was a stranger to the victim, and 13 of the offenders were never detected by the police.

12

Group Rape

Group perversion is the term applied to any sort of sexual activity involving the participation of more than two persons. It includes group masturbation and group voyeurism. Another type of group perversion which sometimes includes rape is the orgy.[1] Still another form is group rape. It is to this latter phenomenon, constantly alluded to in the present study, that the present chapter is devoted.

From a theoretical point of view, it seems clear that there is a difference between a rape committed by a single offender on one victim and a rape in which one or more victims are subjected against their consent to sexual intercourse with two or more offenders. The latter type of rape is what is meant here by group rape (GR).[2]

Explanations of Group Rape

Reviewing the reference in the literature to GR, we note the following important points:

1. Only one study under the heading of "group rape" is found in the literature on sex offenses written in English, and no study is available on pair rape.[3]

1. See, for instance, H. Ellis, vol. 2, pp. 218–24; Partridge. For some journalistic type studies see: Mannix; Symonds.

2. The term implies here both pair rape and group rape (three or more offenders involved). The term group rape is used because of its sociological and psychological connotations. A better term is multiple rape, which will be used in the actual analysis of the Philadelphia data.

3. Blanchard. Only Gillin (*The Wisconsin Prisoner,* p. 121) reports a case of pair rape and mentions the differences between the leader and the nonleader in the situation.

2. The topic of group perversion which may have some bearing on GR is discussed almost exclusively in the psychoanalytical frame of reference; hence it is speculative in nature.

3. Even the studies concerned with "group dynamics" fail to touch upon GR, and only some theoretical clues can be used to examine the problem of group rape.

4. From the criminological literature, GR can be only inferred and then only when:

   a. it is viewed as part of the theoretical discourse on criminal partnership[4] and criminal companionship;[5]

   b. general group processes in gangs and gang behavior are discussed;[6]

   c. references are made to the phenomena in some surveys on sexual offenses.[7]

This dearth of information means that problems of modus operandi, victim characteristics, leadership phenomena, and other important aspects are as yet untouched as far as GR is concerned.

As we have stated, the main explanation of group perversion appears to be psychoanalytically oriented.[8] According to Freud, group structure and group dynamics are developed from two elements; the first of these is the erotic factor which colors group relations and leadership.[9] Group behavior, it is maintained, is actually the behavior of individuals who are enmeshed in a certain kind of social and emotional interaction. However, through such interaction the group can be perceived as a "psychological whole, as having dynamic properties, such as organization, structure ideal and climate."[10] These latter aspects were further developed by Erickson, Redl, Slavson, and others who used psychoanalytical concepts in describing and analyzing group processes.[11] The other root of the theory is the assumption that individuals tend to transform and transfer attitudes evolved in their families to group relations. Therefore, face-to-face groups, like gangs, are apt to symbolize a family with its libidinal ties.[12] The leader, then, unconsciously represents the parental

---

4. Cormier, et al., "Some Psychological Aspects."

5. Eynon and Reckless (companionship as an onset to delinquent behavior is mainly discussed).

6. See, for instance, Short, Jr., "Street Corner Groups."

7. *California Sexual Deviation Research* (1954), pp. 123–27.

8. Blanchard.

9. S. Freud, *Group Psychology*.

10. Scheidlinger, p. 53. A good summary of Freud's concepts of the group.

11. E. H. Erickson, "Ego Development," vol. 2, pp. 354–96; Redl, "Group Emotion and Leadership" and "The Psychology of Gang Formation," vol. 1, pp. 367–77.

12. S. Freud, *Group Psychology*, p. 101.

figure while the other group members assume the role of siblings.

Freud's theory of group formation and dynamics deals exclusively with the emotions and attitudes, primarily unconscious, but sexual. People constitute a group if they have the same model object (leader) or ideals, or both, in their superego. Added to this is the idea of mechanisms of identification through which the group forms when several individuals use the same object (the leader) as a means of transferring internal conflicts (usually around sexuality).[13] Since sexuality is inherent in the group, the expression of regressive elements with their homosexual, aggressive, and sado-masochistic correlates is facilitated. Manifestations of these elements vary, depending on the relation to various factors such as climate and emotional liability of the group.[14]

Blanchard tries, by the use of projective tests, to prove the Freudian assumption about the homosexual element involved in GR. He states: "It is assumed that the erotized adulation of one boy for another is perhaps the primary factor . . . this is connected with the homosexual feelings of adolescents . . . the very idea of sharing a common sexual object and being stimulated together in a group has homosexual implication." More strongly emphasized, group-rape is "just short of being overtly homosexual in its content."[15] These feelings explain the humiliation of the victims by the offenders before and after the rape. The sexual attitudes of these youngsters are colored by the need to defend themselves against feelings of weakness, inadequacy, or lack of masculinity. Bach, too, has suggested the use of mutual over-excitement and group enforcement of members to fulfill expectations regarding certain types of sexual partners. Sperling, in line with analytical theory, also explains the group perversion as an attempt to overcome the homosexual fears which in turn stem from castration anxieties.[16]

In describing gangs, Bloch and Neiderhoffer note the homosexual element in the gang's leisure activities and detail the indicators for such a tendency—group masturbation, feminine colors in clothes, and the adoration of body and appearance.[17] Bettelheim makes the observation that there is sexual anxiety among American youth; and therefore, "the prime

13. Later we shall see that he is not necessarily the leader. This aspect was developed especially by Redl in his "The Phenomenon of Group Contagion."

14. Ibid. Implicit in the psychoanalytic theory is the assumption that all groups have similar characteristics. Thus, crowd phenomena differ only in degree from those of stable, highly organized groups. The differences are in susceptibility to suggestion, and in the forces making for regression and its correlates.

15. Blanchard, pp. 252–53.

16. "Psychodynamics of Group Perversion."

17. *The Gang*, p. 104.

purpose of gangs . . . of one sex, is often mutual protection against forming relationships with the other sex."[18]

Redl summarizes the problem of homosexuality in group behavior, stating that "there is no need for the libido to remain homosexual in its content."[19] Even if we agree that Freud was correct in his assumption, the libido in the group undergoes a change and gains new elements because of the present situation of the group "climate" and its composition.

Thus far, the psychoanalytical approach has given us few factors which might explain GR. These factors are mainly connected with individual members and their relationship with the leader. Even if we grant validity and recognition to the importance of such psychological variables in group behavior, the psychological variables are, in part, products of social determinants. Assuming, then, that people do experience anxiety, hostility, and heightened sexuality, and that in certain kinds of social situations they become susceptible to the influences of others, the sociological question is: Under what social conditions do these psychological variables come into play as parts of collective behavior? How, for instance, does the group elicit the supposed homosexual tendencies of the members and channel them in the direction of GR? What are the characteristics of the group itself which may contribute to the commission of GR?

Still other questions remain about the operation of the group as a group, regardless of the different dispositions of its members, and about group activities which deviate from society's norms especially in regard to sexual offenses.

The works of Bion, Bales, Homans, and others on group dynamics are too well known to be discussed here.[20] These writers do not specialize in gangs or deviant groups, and no application of their observation to gangs in general and sexually perverted group activities in particular has yet been made.

A Sociological Theory of Group Rape

It is clear that a theory of group rape is not available; I intend only to suggest one by identifying some essential aspects crucial for understanding this phenomena. I have borrowed lavishly from the fields of psychoanalysis, social psychology, small-group dynamics, and juvenile delinquency.

Nowhere in the literature is there a sociological study of GR or any

18. *Symbolic Wounds,* p. 107.

19. "Group Emotion and Leadership," p. 588.

20. Bales, *Interaction Process Analysis;* Homans, esp. chaps. 1–3. For a bibliography on group processes and related aspects see Hare, *Handbook of Small Group Research.*

direct attempt to explain it. The explanation can be elucidated from theories of gang behavior, which are given only in terms of the emergence of delinquent subculture because of differential exposure and vulnerability to status frustration in general,[21] or in dominant social institutions in particular;[22] differential availability of illegitimate opportunities (to explain different subcultures);[23] differential socialization and life concerns within the class cultures;[24] class and ethnic structure within the community;[25] or the general dilemmas of adolescents within the social system.[26]

A recent development is noticed in these studies in which a shift of emphasis occurs from broad culturally-oriented explanation of specific group behavior to group-oriented explanation of such behavior and of the classification of types of gang delinquency. Much recent work is also concerned with the social distribution of a particular pattern of gang behavior within a social or cultural framework. Here, the group is taken to be the carrier of criminal behavior, and group pressures and expectations define for its individual members the type of criminal activities in which they will be engaged. This development turned the attention to gang dynamics and structures,[27] to the episodic nature of gang behavior, and to special settings which bring forth episodic nonroutinized delinquent behavior of the whole gang.[28] All these aspects of gang delinquency are seen in connection with the role of leadership, gang goals, and the gang dynamics in crisis situation.[29]

What use can be made of this development for the likelihood of specific gang behavior, including GR? The answer must include three subdivisions: the basis of group affiliation, retention of membership in the group, and the gang processes which might lead to GR.

Cohen,[30] Cloward and Ohilin, as well as others, maintain that certain status problems induce many adolescents to belong to groups and participate in group deviant activities. Both affiliation and participation in

21. A. K. Cohen, *Delinquent Boys;* Schorr.

22. Short, Jr., "Street Corner Groups."

23. Cloward and Ohilin.

24. On the lower class, see W. B. Miller, "Lower-Class Culture." On the middle class, see Cohen and Short, Jr., "Research in Delinquent Subcultures"; Nye, et al.

25. Crawford, et al.; Kobrin; Kramer and Karr; Salisbury; Thrasher; Whyte, *Street Corner Society.* As an example of foreign studies, see Morris.

26. Bloch and Niederhoffer.

27. Jansyn, Jr.; Short, Jr., "Street Corner Groups"; Whyte, *Street Corner Society;* Klien; Short and Strodtbeck.

28. Klein; Rodman; La Mare and Lubeck; Matza; Yablonsky, *The Violent Gang.*

29. Jansyn, pt. 2; Short and Strodtbeck; Yablonsky.

30. A. K. Cohen, *Delinquent Boys;* Cohen and Short, Jr., "Research in Delinquent Subcultures."

a network of peer groups come to meet these common needs for status security or to alleviate and neutralize status threats and frustrations. For Bloch and Niederhoffer, as well as for Miller,[31] such membership is rooted in the quest for a solution of adolescent sexual insecurity and for sexual identity. Whatever the basis for affiliation, we can assume that the attraction of the group will vary with its presumed or proven success in facilitating satisfaction of these needs.[32] From this viewpoint, it seems that the group values and activities in a group are more important than the individual members qua members in achieving their intended satisfaction since they may have various and diverse needs for which they enter the gang. What emerges, therefore, as another explanation for the attractiveness of the gang, is that only by doing things together, that is, through interaction, can the needs of the individuals be satisfied. By offering this satisfaction, the gang itself, regardless of the personality of its individual members and their dispositions, becomes an end rather than a means to meet personal needs.[33] This approach, again, shifts the attention from the personality level to group level and group processes considerations, to explain delinquent behavior within the gang.[34] However, the authority of the group and its pressure are not absolute and are given to consideration by the individual. The individual who wants, or is ready, to engage in deviant behavior may be prevented from doing so by his doubts and internal inhibitions. However, in group situations, through group processes, he can deindividualize himself by having his personal restraints neutralized or reduced.[35]

But what in the group process leads to such de-individualization? Three main factors are advanced as an answer: group norms and goals, emotional group dynamics, and leadership phenomena.

Delinquent gang norms and goals need not be discussed here. This aspect is probably the most documented one in the literature on delinquency.[36]

Redl, in line with the psychoanalytic schools, concentrates on the

31. Miller, "Lower Class Culture."

32. For an experiment to prove this assumption on nondelinquent behavior see Gilchrist; N. Cameron.

33. Jansyn, pt. 2. The distinction between these two explanations is hard to make, if at all possible, but the relative emphasis in each one of them is what is important.

34. Short, Jr., et al., "Perceived Opportunities."

35. Ibid. For nondelinquent behavior see Festinger, et al. For delinquent behavior, see Redl, "The Phenomenon of Group Contagion"; Matza.

36. Cloward and Ohilin; A. K. Cohen, *Delinquent Boys;* Cohen and Short, Jr., "Research in Delinquent Subcultures"; Miller, "Lower Class Culture"; Whyte, *Street Corner Society;* Yinger. See also Matza and Sykes. For a summary and analysis of these normative problems of delinquent value systems, see Bordua; Downs.

emotional processes within a deviant group.[37] He views group behavior as always comprising two closely related sets of factors: individual personalities, mainly their liability to be carried away by the group activities, and group elements such as organization, leadership, and so on. The group becomes a facilitating agent which arouses and reinforces certain emotions, attitudes, and conceptions which members already have.[38] Thus the group can produce certain perceptual and emotional styles towards certain things, including distorted sexual attitudes and conceptions of women.[39] Further, the group eliminates those attitudes and conceptions which run counter to those of its majority and especially of the leader. The group, then, destroys or neutralizes inhibitions against deviant actions and establishes new mechanisms for justifying them.[40]

The existence of psychopathological tendencies among members may explain why they join the group and why some will participate in deviant behavior. However, the very fact of membership in the group and the suggestion, planning, and execution of deviant acts may arouse a realistic fear (of being caught, etc.), as well as further guilt and anxiety. Why, then, do members still choose to retain their membership and participate in fear-and-guilt-arousing activities?

Rationalizations,[41] and the "contagion effect" of the group and of the leader's behavior,[42] are two answers offered for these questions. Other mechanisms are present and should be considered. The gang, through discussing criminal activities, brings cognitive clarity to those aspects involved in committing the offenses which amount to polling of ideas and planning. Through this process courage is bolstered. Also, the variety of noncriminal activities which the gang is engaged in serves as a diverting mechanism and thus allows for indirect reduction of guilt, fear, and anxiety. What is common to all these mechanisms is the existence of strong social influences which the group exerts upon its members. Hence, those who hesitate or refuse to join the activities of the group, or part of them, are put under the process of homogenization, in which their dissenting attitudes are levelled to that of the rest of the group or its significant others.[43] Among the latter, it is leadership which becomes an essential element in gang behavior, because leaders are the creators and/

37. Redl, see all references.

38. For a general discussion, see Heider, esp. pp. 20–58. For such styles among delinquents see Miller, "Lower Class Culture"; La Mare and Lubeck.

39. Whyte, "A Slum Sex Code."

40. See Miller, et al., "Aggression"; Matza; Sykes and Matza.

41. Sykes and Matza.

42. Redl, "Group Emotion" and "The Psychology of Gang Formation."

43. For nondelinquent behavior, see Schacter, pp. 12–42.

or manipulators of the gang's goals, its emotional climate and of mechanisms of guilt and anxiety arousal and dissolution. However, it is not always the command of the gang leader or other "central" members which is necessary to induce a gang member to participate in a delinquent act. He, as well as the leaders, is under the influence of a set of "ought" rules; that is, impersonal standards of what the one must do and feel, which emanates from the group values and is independent from the individual's wishes or his personal preferences. In certain situations, however, other sentiments and values have greater appeals or relevance to the individual, and the validity of the group norms is questioned.[44] Such questioning will occur, for example, when other alternatives are available to the individual and when other factors such as future consequences of the act are not so clear but threatening.[45]

To adapt these ideas to the phenomenon of GR, the following can be assumed. The existence of actual or latent tendencies for aggressive behavior prevails in the lower class adolescents.[46] This comes in a period of life (adolescence and young childhood) when intensified sexual desires and experimentation with sex occur.[47] On the one hand, there is a sexual identity problem and a need to repudiate bonds with the female sex,[48] which may express itself in isolation from a constant relation to females,[49] or in rejection of everything which may have feminine traits. Sometimes it expresses itself in actual aggression toward females and appreciation of sex only for its physical aspects, without the emotional elements which the middle class attaches to the sexual sphere.[50] Episodically, rape and GR will occur.[51]

Of special interest for this assumption, which is important to the whole problem of GR, is Bloch and Niederhoffer's interpretation. They argue that the American boy in all social classes is sexually troubled since he lives in a society which no longer defines his social status in general, and his sexual role in particular. He also lacks the mechanisms of *rites de passage* which allow the adolescent in primitive society to handle his growing sexual needs by a smooth transition to an adult status. Sexual

44. For a different variety of "ought" see Hollingsworth. See also Heider, esp. pp. 232–33.

45. Strodtbeck and Short, Jr.

46. Davis.

47. Fyvel, pp. 133–46; Reiss, "Sex Offenses" and "Sexual Code"; Whyte, "A Slum Sex Code."

48. Mead, *Male and Female;* Miller, "Lower Class Culture"; Parsons, "Age and Sex"; A. J. Reiss, "Sex Offenses."

49. Yablonsky, *The Violent Gang,* chap. 4.

50. Ibid., pp. 198–201.

51. Ibid., p. 199; Ploscowe, *Sex and the Law,* p. 158.

identity becomes one of his most pressing problems.[52] This situation is coupled with anxiety over sex and a long-enforced formal "celibacy." One solution is to pursue a desired self-image and to establish supportive props for the ego through the activities of the gangs which are similar to puberty rites in primitive societies. Part of the *rites de passage* includes aggression and sexual sadism. Group perversion and group rape are one aspect of these rituals; they may be a part of the ordeal of entering the gang(s).[53] This practice also results from another set of values which gives emphasis on aggression toward, and domination of, females. The group code defines females as mere objects in obtaining sexual relief and conquest,[54] and may license infliction of humiliation upon them. Rape also becomes a means to establish a "rep." of masculinity and to gain status within the peer group, especially in lower classes.[55] It seems from all this that the group itself generates and possesses strong elements of eroticism, aggression, and "risk"-taking atmosphere in these spheres[56] and that their handling becomes a regular part of its activities.

Other factors of the group situation should be considered. There comes a stage of inactivity in the group life when the group "must do" something to hold itself together; or the group reaches an "expressive" phase when some personal satisfaction and excitement is sought to relieve boredom, or a crisis may arise in which some members feel potential or actual deprivation of status because of the group inactivity or other events in or outside the group.[57] It follows that when opportunities emerge or they are sought and stimulation is further aroused by initiatory acts and planning, then the chances for group activity in the form of group rape rise. This is why such group activity is episodic in a group,[58] which is not necessarily a cohesive one but an ad hoc one formed for, or only during, the event.[59] However, the group affairs, like GR, can come as an attempt to solidify the status claims of a member as well as the cohesiveness of the whole group.[60] It follows that aggression and sexually aggressive behavior toward women are only parts of the total range of group or gang activities,

52. On lower class boys see: Burton and Whiting; Gordon, et al. On middle class boys see Greenley and Casey; Mead; Parsons, "Age and Sex."

53. Bloch and Niederhoffer, p. 106; Doshay, p. 80; Salisbury, pp. 33–36.

54. Gordon, et al.

55. Gillin, *The Wisconsin Prisoner*, p. 130; Reiss, "Sex Offenses," p. 320; Short, Jr., Strodtbeck, and Cartwright; Yablonsky, *The Violent Gang*, pp. 198–201.

56. Strodtbeck and Short, Jr.

57. Jansyn, pt. 2.

58. Pfoutz.

59. Jansyn, pt. 2; Miller, "Aggression"; Short, Jr., and Strodtbeck.

60. Yablonsky, "The Delinquent Gang."

and one can hardly speak of specialization of a gang in rape or of a "subculture of rape," as is assumed of "predatory" conflict or "retreat subcultures."

To summarize, we have seen these aspects of GR rape: the psychological set of the group member, and the group interaction and process which recruit and mobilize group members to participate in the offense: all these are based on the values and norms of the group and its regular activities. This means that a future special analysis of GR should identify some crucial elements which determine the conditions which make GR possible. These elements are: (1) the structural elements of the gang— that is, the preexistence of the group or gang, its organization, the commitment and loyalty of the members, the set of values and norms toward illegitimate activities in general and in the sexual sphere in particular; (2) the special strains which are experienced by the individual members and by the whole group—problems of status and sexual identity, the attitude toward woman *vis-à-vis* the conception of future marital roles; (3) the critical events or precipitating factors—that is, crisis in the gang structure (leadership status threat), the existence of "ready" victims, or the appearance of opportune situations; (4) situational facilities which enable the GR to be transformed from a potential activity to a concrete group behavior—here, the group "climate" of aggression and sexuality, the knowledge, planning, and availability of victims are of prime importance; (5) the mobilization of the individual members—here, the role of the leader or other members as agitator or magical seducer who can capture the allegiance of the individual member, mobilize his aggression and sexuality, and organize and direct it toward the specific act (in our example, GR) is a necessary condition if GR is to occur.

The combinations among the suggested factors, as well as their occurrence in particular situations, are numerous. Because the police never investigate group rape as a special type of offense, only factors 4 and 5 are to be found in the dossiers since they pertain to any type of rape. It therefore seems possible to compare multiple rape with single rape and to compare the two types of the former (i.e., pair rape and group rape, where three or more offenders were involved).

The Participants in Group Rape

Let us consider for a moment the state of mind of the individual group member who is already aggressive, has certain attitudes toward women and hence is prepared to participate in GR. He may harbor a conflict between aggressive-sexual desires and "controls from within." He also encounters the need to deal with the aggression and sexual attitudes generated by the group itself, and experiences anxiety and fears about the suggestions and plans for GR. He is further confronted with group normative and relational pressures to follow its activities. Then, in certain specific facilitating situations, he becomes sexually and aggressively aroused or he witnesses an anomic moment of breakdown of inhibitions through the actions of other group members. As a result of all these factors, he is likely to find it easy to follow others because the balance between the sexual desires and sexual and other inhibitions are tipped toward an open act.

Group members may vary according to the strength of their inner controls or the relative weakness of their desires. They may vary also according to their commitment or acceptance, at the moment, of group demands of aggressive exploitative sexual behavior; this they do because of their position in the group, or because they perceive of other gang activities rather than the particular act as more important for gang survival and its true nature. While group delinquency is considered to be the result of special circumstances, it does not imply the captivity of the individual in the group and his constant subjection to its demands. Situational contingencies may prevent him from participating in a particular group event, or convert him to it. His self-doubt and inhibitions mean that he can independently assess options, consider appropriate ventures and thus refuse to enter, witness, or actively participate in a particular group affair.

On the basis of these criteria the following typology can be made about participants in GR: (a) Those who will join immediately, for example, the group "core" members[61] who identify completely with the group and its aggressive climate and who are fully committed to the gang since they need it for expressing personality traits and maintaining self-identity.[62] This type of participant will tend to be aggressive toward the victim, subject her to humiliating practices, and he, rather than the leader, may be the initiator of the actual attack. (b) The reluctant participant who will go along after some hesitation. He will wait for more "magical seduction" to operate, by allowing one or two other members to commit the act before him. (c) The nonparticipant who is around the scene of GR. This type may be someone who happens to be on the scene but wants nothing to do with what is going on. He may be a gang member who refuses to participate. The violence and the whole nature of the situation may frighten him, causing enough anxiety to render him unable to have even an erection. He may be highly aggressive but unwilling to have forced sexual relations; or he may have a partially different self-conception of what it is to be a "good member," or of who is a desired or permitted victim. He may also have stronger ego and super-ego than other

61. Jansyn.
62. Gerrard.

gang members, although his sexual needs are as strong as those of his peers.

Parenthetically, it may be noted that nonparticipants may be legally charged with complicity to the act. The same amount of perversion and intent is assumed for them. The punishment they may receive may not be much lighter than that of the full participants in the offense.[63]

The Victim

All the writers who have alluded to the phenomena of GR have commented on two types of victims: those chosen because they were known to be "loose" and easily "put," that is, they consent to group sexual intercourse; and the accidental victims who were attacked by the group at opportune moments.

The first group of victims, in spite of their reputations, or because of them, may be actually raped with the understanding that their reputations may render their later complaints ineffective and possibly inadmissible in the court. This type of victim is well represented also in the literature in single rape.[64] It is her sexual promiscuity which is emphasized in the literature on gang sexual behavior.[65]

To assume that GR victims always have given consent is to err gravely. There are cases in which the victim's consent is not assured, whether or not she is known to the gang. Here, we assume that her behavior and the particular circumstances under which she encounters the group may bring her victimization. She may be an innocent passerby with nothing in her behavior which suggests provocation or she may be a strange drunk or drinking woman wandering in the gang "territory." Another type of victim is the girlfriend of one of the group members. She may be subjected by her "friend" to submit to the rest of the group. Another victim may consent after threat to only one or two members with the hope, or promise, of being spared by the whole group. She soon finds that she was trapped. Lastly, Salisbury describes the type of victim who agrees to be "raped" by the whole gang as an act of her initiation into the gang.[66]

GR involves intense and prolonged humiliation for victims. Verbal insults, beating, and sexual humiliation (besides the rape) are likely to occur. Salisbury and Whyte noted that it is the "pick up" ill-reputed girl

63. For the arguments against such an approach, see Tarde, pp. 471–72. See also Ferri, pp. 431–32; Garrofalo, pp. 321–23.

64. See, for instance, Dunham, pp. 75–83; Goldberg; Meyer; Weisse.

65. Bloch and Niederhoffer; A. K. Cohen, *Delinquent Boys,* pp. 137–47; Cohen and Short, Jr., "Research," pp. 34–36; Grosser; Miller, "Female Sexual and Mating Behavior"; Reiss, "Sex Offenses"; Salisbury; Short, Jr., Strodtbeck, and Cartwright; Whyte, "A Slum Sex Code."

66. Salisbury, pp. 33–76.

who is treated most brutally; there is a complete lack of consideration for her dignity and well-being.[67] In some cases it is not the leader who will show the most brutality toward her. The aspirant or the new member may excel in these acts to prove his claim to reputation and prestige. Also, the individual who experiences a "shock effect" and fails to function sexually may act most aggressively as a reaction to this failure.

Frequencies and Distribution

The actual number of multiple rapes (MR) among the total number of forcible rapes is not known since MR is not separately classified in criminal statistics. Also, no studies are available about the distribution of MR's among racial or class divisions. Since we found that rape is most prevalent in the lower classes and among Negroes (who are concentrated in the lower strata), it can be assumed that more MR's will also occur there. Further, since rape is an adolescence or young adulthood type of crime, MR is more likely to occur in these age groups.

Bloch and Niederhoffer, Reiss, Salisbury, and Whyte, who portray the sexual patterns of lower-class boys, mention the phenomenon of GR but claim it to be a rare occurrence.[68] They imply that the boys have enough access to "loose girls" who are "put up" as "victims" of "gang bang," "gang shag," or "line up," which imply group sexual relations with promiscuous or consenting girls. However, in certain situations the gang will "make a girl"; that is, enforce sex on her.[69] None of these writers specify the type of gang or under what situations group rape will occur, and what types of girls in terms of race, class, age, and so on, are likely to become victims of rape.

In those studies in which GR is alluded to, the frequencies of GR are measured either from a group of arrested offenders or from the population of convicted sex offenders. The California Sexual Deviation Research reports that of 200 delinquents brought before the juvenile court in San Francisco for sexual assault on girls (1947–51), 6 percent used gang pressure to overcome victims' resistance.[70] From another set of statistics and case studies of sexual offenses, we learned that "the majority of these serious offenders were gang-motivated in their sexually delinquent act."[71] Of 26 forcible rape case studies described, 22 were gang rape. These include 54 offenders, an average of about 2 offenders per episode.[72]

67. Ibid.; Whyte, "A Slum Sex Code."

68. Bloch and Niederhoffer, pp. 17–29; Reiss, "Sex Offenses," p. 312; Salisbury, pp. 33–36; Whyte, "A Slum Sex Code."

69. Ploscowe, Sex and the Law.

70. (1954), p. 99.

71. Ibid.

72. Ibid., pp. 122–35.

The *Report of Mayor's Committee for the Study of Sex Offenses* found, however, that of all sex crimes which appeared in the county court or court of general session during 1930–39, most (89 percent) were committed by single individual offenders. In 456 of the 3,295 cases (14 percent) which the committee investigated, 2 or more offenders were involved. Calculating the percentages of multiple offender cases (GR) we found that 53 percent involved 2 offenders, while 43 percent involved 3 or more offenders.[73]

Radzinowicz reports that of all indicted sexual offenders against female victims, 25 percent include 1 victim and more than one offender.[74] What is characteristic for these cases was that the rape was committed by adolescents.

Leadership

The literature on leadership is abundant, and in studies of gang structure and process the role of the leader is repeatedly touched upon.[75] What emerges from these studies is a distinction between two analytically separate but related phenomena: leaders and leadership.

The question to ask, then, is not only "Who is the leader?" but "What are the functions which leadership is supposed to perform for the group?" It is obvious, however, that the kind of leadership function which will be emphasized and the effectiveness of leadership in a particular group, depend on the group's characteristics, such as its code, structure, solidarity, readiness of members to accept leadership, and the relations of the group to its outside environment.

For general purposes, the following definitions are suggested: *Leader* is defined in this study as the occupant of that position in the group which has the greatest influence over group behavior. *Leadership* is defined as that process of influencing the action of other members in critical group situations.[76] The definitions are intentionally broad and do not include techniques of influence, nor do they specify who can be termed "leader." We can speak, then, of "leadership influence," meaning that a variety of persons can execute leadership roles.[77] Implied here is the idea

73. *Report of the Mayor's Committee*, pp. 68–69.

74. Radzinowicz, *Sex Offenses*, pp. 95–96.

75. For a recent summary of the field of social psychology see: Bass, pp. 38–101; Cartwright and Zander, pp. 535–647; Gibbs, pp. 877–920; Hare, 291–334.

76. See Gouldner, pp. 17–18; Stogdill, "Leadership, Membership and Organization."

77. Leadership does not necessarily mean action. It includes situations in which those who symbolize the achievement of a desired role are considered leaders, for example, the "right guy" as a type of leadership role among prison inmates. Such role models contribute to the solidarity and identity of the

that leadership arises not so much out of the attribution of an individual, but rather out of the group in meeting its special circumstances. If any personal characteristics are observed among leaders, they are functions of the group structure and the special characteristics of the events which call for leadership. It follows also that differences among groups in terms of their code, structure, goals, cohesiveness, past performance, and so on, allow the emergence of different leadership types.

Leadership types can be classified in terms of legitimation and accessibility to leadership position. Thus, one can speak of attempted and accepted leadership,[78] of emergent (conditioned by consent of the followers) and assigned leaders[79] (the latter is imposed from above and is synonymous with authority); of the formal and informal leader[80] (the latter suggests an emergent type along the formal one) with personal but not official power over other group members,[81] and of declining leader or leader under "status threat."[82]

Another criterion for differentiating between leaders is "style" of leadership. By this we mean the manner in which the leader mobilizes the group to action, rather than the way he controls the group.[83] The "style" depends, among other things, on the group needs, its readiness to accept his initiated actions in terms of his past performance and the consequences of his suggested actions for the present and the future of the group.[84]

Our next and final theoretical problem is to combine situational and personal elements of "leaders" and "followers" as they are related to leadership functions and group processes. Such a venture, which is closely related to the problem of GR, is attempted by Redl in his "Group Emotions and Leadership." Redl, in this paper, shows the potentiality of

---

group. However, under certain conditions they may assume active leadership roles, for example, in prison riots. On the other hand, rejected personality types (aggressive psychopaths) are always emerging as leaders in the same circumstances.

78. Such a distinction is made by Hemphill.

79. For such a distinction see Carter, et al.

80. For a classic study on informal leadership and gang structure see Whyte, *Street Corner Society*, pp. 255–76.

81. The assumption is that personal characteristics are more important in informal (and emergent) leadership, and that they cease to be as important when leadership is formal and official. A distinction is then made between "authority" and "leadership," but only for analytical purposes, since one person may, of course, have both. See Bendix, *Max Weber*, p. 301; Selznick.

82. Short, Jr., and Strodtbeck.

83. For the classical study see Lippit, and for a more recent study see Hare, *Handbook*, p. 316.

84. Jansyn, pt. 2; Short, Jr., and Strodtbeck; Whyte, *Street Corner Society*.

studying a leader's personality, combined with considerations of group needs and the situational approach.[85] For him the personality attributes of leaders are functional for the attainment of group integration and the mobilization of the group toward a perverted goal.

In certain groups (Redl clearly speaks about gangs), the members are conflict ridden. The conflict is between their norms and group norms and between both sets of norms and repressed drives (sexuality and aggression). On the basis of these perverted tendencies, already existent but repressed in the group, a person arises who shares the same wishes and is able by various acts to resolve the conflict. The nature of these acts is that they "seduce" the members to act out the forbidden drives by showing them that they, like him after his acting out, can be free from guilt and fear. Moreover, by his actions this person not only mobilizes but also directs, under varying situations and for a diversity of people, latent intentions, and still gives these intentions a specific character.

This is clearly a situational-oriented psychology which no longer follows the traditional conception of a leader. Therefore, instead of the term "leader" Redl proposes the term of "central" or "focal" person. This term applies to group members who show a psychological flexibility of acting out forbidden desires and resolving guilt and fear. By their actions, in a specific way, they reinforce or bring about group integration and a common perverted action which otherwise is impossible. Whether or not the "central" person is a genuine pervert,[86] is not the point here, although most likely he is. At least he shares with the other members the same latent forbidden drives.

The mobilization of the members is possible, as far as group formation and group activities are concerned, by two basic behavior patterns of the "central" persons: "initiatory act" and "magical seduction."[87] In the "initiatory act" the means are provided for satisfying repressed desires through supplying ideas, forbidden products, and so on, to the other members. In "magical seduction" acts, the forbidden acts are not only suggested but actually executed by the person who is ready to be the first one to give license to the inhibited behavior of others, to take the risk of internal and external (legal) guilt.

Through both of these actions, impulses are reinforced and directed (especially by the initiatory acts) and inhibitory mechanisms are neutralized; thus unconscious exculpation is brought about. The primary guilt and anxiety (because of the original existence of the repressed

85. For a general interdisciplinary approach using (for a nondelinquent group) personality traits of leaders interwoven in a situational context, see Seeman and Morris.

86. See Sperling.

87. Redl, "Group Emotion," p. 592.

drives), and the secondary one (aroused by the initiatory acts), are eliminated and the conflicts which may be aroused between the suggested acts and reality (ego) considerations and/or conscience inhibitions are all resolved by the act of the central person.[88] This condition has a "contagious effect"[89] on those who are capable of being seduced.[90]

What is implied above is an emotional seduction, unlike the one suggested by Sykes and Matza which emphasizes the cognitive "seduction" by the group code, which provides through rationalizations a way to deal with anxiety, fear, and guilt-arousing events.[91]

Redl distinguishes 10 types of "central" persons. Important to us are 3 types which invoke the two preceding mechanisms of guilt assuagement: the "organizer" (type 6), the "seducer" (type 7), and the "bad influence" (type 9). Common to all of them is that they develop and mobilize common group emotions, provide support to forbidden drives,[92] and reinforce and direct them to concrete activities.

The "organizer" is the "central" person characterized by the initiatory acts. The "seducer" not only initiates acts but is also the first to commit them. Hence, he becomes a model of behavior. In group rape this person will often be the first to rape the victim and will do more to humiliate her.

The "bad influence" is very similar to the "seducer," but he differs from him in the technique of seduction. No initiatory act is implied here, but he supports the potential of the group members for perversion by virtue of the "infectiousness of the unconflicted personality's consultation upon the conflicted one."[93] Through this method the other members are also spared guilt anxiety and conflict.

It is obvious that type mixture occurs; for example, the organizer is also the "seducer" or vice versa, although it is not necessarily so. Also, the typical gang "leader" (Redl's type 2) who appeals more to the member's super-ego and thus becomes their ego ideal can function as the "organizer," and the "seducer" while also being a constant "bad in-

---

88. Scheidlinger (*Psychoanalysis and Group Behavior*) maintains that especially in aggressive groups the "leader" replaces the super-ego of the individual member who is therefore able to be induced to perform everything the leader "seduces" him to.

89. Redl, "Phenomenon."

90. Sperling.

91. If for Redl the emotional seductive devices come before this act and are therefore group-formative mechanisms, Sykes and Matza's techniques can provide guilt assurance before and after the forbidden events.

92. Aggression and sexuality are the two examples which Redl ("Phenomenon," pp. 580–81) gives as being manipulated by the "seducer."

93. Ibid., p. 582.

fluence." In special situations, as when he experiences a status threat, he may forcefully try to wield the three roles together.[94]

It is similarly clear that because of the latent common desires and the submissiveness of the gang members, the "seducer" may have been seduced by the group to become their seducer. This means that a cul-de-sac of clear exemplification of the type of "central" person is not to be made. The intensity of group cohesion and its latent desires, and the existence of status systems within the group should be taken into account in explaining the "central" person role. Finally, the "central" person theory can partly explain the role of the victim in group rape. Although she is an outsider, she serves as a focus for the group, and thus becomes an object of aggressive drives and also of sexual drives. The existence of aggression and sexuality in the group and in each member is mobilized by the appearance of the victim, especially if she is known to the group as having a "bad reputation," or as being passive due to her drinking or mental condition.

In the following analysis of GR and leadership phenomena, the term "leader" is used to designate the offender (1) whom the victim in the interrogation indicated as the one who either attacked her and hit her first or the one who raped her first, or (2) whom the other members pointed to as the one who started it all by his suggestion or the one who commanded the action by suggestion of place, organizing the order they took in raping the victim, and so on. It is obvious that these actions do not necessarily coincide; and, possibly, they may not relate to leadership in other activities of the group. In our cases there were only 6 group rapes committed by gangs known to the juvenile aid division as organized and stable gangs. In all of them the "leaders" were the ones who struck the victim first; in only 3 cases were they the ones who raped her first. As to the group processes which led to the rape, the files were too incomplete to allow a full analysis.

The Philadelphia Data

Data on group rape were collected from the police case files of victims' complaints. The cases, therefore, represent the number of rape events and not the number of offenders. As we saw, about 20 percent of multiple rape offenders were not apprehended; and, therefore, their race and ages were only guessed by the victim and then incorporated by the police into their files.[95]

As a starting point the following statistics provide a general framework within which the data on group rape is to be examined. Of 646 cases

94. See Jansyn, pt. 2.

95. In some cases the victim gave more than this scanty information about her assailants.

of forcible rape 370 (or 57 percent) were single rapes (SR); 105 (or 16 percent) were pair rapes (PR). In 171 cases (or 27 percent) 3 or more offenders attacked one victim (GR). Thus, 276 females (or 43 percent) were victims of multiple rapes (MR).[96] Of 1,292 offenders 370 (or 29 percent) were SR offenders; 210 (or 16 percent) were involved in PR; and 712 offenders (or 55 percent) were participants in GR. Altogether, 922 offenders, or 71 percent of the 1,292 offenders, were involved in MR offense.

Table 65: Type of Rape and Victims and Offenders Involved

	Victim		Offender	
	No.	%	No.	%
PR	105	16.2	210	16.2
GR	171	26.5	712	55.2
MR	276	42.7	922	71.4
SR	370	57.3	370	28.6
Total	646	100.0	1,292	100.0

Whatever may be the causal explanation, these results are amazing, if we remember the silence with which the literature on sexual offenses treated the problem of GR. This reticence, however, is explainable since the literature is dominated by the clinical approach and the survey method, which deals with the individual offender or (rarely) the victim, rather than with the act of rape as a social and group event.

For analysis the PR and GR categories can be combined to form a MR (multiple rape) category, since both subcategories represent incidents of rape in which there are several assailants. The SR and PR categories can also be combined to form an IR (individual rape) category, based on the assumption that for some line of action the dyad is likely to show characteristics similar to the action of single individual rather than the group.[97] However, in other situations the dyad will behave like a 3 (or more) person group. Also a preliminary examination of the data indicated that in certain situations there are similarities in the characteristics of SR's and PR's.

96. The term multiple rape refers to the number of offenders and not to the number of forced sexual intercourses to which the victim was subjected. In our discussion on "sexual humiliation" we termed the latter activity as "repeated intercourse."

97. Simmel, "Number of Members" and *The Sociology of George Simmel.* A two-person group, in order to stay as a group must agree upon a single and similar line of action. On the other hand, the two members may show some variations in the performance of the actions while one of the pair assumes the role of the "initiator."

Race Differences

The striking feature in the comparison of race distribution in forcible rape was the extent to which Negro victims and offenders exceeded whites. This difference disappears in intraracial MR events.

From the figures in table 66, it is clear that, whatever the type, rape is

Table 66: Types of Rape, Leaders and Nonleaders by Race of Offenders and Victims

| | Offender/Victim | | | | | | | | | |
| | Negro/Negro | | White/White | | Negro/White | | White/Negro | | Total | |
	No.	%	No.	%	No.	%	No.	%	No.	%
Offender in SR	279	27.2	60	30.5	18	43.9	13	44.8	370	28.6
Leader in PR	78	7.6	19	9.6	6	14.6	2	6.9	105	8.1
Follower in PR	78	7.6	19	9.6	6	14.6	2	6.9	105	8.1
Leader in GR	140	13.7	26	13.2	3	7.3	2	6.9	171	13.3
Followers in GR	450	43.9	73	37.1	8	19.6	10	34.5	541	41.9
Total	1,025	100.0	197	100.0	41	100.0	29	100.0	1,292	100.0
SR	279	27.2	60	30.5	18	43.9	13	44.8	370	28.6
PR	156	15.2	38	19.2	12	29.2	4	13.8	210	16.2
GR	590	57.6	99	50.3	11	26.9	12	41.4	712	55.2
Total	1,025	100.0	197	100.0	41	100.0	29	100.0	1,292	100.0

mainly an intraracial affair. Among MR, this is the predominant pattern. In MR's involving Negro offenders, 73 percent of the victims were Negroes. In MR's involving whites, 70 percent of the victims were white. Within the MR pattern, it appears that Negro offenders tend more than white offenders to participate in intraracial group rapes. Thus, 58 percent of all intraracial events involving Negroes were GR, while 50 percent of all intraracial events involving whites were GR.

The differences appear to be *significant* when interracial rapes were examined. Examining all cases of PR, Negro offenders tended in 29 percent to attack white victims. When the races of the participants were reversed, white offenders attacked Negro victims in 14 percent of the cases. When GR occurred, a greater proportion of white offenders assaulted Negro victims (41 percent). It seems, therefore, that, while GR is mainly an intraracial event, when we consider interracial attacks, *significantly* more Negro offenders attacked white victims. A possible explanation for this pattern may be that interracial rapes are likely to be the result of special circumstances.

This explanation may be also true for what appears to be the relationship between leadership and the race of offenders and victims in either PR or GR. Leaders and victims in PR's and GR's tend to be of the same race groups, especially delinquent groups tend to be composed of members of the same race. A desegregated group or criminal cooperation between the different races is very unlikely.

Age Patterns

It was previously discerned that the offenders, as a group, evidence the highest incidence of forcible rape in two age groups: 15–19 and 20–24. When the analysis of the type of rape was made according to this age classification (table 67), it was found that, in *significant* proportions, the older the offender the less likely he is to participate in GR. All offenders

Table 67: Types of Rape, Leaders and Nonleaders by Offender's Age

	10–19		20–24		25–Over		Total	
	No.	%	No.	%	No.	%	No.	%
Offender in SR	79	13.9	93	28.0	198	50.5	370	28.6
Leader in PR	45	8.1	27	8.1	33	8.4	105	8.1
Follower in PR	47	8.2	24	7.7	34	8.8	105	8.1
Leader in GR	86	15.1	52	15.7	33	8.4	171	13.3
Followers in GR	311	54.7	136	41.0	94	23.9	541	41.9
Total	568	100.0	332	100.0	392	100.0	1,292	100.0
SR	79	13.9	93	28.0	198	50.5	370	100.0
PR	92	16.2	51	15.3	67	17.1	210	16.2
GR	397	69.9	188	56.7	127	32.4	712	55.2
Total	568	100.0	332	100.0	392	100.0	1,292	100.0

between the ages of 10 to 14 years participated in either PR or GR. GR appears to be the main type of rape. Only 14 percent who committed the offense with one partner (PR) were 10 to 19 years old. When we move to the other "risky" age level (20–24), the proportion of SR increases (it almost doubled), while the percentage of GR decreases equally. The proportion of SR is doubled again in the age group of 25 and over. Now, 50 percent of all the offenders belong to this age group. The percentage of GR in this age group is 32 percent compared to 70 percent in the age group 10–19 years.

Combining the two critical age groups and testing the association between the age groups and type of rape, the same *significant* associations between offender age and the type of rape appear.

To recapitulate, ages 10–19 are the prime ages for delinquency, especially for gang delinquency. These were also the ages during which GR occurs predominantly.[98] The pattern of PR, however, does not change so dramatically with the changes of offenders' age as does GR. PR took place in the ages 10–19 and 20–24, in almost same proportions. From the age of 25 on the proportion is still not significantly higher (17 percent). This result cannot be explained at the moment; factors like victims' age and the situation in which offenders encounter the victim may play some part here.

As to the differences in age between leaders and nonleaders, we can hardly expect any differences since we are dealing mainly with peer groups who tend to be of the same age. In PR events for all age levels, no significant differences were found between the ages of leaders and followers, and both groups were spread almost evenly in the "critical" age levels (table 67). For the GR pattern, although more leaders tend to be in the 20–24 age group (28 percent) than in the age group 10–19 (17 percent), a case-by-case check disclosed that it is the ages 17–19 to which most of these leaders belong. When the leader and nonleader groups were dichotomized at age 30, a *significant* association was found between the age of the offenders and leadership; 24 percent were under 30, while 84 percent were over 30.

In line with the preceding observations it can be hypothesized, that PR, GR, or MR will be the main pattern of rape when the victims and offenders are in relatively the same age group (±5 years). Indeed, this was the case when such a comparison was made (table 68). The proportion of MR was *significantly* higher when the victims were of the same age as their assailants; 78 percent as against 45 percent when the victim was at least 10 years younger than her assailants. Among offenders who are at the same age level as their victims, MR and especially GR occur. By reason of the distribution of victims and offender in the age groups, it is when both were in the age level of 10–24 years that these patterns of rape mainly occur.

In the majority of rape events (66 percent) Negro offenders attacked Negro victims, and in 62 percent of the cases white offenders attacked white victims when both were at the same age level. We are inclined to

98. It should be noted that between the ages of 45 and over only 1 case of GR occurs against 4 cases of PR. Of all the 29 cases of rape occurring in the group, 24 (over 70 percent) were SR.

believe, therefore, that MR is usually an intraracial crime against members of the offender's age cohort.

Turning to the differences between leaders and nonleaders, it is found (table 68) that the leaders and their followers in the PR patterns stand almost evenly in terms of their age relationships to the victim. It is in the GR patterns that some differences appear. More leaders of GR than followers tend to be older than their victims (by at least 10 years).

Table 68: Types of Rape, Leaders and Nonleaders, by Victim-Offender Age Disparity

	Victim Much Younger (−10 yrs.)		Both Same Age (±5 yrs.)		Victim Much Older (+10 yrs.)		Total	
	No.	%	No.	%	No.	%	No.	%
Offender in SR	132	55.0	184	22.5	54	23.7	370	28.6
Leader in PR	11	4.5	68	8.2	26	11.4	105	8.1
Follower in PR	11	4.5	72	8.6	22	9.6	105	8.1
Leader in GR	27	11.5	115	13.9	29	12.7	171	13.3
Followers in GR	59	24.5	386	46.7	96	42.6	541	41.9
Total	240	100.0	875	100.0	227	100.0	1,292	100.0
SR	132	55.0	184	22.5	54	23.7	370	28.6
PR	22	9.0	140	16.9	48	21.1	210	16.2
GR	86	36.0	501	60.6	125	55.2	712	55.2
Total	240	100.0	825	100.0	227	100.0	1,292	100.0

Temporal Patterns

When analyzing forcible rape in terms of the distribution over the days of the week, a definite pattern was discernible. Forcible rape was found to be a weekend affair, with the highest frequencies on Saturdays and Sundays. This tendency is not fully observed when an attempt was made to examine differences in the occurrence of types of rape during the weekdays. From table 69, it appears that the distribution is erratic, especially for PR events, and the same is true for weekend rapes.

While the proportionate occurrence of SR is spread almost evenly over the weekdays, the PR pattern fluctuates. PR occurred 21 percent on Tuesdays and Saturdays and 13 percent on Sundays and Thursdays. In GR and in MR the distribution patterns became *significant*. During the week MR constituted 38 percent of all rape events, while on the weekends they occurred in 47 percent of all events. SR events decreased from 62 percent of the total on weekdays to 53 percent of the total. Even when PR's were subtracted from the MR pattern, GR still contributed a greater proportion to the weekend rapes (30 percent) as against 22 percent in the weekdays. As for the weekend per se, GR and MR events occurred proportionately more frequently on Friday nights, while PR's were proportionately more frequent on Saturdays.

Table 69: Types of Rape by Daily and Weekend Distribution

	SR		PR		GR		Total	
	No.	%	No.	%	No.	%	No.	%
Weekdays								
Sunday	62	59.0	14	13.4	29	27.6	105	100.0
Monday	39	66.2	10	16.9	10	16.9	59	100.0
Tuesday	36	50.7	15	21.1	20	28.2	71	100.0
Wednesday	41	57.7	12	16.9	18	25.4	71	100.0
Thursday	42	56.0	10	13.3	23	30.7	75	100.0
Friday	51	53.7	10	10.5	34	35.8	95	100.0
Saturday	89	52.3	35	20.6	46	27.1	170	100.0
Total	370	57.3	105	16.2	171	26.5	646	100.0
Weekends								
Friday	32	46.4	10	14.5	27	39.1	69	100.0
Saturday	89	52.3	35	20.6	46	27.1	170	100.0
Sunday	62	59.0	14	13.4	29	27.6	105	100.0
Total	183	53.2	59	17.1	102	29.7	344	100.0

In spite of the absence of adequate data to support any assumption, I suggest that the relatively high proportion of weekend GR is due to more leisure time spent in group activities, especially on Friday nights, which mark the departure from weekly routine and the beginning of heavy and social drinking. The data also suggests that it is not likely that groups will confine themselves to committing rape on a particular day, only that the weekend is more likely to be the time for the reasons given above.[99]

Rape, we found, is mainly a nocturnal event. Because evening hours allow more leisure for social relations and drinking it can be assumed that, along with other group activities, group rape is likely to occur. The observed distribution (table 70) shows only a tendency of SR and PR to decline in the evening hours (between 8:00 P.M. and 1:59 A.M.) but to rise again in the late night hours or early morning hours (between 2:00 A.M. and 7:59 A.M.). The GR pattern increases to its peak proportion (32

99. See Miller, "Lower Class Culture," p. 16.

percent) in the evening hours and declines almost one-half (18 percent) in the early morning hours. The difference, however, is not large enough to be significant. When the evening and night hours were compared to daytime hours, the above pattern is observed again.

Table 70: Distribution of Types of Rape by Six-Hour Periods of the Day

	2:00 A.M.–7:59 A.M.		8:00 A.M.–1:59 P.M.		2:00 P.M.–7:59 P.M.		8:00 P.M.–1:59 A.M.		Total
	No.	%	No.	%	No.	%	No.	%	
SR	83	58.8	33	63.4	81	58.6	169	53.6	370
PR	32	22.7	8	15.4	21	15.2	45	14.3	105
GR	26	18.5	11	21.2	36	26.2	101	32.1	171
Total	141	100.0	52	100.0	138	100.0	315	100.0	646

It should be noted, however, that 59 percent of GR events occurred in the evening hours. When this was combined with the night hours, a *significant* difference appeared; 65 percent of GR's were committed at this time while in the same hours, PR occurred in 43 percent of the cases. A tendency of MR's to occur in evening and late night and early morning hours is observed, and is *significant* when compared to the daytime hours, but, again, vis-à-vis the SR pattern the difference was not found to be statistically significant.

The fact that group activities, especially those of adolescents, terminate in the early evening hours due to the "natural death" of group activities and because of the curfew imposed by police ordinances may, in part, explain the fact of no concentration of MR patterns in the evening and early morning hours separately. However, when group rapes did occur in those hours, it was mainly on Friday and Saturday nights, while during the other parts of the week the proportion of MR's which occurred was balanced by the number of SR's occurring at that same time.

Alcohol

Different assumptions can be made as to the relation between the presence of alcohol and the type of rape. However, the results on the role of alcohol in the total rape situations speak for themselves. Presented, first, are findings of alcohol in the rape situation and second, of alcohol in the offender group.

Table 71 reveals that, in terms of all 646 rape events, MR patterns are a *significant* factor when alcohol was present in the rape situation. While 46 percent of SR's occurred when alcohol was present, MR's occurred in 54 percent of the cases. SR's occurred in 63 percent when alcohol was absent from the rape situation compared to 37 percent of MR's. The PR pattern evidences the effects of alcohol in 25 percent of all cases, while GR occurred in 28 percent. When alcohol was absent from the rape situation, PR's were committed in 12 percent of the cases and GR in 26 percent.

Turning to the 217 situations in which alcohol was present,[100] in only one situation was the presence of alcohol found to be *significantly* associated with the type of rape; it is when alcohol was present in the victim and in the victim only. This situation occurred in 37 percent of the cases of GR, compared to 26 percent of the cases when alcohol was present only in the offender or in both offender and victim. In 63 percent of MR situations only the victim in the rape situation consumed alcohol, against 24 percent when it was absent.

Table 71: Types of Rape and the Presence of Alcohol in the Rape Situation

	Alcohol Present Both		Alcohol in the Victim Only		Alcohol in the Offender Only		Total Alcohol Present		Total Alcohol Absent		Grand Total
	No.	%	No.	%	No.	%	No.	%	No.	%	
SR	70	51.5	23	37.1	8	42.1	101	46.5	269	62.8	370
		(69.3)		(22.8)		(7.9)		(27.3)		(72.7)	
PR	36	26.5	16	25.8	3	15.8	55	25.3	50	11.6	105
		(65.5)		(29.1)		(5.4)		(52.4)		(47.6)	
GR	30	22.0	23	37.1	8	42.1	61	28.2	110	25.6	265
		(49.2)		(37.7)		(13.1)		(35.7)		(64.3)	
Total	36	100.0	62	100.0	19	100.0	217	100.0	429	100.0	640
		(21.1)		(9.6)		(2.9)		(33.6)		(66.4)	

When alcohol was present in the rape situation in both offender and victim, PR and GR patterns showed the same proportion (26 percent and 27 percent, respectively) while SR occurred in 47 percent of the cases. Compared to the cases in which alcohol was present, the changes were not significant.[101]

Examining only the group of offenders in which alcohol was present (table 72), again only one type of alcohol situation was found to be *significantly* associated with the type of rape. When alcohol was present

100. Employed here are the same groupings used in the analysis of the alcohol factor in chap. 8, this volume.

101. Turning to the situations where alcohol was present in the offender only, we find that the number of cases in this category is too small (19 cases) for breakdown by percentage distribution. It is, however, observed that when alcohol was present in the offender only, 42 percent of the cases were GR situations. Alcohol was absent in the offender only in 26 percent of the GR situations.

in the offenders only, [102] 78 percent of these offenders committed PR or GR, and only 20 percent committed SR. Compared to the distribution of offenders in the various types of rape in which alcohol was present either in both them and victim or in the victim only, 63 percent of those who drank participated in MR and 37 percent in SR. Again, PR patterns showed less variation. When alcohol was present in the offender only, 35 percent of the offenders were involved in PR compared to 27 percent when alcohol was present also in the victim or in the victim only.

Table 72: Type of Rape, Leader and Nonleader, and the Presence of Alcohol in the Offenders' Group

	Alcohol Present in Both		Alcohol Present in the Victim Only		Alcohol Present in the Offender Only		Total Alcohol Present		Total Alcohol Absent		Total	
	No.	%	No.	%	No.	%	No.	%	No.	%	No.	%
Offender in SR	70	33.3	23	37.1	8	10.3	101	28.9	269	28.6	370	28.6
Leader in PR	24	11.4	10	16.1	1	1.3	35	10.0	70	7.4	105	8.1
Follower in PR	12	5.7	6	9.7	2	2.6	20	5.7	85	9.0	105	8.1
Leader in GR	45	21.4	8	12.9	8	10.3	61	17.4	110	11.7	171	13.3
Followers in GR	59	28.1	15	24.2	59	75.6	133	38.0	408	43.3	541	41.9
Total	210	100.0	62	100.0	78	100.0	350	100.0	942	100.0	1,292	100.0
SR	70	33.3	23	37.1	8	10.3	101	28.9	269	28.6	370	28.6
PR	36	17.2	16	25.8	3	3.8	55	15.7	155	16.4	210	16.2
GR	104	49.5	23	37.1	67	85.9	194	55.4	518	55.0	712	55.2
Total	210	100.0	62	100.0	78	100.0	350	100.0	942	100.0	1,292	100.0

Turning to the problem of the presence of alcohol in leaders, as compared to nonleaders, some questions arise. Does the leader have to be drunk to lead: how drunk must a leader be in order to be able to lead, or to perform the initial act? Is alcohol a more important factor in determining the leader in PR and/or GR? Is a drinking leader used by the followers because of his drinking? These questions cannot be answered here, but the differences in the presence of alcohol among the leaders and nonleaders can be examined. Of the 350 offenders, alcohol was present in

102. This means that either the offender drank alone, with other offenders, or with other persons, but not with the victim from whom alcohol was absent.

71 percent of the MR offenders, only 39 percent of whom were leaders. Testing the association between the presence of alcohol and leadership the following emerge to the level of statistical *significance:*

1. *Leadership and the presence of alcohol in MR offenders.* Alcohol was present in 39 percent of both PR and GR leaders, while in 21 percent of those leaders alcohol was absent. When alcohol was present, it was in 61 percent of the nonleaders compared to 79 percent of them when alcohol was absent.

2. *Leadership and the presence of alcohol in GR.* Thirty-one percent of GR leaders consumed alcohol, while 21 percent did not. Sixty-nine percent of followers drank, compared to 79 percent GR followers who did not consume alcohol.

3. *Leadership and the presence of alcohol in either offender, or victim, or both in MR's.* When alcohol was present in either the offender, the victim, or both, it was present in 49 percent of the MR leaders but only in 25 percent when it was only in the offenders or only in the victim. Of 254 nonleaders who participated in this situation, alcohol was present in 57 percent but absent in 75 percent of them.

4. *Leadership and the presence of alcohol in both offender and victim in GR.* When alcohol was present in both offender and victim, it was present in 53 percent of the leaders and in 47 percent of the nonleaders. Alcohol was absent in 18 percent of the leaders and in 82 percent of the nonleaders.

Previous Record

Can we expect leaders to have a higher proportion of offenses against the person or a higher record of sex offenses? If the answer is in the affirmative, we can assume that they probably tend to violate the law again, but they will be likely to lead the nonleaders into the offense. Table 73 contains the data on this problem:

1. Participants in MR show a *significantly* higher proportion of criminal record of offenses against the person than SR offenders (60 percent compared to 40 percent, respectively).

2. MR offenders have a higher arrest record of sex offenses (with and without forcible rape) than SR offenders (52 percent and 40 percent, respectively).

3. MR offenders also had a higher arrest record for rape than SR offenders (60 percent and 40 percent, respectively).

4. Leaders in PR's, compared to their followers, had a *significantly* higher proportion of arrest record both of offenses against the person and of sex crimes.

5. PR leaders were arrested (73 percent more than their followers)

Table 73: Leaders and nonleaders, Types of Rape by Previous Arrest
Record of Offenses against the Person and of Sex Offenses

	Offense Against the Person		Sex Offenses (except rape)		Forcible Rape		Total	
	No.	%	No.	%	No.	%	No.	%
Offender in SR	52	40.0	15	68.1	23	39.6	90	42.8
Leader in PR	12	9.2	2	9.1	8	13.8	22	10.7
Follower in PR	8	6.1	1	4.5	3	5.2	12	5.7
Leader in GR	28	21.5	1	4.5	10	17.2	39	18.5
Followers in GR	30	23.2	3	13.6	14	24.2	47	22.3
Total	130	100.0	22	100.0	58	100.0	210	100.0

Note: Only crimes against the person, sex offenses (with or without forcible rape) are
included due to their closer theoretical, clinical, and legal connection to the present offense.

for previous forcible rapes. For GR situations, more nonleaders
have been arrested for forcible rape.

Rape Situation Modus Operandi and Group Rape

Areas of Victims' and Offenders' Residence and Crime

On the basis of the results discussed in chapter 7 above and because residential propinquity is the basis of peer relations and of gang membership,
it can be assumed that MR events and especially GR's will be characterized by the two main types of spatial patterns: delinquency and/or
neighborhood triangle. Table 74 shows that when the offender lived in
the area of the offense and within victim's residence, the offense was
mainly MR and GR. The table also reveals that while for SR it is more
important that the offender live in both victim's vicinity and area of
offense, either the GR offender tends to live in either the vicinity of offense or in the area of victim's residence or in both. When the offender
does not live in the area of offense, nor in the victim's residential area, the
proportion of SR offenders decreases (34 percent) compared to 11 percent when he only lives in his victim's vicinity and 10 percent when he
lives in the area of offense. Under these circumstances, the proportion of
GR offenders increases; 86 percent when they live in victims' vicinity
and 74 percent when they live in the area of the offense. A check of those
cases in which the offender lives in the victim's vicinity and the crime is
committed elsewhere reveals that 50 percent of automobile rapes are included here, and in the majority of cases it was a GR event.

Table 74: Types of Rape by Area of Victim and Offender and Area of Crime

	A: Offender Lives In Area of Offense and Not Area of Victim Residence		B: Offender Lives In Victim's Vicinity Rape Committed Elsewhere		C: Offender Lives In Vicinity of Victims and Offenses		D: Offender Lives Not in Vicinity of Victim or Offense		No Information		Total	
	No.	%	No.	%	No.	%	No.	%	No.	%	No.	%
SR	3	9.7	4	11.2	198	32.6	72	33.9	93	22.8	370	28.6
PR	5	16.1	1	2.7	103	16.9	60	28.3	41	10.1	210	16.2
GR	23	74.2	31	86.1	305	50.5	80	37.8	273	67.1	712	55.2
Total	31	100.0	36	100.0	606	100.0	212	100.0	407	100.0	1,292	100.0

An attempt was made to test the importance of residence in victims' area or areas of offenses by combining the following categories (see table 82 below): victims' area $(B + C)$; offense area $(A + C)$.

It was found that no difference existed for SR offenders according to whether they lived in victims' areas; no difference was found related to offender's residence in offense area. In both of these situations, 31 percent of the offenders were SR offenders. Group rape offenders, again, either lived in the areas of offense (52 percent) or in victims' area (42 percent). It means that the GR offenders either moved the crime scene $(B + D)$, or they looked for new areas and potential victims outside their neighborhood triangle. PR offenders were more "lazy" and committed the crime mainly in either their own residential area or potential victims'.

Initial Interaction and Meeting Place

It can be assumed that the street, the scene of group activities, will be the place where MR offenders are more likely to meet their victims (table 75).

Table 75: Types of Rape by Initial Meeting Place

	Place of Acquaintance[a]		In the Streets Proper[b]		
	No.	%	No.	%	Total
SR	232	69.7	138	44.1	370
PR	44	13.2	61	19.5	105
GR	...	17.1	114	36.4	171
Total	333	100.0	313	100.0	646

a. Includes: victim's home, victim's place of stay, offender's place, bar and park, or picnic.
b. Includes: victim in the street walking, in the park, victim in front of a bar, victim in the street waiting for transportation.

Table 75 reveals that GR and MR types of rape are *significantly* associated with the street as the first meeting place between offenders and their victims. The same is true when only the residences of offenders or victims were compared to the rest of the meeting places. Seventy-five percent of the cases when the residence of participants was the place of incipient meeting, resulted in SR as compared with 10 percent PR, and 15 percent GR. MR offenses occurred in 25 percent of the cases in which the offender's/victim's residence was the place of initial meeting. On the other hand, when the streets were the place of first meeting, the proportion of SR cases dropped from 70 percent to 45 percent, PR increased to 21 percent, and GR to 37 percent. MR occurred in 25 percent of the cases in which the victim met her assailants in her home, in one of the offenders' homes, or in the place where she stayed, compared to 55 percent when they met outside on the street. These results indicate the well-documented fact that the street is the place where delinquent behavior takes place, where victims are sought or encountered.

Planning and Types of Forcible Rape

One of the main characteristics of rape is that it is a planned event. In 71 percent of the 646 cases under investigation the offense was planned, while in 11 percent of the cases it was partially planned; only in 16 percent could the offenses be defined as explosive. It seems that GR can hardly be thought of as being "explosive" since any group activity compels a minimum level of planning. However, if by explosive we mean the opportune aspects of the situation leading to further initiatory acts which render the offense possible, then GR and PR can also be considered explosive events.

In the previous discussion on the planning and type of rape, it was found that planned rapes are *significantly* associated with GR and PR situations. A more detailed analysis is contemplated here because partially planned rape was not previously found to be an equally consistent pattern. The combination of partially planned rapes with either planned or explosive rape situations, will not be further tested for their associations with MR and IR (individual rape) patterns.

On the basis of table 76 the following facts emerge to the level of statistical *significance:*

Table 76: Types of Rape by Degrees of Planning the Offense

	Planned		Partially Planned		Explosive		No Information		Total	
	No.	%	No.	%	No.	%	No.	%	No.	%
SR	216	47.0	51	70.0	93	90.0	10	76.9	370	57.3
PR	87	19.0	10	13.7	6	5.8	2	15.4	105	16.2
GR	154	34.0	12	16.3	4	4.2	1	7.7	171	26.5
Total	457	100.0	73	100.0	103	100.0	13	100.0	646	100.0

1. *Types of forcible rape and all degrees of planning.* While SR's and GR's are associated with planned rapes, the difference is reversely *significant* when they are compared to explosive rape events; 90 percent of all explosive rapes are SR's compared to 4 percent of GR events. This association maintained its level of significance when PR's were combined with GR (MR) or with SR (IR). Again,

GR was *significantly* associated with planned rape, while the proportions of PR's appear to oscillate between the different group rape events, according to their degrees of planning. PR appears to be more related to planned rape than to explosive rape (19 percent and 6 percent, respectively).

2. *Between types of forcible rape and planning only* (while partially planned and explosive rapes are combined). Within the planned pattern, SR occurred in 47 percent, PR in 19 percent, and GR in 34 percent. When the rape was either partially planned, explosive or both, SR appeared in 82 percent, PR was observed in 9 percent, and GR also in 9 percent. The association between GR and planning maintained its level of significance when PR's were combined with GR(MR) or with SR pattern (IR). GR, again, seems to be more connected with planned rape than with explosive events.

3. *Between types of forcible rape and explosive events only.* When the rape was either planned, partially planned or both, SR occurred in 50 percent of the cases compared to 19 percent of PR's and 31 percent of GR's. When the rape was an explosive event, SR's were apparent in 90 percent, PR in 6 percent and GR in 4 percent only. The association also maintained its level of *significance* for MR and IR pattern. Again, PR's and GR's appear to be significantly associated with planned rape and partially planned rapes.

These associations between degrees of planning, the offense, and the type of rape have four consistent tendencies. (1) There is an association between the planning of rape and GR patterns. (2) PR tends to be associated with planning too, but with a lower level of significant association than GR. Thus, PR seems to be of a somewhat shifting pattern among planned and partially planned rapes but not for explosive events. (3) Partially planned rapes have more in common with planned rapes than with explosive events (in spite of the ad hoc elements explosive events). (4) The association between types of rape and degrees of planning still maintained its level of *significance* when PR was combined with GR (MR) or with SR (IR). This indicates that PR cannot be considered sharply distinct from SR. Although we cannot explain it at the present time, PR pattern seems to defy its unqualified inclusion as a separate category of group rape behavior.

The Scene of Rape

In examining the scene of rape, the three places previously noted will be used here in the analysis of types of rape: indoors (found to be the most dangerous place, particularly in the participant's residence); the automobile; and the "moving crime scene," that is, when rape occurred other than in the initial meeting place.

How these patterns apply, if at all, to the different types of rape is observed in table 77. A cursory look at the table reveals that a difference exists between GR and SR when the participants' places are compared with other locations. When the place of rape was in some closed structure, but outside the participant's place, GR occurred in almost half of the cases, PR in 14 percent and SR in 36 percent of the cases. When strictly open spaces were the scene of the crime, GR occurred in 28 percent of the cases and SR in 57 percent. SR was the type of rape in 65 percent of the cases when the rape took place in the participants' places, whereas GR occurred in these places in 21 percent. PR occurred in almost the same proportion in all these places (15 percent), except when the place of rape

Table 77: Types of Rape by Place of Offense

	Auto		Open Spaces		Indoors— But Outside Participant's Place		Indoors—in Participant's Place		Total	
	No.	%	No.	%	No.	%	No.	%	No.	%
SR	42	43.8	72	56.7	23	36.5	233	64.7	370	57.3
PR	23	24.0	20	15.7	9	14.3	53	14.7	105	16.2
GR	31	32.2	35	27.6	31	49.2	74	20.6	171	26.5
Total	96	100.0	127	100.0	63	100.0	360	100.0	646	100.0

was the automobile (24 percent). Following the consideration of GR's, residential proximity to the victim, and the street as the meeting ground, the observations about the place of rape and its association with GR pattern are expected and conceivable.

Because of the high proportion of automobile PR's and GR's, the automobile was included in the categories of "outside participants' places." The association between the place of rape and the type of rape is statistically *significant*. When the scene of rape was the participants' places, SR occurred in 65 percent, and GR in 20 percent. When the scene was outside the participant's place, SR was committed in 48 percent and GR in 35 percent of the cases. PR's are almost evenly distributed between both categories of places (15 percent and 17 percent, respectively). This level of *significance* is maintained when SR is compared to MR and IR is compared to GR. However, it is clear that certain PR's are more connected with the participants' places as the scene of crime, than with outside places. For instance, GR occurred in 15 percent when the initial meeting place was the participant's place and the same proportion of PR's are observed when the scene of rape was at the same place.

A comparison of the IR and GR patterns strengthens this statement.

The former occurred in 79 percent of the cases when the rape took place at the participant's place, while the latter occurred in 21 percent of the cases. It can be concluded that GR's are mainly outdoor affairs, compared to SR's and PR's. PR's are either outdoor or indoor affairs, a pattern which is probably a function of relationships between offenders and victims and the circumstances of their encounter.

Turning to the aspect of the "movement of the crime scene," it was previously shown that a significant association exists between the place of initial meeting and the place of rape. When the meeting was in the participant's place so was the rape; when the meeting was outdoors, the rape occurred there. It was also shown that GR and PR are outdoor events and that the initial meeting between offenders and victims occurred there. It is, therefore, more likely that for MR cases a similar pattern will remain for initial meetings and places of rape than for SR. A case-by-case check was made of 126 victims who met the offenders outside but were raped indoors. SR was found in 83 cases, or 67 percent; in 23 cases, or 18 percent, the event was a PR (mainly when the victim and the offender were drinking together or after a party or picnic); and in 20 cases, or 15 percent, the event was a GR (again, mainly after victims or offenders were drinking together). In 31 of the 32 cases, when the victim met the offender in her or his place, but the rape took place outside, the event was a SR.

Means, Methods Used, and Type of Rape

When the concepts of nonphysical force and violence are applied to PR or GR, at least two seemingly contradictory assumptions can be made. First, that only the coercion of slight intimidation is necessary in order to render the victim into submission because of the sheer number of offenders. On the other hand, she must be immediately threatened and subdued in MR situations. Thus, the intimidation would be more extreme in its form. Exceptions may occur when the victim had been drinking, especially when alone, or when she initially encountered only one or more of the participants in the GR and the other offenders came later. To see what actually happened we turn to table 78.

Temptation was used in significantly higher proportion by SR than MR offenders. Offenders in PR's and GR's resorted more to coercion. Of those rape events when temptation was used, 84 percent of them were SR events, 7 percent were PR's and 19 percent were GR's. Among those events where various forms of constraints were used, 53 percent were SR's, 19 percent were PR's, and 29 percent were GR events. When the two forms of intimidation (with and without a weapon) were combined and compared to the other two forms of manipulating the victim (temptation and coercion), it appeared that in situations when various forms of intimidation were used, the proportion of SR's were *significantly* higher (64 percent) than that of PR's (16 percent) and of GR's (20 percent). For, in PR situations the use of intimidation is almost equal to the use of coercion and/or temptation (16 percent and 20 percent, respectively). GR situations occurred in 38 percent of the cases when the victims were tempted and/or coerced, while in 20 percent when intimidation was used. This is clearly colored by the high proportion of coercion (51 percent) used in GR.

Table 78: Types of Rape, Leaders and Nonleaders, by Nonphysical Force Used in the Offense

	Tempting		Coercion		Intimidation without a Weapon		Intimidation with a Weapon		No Information		Total	
	No.	%	No.	%	No.	%	No.	%	No.	%	No.	%
Offender in SR	63	84.0	43	14.5	177	53.2	79	58.1	8	1.8	370	28.6
Leader in PR	5	6.7	35	11.8	40	12.0	25	18.1	...	...	105	8.1
Follower in PR	...	...	35	11.8	...	...	...	...	70	15.5	105	8.1
Leader in GR	7	9.3	83	28.1	49	14.7	32	23.2	...	...	171	13.3
Followers in GR	...	...	100	33.8	67	20.1	...	...	374	82.7	541	41.9
Total	75	100.0	296	100.0	333	100.0	136	100.0	452	100.0	1,292	100.0
SR	63	84.0	43	26.7	177	66.5	79	58.1	8	100.0	370	57.3
PR	5	6.7	35	21.8	40	15.0	25	18.8	...	...	105	16.2
GR	7	9.3	83	51.5	49	18.5	32	23.1	...	...	171	26.5
Total	75	100.0	161	100.0	266	100.0	136	100.0	8	100.0	646	100.0

As to the two forms of intimidation, there is a tendency in PR and GR to add weapons or another object in threatening the victim, but it is in SR situations where both forms of intimidation occurred in *significantly* higher proportion than in either PR, GR, or MR events.

It appears that while SR offenders will use temptation or intimidation to initially overcome the victim, in GR she will be more likely to be coerced by the use of verbal and gestural threats. In PR's, there is the likelihood that the victim will be manipulated like her sister who is accosted by a single offender. These findings qualify our first hypothesis, that is, that a verbal and gestural threat with the fact that the whole group is confronting the victim precludes the necessity to resort to more extreme means of threat.

According to our theoretical discussion the act by which leadership may be assumed or confirmed is the initiatory act, that is, the first to threaten, strike, or rape the victim. Returning to table 78, we are first confronted with the validity of this assumption.[103] The leader alone tempted or lured the victim in PR and GR situations, when the victim was intimidated with a weapon. Of those who intimidated the victim without a weapon, 43 percent of GR leaders did so, compared to 67 percent of nonleaders.

Types of Rape and Physical Force

When, previously discussing the problem of physical force or violence, it was found that in 85 percent of the 646 cases of rape, varying forms of force were used. It was further revealed that violence, especially in its extreme forms, is *significantly* associated with GR. In the following paragraphs a more detailed analysis is intended of the relationship between GR's leadership and violence. A cursory inspection of table 79 suggests that all types of rape have their share of violence. Comparing the type of rape for the differences in violence we observed that it is GR which is *significantly* associated with the use of physical force. When force was used, 30 percent of the rape situations were GR's while force was absent in only 9 percent of GR's. On the other hand, when force was used 54 percent were SR's but when force was absent from the rape situation 78 percent were SR's. PR's were spread in somewhat even proportions; they were observed in 17 percent when force was used and in 13 percent when force was absent from the rape situation. The MR and IR combinations show the same pattern, that is, the proportion of GR's increased when force was used but decreased when force was absent from the rape situation. For SR cases the pattern is reversed.

Various forms of violence (roughness, beating, brutality, and choking) were compared with the different types of rapes, while also noting the timing of the violence, for its relation to types of rape and leadership phenomena. Of all these combinations, the following associations emerge to the level of statistical significance.

1. *Types of rape and degrees of violence.* When degrees of violence were divided between roughness and beating (in all its forms), GR's were found to be associated with more extreme forms of violence, while PR's were almost evenly spread when roughness or beating occurred. Thus, when roughness was the victim's lot, in 23 percent it was in GR, which also occurred in 33 percent when beatings, in one form or another, were administered to her. PR's occurred in these circumstances in 62 percent

103. On 452 offenders we found no data in the files about this aspect of their behavior. The lack of data is for the offenders in PR and GR events; and, therefore, the conclusions drawn from the table are very inaccurate.

Table 79: Types of Rape, Leaders and Nonleaders, by Degrees of Physical Force Used in the Offense

	Roughness		Beaten Not Brutally before Rape		Beaten Not Brutally during or after Rape		Beaten Brutally before Rape		Beaten Brutally during and after Rape		Choked		Total Use of Force		No Use of Force		Grand Total	
	No.	%	No.	%	No.	%	No.	%	No.	%	No.	%	No.	%	No.	%	No.	%
Offender in SR	114	40.0	54	32.9	13	35.2	35	45.5	29	35.7	50	50.0	295	39.6	75	13.7	370	28.7
Leader in PR	28	9.8	28	17.1	1	2.7	9	11.7	14	17.3	13	13.0	93	12.5	12	2.2	105	8.1
Follower in PR	17	6.0	10	6.1	6	16.2	2	2.5	2	2.5	10	10.0	47	6.3	58	10.6	105	8.1
Leader in GR	42	14.7	59	36.0	5	13.5	25	32.5	20	24.7	11	11.0	162	21.8	9	1.6	171	13.2
Followers in GR	84	29.5	13	7.9	12	32.4	6	7.8	16	19.8	16	16.0	147	19.8	394	71.9	541	41.9
Total	285	100.0	164	100.0	37	100.0	77	100.0	81	100.0	100	100.0	744	100.0	548	100.0	1,292	100.0
SR	114	62.0	54	38.1	13	68.4	35	50.8	29	46.1	50	67.6	295	53.6	75	78.2	370	57.3
PR	28	15.2	28	19.9	1	5.3	9	13.0	14	22.1	13	17.6	93	16.9	12	12.5	105	16.2
GR	42	22.8	59	42.0	5	26.3	25	36.2	20	31.8	11	14.8	162	29.5	9	9.3	171	26.5
Total	184	100.0	141	100.0	19	100.0	69	100.0	63	100.0	74	100.0	550	100.0	96	100.0	646	100.0

and 50 percent, respectively. MR types are, therefore, characterized by the use of beatings rather than "roughing" the victim.

2. *Types of rape and degrees of brutality.*[104] When the victim was brutally beaten, 53 percent occurred in SR situations; and in 42 percent, nonbrutal beating was used against her. PR's, again, were observed in these circumstances in equal proportions (18 percent), and GR's in 27 percent and 40 percent, respectively. Therefore, in the SR situation more brutality is used against the victim. It is logical to expect that the lone offender, once he had to use physical force, would beat his victim more brutally to render her into submission. On the other hand, brutal beating of the victim by the group seems less necessary if it is intended to overcome her resistance. In all cases of GR, the victim was held by one or two offenders while one was raping her. The lone offender cannot rely on such help and brutality is, thus, employed.[105]

3. *Type of rape and the time of beating.* In all types of rape, the victim suffered beating (before, during, and after the rape), whether the beating was brutal or not. However, only when the beating was not brutal, a *significant* difference between the types of rape was found. For, when nonbrutal beating was employed against the victim, in 42 percent it was in GR situations before the rape, and in 26 percent during or after. In PR's nonbrutal beating was used in 20 percent before the rape and in 5 percent during or after. In SR situations, nonbrutal beating occurred in 30 percent and 69 percent, respectively. MR situations are characterized by nonbrutal beating, which is employed early in the offense, while in GR's nonbrutal beating was administered during all stages, especially during the offense. Again, we assume that beating is the only way the lone offender can render the victim's submission and complete the offensive act.

Turning to the difference between leaders and nonleaders, the following facts emerge to the level of statistical *significance.*

1. *Leadership and the use of force.* In all PR's, GR's and MR's leaders show a significantly higher proportion of use of force than nonleaders. In the PR situation, when force was used, it was exerted by 67 percent of the leaders, but by half of this proportion of nonleaders. While 35 percent of PR leaders were not violent, 83 percent of the nonleaders refrained themselves from using force. In GR situations, when force was used, it was employed in 52 percent by the leader and in 48 percent by the nonleader. When force was absent from the rape situation, only in 2 percent did the leaders disengage from it, compared to 98 percent of the nonleaders.

104. Brutal beatings including choking the victim; roughness is not included in the nonbrutal beating.

105. The contention that the lone rapist is more aggressive due to his mental or emotional condition may also explain it, but this argument cannot be tested here.

2. *Leadership in MR situations and degrees of force.* In MR situations, when nonbrutality in the form of roughness was used, it was employed by 41 percent of the leaders compared to 66 percent when other forms of force were used. Thus, 34 percent of nonleaders used roughness compared to 59 percent who inflicted beating in one form or another upon the victim.

3. *Leadership in GR's and MR's and beatings inflicted in the rape situation.* Leaders in GR, compared to nonleaders, used in *significant* proportion more beating (brutal and nonbrutal) than roughness. Beatings were inflicted in 64 percent of the GR situations, by the leaders, compared to 33 percent who only roughed their victim. Roughness was used in 67 percent by the nonleaders, who inflicted beatings in 34 percent. Almost the same proportions of roughness were observed for leaders and nonleaders in MR situations.

4. *Leadership in PR and GR situations and the use of brutality.*[106] In 85 percent of the PR situations when brutality was used, it was inflicted by the leaders, compared to 62 percent when nonbrutality (in all its forms) was used by them. Thus, 9 percent of the nonleaders used brutality against the victim while 30 percent did not. In GR situations, when brutality was used in 67 percent it was by the leaders, compared to 40 percent when nonbrutality was employed.[107] The *significant* association between leadership and brutality also pertains to MR situations.[108]

5. *Leadership in PR and GR situations and degrees of brutality.* In PR situations when the victim suffered nonbrutal beatings 65 percent were inflicted by the leaders, while 82 percent of the leaders were responsible when her lot was that of brutality in all its forms (beating and choking). In GR situations when the beatings were nonbrutal, 72 percent of the leaders were responsible, compared to 59 percent who brought brutal beating on the victim.

6. *Leadership and initial act of beating* (brutally and nonbrutally). In GR situations, when the beating was inflicted on the victim before the rape, in 79 percent it was the leader who did it and in 21 percent the nonleaders. In 47 percent, those who resorted to beatings during or after the rape were leaders compared to 53 percent of the nonleaders. Almost the same proportions are maintained for MR situations.[109]

7. *Leadership and initial act of nonbrutal beating in PR, GR, and*

106. Brutality here does not include choking of the victim.

107. Significant associations were also formed when choking was combined with the category of brutal beatings.

108. This occurs when choking of the victim was included or omitted from the category of brutal beatings.

109. PR leaders beat the victim before the rape in 69 percent and during or after the rape in 65 percent.

MR situations. In PR situations, when nonbrutal beating was used against the victim in 74 percent it was the leader who struck first, but he was responsible for beatings during or after the rape only in 14 percent. In GR situations the differences in the proportions are as high: 82 percent and 29 percent respectively. The same is true for the MR situation.[110]

Sexual Humiliation

As previously noted sexual humiliation of the victim, that is, forced, perverted sexual practices, exists in slightly more than one quarter (27 percent) of the rape events. Among these practices either fellatio, cunnilingus, both, and repeated sexual intercourse are the main forms to which the victim was subjected. It can be assumed that when sexual humiliation does occur, the form it will most often take in MR situations will be repeated intercourse. Taking repeated turns is part of what GR can "offer" to the participants.

Also, "magical seduction" is one of the forms of sexual perversion which will appear in MR situations as part or a separate activity of the leader. Let us see what really happened for this aspect of the offense.

From table 80 it is observed that sexual humiliation was *significantly* prevalent in MR's. When sexual humiliation was present, it was in 51 percent SR's which occurred in 56 percent when sexual humiliation was absent from the rape situation. PR's appear in 19 percent and 15 percent, respectively. The incidences of GR's are 31 percent when sexual humiliation took place in the rape situation, and 25 percent when sexual humiliation was absent.

Looking for the differences among types of rape in terms of the sexual perversion to which the victim was subjected, a *significant* association was found between the MR situation and repeated intercourse. It is in GR situations, however, that repeated intercourse occurred in 48 percent of the cases. In only 19 percent was repeated intercourse absent from the GR situation.

Turning to the differences between leaders and nonleaders, the "magical seduction" argument is again assumed, that is, it is the leader who is more likely to commit the perversion upon the victim, and to first rape the victim, repeatedly—then the nonleader may follow.

From table 81 it appears that it is the PR leaders who have, in *significant* proportion, tormented their victims by sexual humiliation. In PR situations, when sexual humiliation occurred 59 percent of the leaders were responsible, compared to 46 percent who abstained. Of the non-

110. For brutal beating only GR leaders showed a tendency to be involved in brutally striking the victim (62 percent), but the differences are not significant when the brutal beating was inflicted during or after the rape (57 percent).

Table 80: Types of Rapes, Leaders and Nonleaders, by Sexual Humiliation

	Fellatio No.	%	Cunnilingus No.	%	Fellatio and Cunnilingus No.	%	Offender Used Prophylaxis No.	%	Pederasty No.	%	Offender Performs More Than One Intercourse No.	%	Total Presence of Sexual Humiliation No.	%	Total Absence of Sexual Humiliation No.	%	Total No.	%
Offender in SR	30	21.0	10	100.0	8	7.5	3	23.1	9	75.0	28	15.8	88	19.1	282	33.9	370	28.6
Leader in PR	16	11.2	...	...	6	5.6	1	7.7	2	16.6	11	6.2	36	7.8	69	8.3	105	8.1
Follower in PR	9	6.3	...	...	2	2.0	3	23.1	1	8.4	10	5.6	25	5.4	80	9.6	105	8.1
Leader in GR	14	9.8	...	...	1	1.0	3	23.1	...	...	39	22.0	57	12.4	114	13.7	171	13.3
Followers in GR	74	51.7	...	...	89	84.0	3	23.1	...	...	89	49.4	255	55.3	286	34.4	541	41.9
Total	143	100.0	10	100.0	106	100.0	13	100.0	12	100.0	177	100.0	461	100.0	831	100.0	1,292	100.0
SR	30	50.0	10	100.0	8	72.7	3	42.9	9	81.8	28	37.8	88	50.9	282	59.6	370	57.3
PR	16	26.7	...	...	2	18.2	1	14.2	2	18.2	11	14.9	32	18.5	73	15.4	105	16.2
GR	14	23.3	...	...	1	9.1	3	42.9	...	...	35	47.3	53	30.6	118	25.0	171	26.5
Total	60	100.0	11	100.0	7	100.0	11	100.0	11	100.0	74	100.0	173	100.0	473	100.0	646	100.0

leaders, 41 percent performed it compared to the 54 percent who abstained.

In the PR pattern leadership and type of perversion were definitely associated. In PR situations, when either fellatio and/or cunnilingus was practiced upon the victim, 68 percent of the leaders performed it compared to 50 percent who abstained, and 33 percent of the nonleaders performed it, and 5 percent abstained. In other types of perversion for GR situations, the nonleaders were in *significant* proportions engaged with it.

Table 81: Leadership Activities in Multiple Rape Situations according to Performance of Initial Acts

Initial Act by the Leader[a] Magical Seduction[b]	Committed by the Leader		Not Committed by the Leader		Total	
	No.	%	No.	%	No.	%
Performed by leader in PR	56	26.1	15	24.6	71	25.7
Not performed by leader in PR	22	10.1	12	19.6	34	12.3
Performed by leader in GR	95	44.1	25	41.1	120	43.6
Not performed by leader in GR	42	19.5	9	14.7	51	18.4
Total	215	100.0	61	100.0	276	100.0
Performed by leader in MR	151	70.3	40	65.6	181	69.2
Not performed	64	29.7	21	34.4	85	30.8
Total	215	100.0	61	100.0	276	100.0

a. Initial action, includes all forms of beatings, thus all degrees of brutality.
b. Magical Seduction includes only first rape and not repeated rapes.

Thus, sexual humiliation is associated with MR situations. The victim's chances to be further brutalized by repeated intercourse, fellatio, cunnilingus or both is greater in GR for the former and in PR for the latter. It seems that "magical seduction" is not operative for these types of perversion, and it is left to each offender according to his inclination or perversion to engage in it.

In table 82 we look for another factor in the leadership role, that of "commanding" the rape situation and its relation to "magical seduction" and "initial act." It is assumed that the leader may not be the one who performs both of these latter activities, but still commands the situation; in the form of arranging and ordering the scene and the activities of the other participants. Interesting to note, though it cannot be explained, are the PR leaders who commanded the situations, while they were not the ones who first struck or raped the victim. However, when they performed both the first rape either with the first beating (55 percent) or without it (3 percent), they controlled the situation.

Table 82: Leadership Commanding Role in Multiple Rape Situations by Leadership Acts

	A: Initial Act (Beating, Rape, and Magical Seduction)		B: Initial Act But Not Magical Seduction		C: Not Initial Act But Magical Seduction		D: Not Initial Act and Not Magical Seduction		Total	
	No.	%	No.	%	No.	%	No.	%	No.	%
Commanding in PR	31	20.7	15	23.4	8	20.0	9	42.9	63	22.8
Not commanding in PR	25	16.5	7	11.0	7	17.5	3	14.3	42	15.2
Commanding in GR	78	51.6	33	51.5	18	45.0	6	28.5	135	49.0
Not commanding in GR	17	11.2	9	14.1	7	17.5	3	14.3	36	13.0
Total	151	100.0	64	100.0	40	100.0	21	100.0	276	100.0
Commanding in MR	109	72.2	48	75.0	26	65.0	15	71.4	198	71.8
Not commanding in MR	42	27.8	16	25.0	14	35.0	6	28.6	78	28.2
Total	151	100.0	64	100.0	40	100.0	21	100.0	276	100.0

Among the GR leaders 83 percent of them commanded the situation when they performed both the "initial" act and the "magical seduction," and in 82 percent when they were engaged in the latter but not in initial act. When they only committed the initial act in 77 percent they also commanded the situation. Of those who disengaged themselves from both initial action and "magical seduction," 67 percent commanded the situation. The "true" leader, then, is the one who performed all 3 actions of leadership roles in GR situations, but he is also likely in *significant* proportion to command the event if he was only the one who first raped the victim.

Victim Behavior

In MR situations it can be assumed either that a victim will submit herself to her assaulters without resisting, because she is aware of the futility of the fight or is unable to fight more than one strong male. Now, it can be further assumed that the victim will fight more in MR situations, since the possibility of humiliation is greater than in SR. From the data, however, it was found that to fight or not to fight depends more on the age, race, temperament, mental and emotional conditions of the victim (including the presence of alcohol), rather than the fact that the situation was a MR event.

From table 83 we attempted to gauge the differences among types of rape according to the victim behavior in these rape situations. We learn

Table 83: Type of Rape by Victim Behavior in the Rape Situation

	Submissive		Resists		Fights		No Information		Total	
	No.	%	No.	%	No.	%	No.	%	No.	%
SR	214	60.3	79	45.7	76	65.5	1	50.0	370	57.3
PR	56	15.8	31	17.9	17	14.7	1	50.0	105	16.2
GR	85	23.9	63	36.4	23	19.8	...	...	171	26.5
Total	355	100.0	173	100.0	116	100.0	2	100.0	646	100.0

that MR situations in general, and SR situations in particular, are characterized by victims' resistance, while SR situations are distinguished by either victim's submissive or fighting behavior. PR's show no definite pattern in terms of victim behavior.

When submissive behavior and resistance were compared to fighting as the form of victim behavior, it is evident that the victim in *significant* proportion fought more in SR situations, while in GR's she was in *significant* proportion submissive. Thus, when the victim was submissive, resistant, or both, in 55 percent it was in SR situations, while she fought in 65 percent of the SR situations. Under these conditions, PR occurred in 16 percent and 15 percent, respectively. In those situations when the victim either was submissive or resistant or both to her assaulters, in 28 percent it was found in GR's and in 20 percent when she fought them.

It seems that "resistance" is somewhat a "vague" term and no wonder it arouses a lot of bickering in the court. Further, it seems that the victim of PR or GR is not likely to resist her attackers, while the SR victim is more likely to fight her assailant.

IV

The Victim in Forcible Rape

13

The Interpersonal
Relationships between
Victim and Offender

Relationships are the starting point of a sociological analysis of all human behavior, including criminal conduct. Thus, most offenses begin with the entering into some sort of a relationship with someone else. It is generally assumed by the public that most crimes involve more or less innocent victims whose person or property is harmed or exploited without their consent by offenders who are strangers to them. Sometimes, the relationship is intimate, and with a special victim (a female in rape); sometimes with an abstract or a detached victim (the department store vis-à-vis the shoplifter). Some crimes do not have an actor separated from an "alter" who is the victim. In a way they are crimes "without victims,"[1] and the offender is both "doer and sufferer." Such is the case in suicide,[2] drug addiction, alcoholism, criminal abortion,[3] and illegal homosexual relations between two adults.

Criminology recognizes that it is not always the offender alone who is to be blamed and condemned as responsible for the offense. Sometimes victims can be equally blamed. The study of victim-offender relationships and the role of the victim in the perpetration of crimes against the person has been the special contribution of Von Hentig, Wolfgang, and Bohannan in their work on homicide.[4]

1. On this concept see Schor.
2. Menninger, p. 71.
3. The "pusher" in drug addiction and the abortionist in criminal abortion are both accomplices. The addict and the woman are at the same time both offenders and victims alike.
4. Von Hentig, *The Criminal,* pp. 404–38, and "Remarks"; Wolfgang, *Patterns,* pt. 3; Bohannan, pp. 27–28, 35–37, 105–8, 168–70.

Sex crimes in general, especially those involving young victims, were studied originally by psychoanalysts emphasizing proneness to victimization.[5] Later Bender and Blau dealt with the child victim of adult sex offenders. The assumption in these psychologically oriented studies is that, like the offender who creates situations in which he is apprehended, and thus becomes the victim of his own doings, the victim of sex crimes, by her relationship to the offender and by her behavior, which is often unconscious, creates the situation of her victimization.

The role of victim in forcible rape is dealt with in Von Hentig's work which is best known for its theoretical implications.[6] Some studies, less well-known, appeared before that, from which "victimology" has been thought to have been developed as a legitimate but separate discipline[7] or as a branch of criminology.[8]

Probably more than in any other crime, in forcible rape the personal relationship between the offender and his victim is of prime importance. This is so because the law and the public recognize degrees of moral weakness and of culpability, depending, partly, on the relationship between the offender and his victim.[9] Thus, in the incest relationship, the girl is always considered to be an innocent victim, and the offender bears the full consequences of the "resistance potential" of the norm, which he violates. Such is not the case in rape if prior to the offense drinking or a close relationship existed between the victim and the offender.

Von Hentig, who dealt with victim-offender relationships (VOR) as that of doer-sufferer, and Mendelson in his "penal couple" relationships, are limited in their approach to the problem of victim-offender relations.[10] First, in their writings, only the dyad type of relationships is portrayed; whereas the prevalence and importance of triads or multiple forms of rape indicate a multiplicity of relationships. Second, Von Hentig emphasizes those types of relationships which grow after the encounter takes place between the victim and the offender. Third, Von Hentig's study

5. Abraham; S. Freud, "Three Essays."

6. Von Hentig, *The Criminal and His Victim*.

7. Mendelson claims "victimology" to be a separate science. He reports the works on the subject, including his own on forcible rape, which anticipated Von Hentig's study. Also included are the various theoretical studies on victimology published in languages other than English. On the problem of victim-offender relationships as reflected in philosophy and fiction see Ellenberg.

8. See Nagel. He argues with Mendelson's attempt to develop "victimology" as a separate science.

9. The law emphasizes her behavior during the offense ("The Consent Problem and That of Moral Reputation"). See *Purdon's Pennsylvania Statutes*.

10. Von Hentig, *The Criminal and His Victim* and "Remarks"; Mendelson, p. 241.

lacks a discussion of the connection between the VOR and other situational elements which may be involved, such as ecological, drinking, and gang relationships, as well as race and age relationships.

A special aspect, important in sexual crimes in general, and rape in particular, is the institutionalization of VOR and the legitimation of sexual relationships within their framework. Thus forced sexual intercourse by a husband on his wife is not considered rape, while between a father and his daughter it is deemed more serious than rape. However, such clarity does not exist when forced sexual intercourse occurs between lovers, petting partners, or drinking companions. The existence of prior relationships with the offender, if established by the court, may cast doubt on the victim's story and on her allegations about the whole event, regardless of her behavior prior to, or during the offense (resistance, etc.) or whatever happened to her as a result of the offense. The suspicion of complicity and consent because of prior relations with the offender may, in the court, transform the victim into an accomplice, or she may even be regarded as an offending party (especially in the case of statutory rape where the machinery of justice will be turned against her as well as against the offender).

An important aspect of the problem of VOR in rape situations is the choice of the victim. She may be "selected" the moment before the offense is perpetrated, or long before it, if a prior relationship exists. If the latter is the case, the fear of the community that unfamiliar offenders will attack victims unknown to them, can be reduced or at least partially alleviated.

Knowledge about VOR is also important for practical purposes. Even when the offender is originally unknown to the victim, if some relationship is established between them, such relationships may help to prevent possible future offenses by identifying potential victims, vulnerable situations, and dangerous relations (especially in the case of young victims warned about associations with strangers, accepting their gifts, and so on).[11]

Criminal violence produces fears and changes in people's behavior. The study of victim-offender relations is therefore important in alleviating community fears that persons attack victims unknown to them. The victim may be "selected" or marked by the very fact she entered a relationship with the offender under special circumstances, for example, accepting invitations for drinking in his or her home or going for a ride in his car.

Victim-offender relationships are important aspects in the problem of victim precipitation of the offense. Because sexual offenses are connected

11. See, for example, Hoover.

with emotions and passion, victim-offender relationships become part of the offender's motivation. The nature and type of victim-offender relationship may mobilize the energy and tendencies toward criminal activities, and may in themselves contain the seeds of crime. Victim-offender relationships are also connected with the victim's role in arousing and directing offender's motivation in a way which culminates in her victimization. The type, duration and intensity of victim-offender relationships may furnish an explanation as to how victim behavior and situational elements led to the offense.

From the public point of view, then, if a high proportion of victims know their assailants, then the fear and the hysteria which stirs most violently the imagination and action of the community—the fear of the stranger who seduces or attacks women—is partly baseless.

Thus far, only a static analysis of rape has been presented. The aspect of VOR introduces a dynamic element to the understanding of rape. True, the analysis of modus operandi indicates some dynamic interactive elements between offender and victim at the time the offense was committed; yet, the victim and offender have been examined as distinct, somewhat separate entities. Now, we intend to see the relationship between victims and offenders before the offense took place, and its implications to the various aspects of the rape situations which were previously touched upon. Two problems are involved here: identifying the victim; identifying the relationship between the victim and the offender(s). The first problem involves factors which have been already discussed, such as: age, race, and proximity of residence to the offender.

As to the problem of actual relationships between the victims and offenders, it may be assumed either that there was no prior relationship between them, or that a previous relationship did exist. In the first case, the offender and victim are assumed to be unknown to each other: the victim never had a chance to know the offender and saw him only when he assailed her. In some cases, however, some relationships may have been established a relatively short time before the offense. When relationships are established just prior to the offense, their content and intensity become important in explaining the offense which followed. Thus, drinking relationships between strangers, or other circumstances of their first encounter, may be highly charged with sexuality. In short, when interpersonal relationships are absent before the offense, or when they are established immediately prior to the act, the situational factors and victim behavior may be the pertinent factors in explaining the offense.

If a relationship existed between the victim and offender(s), the question of how to classify them arises. An objective scale can be formed for this purpose, according to degrees of social distance, anonymity, or degrees of intimacy.[12] Thus, the scale will be comprised of the category of "offender stranger to the victim" on the one end, and of "family relative," on the other. The scale, however, must also classify VOR's according to degrees of interaction on the basis of durability and intensity of the relationship. The two classifying factors must merge since they are not mutually exclusive. Already alluded to is the fact that relationships between victim and offender who are initially strangers can become intensive, although not durable. On the other hand, an uncle can rape his niece the first time he visits her.

The Philadelphia Data

The classifications of VOR used in the present work are as follows:

a. stranger—no previous contact existed, and no acquaintanceship established before the offense;

b. stranger but general knowledge—offender is only known visually to the victim without any other contact between them;

c. acquaintance—offender becomes known to victim just before the offense, or she has some prior knowledge about his residence, place of work, name or nickname, but no specific relationships exist between them;

d. neighbor—close neighbor, or victim saw the offender before and crossed his way many times;

e. close friend or boy friend—offender often in victim's home or dated with her, or having close, direct, or frequent relationship with her;

f. family friend—offender friend of one of victim's family members, often at her home, trusted;

g. offender is a family relative—relationship by consanguinity or legal affinity, but not husband-wife, or any type of incestuous relationship.

This is an ad hoc classification combining type, content and duration of the relationships. It is based on the information given by the victim and the offender (if apprehended) written into the police dossiers. For most of the cases no subjective evaluation of the type of VOR was necessary. Such is the case when offender and victims were relatives or when cross-race events precluded the possibility of kinship relationship. Judgment of degree of personal association, especially for categories (c), (d), (e), and (f) was not always easy, nor was the evaluation about the duration and frequency of contacts between the offender and his victim. The information supplied by those involved in the offense, as well as by others, made the police designation of the type of relationship as valid as can

12. It is possible also to see the social status differences between them. However, this aspect can be easily converted into the interpersonal relationships scale by assuming that the greater status differential between victim and offender, the greater is the chance of anonymity between them.

be expected. Therefore, the terms employed here are those used by the police.

The specific categories of VOR have been combined in various ways in order to distinguish different types of *primary* and *secondary* relationships. The data have been grouped as follows: relationships between strangers (a and b) vs. primary relationships (c–g); primary relationships divided between acquaintanceship (c and d) and intimate relationships (e–g).

Race

On the basis of previous results, especially the proportion of victims and offenders who are of the same race and age group and who live in spatial proximity, it can be postulated that the distribution of interpersonal relationships existing between victims and offenders in forcible rape will show a high frequency of primary relationships. This statement implies that victims and offenders had some knowledge of each other, in varying degrees of duration and frequency of personal contact. It shall be further postulated that primary relations will be more frequent among intraracial rape events and for those rape situations where the victim and offender were of the same age group.

In general, the data (table 84) support the first assumption regarding

Table 84: Type of Interpersonal Relationship between Victim and Principal Offender by Race of Victim and Offender in Rape Events

	Offender/Victim									
	Negro/ Negro		White/ White		Negro/ White		White/ Negro		Total	
	No.	%	No.	%	No.	%	No.	%	No.	%
Stranger	208	41.9	36	34.3	19	70.4	10	58.8	273	42.3
Stranger but general knowledge	54	10.9	7	6.6	1	3.7	...	...	62	9.6
Acquaintance	61	12.3	26	24.8	3	11.1	3	17.6	93	14.4
Neighbors (close)	104	20.9	18	17.1	3	11.1	...	...	125	19.3
Close friend or boyfriend	28	5.6	11	10.5	...	...	...	...	39	6.0
Family friend	26	5.2	6	5.7	...	...	2	11.8	34	5.3
Relative	15	3.0	1	1.0	...	...	...	...	16	2.5
No information	1	0.2	...	...	1	3.7	2	11.8	4	0.6
Total	497	100.0	105	100.0	27	100.0	17	100.0	646	100.0

Note: See table 92 for an analysis of offender position; there the proportion and absolute number of all offenders, rather than only the principal one, are presented.

VOR's and a high proportion of "primary contact"[13] (acquaintance, close neighbors, close friends, or boy friend, family friend, relative). When these are combined, they constitute 48 percent of all VOR's, and constitute 53 percent, or 676 offenders who stood in such relationship to the victim. Categories which involve relationships between strangers (stranger or stranger but general knowledge), when combined, comprise the remaining 52 percent of interpersonal relationships between victim and principal offender, and 612 (or 47 percent) of all offenders who were strangers to the victim.

When the types of primary contacts are divided between "acquaint-anceships" and more "intimate" relationships, categories which involved acquaintance relationships (acquaintance and close neighbors) constitute 34 percent of the cases, and include 43 percent of all offenders who participate in the offense. Categories which involve intimate relationships (close friend and boy friend, family friend, relative) contribute 14 percent of all victim-principal offender relationships and 9 percent of all offenders.

Whereas, strictly acquaintance relationships (acquaintance and close neighborhood) constitute the same proportion as all types of primary relationships (34 percent). Henceforth, we shall present the analysis only for the differences between stranger and the two types of "primary" relationships ("acquaintance" and "intimate relations").

The offender was a complete stranger to the victim in 42 percent of 646 cases, while some knowledge of him, but no previous contact, existed in 10 percent of all categories in interpersonal relationships. Of the "primary contact" types of relationships (33 percent), the two types with the highest frequency are "close neighbor" (19 percent), and general acquaintance (14 percent); and account for a third of all relationships, and for 71 percent of all primary contacts.

It should be noticed that girls who trust their boy friends and those whose families have confidence in their friends or relatives, may not be spared from becoming victims of rape. In 29 percent of primary relationship cases, gentlemen forfeited their positions of trust and committed the crime of forcible rape.

Negro victims were as likely to be raped by a stranger as the white victims (53 percent compared to 50 percent, respectively). Among the victims who had some primary contact with their assailant, the white

---

13. In 4 cases the relationship between victim and offender is not known, and a total of 642 relationships are provided for analysis. Because in all MR cases the offenders were of the same race, and practically in all cases were also of the same age group, these 642 associations include relationships between victim and principal offender, which, therefore, represent the association in rape events or situations.

victim was somewhat more likely to be raped (50 percent) than was her Negro counterpart (48 percent). When an acquaintanceship existed between the victim and the offender, 33 percent involved Negro victims, while 29 percent included white victims. Negro and white victims were equally likely to be raped by those who had had some intimate contact with them (14 percent and 15 percent, respectively).

Significant differences, however, exist for some categories in the distribution of VOR's. For example, Negro victims were more likely to be raped by a close neighbor (21 percent compared to 13 percent for white victims), and white victims were more prone to be raped by an acquaintance (22 percent compared to 12 percent for the Negro victims). Acquaintance relationships with offenders were more prevalent among white victims, and consist of almost half (44 percent) of all primary contacts. For Negro victims as close neighbor relationships with the offender exist in 44 percent of VOR.

The hypothesis which suggests a higher proportion of primary relationships for intraracial rape events is also supported by the data. The frequency distribution of VOR's according to the race of victim and offender in rape events reveals *significant* differences. Categories which involved primary contacts, when combined, constitute 50 percent of all intraracial events, but 27 percent of interracial rape events. Moreover, specific differences among the types of primary relationships are noted for intraracial and interracial rape events. The data show that over a third of intraracial (35 percent), but only 22 percent of the interracial cases were between acquaintances, while intimate contact is observed in 15 percent of intraracial events, but only in 5 percent in interracial rape situations. When primary relationships were further analyzed it was found that intraracial rapes were more likely to occur between close neighbors and accounted for almost a third (30 percent) of all relations, and for 41 percent of all intraracial primary contacts. For, when primary relationships existed between victim and offender, interracial rapes were more likely to occur between those who were strictly acquaintances: in the data they accounted for 15 percent of all relationships and for 54 percent of all interracial primary contacts.

As was expected, the majority of interracial rape events occurred between strangers. In more than three-quarters of these cases, the event occurred when the offender was a Negro and his victim white (77 percent) while 67 percent of the events involved a white offender and a Negro victim. When primary relationships are further analyzed, it was found that acquaintances existed in only 3 cases in both types of interracial events, while between neighbors the rape occurred only when the offender was a Negro and his victim white and, again, only in 3 cases.

As can be expected, no interracial rapes occurred between close friends or boy friends or between relatives.

Age

The hypothesis which suggests a higher proportion of primary relationships between offenders and victims who are at the same age level is partly supported by the data (table 85). The frequency distribution of VOR

Table 85: Type of Interpersonal Relationship between Victim and Principal Offender by Victim and Offender Age Disparity In Rape Events

	Victim Much Younger (−10 yrs.)		Both Same Age (±5 yrs.)		Victim Much Older (+10 yrs.)		Total	
	No.	%	No.	%	No.	%	No.	%
Stranger	55	32.2	145	39.5	73	67.6	273	42.3
Stranger but general knowledge	11	6.4	44	12.0	7	6.5	62	9.6
Acquaintance	16	9.4	58	15.8	19	17.6	93	14.4
Neighbor (close)	48	28.1	73	19.9	4	3.7	125	19.3
Close friend or boyfriend	9	5.2	29	7.9	1	0.9	39	6.0
Family friend	24	14.0	8	2.2	2	1.9	34	5.3
Relative	7	4.1	7	1.9	2	1.9	16	2.5
No information	1	0.6	3	0.8	...	...	4	0.6
Total	171	100.0	367	100.0	108	100.0	646	100.0

according to victim-offender relative age in rape events reveals some *significant* differences. Categories which involve primary contact, when combined, constitute 61 percent when the victim was much younger than the offender, and 48 percent when the two were at the same age level. When the victim was older than her assailant, in only 26 percent of all relationships did primary contact exist between them (of which 50 percent were between older women who established acquaintanceship with their, mainly drinking, would-be assaulters). The latter result is expected if we remember that most of the felony rapes occurred between victims and offenders with this age difference. Specific differences among types of primary relationships are noted for some of the age disparity between victims and offenders in forcible rape events. When victims were younger than the offender or when they were of the same age group, in over a third of the cases they were acquaintances. Acquaintanceship was observed in 21 percent when the victim was at least 10 years older than the offender. When intimate contact existed between them, in 24 percent of the cases it was between victims who were younger than the offenders, by at least 10 years; in 13 percent when they were at the same age level, but only in 5 percent when the victim was at least 10 years older than the offender. The high proportion of intimate relations between victims who were much younger than the offenders is partly explained by the fact that in 14 percent of the cases, the offender was a family friend who took advantage of the young victim. Among these cases, 9 victims were under 9 years of age, and 12 were between 10 to 14 years of age. It is noted that in the combined categories of "primary" relationships, neighborhood relations rank the highest in frequency among cases when the victim was at least 10 years younger than the offender, as well as when they were at the same age level (20 percent).

Alcohol

The assumption can be made that social drinking is more likely to occur between those who already have had some primary relations with each other. Such an assumption is in line with the previous results about the proportion of rape events in which victim and offender had some primary association. On the other hand, another assumption can be that, other things being equal, alcohol is just as likely to be consumed by strangers who establish a drinking relationship with each other immediately prior to the offense. Also, alcohol can be consumed before the offense either by the victim alone or by the offender alone without any relationships existing between them.

Only the third hypothesis is supported by the data (table 86). The highest proportion of the presence of alcohol in the rape situation is in cases involving strangers (69 percent) where it is twice as high as in events involving primary relations (31 percent). Of the types of primary relations, alcohol is present in 16 percent of the cases among acquaintances and in 15 percent among intimates. When the groupings relative to the presence of alcohol are compared with the various categories of interpersonal relationships only the following emerge to the level of statistical *significance:*

1. *Relationships between strangers and alcohol present in the offender only.* Strangers consumed alcohol together in 54 percent, but in 63 percent only the offender consumed alcohol.
2. *Relationships between strangers and alcohol present in the victim only.* Strangers consumed alcohol together in 54 percent, but in 85 percent alcohol was present in the victim only.

Table 86: Type of Interpersonal Relationship between Victim and Principal Offender by Presence of Alcohol in the Rape Events

	In Both Offender and Victim		In Victim Only		In Offender Only		Total Present in the Rape Situation		Total Absent from the Rape Situation		Grand Total	
	No.	%	No.	%	No.	%	No.	%	No.	%	No.	%
Stranger	31	22.8	48	77.4	10	52.6	89	41.0	184	42.9	273	42.3
Stranger but general knowledge	53	31.0	5	8.1	2	10.5	60	27.6	2	0.5	62	9.6
Acquaintance	13	9.6	1	1.6	1	5.3	15	6.9	78	18.2	93	14.4
Neighbor (close)	13	9.6	5	8.1	2	10.5	70	9.2	105	24.5	125	19.3
Close friend or boyfriend	12	8.8	1	1.6	...	...	13	6.0	26	6.1	39	6.0
Family friend	6	4.4	1	1.6	1	5.3	8	3.7	26	6.1	34	5.3
Relative	8	5.9	...	...	1	5.3	9	4.1	7	1.6	16	2.5
No information	...	...	1	1.6	2	10.5	3	1.4	1	0.2	4	0.6
Total	136	100.0	62	100.0	19	100.0	217	100.0	429	100.0	646	100.0

Note: Analysis is made only on those interpersonal relations in which alcohol was present in the rape situation and for which information is available on interpersonal relationships (n = 214).

3. *Relationships between acquaintance and alcohol present in the offender or the victim only.* Acquaintances in 19 percent consumed alcohol together, but rape occurred only in 16 percent of the cases when only the offender was drinking and in 10 percent when only the victim alone was drinking, prior to the offense.

4. *Intimate relationships.* Although the numbers for intimate relationships are too small to be probed, what emerges is that intimate relationships are characterized by offenders and victims drinking together (19 percent compared to 5 percent when alcohol was present in the victim only, and 11 percent when in the offender only.)

It appears that the third hypothesis regarding interpersonal relationships and the presence of alcohol is accepted, while the second one is partly rejected.

Place of Initial Meeting

In the light of the previous analysis about the place of initial meeting between victim and offender, it can be postulated that the closer the relationship between victim and offender, the greater is the likelihood that their initial meeting will be in his or her place of residence or where either one of them temporarily stayed. Indeed, the frequency distribution of VOR's according to places of initial meeting reveals *significant* differences (table 87). The combination of those categories which involve primary contact constitutes 62 percent when the meeting was in the participants' places, but 38 percent outside their places. Specific differences in the type of primary relation are noted for places of initial meeting between victim and offender. However, both the participants' places or outside them are the places where one third of acquainted victims and offenders met (37 percent and 32 percent, respectively), in 25 percent the participants' places were the meeting places for those in intimate relations. The data further show that when the initial meeting was at the place of one of the participants, in 25 percent of all cases of VOR's the rape occurred between neighbors, and it accounted for 40 percent of all primary contact relations.

When the initial meeting was outside the participants' places, it was mainly the street where victim and offender who were strangers met (67 percent).[14] As was expected, a bar, party, or picnic were the places where acquaintanceship was established; over half of the acquaintance relations between victims and offenders were established there.

14. Included are the categories of the street, in front of a bar, the park, and in the street waiting for transportation.

Table 87: Type of Interpersonal Relationship between Victim and Principal Offender by Place of Initial Meeting for Rape Events

	At Victim's Place		Where Victim Stayed		At Offender Home		On Street Walking		In a Bar		At a Party or Picnic		In the Park		In Street in Front of a Bar		In Street Waiting for Bus or Car		Total	
	No.	%	No.	%	No.	%	No.	%	No.	%	No.	%	No.	%	No.	%	No.	%	No.	%
Stranger	66	38.6	20	38.5	1	2.3	138	51.3	13	26.0	...	...	4	80.0	20	90.9	11	68.8	273	42.3
Stranger but general knowledge	11	6.4	3	5.7	...	...	39	14.5	5	10.0	2	11.8	...	...	1	4.5	1	6.3	62	9.6
Acquaintance	15	8.8	14	27.0	3	7.0	24	8.9	24	48.0	11	64.6	...	...	...	...	2	12.4	93	14.4
Neighbor (close)	32	18.7	7	13.5	26	60.4	55	20.4	1	2.0	2	11.8	1	20.0	...	...	1	6.3	125	14.3
Close friend or boy friend	20	11.7	3	5.7	3	7.0	6	2.2	5	10.	2	11.8	...	...	...	...	...	...	39	6.0
Family friend	19	11.1	2	3.9	8	18.6	4	1.5	...	...	...	...	...	...	1	4.5	...	...	34	5.3
Relative	6	3.5	3	5.7	2	4.7	3	1.1	2	4.0	...	...	...	...	...	...	...	...	16	2.5
No information	2	1.2	...	...	...	...	1	0.4	...	...	...	...	...	...	...	...	1	6.3	4	0.6
Total	171	100.0	52	100.0	43	100.0	270	100.0	50	100.0	17	100.0	5	100.0	20	100.0	16	100.0	646	100.0

Place of Rape

The previous analysis of the relation between place of initial meeting and the place of rape, as well as the results about VOR's and initial meeting, provide the basis for the hypothesis that the closer the relationship between victim and offender, the greater will be the proportion of rapes committed indoors. The data (table 88) support the hypothesis. Among

Table 88: Type of Interpersonal Relationship between Victim and Principal Offender by Place of Rape Events

	Auto		Open Spaces		Indoors—Outside Participant's Place		Indoors—Participant's Place		Total	
	No.	%	No.	%	No.	%	No.	%	No.	%
Stranger	45	46.9	69	60.0	47	62.7	112	31.0	273	42.3
Stranger but general knowledge	8	8.3	13	11.4	10	13.3	31	8.6	62	9.6
Acquaintance	22	22.9	12	10.4	6	8.0	53	14.7	93	14.4
Neighbor (close)	3	3.1	15	13.1	8	10.7	99	27.5	125	19.3
Close friend or boyfriend	12	12.5	1	0.9	4	5.3	22	6.2	39	6.0
Family friend	5	5.3	2	1.8	...	...	27	7.5	34	5.3
Relative	1	1.0	1	0.9	...	...	14	3.9	16	2.5
No information	...	...	2	1.8	...	...	2	0.6	4	0.6
Total	96	100.0	115	100.0	75	100.0	360	100.0	646	100.0

victims who were raped indoors, 60 percent of them had primary contact with their assaulters, while among those who were raped outside, 32 percent had such contacts with the offender. The hypothesis is further supported if we look for specific differences in the type of primary relations according to more specific places of rape. The highest proportion of acquaintance relations appear when the rape was committed in participants' residences (42 percent), which are also the places where the second highest proportion of intimate relations appear. The automobile is the place of rape where 46 percent of the victims had primary relations with the offenders, and in 22 percent they were in intimate relations with each other.

Means Methods: Nonphysical Force

Turning to some other features of the offense it can be postulated that the closer the VOR's are, the greater will be the use of nonphysical means to

Table 89: Type of Interpersonal Relationship between Victim and Principal Offender by Nonphysical Force Used in Rape Events

	Tempting		Coercion		Intimidation without Weapon		Intimidation with Weapon		No Information		Total	
	No.	%	No.	%	No.	%	No.	%	No.	%	No.	%
Stranger	18	24.0	72	44.7	104	44.7	75	55.2	4	50.0	273	42.3
Stranger but general knowledge	6	8.0	10	6.2	30	11.3	16	11.8	...	...	62	9.6
Acquaintance	8	10.7	29	18.0	41	15.4	15	11.0	...	...	93	14.4
Neighbor (close)	20	26.7	33	20.5	51	19.2	20	14.7	1	12.5	125	19.3
Close friend or boyfriend	15	20.0	4	2.5	13	4.9	5	3.7	2	25.0	39	6.0
Family friend	4	5.4	7	4.3	21	7.9	1	0.7	1	12.5	34	5.3
Relative	3	4.0	5	3.1	5	1.9	3	2.2	...	...	16	2.5
No information	1	1.3	1	0.6	1	0.4	1	0.7	...	...	4	0.6
Total	75	100.0	161	100.0	266	100.0	136	100.0	8	100.0	646	100.0

Note: Because there are 8 forcible rapes for which no information is available on the use of nonphysical means and 4 cases for which there is no information on interpersonal relationships, only 634 interpersonal relationships are analyzed.

subdue the victim (table 89). The data show the *significant* difference between the types of VOR's and nonphysical means used in the rape situations. In those situations where "temptation" or "seduction" was used, in 68 percent of them primary relations existed between victims and offenders, while 49 percent of such relationships existed when "coercion" was used, and 44 percent when the victim was intimidated.[15] The differences are still *significant;* the category of "coercion" was combined with "temptation" or with "intimidation." The hypothesis is further supported by the specific differences in the type of primary relations which are noted. Categories of those which involve "intimate" relations, when combined, constitute 30 percent of rape situations where temptation was used, but only 11 percent when coercion was employed and 12 percent when the victim was initially subdued by the use of intimidation. In acquaintanceship between offenders and victims, in 38 percent of the cases the offender tempted the victim, but in the same proportions, coercion was used against her.

15. Included are the two forms of intimidation: with and without weapons.

Table 90: Type of Interpersonal Relationship between Victim and Principal Offender by use and Degrees of Violence in Rape Events

	No Use of Force		Rough-ness		Non-brutal Beating		Brutal Beatings		Total No Use of Force		Total Use of Force		Grand Total	
	No.	%	No.	%	No.	%	No.	%	No.	%	No.	%	No.	%
Stranger	35	36.5	65	35.3	64	40.0	109	52.9	35	36.5	238	43.3	273	42.3
Stranger but general knowledge	4	4.2	21	11.4	18	11.2	19	9.2	4	4.2	58	10.5	62	9.6
Acquaintance	10	10.4	24	13.0	26	16.2	33	16.0	10	10.4	83	15.1	93	14.4
Neighbor (close)	29	30.2	41	22.3	31	19.4	24	11.7	29	30.2	96	17.5	125	19.3
Close friend or boyfriend	3	3.1	16	8.7	9	5.6	11	5.3	3	3.1	36	6.5	39	6.0
Family friend	10	10.4	9	3.8	8	5.0	7	3.4	10	10.4	24	4.4	34	5.3
Relative	3	3.1	7	4.9	4	2.5	2	0.9	3	3.1	13	2.4	16	2.5
No information	2	2.1	1	0.5	...	...	1	0.4	2	2.1	2	0.4	4	0.6
Total	96	100.0	185	100.0	160	100.0	206	100.0	96	100.0	550	100.0	646	100.0

Note: Categories of nonbrutal beating before, during, and after rape were combined. Brutal beating includes categories of before, during, and after rape and the category of choking.

Violence

The foregoing results about the association between VOR's and the use of nonphysical force leads to the assumption that the closer the relationship between victim and offender, the less violent be the rapes. The data (table 90), do not support the hypothesis and the differences are *significant* in reverse, i.e., the closer the relationship between victim and offender, the greater is the violence used against the victim. Among those cases where violence was used, 54 percent involved strangers, while among nonviolent cases, in 41 percent the participants were strangers. Among violent rapes, in 46 percent some primary relations existed between victim and offender compared to 59 percent of nonviolent rapes. Among the specific categories of primary relations, the highest proportions of violence were among neighbors and acquaintances.

As for the degrees of violence used in primary relationships, the highest proportion of nonbrutal beatings were among acquaintances (16 percent) while the highest proportions of brutal beatings were among neighbors (19 percent). From this and previous results it seems that neighbors and acquaintances are the most potentially dangerous people as far as brutal rape is concerned. These results which led to reversing the hypothesis may reflect the fact that the offender who is trusted by the victim, establishing or having primary relationships with her, must subdue her instantly, especially when the offense takes place (as found in high proportion) in the residence of one of the participants, or place where he or she stayed. Also, since violence comes after the initial manipulation of the victim by temptation or coercion,[16] the latter were ineffective measures for subduing the victim and made the use of violence necessary.

It should be noted that no differences exist in the distribution of VOR's according to sexual humiliation to which the victim was subjected in the rape situation. Among those cases where sexual humiliation was practiced, in 50 percent of them it was on victims who had some degree of primary relations with the offender, while sexual humiliation was absent from the rape situation in 47 percent when primary relationships existed. Among the specific categories of primary relationships, the highest proportion of sexual humiliation was again between neighbors (19 percent) and acquaintances (16 percent). In 9 percent lovers subjected their girl friends to such practices.

Victim Behavior

The foregoing analysis already tends to discard the assumption that forcible rape is an event where a woman is attacked, without warning, by

16. When the victim was tempted, in 30 percent of the cases she was either beaten brutally or nonbrutally before the rape.

an offender who is unknown to her. On the basis of this it can be postulated that rape situations, where primary relations exist between the victim and offender, will be characterized by less resistance on the part of the victim. The assumption is not fully borne-out (table 91) although some differences do exist in the distribution of victim-offender relations according to victim behavior in the rape situation. Among strangers, in 52

Table 91: Type of Interpersonal Relationship between Victim and Principal Offender by Victim's Behavior in Rape Events

	Submissive		Resistance		Fight		No Information		Total	
	No.	%	No.	%	No.	%	No.	%	No.	%
Stranger	155	43.7	79	45.7	39	33.6	...	...	273	42.3
Stranger, but general knowledge	30	8.5	20	11.6	12	10.3	...	...	62	9.6
Acquaintance	44	12.4	31	17.9	18	15.5	...	...	93	14.4
Neighbor (close)	73	20.6	30	17.3	21	18.1	1	50.0	125	19.3
Close friend or boyfriend	18	5.1	8	4.6	12	10.3	1	50.0	39	6.0
Family friend	21	5.7	4	2.3	9	7.9	...	...	34	5.3
Relative	12	3.4	1	0.6	3	2.6	...	...	16	2.5
No information	2	0.6	...	...	2	1.7	...	...	4	0.6
Total	355	100.0	173	100.0	116	100.0	2	100.0	646	100.0

Note: Because there are 2 cases for which no information is available on victim's behavior and 4 cases for which there is no information on interpersonal relationship, only 640 interpersonal relationships are analyzed.

percent of the events, the victim behaved submissively toward her assailants, while in 57 percent she resisted them. In 48 percent the victim fought. Among those victims who had some degree of primary contact with the offenders, 48 percent submitted without any resistance or fight, 43 percent resisted, and 55 percent fought their assailants. Further rejection of the hypothesis is found in the fact that among those involved in primary relations, a larger proportion of acquaintances (34 percent) and a larger proportion of intimates fought in the rape situation. In general, it appears that the degree of intimacy of personal relationships has little direct association with victim behavior in the rape situation.

Type of Rape

From the previously noted characteristics of multiple rape situations, and from the foregoing discussion of VOR, we may postulate that, com-

Table 92: Type of Interpersonal Relationship between Victim and Principal Offender, by Types of Rape, Leader and Nonleader in Rape Events

	Offender in SR		Leader in PR		Second Offender		Leader in GR		Offender in GR		Total		Single Rape		Pair Rape		Group Rape		Total	
	No.	%	No.	%	No.	%	No.	%	No.	%	No.	%	No.	%	No.	%	No.	%	No.	%
Stranger	147	39.7	54	51.4	54	51.4	72	42.1	127	23.6	454	35.1	147	39.7	54	51.4	72	42.1	273	42.3
Stranger, but general knowledge	19	5.1	17	16.2	17	16.2	26	15.2	79	14.4	158	12.2	19	5.1	17	16.2	26	15.2	62	9.6
Acquaintance	45	12.2	18	17.1	19	18.1	30	17.5	127	23.6	239	18.5	45	12.2	18	17.1	30	17.5	93	14.4
Neighbor (close)	75	20.3	14	13.3	15	14.3	36	21.1	182	33.6	322	24.9	75	20.3	14	13.3	36	21.1	125	19.3
Close friend or boyfriend	34	9.2	1	1.0	...	...	4	2.3	19	3.5	58	4.4	34	9.2	1	1.0	4	2.3	39	6.0
Family friend	32	8.6	...	...	...	...	2	1.2	7	1.3	41	3.4	32	8.6	...	...	2	1.2	34	5.3
Relative	15	4.1	1	1.0	...	...	...	...	...	...	16	1.2	15	4.1	1	1.0	...	...	16	2.5
No information	3	0.8	...	...	...	...	1	0.6	...	...	4	0.3	3	0.8	...	...	1	0.6	4	0.6
Total	370	100.0	105	100.0	105	100.0	171	100.0	541	100.0	1,292	100.0	370	100.0	105	100.0	171	100.0	646	100.0

pared to SR's, more victims and offenders in MR situations are strangers to each other. The homogeneous features of the participants in multiple rape (in terms of race, age, etc.) allow us to assume further that such homogeneity exists for the types of interpersonal relationships, except for the leader or the "central" person. He may be the one who is closer to the victim than his followers. This will be especially true for those situations in which the leader or "central" person allows the subjection of his girl friend to sexual exploitation by the whole group.

In general, the data support our first assumption regarding type of rape and victim-offender relationships. The differences according to types of rape are statistically significant (table 92). When categories which involve relations between strangers are combined, they constitute 62 percent of MR situations compared to 45 percent of SR situations. Thus, categories of "primary" relationships, when combined, constitute 38 percent of MR cases and 55 percent of SR situations. When PR's, GR's, and SR's are compared, it is noticed that PR's indicate a higher proportion of relations between strangers than GR's (68 percent and 57 percent, respectively), the reason may be, partly, that pair rape as a dyad type of relationship is more a homogeneous group than GR, which may include offenders who stand in different relations to the victim. Acquaintance relationships constitute 37 percent of all victim-offender relationships among MR situations, and 32 percent among SR situations. Such is not the case, however, for GR situations for they constitute 39 percent when the relationships are that of acquaintances, compared to 30 percent of PR situations and 32 percent of SR's. Although the total number of intimate relations for MR situations is too small to be statistically significant (2 cases for PR's and 6 cases for GR's), these results point out the fact that MR's are not likely to occur between intimates but mainly between strangers and in cases of primary relationships between acquaintances. As we stated, the main danger to the community is not the lone stranger who will attack indiscriminately (in 55 percent this type had some primary contact and in 23 percent an intimate contact with his victim). Rather, the danger seems to be the groups of 2, 3, or more males who are more likely to seek their victims among women unknown to them. For all types of rape, however, established acquaintanceship or exposure to close neighbors, may lead to the victimization of the female (in over 30 percent and for all types of rape.)

The assumption, concerning the relationships of the leader to the victim as compared to nonleaders, is rejected by the data. A higher proportion of leaders (61 percent; compared to 45 percent of followers), were strangers to their victims. Further rejection of the hypothesis is found by the fact that a larger proportion of acquaintance by intimates were among nonleaders (in PR's and GR's) than among leaders. It appears that the degree of intimacy of personal relationships has little direct association with leaderships in MR situations, but that other variables (some of which already have been analyzed) are involved in leadership phenomena in multiple rape situations.

As to the role of the leader who has closer relations with the victim and who exploits this to subject her to group rape, such was found to be the case in 4 occasions, there the leader was the victim's boy friend and in 5 situations he established acquaintance with a drinking would-be-victim, brought her to his apartment and invited the other males to exploit her sexually.

Victim Offender Relationships Noted in Other Studies

In the attempt to compare the present study with other research, a lack of data became evident; and that which is available poses some major difficulties. First, if relationships are identified at all, they are rarely the same because their classifications are incomparable. Second, most lacking is the connection between the general aspect of victim-offender relationships, their social and personal characteristics, and other dimensions of the crime. What is attempted in the following paragraphs is a review of the general similarities and divergences between the present study and others found in the literature.

In the *Report of the Mayor's Committee* a statement is made and is repeated again in later studies: "In most sex crimes, the fact that a particular girl is a victim of sex assaulters is no accident."[17] This report, however, does not discuss any further the social relationship between victim and offender. Whyte has shown in his study that some girls are less apt to victimization while for others, because of their relationship with boys, rape is a standing threat.[18] A distinction is made between "good girls" with whom sex relationships are prohibited, and girls with "bad reputations," with whom sex, in any form, including use of force, is accepted if not desired. The same findings were reported in studies on adolescent gangs.[19] In these studies the likelihood that certain girls will be exempt from forays against them increases with the proximity to the peer groups, that is, with the increase of contact and duration of the relationship between the potential victim and her assailant(s).

The studies which deal specifically with VOR are numbered, and from some of them we can make only some inferences about this aspect. In

17. *Report of the Mayor's Committee*, p. 72.

18. "A Slum Sex Code."

19. Bloch and Niederhoffer, p. 104; Reiss, "Sex Offenses"; Salisbury, pp. 33–34; Short, Jr., "Street Corner Groups."

surveys emphasis is made on the fact that victims are not strangers to their assaulters. The psychiatric school is mainly interested in the psychological dynamics in the encounter between the girl and the stranger who later victimized her.

One of the California studies found that the victims of juvenile rapists "most frequently make a pick-up date with a stranger or near stranger (and), almost as frequently the girl knew the boy but was not in love with or engaged to him."[20] Another sample found that the girls enter relations with offenders who are not unknown to them. Of a group of all sex offenders convicted in San Francisco Superior Court between 1950 and 1951, in only about one-third of the cases was the victim involved in sex relations with a stranger.[21] In half of the cases the sex partner was a friend or at least an acquaintance, and in 20 instances the participants were more closely related to each other.[22]

One of the purposes of the Michigan study was to dismiss the notion that the rapist randomly strikes women who are unknown to him, a factor which stirs most violently the imagination and the reaction of the community.[23] In searching the files of Detroit police for the year 1949, it was found that among 81 cases of forcible rape, 46 (or 57 percent) of the victims were known to the offender; while in 35 cases (or 43 percent), they were strangers. This means that the hazard to the females in the community of becoming a victim of an unknown attacker is then lessened by 50 percent.

Compared to the Michigan study, the proportion of rapists who were absolute strangers to their victims is greater in the New York study conducted by Glueck.[24] In 67 percent of the rape cases, the offender was a total stranger to the victim. In 10 percent he was either a relative or a close friend of the victim's family, and in 20 percent the offenders were either casual (neighborhood, etc.) or visual acquaintances. The State of Wisconsin attempted to review the results of the enactment of the sex deviate laws.[25] In this study, two aspects of victim-offender relationships were separately surveyed: type of relationship and number and duration of prior contacts between offenders and their victims. It was found that in 28 (or 87 percent) of 33 cases of rape victims and offenders were strangers to one another.[26] Among the 33 cases of rape, in 30 cases (or 91 percent)

20. *California Sexual Deviation Research* (1954), p. 118.

21. Ibid., p. 111.

22. There were 9 cases of rape in the whole sample. The relationship between victims and offenders for these 9 rape events is, however, not specified.

23. Dunham, pp. 37–38.

24. *New York Final Report,* p. 295.

25. *Wisconsin's Experience,* appendix tables 15, 17.

26. Other kinds of relationships were not specified except for three cases of incest.

the contact between the offender and his victim was the first and only contact, and only in one case were there many contacts spread over a period of 6 months.

Among European investigations, Svalastoga's study is the most relevant to our study, since he reports on a study of rape cases only.[27] He hypothesizes that between a rapist and his victim "anonymity or a condition of low interaction prevails prior to the offense." He finds, that "no mutual acquaintance existed in 76, or 54 percent of the samples ($N = 141$)." In 29 (or 21 percent) of the cases, the acquaintance between the offender and the victim was "brief," "superficial" or "indirect." "Long acquaintanceship" or "relations as relatives" existed in 14 percent and 8 percent of the cases respectively.[28]

In two studies which dealt with forcible rape, among other offenses, the relationship between victims and offenders can only be inferred. Goldberg describes the background and circumstances of sexual relations of girls who were involved in forcible rape, statutory rape, promiscuity, and prostitution.[29] All these kinds of sexual involvement he terms "rape." However, more than half of these girls were actually raped, as determined by him, by the fact that they actually resisted their offender. Of these girls, the majority were seduced and attacked by strangers. In almost one-fifth they were victims of relatives or family friends.

Landis investigated the traumatic sex experiences in childhood of 500 college girls. Of the 500 girls, 20 percent were forcibly raped. To 31 percent of these victims the offender was known prior to the offense. An interesting difference was found between city girls and those who came from rural areas. Of the first group 27 percent knew the offender before the offense, while the proportion for the rural girls was 66 percent.

An interesting study is that by Kanin on what might be termed as a "dating" type rape.[30] He investigated coeds who experienced sexual attack when dating males. He found that only in 25 percent of the cases the situations were devoid of sexual intimacies before the unfortunate event. In most of the cases those involved were "steady dates," that is, there was a prior durable and intimate relationship between the boy and the girl. In 25 percent the attack occurred after either mutual drinking, a "wild party," or a tête-à-tête relationship between them in a car. It seems that the higher the level of sexual intimacy which the girl allows herself to enter with her date, the more vulnerable she becomes to being raped.[31]

27. Svalastoga, pp. 51–52.

28. No information in 5 cases, or 4 percent.

29. Goldberg, chaps. 1–4.

30. See also Kanin and Kirkpatrick.

31. Rape as a consequence of intimate sexual play where the offender does not believe the victim's protest and is unable to stand the tension and frustration is suggested as early as 1918 by Huhmer.

Moreover, it is neither the "blind date" with a stranger nor the number of dates she has which determines the chances of the girl to be victimized. Rather, it is the intensity of the relationships which may enhance the probability of victimization (although sexual attack did occur, also, suddenly in a casual date). It seems fair to us to hypothesize that girls walk a tight rope when they try, in a date, to play the dangerous game of posing as a possible "bad" girl who in the end turns out to be a "good" girl. Alas, the situation is likely to have an unfortunate end.[32]

32. See also *California Deviation Research* (1954), pp. 132–35; Coleman, chaps. 3, 4; Ehrmann, "Premarital Sex."

14

The Potential Victim and the Vulnerable Rape Situation

From the patterns of forcible rape described and analyzed previously we can shed some light on two aspects of rape: the likelihood that only certain females will become victims of forcible rape and the choice of victims by the offenders. To state it differently, the question is of the situations or characteristics of certain potential victims which may actually bring about the offense. The rape event may be a confluence of these related analytically separate aspects.

The question of the likelihood of becoming a victim has been dealt with mainly within the psychological framework, but we can distinguish three broad approaches: that of victimization as a potential factor in every woman, stated mainly in psychoanalytic terms, the psychopathological approach which emphasizes emotional and mental disturbances of some females, and the sociological approach which lays stress upon adolescence or status problems of girls. The common element in these approaches is the emphasis on risk factors. The approaches differ in ascribing potentiality for becoming a rape victim first, to the personality structure of every female, and the second and third, to some psychological deviation or social conditions which enhance the potentiality of certain girls to be victimized.

The underlying idea of the psychoanalytic school of thought is the tendency for victimization as a universal condition of every woman. It assumes the idea of "polymorphic perverse" characteristic of humans.[1]

1. S. Freud, "Three Essays."

Reflected in women is the tendency for passivity and masochism,[2] and a universal desire to be violently possessed[3] and aggressively handled by men.[4] Some writers even claim that there is a universal wish among women to be raped[5] or at least to be forcefully seduced by strangers.[6]

Entering the role of a victim may alleviate anxiety and mollify the feelings of guilt which the forbidden wishes evoke,[7] and it will allow a taste of the "sweetness of stolen waters."[8] Sometimes the very fear of rape may activate a "riddance rape," whereby those who suffer from such fear may get rid of anxiety by doing the very thing that is feared, or the victim may yield to being raped in order "to get it over with."[9] Whatever is one's judgment on such views,[10] it follows that rape may be a primarily pleasurable event or provides a secondary gain as a liberating experience.[11]

The psychiatric approach, using the psychoanalytic concepts and reasoning, emphasizes the pathological personality and deviant behavior of victims of sex offenses and rape, especially of young or adolescent girls who are mainly of a lower-class origin.[12] Psychiatry attempts to identify the psychological dynamics which favor the victimization of some girls, who are believed to be, if not actually seductive, at least unconscious participants in the rape event. These girls, who come from homes where they are rejected, or from otherwise "bad" environment,[13] and who lack sexual guidance along with family protection, tend to mature rapidly. As a result, they act out against their homes, their environments and become sexually precocious.[14] Looking for new experiences which afford them a

2. H. Deutsch, vol. 1; Fenichel; Halleck.

3. Jenkins, p. 131; Murray, p. 135.

4. Alexander, *Fundamentals,* p. 127; Ferenczi, "Sex and Psychoanalysis."

5. Eidelberg, chap. 1.

6. Abraham, "The Experiencing of Sexual Traumas"; S. Freud, *New Introductory Lectures in Psychoanalysis,* p. 151.

7. Abrahamsen, *The Psychology of Crime,* p. 161; Alexander, *Fundamentals,* p. 122.

8. Eidelberg, p. 15.

9. Slovenko and Philips.

10. On the logical and scientific merit of psychoanalytic theory see Hook, *Psychoanalysis,* esp. chaps. 1, 4.

11. Devereaux, "Awarding"; Factor.

12. Also dealt with in these studies is the problem of the effect of the offense or sexual trauma on the victim's personality and her later social and psychological adjustment.

13. Abbott; Bender and Blau; Dunham, pp. 75–83; Goldberg, chap. 2; Meyer, "Girls Involved in Sex Offenses," pp. 160–63.

14. Atckeson and Williams; Weisse.

false sense of protection, attention, and status, these girls will easily enter relationships and situations fraught with dangers of sexual exploitation and humiliation.

The sociologists emphasize the status problems of adolescent girls, but they are less specific about the relationships between this condition and the girls' sexual deviancy. However, some inferences can be made from their writings for our present problem of the potential victim. If the boy uses sex mainly as an end in itself, though also to achieve status and prestige by outside manipulation of people and objects (including sexual conquests),[15] the girl emphasizes sex as a means to an end to achieve status in terms of popularity and personal appeal.[16] She does it by using her sex, which is her natural area of competition[17] and which is also appropriate for the values and expectations of the female sex roles.[18] When girls are rejected at home, sex may become for them an avenue to achieve love and intimacy, a sense of being cared for as individuals.[19] They will, therefore, enter unstructured superficial relations with strangers and in these situations use their sex as a means for ego enhancement.[20] The acting out of their resentment toward home through careless sexual behavior is not only a liberating behavior, as it is thought in the psychiatric approach, but carries with it social (status) and material gains. It is Thomas, who suggested that it is not passion which is the important factor in these situations, but the feeling of being free and sophisticated and of participating in a new and adventurous life which is exciting and socially rewarding.[21]

The aspect of rape concerned with the factors which determine the selection of victims by the offender involves many psychological considerations, especially those of the offender motivation and personality. These are factors which are beyond the scope of the present study. For sociologists, the question becomes that of observing those situations where chance factors alone will operate, or those situations where victim's behavior, victim-offender interpersonal relations, and other elements increase the likelihood of certain women becoming victims of forcible rape.

The derivative consideration is whether or not some particular vic-

15. Grosser.

16. Reiss, "Sex Offenses," p. 319; Waller.

17. A. K. Cohen, *Delinquent Boys,* pp. 137–45; Cohen and Short, "Research in Delinquent Subcultures," pp. 34–36.

18. Green, "The 'Cult of Personality.' "

19. Plant, *The Envelope,* p. 121.

20. Grosser, pp. 110–12. The structural "steady" date situation, however, is no less dangerous to the girl: see Kanin.

21. Thomas, p. 109.

tims are specifically sought by offenders because they have assumed special characteristics which attract the offender. Thus, the Negro victim may be chosen by the white offender because of the myth of Negro women's sexuality,[22] or the child victim will be sought by an adult,[23] or by an old offender for various reasons.[24] Again, it is mainly a psychopathological problem which involves "fetish" qualities which the victim may have for a particular offender.[25]

True, there might be some chance factors which are operating in the choice of the victim, many without our being able to prove or qualify them. Also, and for our purpose, unfortunately, in the interrogation, the police rarely ask the offender why he chose a particular victim but only the "when" and "where" and "how" of the offense, as well as how the victim behaved prior to, during, and after the offense. For these reasons, we believe the analysis and the assumptions about the victim's behavior and her "selection" can and must be made on the situational factors, without denying, however, the importance of psychological ones. The offender, for instance, might have been sexually hungry because of his wife's pregnancy (occurred in our study in 2 cases of single rape) or might be just out of prison and, again, sexually hungry (2 cases of single rape and a leader in pair rape), but we are not inclined to look for other cases in which sexual hunger may be the "motive" for the offense.

Before turning, therefore, to the situational factors which make the choice of the victim less haphazard and fortuitous, let us hypothesize what the offender does not find, or does not intend to find, in any victim, whatever the reason she was chosen. It seems to us that the rape situation is the opposite of what may be found in love relationships.

According to Parson's scheme of "modes of orientation" between "ego" and "alter," the relationship of the man to his loved one is "diffuse," "particular," and "achieved."[26] On the other hand in the rape situation rapists may have many motives but one intent; and thus the orientation of the rapist toward his victim is "specific" (sex rather than the whole personality is the major consideration in entering the relationships— disregarding for a moment the view that sexual assault is a symptom of a

22. Dollard, pp. 137, 143–45; Kardiner and Ovesey, pp. 69–70.

23. On the problem of pedophilia see Mohr, Turner, and Jerry.

24. For the reason that the old sex offender chooses a child victim see: Apfelberg, et al.; East; Fox, "Intelligence"; Frosch and Bromberg; Grossberg; Hartman and Schroeder; Henninger; Moberg; Ploscowe, *Crime and Criminology*, p. 7; Revitch and Weiss; Schroeder; Toobert, Bartelmea, and Jones; Wile, "Sex Offenders."

25. For a general but still classic discussion see Stekel.

26. Parsons and Shils, chap. 1.

substitute of another nonsexual emotion) and "universal" (almost any victim will do unless there is a fetish element which may be present and compel the offender to choose a particular victim). Difficult, however, is the distinction between "ascribed" vs. "achieved" modes of orientation. This is so because being a female is being in an "ascribed" status, while certain actions on the female's part may put her in the position of "achieved" status of a victim (a defenseless, drunken woman, or a girl with "bad" reputation, etc.).

Also, in contrast to the case of love relationships, where the well-being of the loved one is of prime concern, the victim's well-being does not interest her assailant. Furthermore, the offender is not interested in bestowing and/or receiving affection from the object, nor is any idealization of her developed.[27] On the contrary, some contempt and hate exist and develop between them. Even the seduction of the victim is likely to be absent, and the niceties of the love game are almost completely abstracted from the rape situation. The ideal of courting, of "pursued" or "pursuer," so paramount in love relationships does not exist in the rape situation.[28] As between lovers, the offender desires to possess the female, but, unlike in the love situation, he enforces this wish upon the victim. In contrast to a love relationship which the male attempts to lengthen to an "ever after" connection, rape is rather short and specific.

We could inquire how the situational or the fetish characteristics which only *certain* or specific victims have for *some* offenders, and the relationships which exist or are established between them actually brought about the offense. To answer such a question one has to analyze each rape event; a venture we did not intend to undertake.

We have already stated that although there is a degree of random selection in the choice of the victim by the offender, the choice is not wholly so. There are conspicuous exemptions in the negative sense; that is, some girls are more likely to be victimized. Some girls are chosen because of their "bad" reputations;[29] hence, their sexual self-determination may be easily brushed aside,[30] possibly with the idea that because of this "reputation" the consequential criminal process won't be involved.[31]

27. For a classical discussion on these aspects of love, see Fraz; for a cynical view, see DeBalzac; for an analysis of the conflict which stems from the welfare orientation toward the idealization of the love object, see Reik, esp. pt. 2; for solutions of the conflict see the "naturalist" stance of Gyon; for the "humanistic" stance see Fromm.

28. For historical development of this aspect see DeRougemount.

29. Whyte, "A Slum Sex Code."

30. On the cognitive aspects of denying the victim see Matza and Sykes; on the more emotional and psychological dynamics see Redl and Wineman, *The Aggressive Child*, pp. 144–56.

31. Goldstein.

Since the analysis involved in this study renders us unable to answer the question of chance and/or fetish choices, let us instead examine the factors emerging from our study which increase the probability of certain females becoming victims of forcible rape. The following is the list of such situational factors:

1. when would-be victims and offenders of single and multiple rape events are either of the same race or age or both; or

2. when the victim is white and at least ten years older than her Negro assailant, who committed felony rape;

3. when offenders, Negro and white, live in the same area where victims of their own race and of the same age level live, in an area which is also that where the crime is committed;

4. when offenders are of the same race and age level as their victims and meet them in the warm months, on weekends, and/or during the evening and night hours;

5. when alcohol is present in both the offender (white) and the victim (either white or Negro) or when alcohol is present in the victim only, especially when her assailant is white;

6. when a Negro woman is a victim of felony rape committed by a Negro offender;

7. when a Negro victim has a "bad" reputation;

8. when an initial meeting place between the offender and the victim is either the victim's home or place where she stayed at that time; a place which allowed or encouraged the development of an acquaintanceship; or when such relationships already existed between close neighbors;

9. when a group of offenders plans the rape on victims of their own race who live in the same vicinity;

10. when primary relations exist between victims and offenders who are neighbors, of the same race and age level, and especially when close neighbor relationships exist between them; or when they establish drinking relationships just prior to the offense; or when a drinking woman is accosted by a stranger (usually of her own race) in the street.

Enumerated here are the factors in the rape situation found to be present in significant proportions. These are situations in which rapes are more likely to occur, but are not to be considered as "causes" of the offense. Thus, not in every instance of their presence will rape occur. Furthermore, they are not mutually exclusive, and some of them may appear together as contributory factors in the same event.

15

Victim-Precipitated Forcible Rape

In a way, the victim is always the cause of the crime; every crime needs a victim or his extension—that is, something which belongs to him. The general model of the victim's role in crime is that of the passive, weak, and vulnerable opposing the doer. The victim is seen as one prospective subject among other alternatives, and some of her characteristics, and situational opportune elements make the offender drawn to her, or he may seek her particularly because of special motives, or she seems to offer the least resistance. In this victim-doer model presented by Von Hentig, the offender is the acting-out agent and the question is why the particular victim was chosen. The concept of victim precipitation (VP) rests on another model: victim-doer-victim. Here, the victim is the one who is acting out, initiating the interaction between her and the offender, and by her behavior she generates the potentiality for criminal behavior of the offender or triggers this potentiality, if it existed before in him. Her behavior transforms him into a doer by directing his criminal intentions which not only lead to the offense but also may shape its form.

We are accustomed to believe that forcible rape is an act "which falls upon the victim without her aid or cooperation, . . . but there is some reciprocal action between perpetrator and victim in such cases; . . . this junction, however, is not specific, and, therefore, presents no changeable and preventable relation."[1] This passage from Von Hentig's pioneering paper, along with his other work,[2] provides the framework for the present

1. Von Hentig, "Remarks," p. 304.
2. Von Hentig, *The Criminal,* chap. 12.

259

analysis. It turns our attention to the fact that once the victim and the offender are drawn together, a process is set in motion whereby victim behavior and the situation which surrounds the encounter will determine the course of events which inevitably leads to the crime. The contingencies of events may not make the victim solely responsible for what becomes an unfortunate event; at least she is a complementary partner, and victimization is not, then, a wholly and genuinely random affair.[3]

Previously, we have discussed the theories which attempted to explain the tendency of some women to become potential participants either passively or actively. From this discussion a typology of victim behavior can be made along a continuum which will include the accidental victim on the one hand, and the consciously or unconsciously seductive on the other (fig. 2).

FIG. 2. A typology of victim behavior

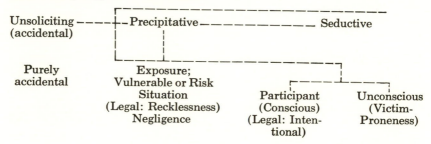

This typology assumes interrelationships and graduated interaction before and during the initial encounter between victim and offender. However, the typology and the process initiated by the encounter should include another category, that of precipitation.

Following Webster, precipitation means "acting out with unwise haste . . . or exhibiting lack of due consideration or care." It is a behavior which is clearly differentiated from "provocation" and outright "seduction." If the dictionary definition is clear, such is not always the case when a judgment is called for or when behavior ceases to be precipitating and becomes provocative or seductive. This aspect of judgment and evaluation will be discussed presently.

Theoretically, victim precipitation of rape means that in a particular situation the behavior of the victim is interpreted by the offender either

3. For a theoretical background on victim precipitated criminal homicide also anchored in Von Hentig's work but containing other classic and modern theoretical statements, see Wolfgang, *Patterns*, pp. 245–46. For the victim-doer-victim model see Reckless *The Crime Problem*, pp. 137–44.

as a direct invitation for sexual relations or as a sign that she will be available for sexual contact if he will persist in demanding it.

Excluded are the situations where no interaction was established between the offender and the victim, and when the offense was a sudden event which befell the victim.

Victim behavior consists of acts of commission (e.g., she agreed to drink or ride with a stranger) and omission (e.g., she failed to react strongly enough to sexual suggestions and overtures). This distinction is made besides the variety of interpersonal relationships which may exist between them. Thus, a "passive" victim like an "active" one, becomes a "mark" if the offender's interpretation leads him to exploit her.[4]

The behavior can be of an outright and overt seduction, or covert and suggestive. Whether it is really so is not as important as the offender's interpretation of her actions within the then current situation. Because even if erroneous, it leads to action. Also, such interpretation helps the offenders to legitimate their behavior and explicate guilt, or neutralize the moral implication of the act by using victim behavior as validation of their image of the victim. "Teasers," "easy mark," are stereotypes of low moral worthiness, and are part of the code under which females become legitimate objects of probable victimization. Thus the offender may see the victim's behavior as being contrary to the expectation about appropriate female behavior as well as conflicting with the whole image of a woman's propriety (that is, rape will be seen as a sort of punishment "she deserved" or "had coming to her").

The situational aspect contains all the elements suggested above in our discussion on "vulnerable situations" and need not be elaborated again. These are risk, victim-exposing and disposing situations which, together with the victim's behavior, become aggravating circumstances. Without them we shall find a potential offender without a victim and/or a potential victim without an offender. With them, we observe a situation in which the victims' behavior and the offenders' imputations make both of them possible candidates for the event.

The relationship between behavior and situation and how it is interpreted assumes the interdependency of culture and individual psychology.[5] The psychological disposition of people embedded in their culture will tend to produce an interrelationship between different modes of verbal expression and behavior in any realm of life.[6] In the sexual sphere, a man can interpret verbal and nonverbal behavior on the part of

4. This is the psychological type of victim called "wanton" by Von Hentig in "Remarks."

5. Bohannan, p. 28.

6. This is the theme of Goffman's work (see pp. 1–16).

a woman in such a way that she will be placed in the category of a sexually available female.[7] Thus, wrongly or rightly, a woman's behavior, if passive, may be seen as worthy to suit action, and if active it may be taken as an actual promise of success to one's sexual intentions.[8] The offender then will react as seems appropriate toward such a woman. Her subsequent behavior and the situation can enhance his interpretation. In short, rationalizations and interpretations "will precede whatever overt sexual gesture toward her that he may make."[9]

Imputations and subjective meanings or actual rationalizations of social situations are a recognized position in understanding social behavior and social interaction.[10] The question is why is the victim's behavior and the situation in which she is placed interpreted to mean her sexual availability? Again, the interrelationship between society and individual,[11] not the logic and the truth about the victim's behavior, is important here. It is highly probable that often the offender will misinterpret the behavior and the situation and draw wrong conclusions about the character of the victim and about the ripeness of the situation for sexual exploits.[12]

There is no problem of validation or of evaluating the truth of the offender's interpretation. Even if wrong, it leads to action. Therefore, whatever is the case, the behavior and its (mis)interpretation made the female enter either symbolically, or actually, a situation in which her behavior and the situations are "suggestive" and from which one can infer sexual accessibility. Thus, her resistance, if made, is not taken seriously; or the situation and the offender "motive" becomes such that her protestations are overridden.

A note should be injected about one type of offender for whom no interpretation of victim behavior or assessment of the situation is ever assumed. He may indiscriminately and randomly attack any victim, no matter what her behavior. This is the so-called compulsive offender, or the one inflicted with "irresistible" impulse. Sociologists and criminologists seek to dismiss this type as a psychiatric entity and to view him in a social psychological framework. Thus, role theory regards "compulsive" behavior as a selective pattern rather than as repetitious uncontrolled con-

7. Dunham, pp. 38–39; Lawton and Archer, p. 111.

8. These distinctions are not mutually exclusive but seem the most typical.

9. Hartung, pp. 159–60.

10. See: Pitt; Thomas, pp. 121–44. For an appeal for a situational sociology, see: Carr, esp. pp. 9–45; Hinkle and Hinkle, pp. 57–66. For criminological studies emphasizing the situational approach see Cressey, *Other People's Money;* Lindesmith. On the court situation see W. G. Elliasberg, "The Acute Psychological Situation."

11. See Lanzer.

12. On the problem of misinterpretation of another's behavior and of situational settings see: Burke; Heider; Ichheiser; Schutz.

duct.[13] Furthermore, the traditional concept of compulsive behavior views the one who "suffers" from it in terms of biological or instinctual manifestations for the existence of which there is no evidence. On the other hand, a sociological approach to the problem of compulsive behavior, as well as of behavior due to irresistible impulse,[14] regards them also as sociocultural learned types of behavior. Such an approach recognizes the importance of cultural mileau in understanding the criminal behavior of repeaters and prior record of offenses or the sequence of their offenses.[15] These offenses are more likely to be an expression of subcultural "themes" rather than merely a matter of personality disintegration.[16]

The investigator, the law officer, and the court may never know why the offender misconstrues the situation, and they will be completely wrong in considering the victim's behavior and the situation as the "motive for the offense." Asking the offender "why" he interpreted the situation and victim behavior as he did implies that there may be an excuse or a rationalization, while emphasis on vulnerable situations enables the investigator to explain why not all males will resort to rape provided they do not suffer from a certain pathology.[17] Also, the investigator, the police, the witnesses, and the court in dealing with cases of seductiveness, all make interpretations and suppositions about seductiveness and precipitations, which are hard to define and difficult to prove or disprove. Another problem is that every aspect in the situation may incur a selective and differential perception which tends to be screened, tainted, and hence, distorted.[18] The end result of all these factors may be that the police, the witnesses, and the court may, in their interpretation of the victim's

13. See: Cressey, "Role Theory"; Wooton, *Social Science and Social Pathology,* pp. 234–35.

14. On the history of this concept see Fink. For proponents of this concept see: Guttmacher and Weihofen, *Psychiatry and the Law;* Weihofen. For critical views, see Hall, *General Principles of Criminal Law,* pp. 472–76. For critical analysis of the claims of psychiatry see Hakeem. Within the field of psychiatry see Szasz.

15. Wolfgang and Ferracuti, "Violent Aggressive Behavior."

16. The issue of "compulsive" crime, irresistible "impulse," and so on, serves also as a theme in the polemics about reintroducing into criminology the aspect of "will" and "responsibility," see Hartung, esp. chap. 6; Matza; Wooton. For a supporter of such an approach in the field of psychiatry, see Szasz' works. For an excellent philosophical background on the problem of "will" and "responsibility," see: Grunbaum, pp. 766–79; Hook, *Determinism and Freedom,* pt. 4.

17. This stance, which accounts for the fact of nondelinquency as a sociocultural process, is exemplified in Reckless' theories of "insulation," see: Reckless, "A New Theory"; Reckless, Dinitz, and Murray, "The Good Boy" and "Self Concept."

18. On the problem of testimony by witnesses as well as by the victim, see: Davidson, "Appraisal of Witnesses"; Elliasberg, "The Acute Psychosexual Situation" and "The Examination"; Kaufman; Luckman; Machtinger; Monahan.

behavior and the situation of her encounter with the offender, be close to the offender's interpretation. This is so because they are bound to the same socio-cultural orientations. However, they, like the offender, may be wrong in their imputations. Even if seduction is found, we must still answer the question of quantity and decide what aspect in this provocation is the causal nexus wherein the act developed. Moreover, no victim will admit seductiveness (provided she is able to recall the event, i.e., if she was not drunk or too young to assume such seductiveness, or did not suffer from past crime amnesia).[19] On the other hand, the offender may claim her seductiveness as a defense. This is likely to occur when some previous relationship existed between them. Thus, the alternative left to us is to look for those rape events where behavior patterns of the victims along with vulnerable situations allow us to consider these victims as precipitators of the event.

The Legal Framework

Unlike the law of criminal homicide, the law of rape hardly recognizes provocation or seduction by the victim as a possible reason for mitigation of the offense, let's say, to fornication or assault with intent to ravish. If the *mens rea* of the victim should be an issue for the court, then a distinction could be made between the conscious seductive victim, and the legal concept of intention and motive, and between the precipitative victim and the legal concepts of negligence and recklessness. In both of them victim behavior increases the risk of being victimized. However, in negligence the victim's conduct is not intentional or reckless, and she is not aware of the danger of her behavior although it increases her chances of being victimized. In reckless behavior she may be aware of a dangerous outcome, but believes that harm will not occur while taking the risk.[20] It does not follow, however, that her conduct increases the danger and so is necessarily a reckless behavior. In each such case it is essential to find if due care was taken and, if not, the victim was reckless in that regard. Some situations, which we term vulnerable, are so fraught with danger that any action on the victim's part would be risky. With relation to that kind of situation, her conduct needs to be judged—that is, did she add

---

19. On the problem and rules of remembering see: Bartlett; D. E. Cameron. Saul (p. 47) maintains that because super-ego needs are dominant in women they will recall those elements in the situations which appeal to "authority figures"—that is, they will recall their resistance and not their consent in the situation or their rejection and not their possible seductive behavior. Kinsey (pp. 35–62) discussed the dangers of relying on reported past experience of rape. On the problem of amnesia see: Arens and Meadow; Gray; Hulbert; Lenox; Moore; Weinstein.

20. Hall, *General Principles,* pp. 215–16.

to the risk without realizing it, or did she know her actions might have consequences but took a chance anyway.

As we stated, the law is not interested in these problems since they pertain to the defendant and not the victim. Even if it is later established that the victim, consciously or unconsciously, set up the situation which ended in rape, the fact remains that she is still the victim. The immediate concern of the law is with the offender's responsibility and not with that of the victim. The major task of the law is to prevent victimization, whatever the responsibility which one may attribute to the victim.

From the Pennsylvania Criminal Code we learn that the immediate concern of the law is whether or not the victim was of bad repute and if the carnal knowledge was with her consent.[21] (By "repute" we mean "reputation of the girl for chastity in the community in which she resides at the time the charge for the crime is made.")[22] "Bad reputation" does not mean "character," which is more related to the "person's conduct in life." The concept of "bad reputation" has bearing on the question of consent,[23] and thus may serve as a defense for the offender, but such is not the case with "character." Therefore he must show proof of bad reputation (though the offender is not asked to prove "bad character").

On the other hand, in a case appearing before a Pennsylvania court,[24] it was ruled that presumption of consent of the woman was made if it is "shown by her prior, contemporaneous, or subsequent conduct."[25]

The law also suggests taking into consideration the situation where consent was given but withdrawn before the act. Such situation, however, is not to be considered as a defense for the defendant.[26]

It seems that the law does not recognize precipitation, provocation, and seduction. Some related factors such as delay in time or reporting the offense and "bad reputation" may be used by the court to infer consent rather than precipitation. Although in the legal process we ask the victim what the offender was doing, a question which allows interpretation on the part of the victim or the witnesses, the law is not equally, or indeed at all, interested in the offender's interpretation of victim behavior and intentions. The closest we have come to such interpretation is when the victim's personality is assessed for establishing previous chaste character or reputation. The problem of consent is the legal issue to be proven by the offender and decided by the court. In short, there is not justifiable

21. *Pennsylvania Law Encyclopedia; Purdon's.*

22. Commonwealth vs. Sam John, 1938, 195A 433, 129, Pa. Super. 179.

23. Commonwealth vs. Eberhardt, 1949, 67A 2d 613, 164, Pa. Super. 591.

24. Commonwealth vs. Goodman, 1956, 126A 2d 763, 182, Pa. Super. 205.

25. *Pennsylvania Law Encyclopedia.* By subsequent conduct it is meant "when," "where," and to "whom" the complaint was made.

26. *Purdon's,* p. 213.

rape in the same sense as we have justifiable murder, and looking for victim precipitation of the offense is the enterprise of the investigator and not the business of the law and court. If any causal connection exists between precipitation and rape, we must assess it with the aim of educating the law to recognize it too.

Working Definition

The term "victim precipitation" describes those rape situations in which the victim actually, or so it was deemed, agreed to sexual relations but retracted before the actual act or did not react strongly enough when the suggestion was made by the offender(s).[27] The term applies also to cases in risky situations marred with sexuality, especially when she uses what could be interpreted as indecency in language and gestures, or constitutes what could be taken as an invitation to sexual relations.

In seeking to identify victim-precipitated cases in police files, we have no objective measures with which to decide upon these cases, as are provided by legal interpretation of homicide.[28] The police dossiers include evaluative statements by witnesses and offenders which give the investigator a feeling that no objective proof exists for what was actually seductive and provocative behavior on the part of the victim. In some files examined the police interrogator recorded his own evaluative opinion, such as "she behaved provocatively," "it seems she was seductive," or "she was irresponsible and endangered herself." Most of these statements referred to adolescent and juvenile victims. For adult women we found such statements as "known as prostitute," or "known in the neighborhood as bad character," but there was no consistency in recording such opinion. It seems that these statements were more related to the problems of reputation and consent to be later used in court, and thus I had to rely on my own interpretation.

The Philadelphia Data

Of the 646 forcible rapes in this study, 122 (or 19 percent) have been found to fit the previous definitions as victim-precipitated (VP) rape cases. The remaining 524, have been stipulated as non-VP rapes. The following analysis attempts to compare VP with non-VP cases (table 93).[29]

27. The aspect of the vulnerable situation is not analyzed here but is assumed to operate in enhancing the offender's interpretation about the victim's availability as a sexual partner.

28. Wolfgang, *Patterns,* pp. 247–52.

29. In some cases the number of VP events are not sufficient for such analysis, and a grouping of cases was made.

Table 93: Victim Precipitated and Nonprecipitated Rape, by Selected Variables, Philadelphia, 1958 and 1960

	Victim Precipitated		Nonvictim Precipitated		Total Victims	
	No.	%	No.	%	No.	%
Victim's Race						
Negro	86	70.5	434	82.9	520	80.5
White	36	29.5	90	17.1	126	19.5
Total	122	100.0	524	100.0	646	100.0
Victim/Offender						
Negro/Negro	69	56.7	428	81.6	497	76.9
White/White	43	35.2	62	11.8	105	16.2
White/Negro	3	2.4	24	4.5	27	4.2
Negro/White	7	5.7	10	2.1	17	2.6
Total	122	100.0	524	100.0	646	100.0
Victim's Age						
0–9	2	1.6	49	9.3	51	7.9
10–14	18	14.7	105	20.5	123	19.0
15–19	44	37.1	117	22.3	161	24.9
20–24	19	15.6	68	12.9	87	13.5
25–29	14	11.2	54	10.3	68	10.5
30–34	12	9.6	38	7.2	50	7.7
35–39	4	3.2	40	7.6	44	6.8
40–44	3	2.4	18	3.4	21	3.3
45–49	3	2.4	15	2.8	18	2.8
50–54	2	1.6	7	1.3	9	1.4
55–59	...	...	1	0.3	1	0.2
60–over	1	0.8	12	2.3	13	2.0
Total	122	100.0	524	100.0	646	100.0
Age Disparity						
Victim much younger (−10 yrs.)	24	19.6	147	28.2	171	26.5
Both same age (±5 yrs.)	71	58.2	296	56.4	364	56.8
Victim much older (+10 yrs.)	27	22.2	81	15.4	108	16.7
Total	122	100.0	524	100.0	646	100.0
Alcohol during the Offense						
Present	64	52.5	153	29.2	217	33.5
Not present	58	47.5	371	70.8	429	66.5
Total	122	100.0	524	100.0	646	100.0

Table 93 Continued

	Victim Precipitated		Nonvictim Precipitated		Total Victims	
	No.	%	No.	%	No.	%
Alcohol in the Victim and/or Offender						
Present in both	42	35.1	94	17.9	136	21.1
Present in victim only	22	18.0	40	7.6	62	9.5
Not present in both or in the victim only	58	46.9	390	74.5	448	69.4
Total	122	100.0	524	100.0	646	100.0
Victim's Reputation						
Bad reputation	40	32.9	88	16.7	128	19.8
No reputation or no information	82	67.1	436	83.3	518	80.2
Total	122	100.0	524	100.0	646	100.0
Victim's Arrest Record						
Sex offenses	8	6.4	62	11.9	70	10.8
Other offenses only	16	(33.3) 13.2	38	(62.0) 7.2	54	(56.4) 8.4
Total, previous arrest record	24	(66.7) 19.6	100	(38.0) 19.1	124	(43.6) 19.2
No previous arrest record	98	80.4	424	80.9	522	80.8
Total	122	100.0	524	100.0	646	100.0
Proximity of Victim-Offender Residence and Offense						
Victim lives in area of offender's residence, not area of offense	3	2.4	160	30.5	163	25.3
Victim lives in area of offender, not of offense	35	28.7	92	17.4	127	19.7
Victim lives in area of offender and offense	70	57.4	258	49.5	328	52.3
Victim lives not in area of offender or offense	14	11.2	14	2.6	28	2.7
Total	122	100.0	524	100.0	646	100.0

Table 93 Continued

	Victim Precipitated		Nonvictim Precipitated		Total Victims	
	No.	%	No.	%	No.	%
Place of Initial Meeting						
Victim's place	22	18.0	149	28.4	171	26.5
Where victims stayed	12	9.6	40	7.6	52	8.0
Offender's place	8	6.4	35	6.8	43	6.7
In a bar, at a picnic	29	23.8	38	7.2	67	10.3
In the street	51	42.2	262	50.0	313	48.5
Total	122	100.0	524	100.0	646	100.0
Place of Rape						
Participant's place	23	19.4	337	74.5	360	55.7
Outside participant's place (not in car)	76	62.2	114	11.7	190	29.4
In a car	23	19.4	73	13.8	96	14.9
Total	122	100.0	524	100.0	646	100.0
Use of Nonphysical Force						
Tempting	17	13.9	58	11.1	75	11.7
Coercion	33	27.0	123	13.4	161	25.2
Intimidation	72	59.1	330	75.5	402	63.1
Total	122	100.0	524	100.0	638	100.0
Use of Violence						
Roughness	46	37.7 (40.7)	136	15.9 (31.7)	182	29.0 (29.9)
Nonbrutal beating	26	21.3 (23.1)	131	36.2 (30.4)	157	24.1 (30.7)
Brutal beating	41	33.7 (36.2)	163	31.3 (37.9)	204	31.9 (39.4)
Total use of force	113	92.7	430	83.4	543	85.0
No use of force	9	7.3	87	16.6	96	15.0
Total	122	100.0	524	100.0	639	100.0
Interpersonal Relationships between Victim and Offender						
Strangers	35	28.7	300	57.2	335	51.9
Acquaintance	28	22.4	65	11.4	93	14.4
Neighbor (close)	33	27.9	92	11.4	125	19.3
Close friend or boyfriend	18	14.6	21	6.0	39	6.0
Family friend	6	4.8	28	5.3	34	5.3
Relative	2	1.6	14	2.6	16	2.5
Total	122	100.0	524	100.0	642	100.0

Table 93 Continued

	Victim Precipitated		Nonvictim Precipitated		Total Victims	
	No.	%	No.	%	No.	%
Type of Rape						
SR	66	54.1	304	58.0	379	57.3
PR	25	20.5	80	15.2	105	16.2
GR	31	25.4	140	26.7	171	26.5
Total	122	100.0	524	100.0	646	100.0
Sexual Humiliation						
Performed	75	61.5	98	18.7	173	26.8
Not performed	47	38.5	426	81.3	473	73.2
Total	122	100.0	524	100.0	646	100.0
Victim's Behavior						
Submission	62	51.3	293	55.9	355	54.9
Resistance	32	26.3	141	26.9	173	27.1
Fight	28	22.4	88	17.2	116	18.0
Total	122	100.0	524	100.0	644	100.0

Race Differences

Because Negro women have been found to be involved in more rape cases, we expected to find them also more represented than white women among the VP cases. The data does not confirm this inference. While 71 percent of VP cases involve Negro victims, as compared to 83 percent of non-VP cases, the proportion of white victims who were involved in VP cases is *significantly* higher than their involvement in non-VP rape situations (30 percent and 17 percent, respectively). One explanation offered for this result is the greater proportion of white victims who entered drinking relationships with white males who were strangers to them and who later attacked them. This explanation is further confirmed by the observation that white intraracial events are *significantly* associated with VP events (36 percent compared to 12 percent of non-VP cases). Although there is no difference between VP and non-VP cases for intraracial events, intraracial rapes constitute the majority of cases (over 90 percent) of VP events. Again, only white intraracial rapes are *significantly* associated with VP rapes.

Age

The age distribution of victims in VP or non-VP cases is similar except for age groups 1–10 and 15–19 years of age. The first group contains 2 VP cases compared to 49 cases of non-VP cases. It is very unlikely that girls that young will be overtly seductive or will be found in vulnerable situations. The opposite can be stated about age group 15–19,[30] which shows *significantly higher* involvement in VP rapes than any age group, though it should be remembered that this is the age group with the highest proportion of victims who were involved in the offense in general (25 percent). The median age of VP victims is 19.2 years, while that of non-VP victims is 16.7 years. Since rape involves mainly victims (57 percent) and offenders who are at the same age level, it was expected to find the same proportion in VP events, and such were the results. However, no differences exist between the proportion of VP and non-VP cases with respect to any of the three groupings of victim-offender relative age.

Alcohol

A *significant* association was found between VP rapes and the presence of alcohol. Alcohol was present in the rape situation (alcohol present either in the victim alone or in both the offender and the victim), in 53 percent of the VP cases and in 25 percent of the non-VP cases.

Because we are interested mainly in the contribution of the victim to the offense, the important factor of alcohol here is its existence in the victim or in both victim and offender. Victims had been drinking immediately prior to the offense in *significantly* more VP cases (18 percent) than in non-VP cases (8 percent). A *significant* relationship was also found between VP events and the consumption of alcohol by both offender and victim. Thus, alcohol was present in both offender and victim in 35 percent of VP cases compared to 20 percent of non-VP rape events. It seems that when alcohol is present in both offender and victim, the situation is more "risky" than when it is present in the victim only. When alcohol was consumed by both participants, it was more likely to occur in his or her home. However, when alcohol was present in the victim only, she was more likely to "be in outside places," such as the street "protected" by what the street can offer in that respect (other people around, etc.).

Victim Reputation and Previous Arrest Record

Previous observation showed residential propinquity of victims and offenders and of the close interpersonal relationships between them as neighbors. It can be expected, therefore, that if the victim has a "bad reputation" it is known to the offender, and therefore contributes more strongly to the offender's imputation that she is sexually available. Hence, it is necessary to determine whether an association exists between VP rapes and victim (bad) reputation. Such association was, indeed, found

30. This is also the age group in which the various studies found the "seductive" or "participant" victim.

to be *statistically* significant. Thus, in VP cases the victim is more likely to have a bad reptuation (33 percent) than in non-VP events (17 percent).

If in homicide the victim's record of previous arrests, especially of offenses against the person, is considered a direct contributory factor to precipitation of the offense,[31] record of sex offenses or sexual misconduct (for juvenile) may have an analogous importance in forcible rape, provided the offender knows about it. Or, just knowing that the victim has a bad reputation in terms of her sexual behavior may have the same effect.

In testing this hypothesis, no association was found to exist between VP rapes and victim's previous record of arrests for sexual offenses and juvenile (mainly sexual) misconduct, or, indeed, for any other offenses. Obviously the importance rests not with the objective fact of being promiscuous or having been charged with such behavior, but, rather, with the fact that the offender was led to believe or assume that the victim had a bad reputation.

Residential Proximity

Residential proximity offers the first condition for encountering the victim, establishing relations with her, and/or knowing her reputation. It allows the possibility of being together in his or her residence or place of temporary stay; in the latter case without his being an unwelcome intruder. It is more likely, therefore, that compromising situations will arise between those who live close to each other. On the other hand, it can be assumed that anonymity due to ecological distance affords some "protection" from later consequences of the offense if intended by the offender(s). In the light of the previous results we can more readily accept the first hypothesis of association between residential proximity between victim and offender and VP rapes. Testing each hypothesis by its collated data shows that in VP cases the victim is more likely to live in offender's vicinity. Thus, 29 percent of VP victims live in offender's vicinity but not in the area of offense, compared to 17 percent of non-VP victims. Fifty-seven percent of VP victims live in offender's vicinity and offense area, as compared to 50 percent of non-VP victims. Taken together, 86 percent of VP victims live in offender's vicinity (which either includes the offense area or does not) as compared to 67 percent of non-VP victims.

Place of Initial Meeting

The previously established relationships between place of initial meeting and place of rape, especially when the place was that of either the residence of victims or offenders, point to the vulnerability of such situations.

31. Wolfgang, *Patterns*, pp. 262–64.

The offender may interpret his staying in her home, and especially her presence in his residence, either as a sign that the victim is ready to take the risk of encountering his sexual overtones, or as an indication of outright readiness to allow sexual relations. In either case she puts herself in a precarious position (discounting for the purpose of gross analysis felony rape situations). The situations may be even more dangerous for her if the meeting place is a bar, or a picnic where alcohol is present. Whatever the victim then does or fails to do may rightly or wrongly contribute to the offender's imputations of sexual accessibility to the victim. To test this hypothesis, the places of initial meeting were divided between participant places—offender's and victim's residence or place of sojourn, the bar, picnic or "party" locales; the outside places—all places which previously were designated as the "street." No association was found between the meeting place in his or her residence or place of sojourn and VP events. For the events where the victim's residence was where the initial encounter took place, the association is reversed, that is, *significantly* more non-VP cases occurred there (28 percent) than VP events (18 percent). The bar as a meeting place is found to be more important as a precipitative factor. In 24 percent of VP rapes, the bar, picnic, or party was the initial meeting place, compared to only 7 percent of the non-VP rape events. The street was found to be more associated with non-VP events than with VP cases.

Place of Rape

The previously observed relationships between place of initial meeting and place of rape, and the last mentioned results associating the street as an initial meeting place with VP rapes, can explain the associations which are found between VP events and place of rape. In *significant* proportions VP rapes occurred outside participants' residence (82 percent including the automobile as the place of rape, as compared to 25 percent of non-VP rapes which took place in these places). Only 19 percent of VP cases occurred in participants' place or place of temporary stay, while 75 percent of non-VP events took place there. In the light of these results (when the rape took place in his or her place, and especially when those involved also met each other there), the police may suspect, after establishing a nonfelony rape, some seductiveness or gross reckless behavior on the victim's part.

The Use of Nonphysical Force

If the offender deems the victim accessible, he may find intimidation unnecessary to render the victim into submission, and temptation or coercion will be the form used against her. The data partly supports this assumption. While the occurrence of temptation among VP and non-VP cases shows no *significant* association, coercion accounts for 27 percent of all VP cases, but only 13 percent of non-VP events, a difference which is *significant*. The assumption gains further support by the finding of higher frequencies of intimidation among non-VP cases (75 percent compared to 59 percent of VP events). However, VP victims are not spared from being terrorized by the offender, because an interpretation of sexual accessibility may not diminish the offender's notions that he may be mistaken, and in order to effect the act itself, he may not take "chances." He therefore will behave toward the victim like those offenders who do not have to believe their interpretation of the situation that the victim is an easy "make."

Violence

The above result and the result of the relationship between nonphysical methods and VP events are further supported by the observation about the use of violence in VP rape events. In 113 (or 73 percent) of the 122 VP rapes violence was used, compared to 430 (or 83 percent) of non-VP events. When the specific methods of violence are analyzed, it is found that the incidence of "roughness" used against the victim is *significantly* greater in VP cases (41 percent) than in non-VP cases (32 percent). The relationship is reversed for nonbrutal beatings (21 percent in VP cases compared to 30 percent in non-VP cases). The frequency of brutality is equal in VP and non-VP cases.

Sexual Humiliation

Subjecting the victim to forced sexual intercourse means that the imputation of sexual availability was a false interpretation on the offender's part. He may still hold to his views and try to prove them by subjecting her to sexual humiliation, other than forced intercourse, or he may humiliate her as a revenge just because of the failure of his imputation. It is therefore inferred that the frequency of sexual humiliation is greater among VP than among non-VP cases. The data support such an inference and reveal that rapes accompanied by sexual humiliation account for 61 percent of VP cases but only 19 percent of non-VP cases, a difference which is *significant*.

Victim Behavior

Imputations and interpretations of a victim's availability for sexual relations come before the act. Once the offender tries to "prove" them, the victim's behavior may make the difference in how the encounter is ended: with the withdrawal of his plans or with his trying to force sex on her. Hence, we may expect that victims would more resist or fight the offender in VP cases, to convince him that he erred in his assumption. The data does not support such expectation. The distribution of all forms of victim behavior among VP and non-VP cases shows no difference. VP victims do tend in a slightly larger share to fight their assailant than victims who are involved in non-VP events (22 percent compared to 17 percent, respectively). These results show that the victim's behavior after the offender attempts to force sexual relations on her makes no difference in the outcome of the event.

Victim-Offender Relationships

Assuming that either seductiveness or the insinuation of such an attitude about the victim is more likely to occur when victims and offenders are closely related, or at least, acquainted, leads to further assuming that VP rapes will be characterized by close interpersonal relationships between victim and offender. The data support this assumption and reveal that primary relationships (from acquaintance to family relative types of relationships) account for 71 percent of VP cases but only 43 percent of non-VP cases, a difference which is *significant*. Victims were acquaintances of their assailants in 22 percent of the VP cases compared to only 11 percent of non-VP cases. Also, in *significant* proportion more VP victims were either close neighbors or close friends of the offender. Finally, in only two VP events, compared to 14 non-VP cases, were the victims relatives of their assailants. It seems, therefore, that the closer the relationship between victim and offender, the greater the likelihood of victims being conceived as "easy marks" or their behavior's being interpreted as precipitative.

Type of Rape

The number of offenders involved in the offense is not directly associated with VP rapes. Other things being equal, it may be only a matter of chance how many offenders the victim will encounter. Her behavior may be conceived as "inviting" only by one or more in a group but not necessarily by all members. The situation of differential interpretation of victim availability, if it exists at all, will depend on, among other things, the "initiatory" act or the "magical seduction" of one of the members of the group. Thus, we expect to find no differences in the frequencies of types of rapes among VP and non-VP events. Indeed, there is no difference between VP and non-VP rape with respect to type of rape; that is, the number of offenders who participated in the event has no relationship to VP events.

These results point to the fact that the offender should not be viewed as the sole "cause" and reason for the offense, and that the "virtuous" victim is not always the innocent and passive party. Thus, the role played by the victim and its contribution to the perpetration of the offense becomes one of the main interests of the emerging discipline of victimology. Furthermore, if penal justice is to be fair it must be attentive to these problems of degrees of victim responsibility for her own victimization.

V

The Post-Rape Situation

16

Unsolved Rapes

Adolphe Quetelet has divided crime into three classes: those that are reported and whose perpetrators are detected; those that are known but committed by undetected offenders; and those that are completely hidden —that is, the offenses and their perpetrators are not known.[1] It is with the second group of offenses that we shall deal in the present chapter.

It is well known, although students in the field are in disagreement as to the volume, that a large number of forcible rapes are never reported, and even when reported to the police, some forcible rapes are never solved—that is, the offenders are not apprehended.

The *UCR* for 1960 shows that, for the years 1958, 1959, and 1960, a little more than one-quarter of all forcible rape cases reported to the FBI were not solved or "cleared by arrest."[2] Almost the same holds true for the proportion of offenders charged with the crime.[3]

A much lower proportion of clearance by arrest exists in Philadelphia on the basis of the 1961 *Annual Report* of its police department.[4]

1. Quetelet, p. 324 (reported in Sellin and Wolfgang, p. 26).
2. *UCR* (1960), p. 12.
3. *UCR* (1958), p. 75, table 12; (1959), p. 81, table 12; (1960), p. 83, table 8.

	1958	1959	1960
Offenses cleared by arrest	73.0%	73.6%	72.5%
Persons charged	78.9%	75.6%	74.2%

4. *Annual Philadelphia Police Report* (1962), p. 5.

	1958	1959	1960
Offenses	573	666	529
Clearances	382	466	438
	(66.7)	(67.1)	(82.8)
Arrests	522	601	559

Radzinowicz, in the only study which has dealt with the problem, found that in heterosexual offenses the proportion of undetected offenders was as high as 37 percent.[5] Although we are unable to determine how rapes fare in this proportion, the results point to the fact that the number of persons arrested has no direct relation to the volume of offenses reported or known to the police. An offender may commit more than one rape or several persons may commit a gang-type rape which will be recorded as one offense.

In view of these numbers of rapes which are not solved, or for which the offenders are never discovered, it seems desirable to analyze our data on unsolved rape for both criminological reasons (especially for crime measurement considerations) and for practical reasons (for police and community interests).

The problem of estimating the number of offenses committed, let us say, by local residents of the community and those committed by nonresidents, is important in the building of an index and computing the general rate of crime committed in the community. Since this estimate of crime committed in the community is part of the problem of validity and reliability of criminal statistics, then, when the offender is not arrested, these problems are far from being solved. Moreover, if specific crime rates and other important social and psychological data are to be obtained, we have to know what types of offenses are committed by what age, racial, occupation, or criminally recidivist group. Again, the high proportion of unsolved rapes, such as one-third in Philadelphia, makes such attempts an almost impossible task.

From a practical point of view, the unsolved cases not only present a problem of valid police statistics, but they can also serve as an index of police efficiency, and as an indicator for a need to enlarge and improve police and other protective and preventive services.

Various situations influence detectability of offenses.[6] Low detectability may indicate ineptitude of the police. On the other hand, even if the police force is free from such criticism, it may be understaffed so that the police are unable to investigate adequately the crime and those involved as well as witnesses, and so on. A low standing of the police in the community may amount to a reluctance to help them in the investigation. Despite diligent police efforts, the police may fail to solve the offense when in a large community, like Philadelphia, the perpetrator is able to disappear into the shadows of anonymity of the city.

Some elements in the reporting of the offense may affect the chance of detecting the offender; among them are the following:[7]

5. Radzinowicz, *Sexual Offenses*, p. 26.

6. Sellin and Wolfgang, p. 32.

7. Wolfgang, *Patterns*, p. 285. See also Radzinowicz, *Sexual Offenses*, pp. 28–32.

1. A delayed report diminishes the chances of apprehending the offender. For instance, young victims may report the case first to their parents, who for some reasons may delay in reporting the offense to the police.
2. Inadequate description of the offender or conflicting stories given by the victim or witnesses about the offense increase the chances that the assailant may not be found.
3. The description of the offender or the knowledge of the circumstances of the offense may be vague because the victim is young, retarded, intoxicated, or shocked immediately at the beginning of the attack.
4. The victim or her guardians, after reporting the event, may refuse to continue cooperating with the police or to pursue the case further.

We must remember that sometimes a quick report or what seems an adequate and reasonable report eventually turns out to be inaccurate when the offender is later apprehended.

In the Philadelphia police files the term "active" was used to designate "unsolved cases." These "active" files included two types of cases: the undetected—those cases for which the police could not attribute the recorded offense to an identified offender(s) so that he will be arrested if located; and the vanished[8]—those cases about which the police have some information on suspected, identified, or alleged offender(s), but suspect is still at large. These two types are distinguished from the "solved" cases: those in which the police are satisfied as to the identity of the offender, who has been arrested but has either not yet been brought to trial, or not yet been convicted.[9]

In the following study, cases in both groups will be considered. It should be pointed out that persons in the second group, the vanished, are not necessarily sufficiently suspected; that is, there may not be enough evidence to bring them before the grand jury for preliminary hearing, or to justify a conviction upon a trial.

The Philadelphia Data

Of the 646 forcible rapes studied 124 (or 19 percent) can be classified (table 94) as undetected, and 24 (or 4 percent) as vanished. Together they present 148 (or 23 percent) of the unsolved cases. Of 1,292 offenders, 405 (or 31 percent) can be classified as undetected and 40 (or 3 percent) can be classified vanished. Together they represent 445, or 34.4 percent of undetected offenders.

Since the "vanished" cases differ from the "undetected" ones only in

8. The terms "undetected" and "vanished" have been coined to summarize the reasons for the designation of the cases as "active."

9. Since only 92 offenders of the total 1,292 were brought to trial, the aspect of adjudication will not be pursued in the present study.

the fact that some data about the offender is known to the police,[10] we shall treat the two types of cases as a combined class except when it seems pertinent to treat them separately.

Comparison of the unsolved with solved forcible rapes in Philadelphia reveals the following differences (table 94): a larger proportion of the victims of unsolved than of solved forcible rapes are Negroes; but in terms of the total rape cases, the proportion of Negro or white victims of unsolved rapes does not differ from their representation in the total group. Thus, Negro victims (520) who represent 80.5 percent of all victims, are found to comprise 82 percent of the unsolved cases. The proportion of white victims is 20 percent and 18 percent respectively.

Table 94: Unsolved and Solved Rapes, by Race of Victims and of Offenders

| | Unsolved | | Solved | | Total | |
	No.	%	No.	%	No.	%
Victim						
Negro	122	82.4	398	79.9	520	80.5
White	26	17.6	100	20.1	126	19.5
Total	148	100.0	498	100.0	646	100.0
Offender						
Negro	402	90.3	664	78.4	1,066	82.5
White	43	9.7	183	21.6	226	17.5
Total	445	100.0	847	100.0	1,292	100.0

As to offenders, a larger proportion of offenders of unsolved than of solved forcible rapes are Negroes; but in terms of the total number of offenders (1,292) who participated in the rape cases, the proportion of Negro offenders in unsolved cases is higher than their representation in the total offender population—90 percent and 82 percent, respectively.

Some questions arise in explaining such race differentials: Are white victims or their guardians quicker to report the offense to the police than Negro victims? Are white witnesses more willing to testify to police? Are white accomplices in group rape more willing to implicate their partners to the crime? Do the differences in the circumstances of the offense make any difference? Are more Negro victims drunk, raped more by single offenders, younger than their white counterparts? Are Negro offenders more astute in escaping detection than white rapists? Or, are the police less diligent in searching for the Negro offender than for the white one?

10. Usually nickname, address, or place of work are known. It is with the type of relationship between these offenders and their victims that the "vanished" group mainly differs from the "undetected"—a factor which will be analyzed later.

Before answering these questions, we must see if unsolved rape events, like the solved ones, are mostly intraracial events or not (table 95).

Indeed, we find that as in the total sample, where intraracial rapes totalled 93 percent, as well as in the solved cases, where they accounted for 94 percent of the total, the group of unsolved rapes consist mostly of intraracial events. In fact, some differences are noticeable, especially with respect to those cases which involved a white offender. The proportion of unsolved white intraracial events is lower than the solved ones (13 percent as compared to 17 percent). It is not a large difference, but it may suggest that white victims were quicker and more willing to report the event or that white offenders were more clumsy in escaping. Another difference appears in those cases involving a white offender and a Negro victim—the proportion of unsolved cases is higher than the solved ones. In checking these cases, we find that each involved a child victim.

Table 95: Unsolved and Solved Cases, by Offender and Victim Race in Rape Events

Offender/Victim	Unsolved		Solved		Total	
	No.	%	No.	%	No.	%
Negro/Negro	116	78.4	381	76.4	497	76.9
White/White	19	12.8	86	17.2	105	16.3
Negro/White	6	4.1	21	4.4	27	4.2
White/Negro	7	4.7	10	2.0	17	2.6
Total	148	100.0	498	100.0	646	100.0

Victims of unsolved rapes have a median age of 22.4 years compared to 19.16 for all victims, and 18.5 years for solved rape events (table 96). Offenders of unsolved rapes have a median age of 21.4 years compared to 23.5 for all offenders, and 20.3 years for offenders who were detected.[11] The most striking difference concerns the offenders of the age 25–29. The proportion of offenders in this age group among the undetected (24 percent) is twice as high as that of detected offenders in this same age group (12 percent).

In the victim group, the examination of age differences among solved and unsolved cases shows that generally up to the age group 40–44 years, for each age group, the proportion of unsolved cases is greater than that of the solved ones. In the age group 40–44 years, there is an excess of 5 percent of unsolved cases over the solved ones (7 percent and 2 percent, respectively). The proportion declines from 14 percent of unsolved cases compared to 24 percent of solved ones in the age group 10–14.

11. The age of undetected offenders was taken as that reported by the victim, who made a guess about it.

One explanation for these results may be the age differences between the offender and his victim. Thus, we may at first assume that those rapes in which the victim is much younger (at least by 10 years) than her assailant are likely to be unsolved, especially since in those cases the victim tends to be a child. The data does not confirm this assumption. When the victim was much younger than the offender, or was in the same age group, the proportions of unsolved and solved cases were the same

Table 96: Unsolved and Solved Rapes, by Age of Victim

	Unsolved		Solved		Total	
	No.	%	No.	%	No.	%
Victim's Age						
0–10	12	8.1	39	7.8	51	7.9
10–14	20	13.5	103	20.6	123	19.0
15–19	27	18.2	134	26.9	161	24.9
20–24	26	17.6	61	12.2	87	13.5
25–29	19	12.8	49	9.8	68	10.5
30–34	9	6.1	41	8.2	50	7.7
35–39	12	8.1	32	6.4	44	6.8
40–44	10	6.8	11	2.2	21	3.3
45–49	4	2.7	14	2.8	18	2.8
50–54	4	2.7	5	1.0	9	1.4
55–59	...	...	1	0.2	1	0.2
60–over	5	3.4	8	1.6	13	2.0
Total	148	100.0	498	100.0	646	100.0
Offender's Age						
10–14	9	2.0	38	4.4	47	3.6
15–19	173	38.9	348	41.1	521	40.3
20–24	108	24.3	224	26.4	332	25.6
25–29	107	24.0	100	11.8	207	16.0
30–34	32	7.2	66	7.7	98	7.7
35–39	6	1.3	31	3.6	37	2.8
40–44	7	1.6	14	1.6	21	1.6
45–49	2	0.4	6	0.7	8	0.6
50–54	1	0.2	10	1.0	11	0.8
55–59	...	...	5	0.5	5	0.3
60–over	...	...	5	0.5	5	0.3
Total	445	100.0	847	100.0	1,292	100.0

Note: Victims' median age—unsolved, 22.38; solved, 18.49. Offenders' median age—unsolved, 21.37; solved, 20.34.

(17 percent and 16 percent, respectively). It is in those cases in which the victim is at least ten years older than the offender that the proportion of unsolved cases is greater than the solved ones (21 and 15 percent, respectively).

Due to the fact that not all multiple rape offenders are of the same age, the disparity between all offenders and their victims was checked. Again, the attempt to explain unsolved rapes by citing age differences between victim and offender was not borne out. Actually, of 445 undetected offenders, 60 of them were much younger than their victims, as compared to 180 (or 21 percent) of the 847 detected offenders.

We have shown that felony rapes are apt to be events in which witnesses are not present, and as shown in most of these cases, the victim tends to be older than her attacker. Therefore, we were not surprised to find that 50 percent of the explosive rapes were unsolved, and that all of these unsolved cases were felony rapes. Furthermore, partially planned rape and explosive rape combined furnish 41 percent of the unsolved cases, as compared to 25 percent of solved events.

It was assumed that since most of the open-space rapes were committed by offenders who were strangers to the victims, they will include a higher proportion of unsolved cases than solved ones. Indeed, open-space rape events furnish 43 percent unsolved rapes compared to 12 percent solved. Also, since it can be assumed that, in rapes committed at the residence of one of the participants, more sustained acquaintance had been established between offenders and victims—if such relationships did not exist before the offense—then the proportion of solved cases should be higher than the unsolved ones. Again, this assumption was confirmed. In 67 percent of the solved cases (compared to 14 percent of unsolved rapes), the event occurred in the place of one of the participants.

Turning to the association between unsolved rapes and offender-victim relationship, we must distinguish between undetected and vanished offenders. The closer the interpersonal relationship between the victim and the offender, the more information she may have about him which, upon her complaint to the police, would make it easier for them to apprehend the offender. Indeed, table 97 speaks for itself.

In terms of the overall comparison between unsolved and solved cases, the closer the offender's relationship to the victim, all things being equal (speed of complaint, etc.), the more likely it is that the offense will be solved. Such is the case in all categories of offender-victim relationships. For the situation in which the offender was a stranger to the victim, however, the difference was much more revealing. Among unsolved cases, in 124 (or 82 percent) victims and offenders were strangers, compared to 42 percent of solved cases. Sixteen percent of the cases were unsolved when primary relations existed between victim and offender, while 58 percent of the rapes were solved when offenders and victims had primary contacts between them.

In terms of overall cases, no difference was found between unsolved and solved cases when alcohol was present in the rape situation (32 and 34 percent, respectively). The relationship between these two variables was therefore examined only for those rape events where alcohol was present in the rape situation. A drunken victim is less able to identify her attacker and to remember his features and other characteristics important to the police. She is also likely to be late in reporting the offense. Our files reveal that when alcohol was present in the victim only, 47 (or 64 percent) of the cases were unsolved, compared to 70 (or 18 percent) of all solved cases where alcohol was present in the rape situation.

It seems that drinking offenders were able to elude the police. Of the undetected group, 39 percent consumed alcohol alone as against 14 percent in the detected offenders. Combined with those cases where alcohol was present in both offender and victim, the difference was between 55 percent undetected offenders and 84 percent detected.

Table 97: Unsolved and Solved Rapes, by Victim-Offender Interpersonal Relationship

	Undetected		Vanished		Total Unsolved		Solved		Total	
	No.	%	No.	%	No.	%	No.	%	No.	%
Stranger	101	81.5	...	...	101	68.2	172	34.5	273	42.3
Stranger, but general knowledge	15	12.1	8	33.2	23	15.5	39	7.8	62	9.6
Acquaintance	8	6.4	2	8.3	10	6.8	83	16.7	93	14.4
Neighbor	...	...	6	25.3	6	4.1	119	23.9	125	19.3
Friend	...	...	4	16.6	4	2.7	35	7.0	39	6.0
Relative	...	...	2	8.3	2	1.4	14	2.8	16	2.5
Family friend	...	...	2	8.3	2	1.4	32	6.4	34	5.3
No information	...	...	...	...	...	...	4	0.9	4	0.6
Total	124	100.0	24	100.0	148	100.0	498	100.0	646	100.0

No difference was found between the proportions of solved and unsolved cases as far as the use of physical violence was concerned. In 85 percent of the unsolved cases force was used on the victim, and the same proportion prevailed in the solved group. However, when the victim was beaten brutally, the number of unsolved cases was higher than that of solved cases by 8 percent.

Since the major criterion of unsolved rape is the disappearance of the offender, and since in 43 percent of rapes more than one offender was involved, it seems reasonable to expect that, in terms of rape events, single rape would be less likely to be solved than multiple rape; provided we assume that if one offender was apprehended, the case was solved.[12] Indeed, we found (table 98), that of 445 in the undetected group, the number of single rape offenders who escaped detection was four times greater (80 percent) than that of multiple rape offenders. The difference in the detected group was this: twice as many multiple rape offenders (67 percent) were arrested as single rape offenders (33 percent).

In terms of rape events, again, the percent of unsolved single rape events (60 percent) exceeded that of unsolved multiple-offender rape events (39 percent) and that of solved single and multiple events (56 percent and 44 percent, respectively).

Table 98: Unsolved and Solved Rapes, by Type

	Undetected		Detected		Total	
	No.	%	No.	%	No.	%
SR	87	80.4	283	33.4	370	28.6
MR	358	19.6	564	66.6	922	71.4
Total	445	100.0	847	100.0	1,292	100.0

It is interesting to note that among the undetected offenders, differences exist in terms of the offender's position in the rape situation. Of the undetected group, 10 percent of the nonleaders in pair rape and 57 percent of rank and file offenders in group rape were arrested, while only 6 percent of the leaders in pair rape and only 7 percent of group rape leaders were apprehended. The leader may have had the protection of his accomplices who did not "squeal on him" or he may have been more astute in escaping detection.

For determining the reasons underlying solved and unsolved offenses, the records were searched for what we have previously suggested as detectability variables, as well as for some characteristics of victims and offenders which may have been among the reasons for the inability of the police to attribute the offense to an identified offender. The most important ones were: the reporting agent, the interval of time between the commission of the offense and its reporting to the police, and the adequacy of the information.

How the Offense Became Known to the Police

Table 99 shows the various ways in which the offense was made known to the police. The figures point to an interesting situation. First, in 49 per-

12. This assumes that persons who participate in pair or group rape are not strangers to one another, and it is only a matter of time until the offender who was apprehended will implicate his accomplices who will then be apprehended.

cent of the cases people other than the victim reported the case to the police, which may explain some of the delay in reporting. Also, in 90 cases (or 14 percent) the police found the victim and the offender on the scene (87 of them were found in flagrante delicto). The age of the victim correlates with the proportion of cases reported to the police by the victim's parents or other family members. The younger the victim, the more often it was the mother who reported the offense to the police. For victims under 10 years of age, in 72 percent of the cases, the case was reported to the police by the parents or relatives. We note that reports by strangers and actions of the police themselves led in 68 percent of gang rape events to the arrest of the offender.

Table 99: Reporting of Rape Events to the Police

Reporting Agents	No.	%
Victim	237	26.8
Mother	152	23.5
Father	33	5.1
Other family member	36	5.7
Husband	16	2.5
Friend (including neighbor, teacher, etc.)	33	5.1
Stranger	40	6.1
Police found at scene	90	13.9
Hospital	9	1.3
Total	646	100.0

Lapse of Time between the Offense and Its Reporting to the Police

The assumption was made that, all things being equal, the greater the time interval between the offense and its reporting to the police, the greater the chance that the case would be unsolved. The intervals were grouped in the following manner (table 100).

We note that discovery by police does not assure the apprehension of offenders. In 39 (or 26 percent) of the unsolved cases, the police found the victim at the scene of the crime, but the offender had already disappeared. Such cases involved almost exclusively single rapes (only 3 cases of pair rape and 1 case of group rape). Time intervals of 30 minutes after the offense was reported were used since on the average, it took that amount of time for the police to arrive at the scene of the crime and start searching for the offender. Also, many older victims reported that it took them about this time to recover from the initial shock, to douche themselves in order to prevent pregnancy, to reach a telephone, or to tell parents or somebody else who then reported the offense. As for the unsolved cases, it seems that after a one-hour lapse between the offense and its reporting, there is not much difference in the proportion of unsolved cases. However, if the report was made after one week, the proportion of unsolved cases rose from an average of 7 percent to 10 percent of unsolved cases. It seems, therefore, that delay in reporting, however slight, may be an important reason for the failure to detect the offender.

Table 100: Time Intervals before the Offense was Reported to the Police, in Solved and Unsolved Rape Events

| | Unsolved | | Solved | | Total | |
	No.	%	No.	%	No.	%
Found by police at time of occurrence	39	26.4	51	9.5	90	13.9
Reported 30 minutes after occurrence	24	16.2	265	53.2	289	44.7
Reported after 30 minutes and under one hour	11	7.4	22	4.8	33	5.1
Reported between one hour and under two hours	10	6.7	23	5.1	33	5.1
Between two hours and under four hours	8	5.4	28	5.6	36	5.6
Between four hours and less than 24 hours	8	5.4	67	13.2	75	11.6
Between one day and less than three days	11	7.4	15	3.0	26	4.0
Between three days and less than one week	6	4.1	4	0.9	10	1.6
Between one week and four weeks	17	11.5	12	2.4	29	4.5
After four weeks	14	9.5	11	2.3	25	3.9
Total	148	100.0	498	100.0	646	100.0

Reasons for Failure to Report Promptly

In examining the files we were able to find those reasons given by the victim for their delay in reporting the offense. We observed two main groups of reasons: those given by the victim herself, and those which were connected with other persons who reported the offense. Table 101 summarizes these reasons.

It appears that fear of the offender, fear of parents, or both, occurs in one-fourth of the unsolved cases in which the victim was late in reporting the offense promptly. If we add the cases in which fear of pregnancy, or some other kind of fear, was present, the proportion of unsolved rape is 40 percent. However, in terms of the contrast with solved cases, it is fear of the offender and suspicion of pregnancy which differentiate the unsolved from the solved rapes. It is not unexpected to find that victims who delayed reporting the offense due to suspicion of pregnancy constituted the 14 unsolved cases which were reported after four weeks had elapsed.

Table 101: Reasons for Failure to Report the Offense Promptly in Unsolved and Solved Rapes

	Unsolved		Solved		Total	
	No.	%	No.	%	No.	%
Police found at scene	39	26.4	51	9.5	90	13.5
Reported promptly	24	16.2	265	53.2	289	44.5
Fear of offender	20	13.5	32	6.2	52	8.0
Fear of parents	13	8.8	37	8.2	50	7.5
Fear of both	7	4.7	13	2.7	20	3.0
Parents were late to report	4	2.7	6	1.3	10	1.5
Victim was not able to report (drunk, shock, waiting for parents or husband)	11	7.4	42	8.4	53	8.4
Hesitation (publicity, etc.)	5	3.4	44	8.9	49	7.5
Late to report—after suspecting pregnancy	14	9.4	4	0.8	18	3.8
Late— search for offender first	2	1.4	...	...	2	0.3
Victim in hospital	9	6.1	...	...	9	1.4
No information	...	...	4	0.8	4	0.6
Total	148	100.0	498	100.0	646	100.0

Another group of reasons for late reporting of the offense by the victim concerns those situations in which the victim is not able to report the offense: due to the physical effects of the offense (shock, injury, hospitalization, etc.); because of such reasons as the presence of alcohol in the victim or her delay in order to tell parents or husband about the event first; or because she alone or with parents or husband searched first for the offender before reporting. This group of reasons comprised 15 percent of the unsolved cases, as compared to 8 percent of the solved ones.

In those cases in which parents or guardians were late in reporting to the police, the unsolved cases contributed 3 percent as compared to 1 percent in the solved group.

Inadequate Description of the Offender

Besides the problem of delayed reporting, there exists the question of the adequacy of the description of the offender and the whole event to the police. We have to bear in mind the age of some victims and the fact that in almost 50 percent of cases it was not the victim who reported the offense to the police.

In each "active" case the police gave a summary statement for designating the file as active. Table 102 gives the groupings for these statements for the 148 cases of unsolved forcible rapes.

Table 102: Reasons Given by Police for Unsolved Rapes

	No.	%
Victim gives inconsistent stories	41	27.7
Victim refused to cooperate	33	22.3
Victim's inability to describe the offender accurately (victim child, disturbed)	26	17.6
Victim intoxicated	15	10.2
Victim retarded, emotionally disturbed, etc.	14	9.5
Parents refuse to cooperate	10	6.8
Victim in hospital and cannot give further information	9	6.1
Total	148	100.0

A vague description of the offender due to conflicting stories of drunken, young, or retarded victims, was a major cause for police failure to detect the offender. The fact that 28 percent of the victims gave conflicting stories of the offense raised problems for them in court.[13] Almost another quarter of the unsolved cases stemmed from refusal of the victim to cooperate with the police (22 percent). This group consisted mainly of adult women (90 percent Negro) who wanted to avoid further embarrassment and inconvenience by appearing in court, and so on. They said that they wanted to forget the whole unfortunate event. Such especially is the case with those victims who were drinking with the offender (22 percent in this group). Parents who refused to cooperate with the police (in 7 percent of the unsolved group) did so, mainly, to avoid further exposure of the child victim to interrogation, court appearance, and so on.

13. Forty percent of these victims were submissive to the rape; 32 percent were afraid of the offender; 28 percent were below 14 years of age.

17

Theoretical Considerations

The patterns of forcible rape, disclosed and analyzed in the present study, call for some theory of causation. At the outset it should be stated that it is within the sociological orientation—the variables and changes in crime rates and empirical patterns observed in a given community at a given time—that the answers are sought to such questions as why rape involves mainly Negro victims and offenders, why it involves mostly those at the lower end of the occupational and social hierarchy, and why it occurs more frequently among certain age groups. The sociological orientation has been adopted not merely because of a bias on my part, but because of the limitations of the main rival approach—the psychological one. Nevertheless, the psychological approach to the phenomenon of rape, for all its weaknesses, still dominates the literature. It seems, therefore, necessary to discuss this approach and its contribution to the understanding of the offense under study.

The Psychological Approach

In the present study no special data was assembled to check and explain psychological hypotheses about causes for the committing of the offense among individual offenders. Since the data was collected from police files, the paucity of psychological data is understandable. However, existing notions about the psychological aspects of sexual deviation, in general, and rape, in particular, will be discussed.

No unified theory of the psychology of rape exists; it can only be inferred from the existing writing on sexual deviation and sexual crimes.

The Psychoanalytic Theory of Sexual Deviation

For the psychoanalyst, rape is to be understood mainly within the context of the theory of perversion[1] and theory of symptom formation. In contrast to the nondynamic theories, particularly those which regard perverts as constitutionally inferior, the psychoanalytic theory emphasizes the universality of the instincts from which perversion may develop. According to Freud's early theory,[2] perversion means, essentially, the persistence in the adult of infantile sexuality at the expense of adult genitality. In the pervert, infantile traits fail to undergo the normal process of integration during puberty, but are not converted into neurotic symptoms.

Fixation on early forms of sexuality can be the product of strong, inborn drives, or of pathological experiences in infancy or early childhood.[3] In the latter cases, childhood conceptions of relations between the sexes as being aggressive and sadistic and the idea of sexual pleasure as a negative process, essentially achieved by a relief from a state of "unpleasure," are carried into adulthood.

Further, Freud made a distinction between the sexual object and the sexual aim, which might explain the differences between different kinds of perversions. Maturation involves leaving early sexual aims and objects and choosing new aims, such as propagation infused with feelings of love. Perversion can, therefore, be conceived of as distortions of sexual aims and objects and in the absence or distortion of appropriate feelings toward these objects.[4] Fenichel consolidated the approach that aggression arises from castration fears, which, in turn, are derived from earlier oral sadism. This was later accepted by most psychiatrists as a possible explanation of the etiology of perversion, in particular rape. This theory was especially welcome, because it was supported by the clinically established fact that there is a higher incidence of perversion among males than among females.

A discussion of the dynamics of perversion has included the objects of sexuality, aggression, and the operations of the ego and the superego. One theory suggests that the ego is "split" in perverts;[5] another that through ego mechanisms the sexual object splits. Klein suggests that a "good" sexual object is idealized by the pervert, while he uses aggression, phobia, or denial toward a "bad" object.[6]

1. Fine; Gillespie, "Notes."
2. S. Freud, "Three Essays."
3. A. M. Johnson, "Parental Influences."
4. S. Freud, "Three Essays," p. 146.
5. Gillespie, "The Structure."
6. M. Klein, "Note." For a case study of a murder-rape interpreted as an "object-split" of the mother figure see A. H. Williams.

Freud also suggested another factor in perversion: the conflict between love and sexuality. In perverts and neurotics there is a breakdown of the relationship between sexuality and affection; feelings of authority and the dependency become predominant in the relations between the sexes. Putting it differently, in extreme cases, such as rape, sex is devoid of affection, while in neurotics affection is devoid of sex.

The theory of "surplus sexuality" and "surplus aggression" serves to explain the conditions under which impulses are discharged sexually or aggressively. The sadistic rapist is unable to sublimate his aggression, which is, therefore, discharged in his sexual behavior. The intercourse itself may bring him sexual satisfaction, or the satisfaction may be derived from the act of humiliating the victim. This theory brings us nearer to a psychocultural exploration of perversion. Because culture serves as a background to the function of the personality,[7] regressions can be assumed to have a cultural content, that is, the psychopathology of the sexual deviant is also that of the culture. Thus, "sexual offenses are stimulated, aided and abetted by our . . . cultural attitudes and social structure."[8]

The Psychiatric Approach

The psychiatric explanation of sexual deviancy and sexual crimes is based on the psychoanalytic concepts of normal and abnormal sexual behavior. However, it incorporates dimensions ignored by the parent discipline. Like psychoanalysis, the psychiatric approach assumes the instinctual nature of sexuality, its synthesis with other components of personality, and the importance of childhood experiences, especially of traumas, which determine subsequent sexual behavior. But the psychiatric approach emphasizes the problem-solving aspect of behavior: the origin of internal conflict and the adaptive and learning mechanisms which produce substitute and symbolic behavior. According to this theory, crime in general is seen as a substitute and symbolic expression of instinctual drives contrived by the ego and superego, and rape appears as an attack on the mother figure or a distortion of that figure. In rape, the hostility is considered reactive and secondary rather than a primary instinctual component of the personality.[9] The psychiatric approach also emphasizes the inhibitions and defense mechanisms of the person with an undeveloped or distorted ego or superego, who may act out his aberrant sexual impulses when other substitute outlets are not available. Such mechanisms are the basis for some suggested legal definitions of sexual offenses, which

7. Abrahamsen, *Psychology of Crime*, p. 10; Alexander and Healy, p. 4.

8. Alexander, "A Note," p. 17.

9. Abrahamsen, *Who Are the Guilty?*, pp. 184–85; Glueck, Jr., *New York Final Report*, p. 58; Lofan, et al.

take into account the degree of consent between partners, the nature of the sexual act, the nature of the object of sexual gratification, and the setting in which the act occurs.

Also important for the psychiatric viewpoint are the fantasies surrounding the target of the sexual attack. Fantasies may be associated with nonsexual factors or situations leading to sexual passion, which in turn may be connected to wishes to dominate, the arousal of which may neutralize all inhibitions and lead to violence.[10] Or, fantasies may create psychic conditions and arouse a tension which is only relieved by the sexual attack.[11] In this process of "symbolic equation" an external, concrete form of symbol is experienced as would be the thing symbolized.[12]

The Group for the Advancement of psychiatry attempted to summarize the psychiatric viewpoint in the following definition: "Perversion is a personality pathology if it is repetitive, compulsive, accompanied by the use of violence, without consideration for the partner. It is part of a whole personality disturbance."[13] Perversion is a means of solving psychic conflict when the compelling (instinctual) forces, conscious and unconscious, overwhelm the controlling mechanisms. Through the commitment of the perversive act an equilibrium is reached and relief is gained from general mental and sexual tension.[14] Rape is a crime because of its special elements of "social danger" and of "gross" misconsideration for the victim, which point to the lack of inhibitions curbing sexual and aggressive behavior.

Aggression: The Psychoanalytic and Psychiatric Approaches

Aggression is recognized as a basic element in the personality structure. It is accepted via psychoanalysis as a factor in social relations among people, especially between the sexes.[15] Existing in the Western world is the perception of the aggressive male and the passive woman and relations between them, which may sometimes take the form of direct aggression of male upon female.[16] The question arises about the origin and the direction of the aggression. It is this aspect of the psychoanalytic theory to which the discussion will now turn.

In psychoanalysis aggression is considered as part of the sado-

10. Reinhardt, "The Gentle Sex Murderer."
11. Curran: DeRiver, pp. 14–18.
12. This is something similar to what was found in schizophrenia; see Segal.
13. *Psychiatrically Deviated Sex Offenders,* pp. 12–14.
14. Curran, et al.; Roche.
15. Alexander, *Fundamentals,* p. 260; Reik, pp. 38–43.
16. A. W. Maslow, et al.

masochistic complex of psychosexual development; and it has, consequently, become one of the significant aspects of all psychoanalytic theories of perversion. Freud's ideas about aggression changed in the course of his writing. In the beginning aggression was relegated a minor role vis-à-vis the sexual libido, but like the latter it was considered also an innate instinct.[17] The second theoretical formulation of aggression plays a role along with the sexual instinct, but the emphasis is on the target of aggression. Thus, the interplay between aggression and sexuality may lead to sadism, where satisfaction is achieved by causing humiliation to the love object.[18] Aggression is still conceived in this phase as innate; learning can only modify aggression. In this phase of his theory, the origin of aggression is explained by Freud in terms of ego mechanisms of self-preservation, as a reaction when the ego is threatened. In the third stage, aggression was made a pole in the personality structure. The "death" wish concept was developed to explain aggression turned inside in the form of suicide.[19]

The second phase is more pertinent to our problem of sex crimes. Aggression is described like the sexual libido, in terms of conflict, suppression, sublimation, guilt, and so on. Thus, aggression can be "sexualized" and attached by projections to some targets. Under certain conditions aggressive sexual fantasies will erupt into violent sexual attacks, while in other cases sexual dominance becomes connected with aggressive conceptions of sexual relations.[20] Aggression, like sexual drives, is acted out when fears about sexual adequacy or latent homosexuality exist.[21] Such is the case when hostility to the mother, due to feelings of being deprived of her sexual favors, is projected onto other women.[22] It is possible, however, that an aggressive sexual attack will occur as a reaction, not to problems of such an historical origin, but as a reaction to failure in gaining the responsiveness of a woman. She may personify the mother or just frustrate his wish for relieving sexual tension.[23]

In both of these situations—primary (reactive-sexual aggression) and secondary (situational, aroused aggression)—violent relations could become an end for themselves, with the sexual element being overshadowed

17. S. Freud, "Three Essays."
18. S. Freud, "A Child Is Being Beaten."
19. S. Freud, "Thoughts."
20. DeRiver.
21. Bromberg, "Emotional Immaturity"; Gardner, "Aggressive Destructive Impulse"; Glueck, Jr., *New York Final Report,* p. 85; MacDonald.
22. Freund, chap. 4.
23. Jenkins.

and with feelings of domination rather than sexual satisfaction coloring the relationships.[24]

A "surplus" theory of aggression was also developed. Alexander and Ferenczi pointed to the conditions under which aggressive impulses assume a sexual content when discharged.[25] This occurs in cases in which an excess of aggressive impulses exists, that is, more than is useful for survival, or when a neurotic ego cannot absorb the impulses and they erupt, either in the form of perversion or neurotic symptoms. Thus, the same mechanisms operate in the socialization of sexual impulses as in the socialization of aggression. The rapist, or sexual sadist, is unable to sublimate his aggression. It is released in the form of humiliating his victim or partner; sexual satisfaction may be accidental.[26]

This sketchy description on the psychoanalytic approach to aggression points to some questions left unanswered. First, aggressive sexual behavior, and as a matter of fact any type of aggression, is considered by psychoanalysis as a negative form of behavior, as a sign of some personality disturbances. However, sexual aggression was found to be the case among those presumably normal.[27] Second, neither the relationships between the immediate situation, the specific object, nor the historical antecedence to the aggressive reaction is specified. Thus, factors which may weaken or strengthen the aggression or deflect it, are not explained.

It is this set of problems, of the concrete and immediate antecedence to aggressive behavior, which the theory of "frustration-aggression" comes to answer.[28] We shall deal with this theory later.

Some Critical Notes on the Psychoanalytic and Psychiatric Explanations

Many illustrations can be given of the shortcomings of the theory, methodology,[29] and diagnostic tools[30] of the psychiatric approach to perversion. The psychiatric and psychoanalytic theories contain tautological or circular reasoning; in tests of the theories, hypotheses meant to explain the evidence are themselves treated as evidence.[31]

24. Karpman, *The Sexual Offender,* p. 362.
25. Alexander, "A Note"; Ferenczi, "A Theory of Genitality."
26. Cushing.
27. Kanin.
28. Dollard, et al.
29. Coldwell; Hakeem; Trasler, *The Explanation of Criminality,* pp. 660–68.
30. *California Sexual Deviation Research* (1954), p. 88; Dunham, p. 29.
31. Vold, *Theoretical Criminology,* pp. 155–56.

The psychiatric approach to sexual deviation and offenses still contains disagreement over the nature and causes of sexual offenses. Hence, it is impossible to specify the conditions under which we can expect rape or any other sexual offense to occur. We know, for instance, very little about the connection between specific types of family relationships and community life and specific pattern of sexual deviation.

A noteworthy characteristic of the psychiatric approach is the distinction between sexual deviant and sexual offenders, both of whom are viewed as "sick."[32] Sexual deviations are, then, not by themselves pathological entities, but represent an underlying neurosis and should be considered as a substitute gratification. The mere fact of the commission of the offense is taken as proof of the underlying pathological conditions.[33]

The term "deviation" implies a departure from an establishment code of behavior, but it does not necessarily imply a criminal offense. One way the problem has been resolved is by letting the law define deviation. This is the reason why the terms "sexual offender" and "sexual deviate" are often used synonymously.

However, the legal definition of these terms provides no clue to the offender's personality, the significance of the offense for him, his background, or the society in which he lives.[34] "To name the crime," said Healy, "does not elucidate the diagnosis, neither the prognosis, nor does it suggest the best treatment."[35] Also, from data collected on isolated illegal acts, committed by otherwise law-abiding citizens, psychiatrists try to generalize about "habitual" criminals and criminals in general, viewing them as if they represent a clear and definite special personality system.[36] They are deceived by the phenomenological similarities in the structure and commission of the crime.[37] Sociologists show the variety of motivations and psychological defenses which operate in the same antisocial and illegal acts.[38]

Another shortcoming of the psychiatric approach is the lack of dis-

32. C. Allen, *The Sexual Perversions;* London and Capiro. These are but two examples of the voluminous literature, books, and papers which make the same point.

33. Karpman, *The Sexual Offender,* p. 562.

34. Schuessler and Cressey.

35. Healy, p. 402. The same point was made by Sellin (*Culture Conflict and Crime,* p. 44), who states that "etiological conduct research is not greatly interested in the legal label." It means separating legal from behavioral classification. Such a position is taken also by Korn and McCorkle (pp. 45–47). For a recent discussion on this problem see: Trasler, "Strategic Problems"; Turk.

36. The characteristics assumed are not generic to all offenders.

37. Devereaux, "Neurotic Crimes."

38. A. K. Cohen, *Delinquent Boys,* pp. 147–57.

tinction between cases in which a perverse act is a symptom and cases in which perversion is a psychopathological condition, a neurosis per se. In the former, an individual might try a certain mode of gratification, which in itself may be classified as perverse but which is only an addition to his regular, normal, sexual behavior. In the latter, perverse acts dominate the sexual life of the individual. But, again, the assumption is often made that both sorts of cases indicate illness.[39]

The psychiatric approach elaborates on the operation of psychological mechanisms which explain the dynamics of perversion formation. The list of mechanisms is rich and varied. The question of which mechanisms to choose in explaining the causes of rape in general and its variations among different groups and why a particular person committed the offense, remains.

Sociologists accept the view that current definitions of "normal" and "abnormal" sexuality are culturally and historically determined,[40] but psychiatrists, in their treatment of the concept of a symptom, overlook the possibility of distinguishing symptoms belonging to individuals from "group symptoms." An individual deviates from the accepted code of his group, or an entire group or subculture may tolerate or condone types of sexual behavior condemned by the general culture.[41] Culture determines not only the specific nature of the inner conflicts but also the nature of the defenses permitted to deal with them and their behavioral manifestations.

Another aspect virtually neglected by psychiatrists is that of sexual offenses committed in groups. They fail to see that sexual behavior of an individual may arise not because he is psychiatrically "sick" and not only from what he thinks of as pleasurable, but also to a great extent from his conception of what is expected from him in his group, which may encourage, for instance, the use of force even though the members do not act from a "highly specific and grossly deviated sexual motivation, but as a part of a broader behavior system in which force may be used to attain their goals."[42] Whatever the variables chosen by psychiatrists to explain the offense, they are always looked upon as "sources," they are mostly

39. Often the assumption is made by psychiatrists that crime and perversion are "evil," and that "evil" is illness. They fail to understand that they are treating cases from different stratified sociocultural systems with different conceptions of illness; see Nettler. For a bitter, but succinct plea for differential perception in the case of illicit pregnancy, see Vincent, *Unmarried Mothers,* p. 12.

40. See Ford and Beach. We cannot say, however, that toleration exists for all types of sexual behavior. Incest and rape are not tolerated in almost all societies. See J. S. Brown.

41. Devereaux, *Normal and Abnormal.*

42. Wheeler, p. 276.

imputations, frequently circular, whereas they may actually be created by the action of the offender himself and his contact with the reaction of the "labeling" or "defining agencies."[43]

Psychiatry in general is concerned with the individual and his behavior in terms of inner motivations. This may well explain why such factors in sexual deviation as the role of the victim in sexual offense and class, minority, and subculture differences have not been accounted for sufficiently in psychiatric research on sexual crimes.[44] Another possible explanation is that sexual behavior has not been considered as belonging to the realm of regular academic pursuit, pertaining rather to the sphere studied by clinicians whose work is limited to problems of childhood in the family circle.[45]

Psychiatrists have also failed in their attempts to define the personality characteristics of the sexual offender. Either they make an a priori list of characteristics on the basis of some theory,[46] which they try to prove on data selected from groups of offenders (with or without a control group), or they concentrate on specific characteristics connected with the offense and not with the offender; for example, the choice of victim. When no definite personality factor is detected for explaining the offensive or perversive act, there is a tendency toward speaking of "multiple" causation,"[47] or about "maladjusted," "neurotic," or "psychosexual immaturity." The reasons for using such vague terms is that sexual offenders do not comprise a group suffering from a single neurosis[48] or a single type of sexual pathology.[49] Hence, one type of offense might be committed by persons with a variety of personality types, while other persons of a single personality type might commit a variety of offenses.[50]

From the sociological standpoint, the component in rape most overlooked by psychiatrists is the epidemiological aspect of crime. Even if they are aware that different offenders may share the same basic problems, psychiatrists cannot explain why all the offenders in, for instance,

43. Emphasis on the "feed back" process in crime, particularly sexual deviation, is totally lacking. Hostility and sexual hunger due to imprisonment may be decisive factors in some cases of rape.

44. "In the present there is a trend in studies on sexual deviation to show greater recognition to diversity of their social background"—Spencer, p. 482.

45. This was clearly brought out by Kinsey in his studies, as well as by Whyte in his "A Slum Sex Code."

46. For a general critique of the personality characteristics of offenders, see Schuessler and Cressey.

47. Group for the Advancement of Psychiatry, p. 1.

48. Ellis and Brancale, pp. 37–41; *Report of the Mayor's Committee,* pp. 73–74; Tappan, *The Habitual Sex Offender,* p. 15.

49. Hirning, pp. 238–39.

50. Brancale, et al.

one neighborhood, are driven to the same deviant solution. As psychiatrists claim what causes criminal activity may also, and instead, cause neurosis,[51] why was the criminal solution chosen by so many individuals? Was it considered independently or was it because they were of the same age or ethnic or class position within the social structure?

Methodologically, the psychiatric approach suffers from lack of reliability in diagnosis and in the diagnostic tools.[52] Periodically, a few clinical—for example, psychopath or neurotic—concepts dominate the diagnosis and classification of deviates. Even then, there is disagreement not only about the definition and characteristics of the concept, but also in regard to the means of diagnosing persons classified as deviants. One gets the impression that clinical presentations are regarded by psychiatrists as facts rather than as hypotheses requiring further tests of an experimental nature, in spite of the fact that the psychiatric approach relies heavily upon the "case history" method of proving assumptions and, upon conclusions gained through analytic insights. Information gained by the former method is tainted by conscious or unconscious drives, and its analysis is retrospective and liable to be distorted.

Psychiatrists, by adopting the "survey approach" may have enriched the field by providing provocative hypotheses, but this approach does not provide a sound basis for generalizations. Even the "survey studies" cannot be considered research reports, since they consist only of the study of selected groups (apprehended, convicted, offenders, or those undergoing treatment) without control or comparison groups and without specific research designs. Thus, the lumping together of a variety of sexual offenses or sexual offenders and their characteristics, and the subsequent averaging of figures make comparisons with normal or atypical groups almost impossible.

Since the proportions of psychiatrically disturbed sexual offenders varied from survey to survey, the question arises as to what distinguishes the psychiatrically normal from the abnormal sexual offender.[53] The samples do not indicate if, and how much, those surveyed differ from those who are imprisoned but are not investigated or from those who have not been caught at all. It is also not known whether the diagnostic tools employed are sensitive enough to separate personality "difficulties" from reactive behavior to prison life.[54] The samples included a variety of sexual offenders but very few rapists. Moreover, the assignment of characteristics to the offenders is influenced by the knowledge of the type of

51. Zilboorg, p. 1.
52. Hakeem.
53. Group for the Advancement of Psychiatry, pp. 1–2.
54. Bendix, "Psychiatry in Prison."

offense they have committed. These characteristics are, therefore, use-less for prediction.[55] This criticism is not intended to eliminate certain psychiatric concepts from use in arriving at some pertinent generaliza-tions in psychiatric studies of sexual crimes, but these studies do not help to elucidate the causes of such crimes. Psychiatric case studies have an heuristic value, and the psychiatric approach has helped in pointing out misconceptions about sexual offenders, for instance, that they are "over-sexed," that they progress from minor to serious offenses, or that they stick to one type of crime, and so on.[56]

In the following pages will be summarized the different concepts used and interpretations given by various scholars or psychiatric aspects of aggressive sexual offenses. Only a few of them, however, touch specifically on forcible rape.

Socialization and Sexual Deviation

The cornerstone of current psychoanalytic and psychiatric theory is that sexual behavior, normal or deviate, is a result of the socialization process. Yet, as Child stated after reviewing the evidence up to 1954, and as McCord and McCord reported in 1962, ". . . while socialization variables are thus shown by elimination to have great importance as antecedents to adult sexual behavior, we do not have as yet an adequate scientific basis for stating the exact relationships involved."[57]

In other words, we lack definite evidence for concluding that the vari-ations in adult sexual behavior are to be ascribed directly to variables in sexual socialization, rather than to variables pertinent to other aspects of behavior or to experiences which occur later than the primary socializa-tion process.

McCord and McCord attempted to formulate specific hypotheses about the relationship between distinct types of sexual deviants and the type of authority their parents represented, the sexual behavior of the parents, and the subjects' early sexual experiences. They identified one type of sexual deviant, which comes near to the aggressive sexual offender and the rapist. This is the "extrapunitive perverted" type, who partici-pates in overt sexual experiences and exhibits unrestrained aggressive tendencies. The specific background of this type is as follows: strong maternal encouragement of dependent behavior; father sexually promis-cuous, who drank excessively and was a brutal disciplinarian; and pre-mature sexual heterosexuality.[58] While the boys were subjected to sexual

55. Wheeler, p. 275, n. 66.
56. Ellis and Brancale, pp. 33–37.
57. Child, p. 667; McCord and McCord, p. 165.
58. McCord and McCord, pp. 171–72.

repression by the mothers, their sexual drives were heightened by the fathers' examples of uninhibited sexual behavior and alcoholism, which can partially explain their premature heterosexual relations.[59]

The McCords' study indicated the existence of a correlation between specific conditions for specific deviations. However, since not all of those who undergo these particular socialization patterns show such deviation, the question arises as to the specific conditions in which a predisposition for deviation actually results in deviant acts. The McCords dealt with lower class sexual deviants and suggested, as did Whyte, the existence of a "slum sex code." Their findings point to the importance of events and conditions beyond the "latency" or "prepuberty" periods which are considered by psychoanalysts as the upper limits of the socialization period.

The Traumatic Factor

Within the socialization process the psychological approach identifies various conditions and experiences from which the various psychological impairments ensue and which may lead to perversion. In general, they are looked upon as traumas which either, in one way or another, deprive the boy of three basic needs—security, affection, and suitable identification[60]—or they increase his fears and anxieties.[61] A number of studies on sexual perversity have stressed the fact that in some instances perversity is the result of a pleasurable or negative traumatic experience in the early stages of psychosexual development.

The influence of the trauma leads to the basic assumptions of psychological mechanisms of generalization and displacement of feelings toward females, in general, because of a traumatic event with a particular female. The function of perversity is to undo the results of such negative experiences.[62] It is possible, however, that when trauma results from a pleasurable experience the individual will attempt to repeat it.[63] Both kinds of incidents could lead to the individual's having certain attitudes toward sexual relations and relations between the sexes. He will be driven to search for certain types of victims or to enter into certain types of sexual relations.[64] Explanation of perversion and rape through the use of the concept of trauma would be more satisfactory if there were not so many questions left begging for answers: for example, is the traumatic

59. It is interesting to note that Bandura and Walters' (*Adolescent Aggression,* chap. 5) independent study on the aggressive adolescent shows that the aggressive boys had the same pattern of family background.

60. Henry and Gross; Piker; Wertham.

61. Pearson, p. 198.

62. B. Karpman, "A Case of Pedophilia."

63. Curran, et al.

64. Rabinovitch.

factor a universal one, or is it culturally bound;[65] is the trauma always a result of childhood experience and always deleterious;[66] what traumas, in particular, are "cataclysmic" events[67] or long and spread traumatic events;[68] what is the connection between trauma and perversion, in general, and rape, in particular?

Dunham maintained that, although all the sexual offenders in his sample had a traumatic parent-child relationship (hostilities or seductiveness), many who had suffered such experiences became reasonably adequate adults.[69] Bernard Glueck, found that among the rapists only 27 percent showed fear due to sexual trauma, such as witnessing the primal scene, seduction, sex play with adults, or undue punishment for normal sexual curiosity or behavior.[70] Thus, like any single explanation for a sexual offense, trauma may be a necessary factor but not a sufficient one.

Among the sexual traumas and infantile sexual experiences which are stressed by the psychiatric approach as conducive to sexual deviation are early sexual experience with adults, unconscious seductiveness on the part of parents, and inhibitions of sexual interests and experimentation. Rabinovitch discloses that one of the most common findings in the case histories of boys guilty of sexual delinquency is the compulsive need to reexperience gratification at a genital level which they had experienced as children with an adult person.[71]

Much emphasis is given by psychiatry to the kind of sexual trauma where the attitude of the mother is seductive toward her son,[72] which may even reach the extent of unconsciously sanctioning and encouraging the child's delinquency.[73] The seductiveness of parents reactivates oedipal feelings, castration fears, and homosexuality. Such seductiveness also generates hatred toward the mother and, thus, creates an image of women rejecting men and being conquerable only by force. This complex, according to one theory, explains the aggressive behavior of the rapist,

65. Devereaux, *Normal and Abnormal; Kinsey.* See also Erickson, *Childhood and Society,* for the theme of how three cultures are organized around a specific traumatic event in the life of every child within his respective culture.

66. Pearson, p. 198.

67. Ibid.

68. Abrahamsen, "Rorschach Test"; Volberg, p. 125.

69. Dunham, p. 23.

70. Glueck, Jr., *New York Final Report,* p. 28.

71. Rabinovitch, pp. 614–15.

72. Glueck, Jr., "Psychodynamic Patterns"; A. M. Johnson, "Parental Influences"; Johnson and Szurek; W. F. Wile.

73. A. M. Johnson, "Sanction," 225–46. For the classical statement see Ferenczi, "Confusion of Tongues."

who harbors ambivalent feelings of fear, rage, and sexual attraction toward women who are mother images in his eyes.[74]

If, according to the previous explanation, the early trauma experienced by perverts was a somewhat pleasurable experience, other scholars explain perversion and rape as results of traumatic experiences which were not unpleasant.[75] In cases in which the mother is seductive, emphasis is placed on the fact that the young child is also sexually denied by the mother. This experience fosters within the child insecurity and the fears which are liable to strengthen homosexual tendencies[76] and tendencies toward aggression in his relations with women as the sole means of overcoming the aforementioned fears. Some psychiatrists attach primary importance to the trauma of the boy who witnesses his parents engaging in the sexual act,[77] which to him seems to be an assault made by an aggressive man upon a passive woman. There is a tendency for such a boy to generalize and see all sexual relations as relations between an aggressive man and a passive or resisting woman.

A more common traumatic experience than the overly seductive or suggestive attitudes of the parents is the inhibition of normal sexual interests and experimentation. Verbal inhibition and sexual experimentation may be combined and may together produce trauma. Such trauma leads to preoccupation with sex, guilt, and sexual conflict.[78] Psychiatrists also place importance on the relationships between parents and children with respect to discipline and "power." A younger boy who is subjected to a strict disciplinary regime and severe punishments or to unsystematic disciplinary measures may indulge in rape or some other manner of sexual deviation as a sort of revenge upon his mother.[79] Or, sexual deviation may result when the boy feels rejected because of his mother's overindulgence and permissiveness, which contains unconscious elements of seduction and stern discipline, depriving him of independence.[80] Usually such a boy has either a strong but affectionless father or a weak father and mother-dominated family.[81] In other instances, the father may be found to be tyrannical and narcissistic and the mother extremely neurotic.[82]

The last type of trauma discussed leads us from the specific realm of

74. Bak; Glueck, Jr., *New York Final Report,* p. 78.
75. Karpman, "A Case of Pedophilia."
76. Cassity.
77. Karpman, *The Sexual Offender,* p. 604.
78. Rabinovitch, p. 616.
79. Glueck, Jr., *New York Final Report,* p. 78; Hartog.
80. A. M. Johnson, "Permissiveness"; Waggoner and Bond.
81. Bandura and Walters, chap. 5.
82. McCord and McCord.

the study of trauma to the larger realm of the continuative parent-child relationships and their contribution towards the hardening of sexual deviation. These relationships can be subsumed under a few basic headings: perversion of emotional needs, excessive sexual excitation, and overly strict and cruel disciplinary measures. All the above create a constantly oppressive atmosphere in which healthy sexual identification is impossible.[83] This in turn leads to hyperaggressiveness, an inadequate superego,[84] and confused notions and feelings about sexual relations.

A Defective Superego

The problem of the superego and its relationship to crime and rape is connected with the problem of the importance of innerpersonal controls. Since, according to psychiatric theory, a superego is a resultant of the Oedipus complex and perversion is often considered to be an outcome of the same complex, it is sometimes assumed that there is a relationship between a defective superego and rape:[85] the superego may be so defective as to be unable to control sexual and aggressive impulses when such impulses are misdirected.[86] Different explanations are given for such defects in personal control. It may be the result of neurosis due to parental condoning and unconscious encouragement of the child's acting out.[87] It may also arise from the disruption of the child's dependency relations with his parents.[88] A special type of superego is that which is developed by members of a peer group or subcultural influences.[89] Such a superego condones violence and perversion and is found in the type of offender classified alternately as the "subcultural offender,"[90] the normal non-neurotic criminal,[91] the "socialized delinquent,"[92] or the "true criminal."[93] All of these terms indicate a delinquent without a disturbed superego. It is possible, however, that he suffers from "character disorders," which are symptom free. This is where part of the confusion lies in determining whether he is "sick" or not.

83. Henry and Gross; Piker; Waggoner and Bond.

84. Hammer and Glueck, Jr.

85. Arlow.

86. Hammer and Glueck, Jr.

87. Johnson and Szurek.

88. Bandura and Walters, "Dependency Conflict"; A. Freud, pp. 124–26.

89. A. K. Cohen, *Delinquent Boys;* Matza and Sykes; Redl, "Group Emotions," pp. 583–84; Whyte, *Street Corner Society*. For a summary of research see Berkowitz, pp. 289–93.

90. Bloch and Flyn.

91. Alexander and Staub, pp. 145–52.

92. Jenkins and Hewitt, pp. 28–30.

93. Friedlander, pp. 184–87.

The contribution of a defective or weak superego to the crime of rape is best seen in a person whose superego may lose its control in certain situations,[94] for example, under the influence of alcohol or upon encountering temptation in the form of seductive behavior from a woman. These situations may stimulate violent and deviant sexual impulses and permit their expression. For example, the seductive behavior of a woman may cause the rapist, because of his weak inner controls, to carry the fantasy of seduction or the feeling which a real seduction would elicit to its logical conclusion by raping her.

What is more important for the study of rape is not the fact of sexual stimuli and tensions but the actual expression of aggressive sex behavior. Studies have shown that weak personal control and aggression toward others are related.[95] However, we do not know from these studies the relationship between a defective superego and specific types of aggressive behavior. To solve this problem, there is a tendency to show that child-rearing practices in lower social strata[96] tend to make children feel that expression of aggression toward others is legitimate, while practices in the middle class permit only the expression of aggression toward the self;[97] the direction of the aggression indicates the strength of the superego.[98] There is still dispute as to whether a strict superego, or a weak or defective superego, results from severe parental discipline; but it has been definitely established that the types of frustration, reward, and punishment used in parental discipline influence the strength of the person's inner control. How it affects attitudes toward women and toward aggressive sexual behavior remains to be shown.[99]

The Failure to Solve the Oedipus Complex

Psychiatrists tend to view rape and all other sex deviations as neurotic symptoms, expressing the failure of the offender to solve the Oedipus complex.[100] The act of rape is an attack on the mother,[101] and the victim is imbued, through the mechanism of projection, with all the feelings the boy had with respect to his mother: fear, aggression, incestuous wishes,

94. Rado.

95. Aichorn, pp. 223–24; A. J. Reiss, "Delinquency."

96. Bandura and Walters; Davis and Havighurst; M. C. Erickson; Whiting and Child.

97. Green.

98. Bandura and Walters; McCord and McCord; Henry and Short, chap. 7.

99. Berkowitz, chap. 10, containing a literature summary.

100. S. Freud, "A Child Is Being Beaten"; Hammer, "Psychoanalytical Hypothesis."

101. Abrahamsen, "The Psychology of Crime," pp. 116–67.

and anticipation of punishment in the form of castration.[102] Thus, the rapist tries to extract responsiveness from the mother-victim, which he is afraid will not be given.

Castration Fears

The classic psychoanalytic theory maintains that the failure to solve the Oedipus complex creates castration fears, fears of impotency, sexual inadequacy, and homosexuality.[103] These are coupled with the failure to integrate aggressive elements within the ego structure and may be acted out in the form of rape.

Hammer, through the use of projective techniques, tried to prove that the castration complex is the factor which explains the psychological background of rape.[104] He tested two groups of rapists, pedophiles and those who raped mature women, and compared the results with those obtained from a control group consisting of aggressive offenders who had committed nonsexual crimes. He found the existence of castration fear in 90 percent of the rapists as compared to 55 percent among the other offenders. For the rapist who attacks a mature victim, rape is an attempt to negate castration feelings of sexual inadequacy which the castration fear generates.[105]

Feelings of Sexual Inferiority and Inadequacy

Feelings of sexual inadequacy, inferiority, and psychic impotency were suggested as underlying factors in crime[106] as well as in aggressive sexual behavior,[107] and rape (especially in the form of heterosexual pedophilia) in particular. Various traumas were suggested as underlying these feelings: childhood traumas within the family, especially the failure to solve the Oedipus complex and being rejected by the mother;[108] the trauma for the boy of being thwarted in his first sexual experimentation with his masculinity by being rejected by the female; the trauma resulting from social inferiority which is translated into sexual inferiority.[109]

---

102. Bromberg, *Crime and the Mind;* DeRiver; Glueck, Jr., *New York Final Report;* Hirning. Almost all the psychiatrists who deal with sexual deviation cling to this factor as an independent one, while they also look at the resultant of the failure of oedipal solution, castration fears, sexual inferiority, or latent homosexuality.

103. Karpman, *The Sexual Offender,* p. 347.

104. "A Comparison" and "The Relationships."

105. Bak; Banay, "Profile"; Oltman and Freedman.

106. Reinhardt, *Sex Perversion,* pp. 188–89.

107. MacDonald; Pasco; Roth.

108. Banay, "Profile"; Karpman, "Criminality."

109. Henry and Gross; Selling, "Significant Factors."

Bromberg explains rape as a compensatory sadistic reaction to feelings of inadequacy toward women which result in hostility toward them.[110] These feelings of inadequacy originate in the feminine tendencies of the male. By aggressiveness toward the victim, the rapist can mask his rejection of women or his uncertainties about and fears of accepting social standards of masculinity. Humiliating the victim means putting her in an inferior, degrading position, which enables the offender to satsfy his need for sexual dominance. Rape, then, is a reflection not only of sexual feelings but also of social feelings. Thus, aggression toward the victim is far more significant than the sexual satisfaction per se. Through the forcing of the victim to sexual relations the rapist expresses, proves, tests, and gains his image of masculinity, which involves sexual as well as social dominance over women.[111] Also, some sexually inadequate persons can achieve and maintain erection only when they perform aggressive acts.[112]

Granted that psychiatrists may be right about this point, but the questions arise: in which specific situations do feelings of sexual inadequacies lead to rape rather than to passive homosexuality, and how does being hostile and aggressive affect the rapist's attitude and behavior toward women?

Homosexual Tendencies

Karpman, in line with orthodox psychoanalytic theory, maintains that the feeling of inadequacy toward women is not the cause of rape.[113] Inferiority is secondary to something more profound, the incestuous desires which cause castration fears resulting in homosexual tendencies. Rape is an irrational attempt to deny these latent homosexual tendencies[114] by acting out those signs which are considered the marks of masculinity, aggression, and sexual conquest.[115]

Ideas which attribute rape to any of the three factors just discussed—castration fears, feelings of sexual inadequacy, and latent homosexuality—share the assumption that rape is a projective and compensatory reaction to a neurotic inhibition. This particular symptom of neurosis appears because of early sexual development which brought on the regression toward, or made the person fixate on the pregenital level in which aggression and sex were not yet integrated into the ego.

110. Bromberg, *Crime and the Mind,* chap. 4.

111. DeRiver.

112. Haines, et al.

113. *The Sexual Offender,* p. 347. See also Guttmacher, pp. 116–18; Reinhardt, *Sex Perversions,* p. 188.

114. Herman. See also: Bromberg, "Emotional Immaturity"; Guttmacher and Weihofen.

115. Bender and Curran.

An element of compulsion is thought to be involved as well.[116] The rapist feels compelled to go through the act of seeking either assurance or relief from anxiety. If he is a pervert, the very fact of relief of tension is pleasurable; but, if he is a neurotic, the act is in itself painful and gives no pleasure. So far, no explanations of the decisions made by the rapist about the act itself have been offered. Why, for instance, do some rapists victimize only small girls (pedophiles)? Here the emphasis is on the meaning of the child victim for the older sex offender.

The Fetish Factor

The fetish element in sexual deviations has been investigated, especially in terms of the selection of the victim. The victim is termed "fetish" when she is a highly sexualized special object toward which the offender feels great emotion and which may arouse the fantasy of sexual gratification.[117] Some authors include within this concept a personal disposition toward a certain female without any connection to genital sexuality or even to eroticism.[118] The main emphasis in the fetish theory is that the fetish arouses sexual stimulation and sexual gratification connected with the woman[119] or with certain parts of her body or attire.[120] The elements of fantasy and the compulsive anticipation of sexual gratification, regardless of whether the first sexual experience was pleasurable[121] or frightful,[122] are considered important. The choice of the fetish victim can explain much about the psychodynamics of the offender, and knowledge of this choice is very helpful in formulating a diagnosis.[123]

The Organic Factor

Von Kraft-Ebing[124] and other leading psychiatrists of the late nineteenth and early twentieth centuries considered sexual perversion to be essentially a form of "degeneracy" caused by hereditary "taint" and often associated with physical stigmata of degeneracy. In his later writings, Von Kraft-Ebing modified his views by placing greater emphasis, as did Bloch,[125] upon accidental and social causes.

116. Karpman, "Felonious Assault" and "The Obsessive Paraphilias."

117. Fairbairn.

118. Curant; Grant.

119. East, "Sexual Offenders"; Reinhardt, *Sex Perversions,* chap. 11; Stekel.

120. De River, pp. 7, 10, 51, 82, 142, 223; Von Kraft-Ebing, pp. 218–86.

121. Hadly.

122. Karpman, "A Case of Pedophilia."

123. Grossberg.

124. *Psychopathia Sexualis,* chap. 5.

125. I. Bloch, chap. 7.

The search for organic causes for rape continued. Such causes were divided into two groups: brain damage due to senile dementia in elderly offenders; general paresis due to alcoholism, epilepsy, or postencephalitis, and other organic psychoses; and, physical defects and handicaps.

It has been shown that many of the elderly rapists suffer from senile dementia, which causes degenerative brain changes.[126] Karpman stated that brutal sexual crimes are associated with epilepsy or general paresis due to alcohol, and it is frequently observed that rape is associated with postencephalitis brain damage.[127]

On the other hand, Sutherland and Cressey argue that the connection between sexual crimes and these factors is not direct.[128] First, the effect on the person's efficiency and inhibitions after the disease is more important than the disease itself. Second, there is the reaction of peers, parents, and teachers which affects the child and drives him to desperation, since his lack of ability and his behavior produce in him feelings of inferiority.[129] Third, the encephalitic child, for instance, comes from a family which manifests other symptoms of maladjustment. In short, Sutherland hypothesized an association between organic factors and crime involving social learning through the after-effects of the disease on the emotional and intellectual functions.

In surveys on sexual offenders, the percentage of organically defective offenders has been very small, although, of course, it varies with the size and composition of the sample. Ellis and Brancale found that among 300 sex offenders, none of whom were rapists, only 0.8 percent were diagnosed as being psychotic and having organic defects or problems, and not a single case of organic disorder was found in the Wisconsin survey.[130]

Glueck found in his survey that 20 percent of the rapists were suspected to have some kind of cerebral damage, while 27 percent had suffered from a traumatic accident and 10 percent from prolonged illness.[131] Ruskin in his survey found that only 23 percent had organic disorders.[132] Almost all of them were among the senile patients. It seems that there is no evidence of any consistent relationship between organic brain damage and rape, but it may be an important factor in cases of pedophilia.

In considering the role of physical handicaps and deformity in the causation of rape, we again observe inconsistency in the findings and dis-

126. Henninger.
127. "The Principles and Aims."
128. *Criminology* (5th ed.), p. 124.
129. For a general statement on this problem see L. A. Dexter.
130. Ellis and Brancale, pp. 45–48; *Wisconsin's Experience,* p. 1.
131. Glueck, Jr., *New York Final Report,* pp. 166–68.
132. Ruskin, p. 958.

agreement as to the significance of the factors. Gillin in his study of rapists in Wisconsin prison population, found that many of them had physical handicaps and that this constituted an important factor in their sexual maladjustment.[133] The importance of this factor was argued by many others. Some thought its effect was to deprive the individual of normal contact with women.[134] Others doubted whether such direct and narrow relation existed in all cases.[135] These defects have not statistically been shown to be significant. Their significance in certain cases is direct, but generally, as in the case of organic brain damage, their consequences for efficiency and social learning, and the reaction of other people, are more important than the deformities per se.

It is reasonable to conclude that there is no evidence of a consistent and direct relationship between organic factors and the crime of rape, although their importance is unquestionable in certain cases. The consequences of such impairment for emotional and social functions make them selective factors rather than direct causes.

Mental Deficiency

Various statements have been made about the prevalence of mental deficiency among sexual offenders. At least three authors state categorically that the I.Q. of the rapist is low.[136] Guttmacher and Wiehofen make the following generalization: "Worldwide studies of the correlation of intelligence with the type of offense, has consistently shown that . . . sex offenders are at the bottom of the scale."[137] Bowling adds that the I.Q. of rapists is lower than that of other types of juvenile offenders.[138]

On the other hand, surveys have been made of arrested or convicted sexual offenders, including rapists, which report the contrary; that is, the intelligence of sexual offenders and of rapists follows a normal curve, with the greatest number (about 32.8) percent being of average intelligence.[139]

Another index of mental deficiency is a correlation with scholastic achievement. The New York survey by Glueck, Gillin's study on the

133. *The Wisconsin Prisoner,* p. 129. See also: Doshay; Waggoner and Bond.

134. Leppman.

135. Banay, "Physical Disfigurement."

136. V. Fox, "Intelligence"; Pollens, p. 33; Selling, "Results."

137. Guttmacher and Wiehofen, *Psychiatry and the Law,* p. 148. See also, Von Hentig, *The Criminal,* p. 104.

138. "The Sex Offender and the Law" and "Note."

139. *California Sexual Deviation Research* (1954), p. 120; Ellis and Brancale, pp. 67–69; *Report on the Study,* p. 22–23; *Wisconsin's Experience,* appendix, table 8.

Wisconsin prisoner, the Dunham report on Detroit court cases, and Radzinowicz's study, as well as the reports quoted above, all mention the fact that sexual offenders, and the rapists among them, almost invariably show lower educational attainment than that of the general popualtion.[140] There is, however, disagreement among scholars about mental deficiency among sexual offenders and agreement about their educational achievement, in spite of the different size and composition of the sample used in the different surveys. However, since the tests used are seldom mentioned, one might suspect the use of different tests. Furthermore, the selectivity of the sample of arrested or incarcerated offenders should be noted. Even if there is a correlation between low I.Q. and low educational achievement and the crime of rape, does this necessarily imply a causal relationship? Most psychiatrists feel that the feeble-minded, as a group, are no more likely to commit sexual offenses than are others and that mental deficiency plays a minor role in the causation of sexual offenses.[141] "The sexual offense," says Rabinovitch, "is only one manifestation and one outcome of mental retardation."[142]

We saw that when the same standards of mental capacity were applied to the general population and to arrested or convicted sex offenders, including rapists, the number of rapists of low mental capacity is not disproportionally large. One can say, however, that the feeble-minded and uneducated are more likely to be apprehended and committed. We must look to other factors and regard mental deficiency and low educational achievement as being more important in the treatment of these types of offenders than in the explanation of their specific crime, or of criminality in general.[143]

It is also possible that social learning and its social and emotional concomitants are more important in causing antisocial deviation and crime than is mental deficiency alone.[144] It should be remembered that in the present study we have no information on the mental state and educational attainment of the offender.

When we surveyed the reports on the clinical profile of sexual deviants and sex offenders, the limitations of the psychological approach discussed previously become still clearer. Especially noted were the differences in the proportions of those sex offenders who show mental or emotional dis-

140. Glueck, Jr., *New York Final Report,* p. 26; Gillin, *Wisconsin Prisoner* and "Social Background"; Dunham, pp. 50–51; Radzinowicz, *Sexual Offenses,* p. 122.

141. Abrahamsen, "Study"; Bowman, *The Challenge of Sex Offenders;* Frosch and Bromberg; Karpman, "The Principles and Aims"; Wortis.

142. Rabinovitch, reported in Karpman's *The Sexual Offender,* p. 550.

143. Vold, *Theoretical Criminology,* pp. 88–89.

144. Sutherland and Cressey, *Criminology* (5th ed.), p. 124.

turbances. The differences are partly due to differences in the sample used, for example, some deal with offenders and others with offenses. The reason that psychiatric disturbances were observed at all is that these were groups who were selected for diagnostic and prognostic purposes in hospitals, prisons, or clinics.

These studies indicate that sex offenders do not constitute a unique clinical or psychopathological type; nor are they as a group invariably more disturbed than the control groups to which they were compared. The typical rapist appears from these reports to be from a lower-class background, and when ethnic differences are compared, he is a member of the Negro group. As for his personality profile, he was found to have a normal personality and normal sexual instincts as measured by his choice of victim for sexual gratification.[145] However, almost all of the studies show that he has a pronounced tendency to be impulsive, aggressive, and violent. It is this fact which makes him a danger to the community. Another characteristic emphasized by the studies is the rapist's tendency to be influenced by his immediate environment and to reflect its aggressiveness.[146] The rapist also tends to succumb to factors of circumstances such as encouragements by peers, alcohol, or temptation.[147] It is this complex of sexual aggression among members of certain groups within the social structure where aggression is tolerated, condoned, or even encouraged, which becomes the main focus of the sociological explanation of forcible rape.[148]

Classification and Typology of Sex Offenders and Rapists

While criminologists have only recently turned to descriptive and explanatory classifications of specific crimes,[149] such typological efforts in the study of sex deviations are as old as the interest in the subject itself. In contrast with typological statements in criminology, the psychiatric typology of sexual deviation shows some sophistication. First, psychiatric typologies are based more or less on a unified theory, the underlying assumptions are spelled out and serve diagnostic and treatment purposes. They include the processes by which the offenders are placed in the categories of the classification.

Second, although in surveys the psychiatrists rely on the offensive act for classification purposes, in the analysis of individual cases they go

145. Apfelberg, et al.

146. Gillin, *The Wisconsin Prisoner,* pp. 128–31; Waggoner and Bond.

147. Gillin, *The Wisconsin Prisoner,* p. 128; Glueck, Jr., *New York Final Report,* p. 78.

148. Wheeler, pp. 277–78.

149. Ferdinand; Gibbons, p. 24.

beyond the act, and hence are able to separate the legal classifications from those which are based on the characteristics of the act and its collated antecedent factors. Such separation also enables them to distinguish between those who commit occasional acts and persistent (compulsive) offenders.

Third, psychiatrists even manage to explain the changes in criminal acts, by using the theory of the substitutive and symbolic nature of human conduct. In addition, the aspect of "self-conception" is also included in some psychiatric typologies. By probing into the meaning of the act for the offender—for example, his self-image as a sexually adequate man—they are able to relate this element of self-conception to the dynamics of the personality and the form of the offensive or deviant act.

In spite of these advances, psychiatric classification of sexual deviations and sexual crimes suffers from some basic limitations. While the variables are specified (different traumas, etc.) their indicators are not. Also, as we know, psychiatrists still disagree among themselves as to these variables.[150] This means that the same person may be placed in different groups according to who happens to classify him. Although not conforming to legal categories, psychiatrists often use them as a basis for their classification. When legal categories are used, not all who are supposed to fall into some categories are placed there because of court bargaining factors,[151] or because of the process of normalization and stereotyping.[152]

Also, legal terms do not sufficiently reflect the various dimensions of the criminal act which may differentiate between offenders and their offenses. We saw in our study that rapists differ in terms of the force used and in their interpersonal relationships with the victim, as well as in the number and types of crimes contained in their criminal record.

When avoiding legal categories and using strictly psychiatric ones, many psychiatrists fall into other traps. In using such terms as "neurotic" they are lumping offenders together and reviewing them as total personality systems rather than distinguishing between those who may not be pathological at all but criminal, and those who suffer from some affliction and commit the offense sporadically, and those who commit the offense rarely because of subcultural influences. Such confusion stems from the fact that psychiatric designations presuppose certain psychic dynamics which can explain a variety of offensive acts by the same personality process, which may also operate in persons who do not deviate.

Further, although some "case studies" mention the involvement of the

---

150. They do agree, however, on a standard nomenclature for sexual as well as for other psychiatric disorders. See Committee on Nomenclature.

151. Newman, "Pleading Guilty."

152. On minor sex offenders, see Sudnow.

offender with peer groups or reference group orientation, such factors are not included as variables in the typology. In their attempt to go beyond motivational factors, psychiatrists limit themselves to certain phases of psychosexual development (mainly childhood and latency) within one institutional setting: the family, other, and later situational and institutional frameworks are viewed only either as triggers of an already existing disposition to deviate or as scenes or targets for projections of these tendencies. The possibility that these later situations can induce deviating factors or support and maintain an existing pattern of deviation is ignored.

The following is a list of the variables and their indicators used in the psychiatric classification of sex offenders within which we shall try to identify and place the rapist.

I. The deviant sex offenders
   A. Motivational syndromes
      1. The sources of sexual stimuli; biological sources, fantasies, compulsions, and situational factors (alcohol, seduction, etc.) [153]
      2. The intensity of the sexual urge; inhibited, augmented, etc.[154]
      3. Deflections in the sexual urge:
         a. in the aim;[155] release of tension, anxiety over sexual adequacy, or homosexuality;
         b. in the object of the sexual act; age disparity, etc.;[156]
         c. in the amount of aggression in the attack.[157]
   B. General psychiatric categories; neurotic, psychotic, etc.[158]
      1. The stage of fixation or the level to which the offender regressed[159]
      2. Prognostic and treatment considerations[160]
   C. Modus operandi of the offense; degree of violence[161]

153. Ellis and Abarbanel, pp. 802–11; Karpman, *The Sex Offender,* p. 121; Wortis.

154. Banay, "Profile"; Cushing; Glover, "The Social and Legal Aspects"; Herman; I. S. Wile, "Sex Offenders and Sex Offenses."

155. Alexander, *Fundamentals of Psychoanalysis,* p. 260; Sieverts.

156. Argow; Glueck, Jr., *New York Final Report;* Walker and Straus.

157. G. Allen, *Sexual Perversions;* Guttmacher, pp. 116–18; Hartwell; *Report on the Study of 102 Offenders.*

158. See the exhaustive list of references in Karpman, *The Sexual Offender,* pp. 10–18.

159. C. Allen, *Sexual Perversions;* I. S. Wile, "Sex Offenders."

160. Dunham; *New York City Report.*

161. Argow; Bowman; Dunham; Hartwell; Magnus, "Sexual Deviation Research"; *Report of the Mayor's Committee;* Tappan, *The Habitual Sex Offender.*

    D. Danger to the community
       1. Violence used in the commission of the offense or deviant act
       2. Repeated offenses[162]
II. The normal sex offender
    A. Those falling under the legal definition
    B. The occasional offender; alcohol, seduction in felony rape, sexual experimentation, intimate relationship with the victim, etc.[163]
    C. The offender who belongs to a subculture; the influence of subculture, peer group, etc.[164]

In almost all the classifications, the rapist is placed among those sex offenders who show the following characteristics: They are psychiatrically normal, but antisocial, impulsive, and lacking of inner controls over their pent-up aggressive and sexual drives.[165] They tend to have a criminal record of offenses against the person, of which rape is but one. They usually commit the offenses with brutality and violence. They generally commit the offenses under special provocative situations. They tend to be members of lower-class delinquent or criminal subcultures in which masculinity is expressed in general aggressiveness, including exploits of females in the form of sexual conquests.[166]

The literature on sexual pathology contains descriptions of kinds of rapists who have captured the mind of the public, the clinicians, and the police, because of their assumed special characteristics and the consequences of their crime for their victims. These are the sadists, the "satyriasists," and the libertines (or intellectual rapists).

It is the sadist who arouses most fear and concern among the public. This type of rapist is described as the one who bears tremendous hostility and hate toward women and is obsessed with the need to prove his mastery through sexual conquest. Such a rapist is compulsive and enjoys causing pain to his victim by great violence. Only by such methods can he feel and actually be sexually adequate.[167] In many instances the death of the victim is accidental, for example, when the victim cannot stand the blows or when the offender panics and tries to cover his offense

162. All those who conducted surveys included this category. See V. C. Branham in Karpman, *The Sexual Offender*, p. 18.

163. D. C. Allen, *Sexual Perversions;* Argow; Bowman and Engle, "Sex Offenses"; Cushing; Guttmacher; Henry and Gross; Kanin; Mayer; I. S. Wile, "Sex Offenders and Sex Offenses." All those who conducted surveys on sex offenders included this type in their typology.

164. Argow; Jenkins; *Report of the Mayor's Committee.*

165. Bonger stated (*Criminality,* p. 612), that "this crime is not the act of a pervert, but that of a brute." This allows a sociological rather than a psychological discussion of the crime.

166. Argow; Ellis and Brancale; Guttmacher.

167. DeRiver; Hirning; Jenkins; Reinhardt, "The Sex Killer."

by murdering the victim.[168] For others, the stronger the resistance of the victim, the stronger their excitement.[169] Sometimes, the very voice of the victim is fetishistically bound up with compulsions and fantasies inter-woven with other psychic components.[170]

The male "nymphomaniac," or satyr, is mentioned as another special type of rapist. He is thought to be either the "Don Juan" type, whose sexual desires are insatiable,[171] or a victim of latent epilepsy senile dementia.[172] In some cases satyriasis is not the outcome of purely bio-logical drives, but a secondary symptom, such as homosexual fears or feelings of inferiority.[173]

Another type described in the literature is the libertine or intellectual rapist. This person rejects the standards of affection toward women as not becoming to or binding him.[174] He feels that he must reject women and show his superiority and virility by taking passive women by force.[175] For this kind of person forced sexual relations also serve as a new avenue of sexual experimentation,[176] or offer a new sense of thrill.[177]

It seems to us that the last two types indicate the possibility of a better typology of rapists than that offered by psychiatrists. This is not so be-cause these types are common, but because they suggest a typology ac-cording to roles rather than according to personality factors which may not exist or are not necessarily common to all rapists. According to this new typology, rapists can be classified into three types.

1. Offenders for whom the crime is a symptom or an idiosyncratic act either psychopathological or due to special circumstances; it is devoid of direct social role significance. This type of offender is treated with most concern.

2. Offenders for whom the crime is mainly a "role-supportive act," usually part of a youth culture role, that is, the act is performed for the purpose of maintaining membership in a group or for sheer sexual gratification, while pathology is absent.

3. Offenders for whom the crime is mainly a "role-expressive act." It

168. Bromberg, "Emotional Immaturity."

169. VonKraft-Ebing, p. 87.

170. Ibid., p. 362.

171. Hirschfield.

172. Huhmer; Von Kraft-Ebing, pp. 481–82.

173. Herman; Rosaneff.

174. Hyde; Leppman.

175. Abrahamsen, *Mind and Death,* pp. 148–49; Mann, chaps. 24–25.

176. Laurenson.

177. I. Bloch; Henry and Gross; Walbarst. For an accusation that such attitudes are invading the contemporary American sex mores see: Sorokin; Wolfstein.

is performed not so much for the sexual satisfaction as because of participation in the context which it occurred, for example, group rape.

The act serves as a vehicle to express sentiments and codes appropriate to the group of which the offender is a member and which he has incorporated. While rapists of the other type—for whom the crime is a symptom or an idiosyncracy—may not be conscious of the purpose of the act, such consciousness can be assumed in the other two types. Also, the first type may be a compulsive repeater, while the other two types usually commit the crime under special circumstances. Their aggressive behavior is not a result of deviant sexuality,[178] but can be viewed as originating from participation in a group which condones the use of force in attaining goals.[179]

The Emergence of Sociological Interpretations

A broad phenomenological approach has been adopted for the present study. It not only assumes the study of the crime but also calls for "uncovering of recurring patterns in which particular groups of people are found to commit a particular type of crime in particular types of circumstances."[180] Thus witnessing the failure of the clinical approach to explain rape, especially the epidemiology of the offense, we have used the Durkheimian model; that is to find the relationship between the rates for the offense and the participants, and other various social facts to which they may be connected. Such an approach assumes, among other things, explaining the differential distribution and patterns of the crime and those involved,[181] not in terms of the individual's motivations and nonduplicable mental processes which may have led to the crime, but in terms of variations among groups in their cultural norms and social conditions.[182] Because the highest rates of the offenses studied occurred among relatively homogeneous groups, it is, therefore, assumed that these groups situated in a subculture,[183] hold a particular set of conduct norms which emphasize and condone aggressive behavior, and have also the

178. Ellis and Brancale, p. 94; *California Sexual Deviation Research* (1954), pp. 132–35; Guttmacher, p. 50.

179. Wheeler, p. 276.

180. Wooton, *Crime,* p. 23.

181. Durkheim. On the empirical approach, see Selvin.

182. This sociological approach also assumes: variations in cultural integration; variations in social integration; malintegration between cultural and social structure; variations in the integration of conventional and deviant values, as well as the differences in the manner with which individual members are integrated into their groups. See Stein and Cloward, pp. 478–81.

183. On the meaning and problems of subculture see: Arnold; Bordua's works; Short, Jr., "The Sociological Context." For a recent study of delinquent subcultures which emphasizes ecological factors see Spergel.

least "resistance potential"[184] toward aggressive sexual behavior. Thus, under special circumstances, violence, including sexual violence toward women, is more likely to occur. Furthermore, it is contended that members of these subcultures are more likely to react aggressively than nonmembers. Hence, individual differences in aggressive behavior may also reflect different degrees of integration with the subculture rather than only personality differences of a pathological nature.[185]

It is not contended, however, that there is a unique subculture of rape. Rather, there exists a ubiquitous or "parent" subculture of violence. Rape is, therefore, only an epiphenomenon occurring under special circumstances. Members of these groups are not constrained by their subculture allowing for rape whenever the group demands, but they are influenced by the group, and accept, more readily than nonmembers, the idea of the offense and the justification of the act before and after its commission. They are also more apt to view certain females as appropriate victims, and certain situations as suggestive of, even opportune for, rape.

In adopting this sociocultural approach, we have assigned to other approaches a relatively minor role in explaining the offense. The clinicians, who tend to view rape largely as a consequence of a variety of intrapsychic conflicts and pressures, produce at best only a variety of special cases and individual profiles of offenders. The very nature of their approach precludes explanation of the epidemiological nature of the crime, and the regularities and uniformities empirically established by the present study. Nevertheless, we do not intend to repeat Durkheim's error of rejecting the importance of personality factors in the commission of crime[186] and by this to ignore the role of personality in a subculture. Of course, it is always people who commit rape, but the rate of rape is conditioned by the cultural norms and social organization or disorganization of the groups to which they belong. The rates are not "psychological." Our view is that sociocultural framework precedes, and to a great extent determines, personality.[187]

Attempting to explain the crime in terms of the whole social system, leads to difficulties in detecting those dynamic elements in society which are related to the crime and their distribution within it. On the other hand, a narrow ecological explanation of the offense is insufficient. Ecological factors are only indicators of the distribution of the phenomenon, and can be, at best, only a part of a theory of subculture. In

184. Sellin, *Culture Conflict and Crime,* p. 34.

185. Ferracuti and Wolfgang, "The Prediction," p. 293.

186. Alpert.

187. Malinowski. For a recent summary review on the problem see: Inkeles; Smelser and Smelser.

interpretive analyses the role of ecological factors can only be inferred, for it is within ecological boundaries that personal dispositions to commit crime are developed; crime-evoking situations arise; and criminal solutions are learned and supported.

Trying to explain the crime by using the concept of anomie poses many questions, for instance, those of the validity of assuming a dominant value system: the location of anomie within the individual or the normative system, and the nature of the conflict between the norms of the general culture and those of the subculture.[188] The attempt to explain forcible rape by using the "frustration-aggression" theory is not less frustrating.[189]

What are the assumed frustrations which may explain the act of rape? What are their dimensions and measurements? If status frustration is the cause, when does it lead to rape and when does it lead to other forms of aggression?[190] If it is "sexual hunger," we already alluded that lower-class boys are not deprived of sexual outlet. Also, rape is not highly approved among lower-class boys.[191] If it is the act of an individual boy which is to be explained, we found no study which attempts to explain aggressive sexual behavior by correlation with a particular type of frustration. Usually in studies on the genesis of sexually aggressive behavior, frustration is depicted in terms of broad adverse family conditions, rather than in terms of the specific contribution of each condition to the specific act.

The emphasis on psychological factors to explain the processes of frustration overlooks another factor, that of norms which may define the mode of aggression and give it legitimation. Thus, in a culture which is integrated around what might be called "masculine complex," it is more likely that boys will expect to be sexually aggressive.[192]

Failing to use the concept of displacement, the "frustration and aggression" theory overlooked the cases in which aggression can be an instrumental act for aims other than causing injury or pain. Thus, sexual conquest may be the sole reason for rape with aggression only incidental, or sexual conquest may be used for gaining status, while the sexual satisfaction is but a minor element.[193]

188. For a discussion of the failure of anomie theory to explain homicide see Wolfgang and Ferracuti, "Violent Aggressive Behavior." On the general position of anomie theory in relation to deviation see: Clinard, *Anomie,* pp. 1–57; Matza, *Becoming Deviant,* esp. pp. 87–143. On Anomie theory in relation to juvenile delinquency see Short, Jr., "Gang Delinquency and Anomie."

189. Dollard, et al. On a new attempt to modify the theory see Berkowitz, esp. pp. 26–50. For a critique and bibliography see Buss, pp. 217–29.

190. Cohen, *Delinquent Boys,* pp. 193–94.

191. A. J. Reiss, "Sexual Code," pp. 312–13.

192. Miller, "Lower Class Culture"; Parsons, "Age and Sex."

193. Miller, "Lower Class Culture."

Finally, frustration-aggression theory cannot explain the epidemiological aspect of the offense. To overcome these deficiencies, suggestions were made to differentiate between reactive type of aggression and habitual learned aggression which receives situational reinforcement and facilitation.[194] In the latter case aggression becomes customary, persistent, and not just an ad hoc reaction. This learning and being exposed to aggressive modes of behavior creates an aggressive view of the world. The process "aggression" creates counter-aggression, and a vicious circle is thus established.[195] Such can happen only when the value system is aggressive and is accepted by the members who behave accordingly.[196]

If there exists a subculture in which violence and sexual aggression prevail, our empirical data should indicate its existence. I believe that the data do indicate the existence of such a subculture. The study, along with Wolfgang's conducted on the same area, shows that the rates for forcible rape are highest among Negro males (591.25), as compared to whites (41.9) and adolescents ages 15–19 and young adults ages 20–24, and those who are maritally unattached and belong to the lower socioeconomic class.[197] The data are also related to marital status, indicating the correspondence between age and "marginal" social status as "risk" categories for involvement in the crime.[198] Offenders as a group, but Negroes more than whites, show the highest rate in the "single" (unmarried) category of marital status.

Another important social fact is the lower-class position to which offenders belong. In the present study, our analysis reveals that offenders of both races belong to the lower end of the occupational ladder from skilled workers to the unemployed.

A lower-class subculture of delinquents has been described as primarily ecologically bound,[199] for the offenders and their victims. Statistics from police reports and census tracts revealed that those police districts which rank high according to the frequencies of offenses against

194. Berkowitz, p. 203; Buss, pp. 1–2.

195. Berkowitz, p. 137.

196. There are other forms of aggressions: those which stem from repression of aggression; those which serve as "tension management" (a catharsis), and that of the genuine pervert-sadist.

197. Wolfgang, *Patterns*. The description is centered on the Negro group because of the higher proportion of Negroes in the study. No claims are made that the white offender is different from the Negro offender in terms of "inherent criminality," and so on. What is important, and therefore emphasized, is a "social fact"—the over-representation of the Negro as a group in our sample. See also Wolfgang, *Crime and Race*.

198. Reiss, "Sex Offenses."

199. See the review of the literature in Morris. For later literature see: Boggs; Simpson and Van Arsdol; R. S. Stern.

the person and forcible rape, committed within their boundaries, are also the areas where Negroes are concentrated. The data showed that offenders and victims lived in the same vicinity, and in the majority of the cases offenders lived in vicinity of both victim and offense. Moreover, it was found in the study that rape is mainly a Negro intraracial event. The ecological factor is introduced to enhance the argument of subculture interpretation of forcible rape. Residential proximity serves to maintain and strengthen the idea of interaction between those who are differentially associated in terms of being members of the same race and the same age level.[200] The assumption of subculture gains support because it is within the neighborhood that favorable attitudes toward violence and the use of violence are learned in "a process of differential learning, association or identification"[201] with a reference world of shared expectations, explicit life style, affiliation and participation in urban, lower-class Negro youth subculture.

The data on previous arrest records, when used cautiously, may allow us to accept the assumption that such a record to a large extent reflects the development of a potential for aggressive reaction to situations, where such reactions are learned and supported by the normative system and the peer-group interaction.[202] The analysis of our data shows that half of all offenders had an arrest record for crime against the person. Negroes had a higher proportion of record for two or more offenses, and as a group had a higher proportion of persistent offenders.

The theory of subculture assumes, among other things, that criminality is learned in a sociocultural framework, with the ecological factor an important asset for such learning. Moreover, the sociological theory of lower-class criminality contends that the process of learning and maintaining criminal behavior occurs primarily in the peer group.[203] The present study indicates that of 646 rape cases, 276 were group-rape events. Moreover, group rapes were predominantly intraracial events.

A note should be injected here. It is contended that females are members of the subculture. Studies on lower-class, mainly on Negro delinquency, indicate the lower-class origin of these girls[204] and their in-

200. On the theory of differential association and criticism see: Cressey, *Delinquency;* Glaser.

201. Ferracuti and Wolfgang, "Prediction," p. 296.

202. Hartung, p. 47. As a matter of fact this assumption runs through almost the entire field of literature on subcultures of lower-class delinquency, and it seems unnecessary to quote it directly.

203. The data also show that 19 percent of the victims had a prior arrest record, especially of sexual misconduct, and 20 percent had a "bad" reputation (i.e., of promiscuity).

204. Ball and Logan, and see summary of the literature there.

tensive involvement in the life of the male-dominated peer group. It seems that the girls contribute to the dynamics of the male peer group, especially to its activities in the sexual realm.[205]

However, since we deal with the interpretation of the act of rape, we are emphasizing the offender rather than the victim. In chapters 14 and 15 we have dealt with various nonaccidental situations which favor the coming together of offenders and victims and result in rape. We found that in most of the cases victims and offenders lived in the same neighborhood; they were of the same race and of the same age. It was also found that in over half of the cases the victims were not strangers to their assailants; they were actually neighbors or close friends. These results lead us to assume that both victims and offenders are members of the same subculture. However, because the female is the subject of the male's aggression, and because it is the act itself with which we are concerned, it is the male-dominated subcultures that we came to discuss. We are well aware of the role of the female as transmitter of the subculture (mother role), as one who reflects some of the subcultural "themes" (sexual promiscuity, etc.), and as one who participates in victim exposing subculture and victim disposing life styles.

The data presented indicate those elements which can be inferred from previous studies on subculture and which seem to be linked to our perspective. If any support is to be given to the subcultural interpretation of forcible rape it will appear in two forms: in studies which will show the same social groups as those included in our sample, and as having a high rate of involvement in crimes against the person and in replicated studies of the same groups in the same area after a passage of time.[206] For the first approach we can use Wolfgang's study on *Patterns in Criminal Homicide,* conducted in Philadelphia and ended in 1958, when the present study begins. For the second type of support we can use Kupperstein's *An Analysis of Sex Offenses Committed in Philadelphia during 1962.*[207]

In the first study, homicide data indicate *significantly* high rates among Negro males, participants of the ages 20–24, from the lower socioeconomic class. These are the same groups which emerged in our study as having the highest rates of involvement in forcible rape.

In the second study, conducted two years after the present study ended its data collection phase, Kupperstein discloses that "most of those arrested by the police for the crime of forcible rape and assault with intent to ravish, were young men between the ages of 15 and 19 years."[208] When

205. See: Hanson; Salisbury, p. 32; Short, Jr., Strodtbeck, and Cartwright.
206. Sellin, "The Sociological Study of Criminality."
207. Kupperstein, pp. 25–37.
208. Ibid., p. 29.

crime rates were computed, the highest rate (190.1) appeared for offenders between 15 to 24 years of age. A breakdown by race shows that "the rate for arrest for non-white offenders is about nine times greater than for whites."[209]

The theory of subculture that we adopted combines the theories of Downs, Kvaraceus, Matza, Miller, Redl, but not that of Cohen.[210] The means-end assumption in Cohen's theory is not tenable, since, as we have seen, lower-class boys are not deprived of heterosexual outlets.[211] Second, the assumption about the constraining element of subculture is questionable in the light of the fact that rape, although a prevalent activity, is not a frequent and sustained one.[212] Granted that theories of subcultural descriptions consider the etiology of certain delinquent acts, the process leading to the particular acts is not discussed. The approach which describes the acts and their specific nature needs to be integrated with the theory of subculture; this was attempted in the present study.

The existence of subcultures of aggression and violence and its ecological distribution is well-documented in criminological literature.[213] Also documented (see any recent textbook) are the high rates of aggressive and violent crimes among young males located in the lower-class sectors of the American social structure; especially notable are the rates among lower-class Negro men in their adolescence and early adulthood.[214]

The literature on subculture also indicates the prevalence of aggressive and violent behavior, in general, as well as towards women. This prevalence occurs especially among lower-class adolescents and young men who are members of gangs.[215]

Studies in socialization show that lower-class boys learn overt and direct aggressive attitudes and conduct from their families,[216] as well as from peers. As a result of these processes of socialization, the subculture

209. Ibid., pp. 32–33.

210. Downs; Miller, "Lower Class Culture"; Redl, "Psychology of Gang Formation" (Redl emphasizes the importance of the gang rather than the peer group and, by implication, the neighborhood subculture). A. K. Cohen, *Delinquent Boys.*

211. Reiss, "Sex Offenses"; Whyte, "A Slum Sex Code."

212. Matza's *Delinquency and Drift* is another adapted example.

213. For a recent documentation see Ferracuti and Wolfgang, "Design."

214. See Savitz, chaps. 3, 7; Wolfgang, *Crime and Race,* pp. 29–32, and *Patterns.*

215. Bloch and Niederhoffer; A. K. Cohen, *Delinquent Boys;* Miller, "Aggression" and "Lower Class Culture"; Short, Jr., Strodtbeck, and Cartwright; Short, Jr., and Strodtbeck; Whyte, "A Slum Sex Code"; Yablonsky, *The Violent Gang.*

216. For a summary on the socialization of aggression and sex drives in the lower class see Berkowitz, chap. 10, bibliography.

becomes part of their perceptual and motivational structure. They become sensitive and habitually responsive to its expectations and definitions of situations.[217] Under these conditions, aggressive and exploitative behavior toward women become part of their normative systems, for those members who do not conceive such behavior as wrong or as a deviation from the normal.[218] Moreover, the pressure of certain stimuli (special situations) precipitates the potential violence and sexual aggression that exist in each one of them, which leads them to see many situations as opportune to sexual conquest.

Subculture: The Sex Aspect

In approaching the subject of subculture, it is necessary to consider those parts of the value system concerned with sex which can be assumed to permeate more or less all social classes and ethnic groups of American society.[219] Presumably, any subculture is influenced by the beliefs that flourish in influential sectors of the normative order.

Since World War II, a multitude of studies have been conducted to measure the changes in attitudes towards sex, especially toward premarital sexual conduct,[220] while other studies have looked into other aspects of sexual behavior.[221] Almost all the studies have detected a tendency towards: a rejection of the puritanical attitudes toward sex; the elimination of the double-standards for the sexes; the existence of a split in the American middle class between ideal norms and real practice, and between maximum stimulation and titillation and minimum outlet.[222] Within the American society differences were found in the socialization of

217. Wolfgang, *Patterns,* p. 329.

218. See, for instance, Reiss, "Sex Offenses," which provides a good summary of the literature on this aspect of lower-class subcultures.

219. On the changes in sexual morality in Europe and some broad sociological explanations of its occurrence see: I. Bloch; Seward; papers by Von Bemmelen and by Sieverts in Grunhüt, *Sexual Crime Today.* For a comparative study on sex crimes see Hsu. It is unnecessary to document the voluminous writing on sexual patterns among other cultures, usually among primitives, but Margaret Mead's and Montegaza's writings can serve as an introduction to this literature. On the history of sexual mores in the Western world see: De Rougemount; Lewison; Tylor.

220. I. L. Reiss, *Premarital Sexual Standards* and "Sociological Studies of Sexual Standards."

221. Ehrmann, *Premarital Dating Behavior;* Ellis, "Recent Studies"; Hohman and Schoffner; Kinsey, et al., "Concepts"; Vincent, "Ego-Involvement"; Wood, chap. 10.

222. Ditzion; Drucker and Christensen; Ellis, *American Sexual Tragedy, Folklore,* and *Sex Habits;* Foote; Hacker; Himelhoch and Fava; Kardiner; Mead, *Male and Female;* Mores; Porterfield and Salley; Riesman, et al., pp. 172–75, 319–22; Schmolhausen; Sorokin; Whitman.

sex, in the means and severity of control over sexual expression, and in the areas of sexuality which are supervised.[223]

Students have also observed the differences in attitudes and practices concerning sex among adolescents and adults. The general impression gained from the literature is that lower-class people tend to show more freedom in sexual experimentation, which starts earlier in their life.[224] There is a tendency to exploit promiscuous girls in order to establish status within their peer group.[225]

Turning to that section of the Negro lower-class subculture which produced the highest rates of the offense and of those involved in forcible rape, again it is assumed that its structural features and patterns of cultural learning of aggressive sex behavior produced selective perception of, and kinds of interactions with, women, which may partially explain the over-representation of lower-class Negroes in our sample.

The Lower-Class Negro Subculture

The concept of subculture has the advantage of avoiding a priori assumptions about differences between strata within the subculture or variables connected with these differences. However, a distinction must be made between racial, ethnic, and class subcultures.[226] Most of the studies on subcultures have emphasized the class element and considered occupation and family as the most important determinants in understanding and describing the subculture.[227]

The Negro subculture is an historically unique subculture which embodies all the characteristics of a lower-class subculture but has some of its features in a more pronounced form. What follows is a description of the characteristics most important for our purposes. The Negro subculture is characterized by the revolving of life around some basic "focal concerns," which include a search for thrills through aggressive actions and sexual exploits. One-sex peer groups exist "who pursue these activities and who constitute the psychic focus and reference group for those over twelve and thirteen."[228] The emphasis is given by males to masculinity, and their need to display and defend it through brief and transitory relations with women.[229] Such needs, and the subsequent con-

223. Davis and Ginzberg; Havighurst; Sears, et al., chap. 6.

224. Breed; Crook's works; Hollingshead, pp. 110, 416–24; Kinsey, Pomeroy, and Martin, pp. 497–516, 549–62; Neiman; Rabban; Vincent, *Unmarried Mothers;* Whyte, "A Slum Sex Code"; F. G. Wood.

225. Hollingshead, pp. 412–16; A. J. Reiss, "Sexual Code," p. 312–13.

226. See the latest attempt for such distinction by Gans, pp. 229–63.

227. For a review of the literature see Downs.

228. Miller, "Lower Class Culture," p. 14. See also, Miller and Riesman.

229. See Gans, p. 246; Rainwater, p. 69.

cern with sex, stems from growing up in a family in which the mother is dominant and the father has a marginal position.[230] Being socially and economically powerless, the Negro father becomes a negative model of identification for his sons, who can emulate only his aggressive and sexual behavior.[231] Young boys are imbued with negative, or at least ambivalent, feelings toward masculine functions. Sexual and aggressive behavior becomes the main vehicle for asserting their worthiness. They, therefore, idealize personal violence and prowess which substitute for social and economic advantages.[232] Moreover, because the lower-class subculture stresses male dominance outside the family circle, it allows women to enter relationships with men mainly via sex and in situations of an episodic and instrumental nature.[233]

Among lower-class Negroes there has usually been found permissiveness in sexual socialization and control, early sexual experience among boys and girls, promiscuous behavior of girls, and the use of sex by boys for achieving status and as an indication of masculinity; for girls sex provides prestige and a way to enter the boys' peer groups.[234]

The emphasis on physical discipline and the lack of self-control on the part of adults were considered the main reason for the prevalence of aggressive behavior and for expressing anger by violence.[235] This aggressive behavior is further learned and supported by the peer group.[236]

The Subculture: The Age Factor

The analysis in the present study reveals that most of those who are involved in the crime of rape are adolescents and young adults. Hence, sexual aggression should be considered also from the perspective of age. It can be assumed that the natural development processes *together* with

---

230. Dollard, p. 276; for a historical account of this phenomenon see Frazier, *The Negro Family.* For the results of such family structure see: Gans, chap. 11; Kardiner and Ovesey; Miller, "Lower Class Culture," p. 9; Rosen.

231. For a recent perceptive view see Lewis.

232. Dollard, p. 224; Gans; G. B. Johnson; Kardiner and Ovesey, pp. 76, 97, 109.

233. Breman; Short, Jr., Strodtbeck, and Cartwright, p. 190.

234. Childers; Davis and Havighurst; Frazier, "Negro Sexuality" and "Sex Morality"; Hohman and Schoffner; Short, Jr., Strodtbeck, and Cartwright.

235. See, esp.: Bandura and Walters, *Adolescent Aggression;* Broffenbrenner; Davis and Havighurst; Dollard, p. 274; McCord and McCord; Miller and Swanson; Sears.

236. A. K. Cohen, *Delinquent Boys,* p. 131; A. Davis; Miller and Swanson, p. 330; Miller, "Aggression" and "Lower Class Culture."

the manner by which lower-class subculture handles them, partially explains the extent to which these age groups resort to sexual aggression.[237]

Adolescence is a period of preoccupation with sexual matters.[238] The sexual behavior of adolescents reflects the heightened intensity of their sexual drives and the desire for sexual experimentation.[239] However, it may reflect negative childhood experiences which may reactivate infantile aggressive sexuality, latent homosexual inclinations,[240] fears and doubts about sexual potency,[241] and a pressure to execute masturbation fantasy.[242] These statements, by psychiatrists, are made on the basis of selected groups of disturbed adolescents who appeared before the court or clinics.[243] The merit of such generalization need not be again discussed. However, in all of these studies the lower-class origin of the majority of the adolescents is noted.

Sociologists who study the adolescent problems emphasize not so much the psychopathological profiles of a limited sample of boys, but the common aspect of all growing youngsters—that is, problems of status discrepancy between biological and social maturation,[244] which lead, among other things, to the need to prove through sex their adequacy and maturation.[245] Such sexual experimentation usually takes place in the peer groups,[246] and in the lower-class it involves promiscuous relations with girls who are targets for such exploits.[247] These lower-class patterns are part of the general pattern of delinquency;[248] and they are aided by the availability of "marked" girls in the milieu, who are not themselves devoid of aggressive sexuality. The sexual conduct of adolescents partially

237. On the general problems of adolescence and sexual development see Blos. Of the classical works concerned with psychosexuality and the reaction-ego defenses of youth, see A. Freud.

238. For a survey see Sherif and Sherif, pp. 48–67.

239. Grossberg; Karpman, "Crime and Adolescence"; Leppman.

240. Blanchard; Karpman, "Felonious Assault"; Mayer.

241. I. S. Wile, "The Sexual Conduct of Adolescents."

242. Waggoner and Bond.

243. Atckeson and Williams; Doshay; Markey.

244. Davis, "The Sociology of Parent-Youth Conflict"; Erickson, "Youth"; Hollingshead, pp. 239–41; Parsons, "Age and Sex."

245. Griffith, "Sex Problems"; Plant, "Understanding Sex Delinquency"; Reiss, "Sex Offenses," pp. 309–10.

246. Bloch and Niederhoffer; *California Sexual Deviation Research* (1954), pp. 122–36; Hollingshead, pp. 110, 142, 421. For extensive references on this phenomenon among lower-class delinquents see Sherif and Sherif, pp. 57–67. On the general problems of youth culture in America see Parsons, "Youth."

247. Miller, "Lower Class Culture"; Reiss, "Sex Offenses," pp. 312–314; Whyte, "A Slum Sex Code."

248. Gibbens.

reflects the general aggressiveness which prevails in other aspects of the subculture.[249]

The Negro male's aggressive sexuality seems to be more problematically due to the strong need to overcome problems of masculinity and of sexual identity. This is so because of the Negro family structure (mother-based family) and the need to overcome general social disadvantages,[250] by substituting sexual aggressive masculinity for failures as a man in the economic and social status spheres.

The description of a subculture of violence presented above is schematic and sketchy. It is an attempt to furnish some explanation of the origin of such a subculture and the persistence and readiness of its members to maintain their membership. The ecological factor—residential proximity and homogeneous life conditions—can be supposed to contribute to such persistency of the subculture. Family influences and peer group membership are other factors important in understanding the persistence of subcultural solutions of personal and collective problems.[251]

However, "to establish the existence of a subculture of violence does not require that all persons sharing in this basic value element express violence in all situations."[252] What is contended in the theory of subculture is that aggressive modes of behavior are a frequent response which is expected in certain kinds of situations,[253] and that the normative system of the subculture makes it likely that members will interpret a situation as being of a kind calling for violence including forceful sexual exploitation of a female.[254]

Individual differences, for instance, in the intensity of sexual drives,[255] and differential involvement in the subculture and in the peer group

249. Miller, "Female"; Short, Jr., Strodtbeck, and Cartwright; Wheeler, p. 276.

250. Kardiner and Ovesey, pp. 258–83; Pettigrew.

251. For an attempt see: A. K. Cohen, *Delinquent Boys,* chaps. 4, 5; Henry and Short, chap. 5; A. L. Wood.

252. Ferracuti and Wolfgang, "Prediction," p. 295. See also Matza, *Delinquency and Drift.*

253. We are echoing here Matza's objection to the term "delinquent subculture," replacing it with the term "subculture of delinquency" into which juveniles are drifted; see *Delinquency and Drift,* esp. pp. 19–30.

254. Martin (pp. 71–89) viewed such situations and their consequences as giving rise to special patterns of juvenile vandalism ("vindictive vandalism"). Thrasher (chap. 2) called this phenomenon the "ganging process." For crimes of violence see: McClintock, pp. 27–33; Wolfgang, *Patterns,* chaps. 5–14.

255. Bonger (*Criminality,* p. 620) already made this point to explain why, within the same conditions of poverty, only some persons will commit rape. Self-concept and critical effects of past experience can be added in explaining why such people do not resort to violence.

can explain why only some who live within the same subculture resort to violence or to rape as a solution for their sexual problems. The reverse proposition is also true: some people, regardless of whether they belong to a subculture of violence, will be aggressive because of their personal psychopathology, and not because of their membership in it.

In this chapter we have merely outlined a theory for explaining the empirical data derived from the study on forcible rape. It was based on a phenomenological study which established the parameters and the recurring patterns of the offenses. Thus, it entails the reduction of the phenomenon to its objective characteristics, which appeared regularly alone or as part of a pattern. I have explained the offense by a subcultural perspective but, again, providing only the most visible demographic and ecological elements of this subculture. Such a reduction of the phenomenon means overlooking the internal subjective nature of the offense; that is, its meaning to those involved in it. It is my contention that in order to move out of such a reductionist approach, toward a subjective level of the phenomenon, it was necessary to provide the essential features, demographic, ecological, and modus operandi, which are the boundaries of the phenomenon. Before this, any phase is premature. A more refined description, methodology and theory, encompassing more subtle sociological and psychological elements, are now called for.[256]

Where do we move from this stage of our knowledge? We can at this point only suggest some directions: The "dark figure" of unreported rapes is unknown. Some new methods can be used to elucidate more fully and accurately the quantitative and qualitative elements of the offense, their fluctuations and the variables which are related to the unknown number of rapes. For this, use can be made of the "victimization survey research." This method can also better indicate the true nature of the correlates of the offense, which at this stage were based on the fact of underreporting.[257]

Once more accurate rates of rape are provided; studying their changes through time is a worthwhile venture. Rate fluctuations may reflect normative and demographic changes in the community or in its climate in the realm of sex, or of special events which occurred in the community.[258] Measuring changes in rates allows not only the move from variable to causal analysis but also establishes the basis for comparative study, provided we know the demographic social and normative char-

256. For such an attempt in the study of homicide see Ferracuti and Wolfgang, "Design."

257. For example, see: Biderman, et al.; Ennis; Glaser, "Victim Survey Research."

258. As an example of changes in penal policies on rates of forcible rapes see Schwartz and Post.

acteristics of the communities involved.[259] Since the victimization survey method, changes of rates through time and comparative studies will depend on police statistics, the study of the role of the police in reporting, recording and initiating the prosecution, is of prime importance.[260]

Although I have sought mainly to uncover categories and degrees of risks to be involved in rape, throughout this study I constantly referred to psychological—perceptual and emotional—characteristics of those involved, and to special situations in which rape events were more likely to occur. These aspects should be developed as another, complementary theoretical approach to the subcultural one. One such orientation is that of "symbolic interaction," which developed some conceptual and methodological tools to elucidate meanings of the involvement of persons in their subjective situations, including others therein.[261] Methodologically, only a small sample is needed for interviewing, unlike the larger one for the phenomenological approach.[262] Subjects for such a study can be drawn from the prison, without worry that the "representativeness" argument will be invoked. We want to know more about the kinds of interactions, negotiations which occur between the partners before, during, and after the event, and how they are related to the setting of their initial encounter. Or, we would like to know more about changes in the sequence of their interactions, up to the point of no return, where conflict between trust (e.g., in drinking relations), and perceptions of opportune situations and potential victims lead to what seems to the offender, retrospectively, as an unavoidable course. Such methodological and theoretical effort may help to disclose those rape events which are rooted in the psychopathology of their perpetrators, others which are the consequences of idiosyncratic, nonduplicable, accidental situations, and those rape events which can be conceived as, more or less, a part of a normal pattern of aggressive conduct in which sexual violence is but one form.

Much more refined statistical manipulation of our data may yield some clusters of variables which lead to new typologies of offenders, vic-

259. For a recent attempt at a comparative study of rape see Schafer and Geis.

260. On the use of victimization survey research to understand the relation between police and underreporting see Glaser, "Victim Survey Research." On the relations between police organizational variables and prosecution of rape cases see Skolnick and Woodworth.

261. On the interactionist approach to the study of deviation see: Denzin; Matza, *Becoming Deviant.*

262. For an example of the two approaches in the study of the same offense (armed robbery) see Einstader for the symbolic interaction approach and Normandeau for the phenomenological orientation. The first interviewed a sample of convicted armed robbers and the other conducted a phenomenological—area and epidemiological—study using police arrest statistics. On using the "cognitive dissonance" approach to the study of robbery see Syvrud.

tims, and rape events other than those presented before. For instance, types of offenders, like the adolescent, elderly, married or the "ideological" rapist can be investigated.[263] Likewise we may want to understand better certain types of victims, like the ones who showed utmost resistance, the one who is known to the offender, the late or nonreporting victim, or the types of victims more vulnerable to be attacked due to age, residence, or occupational factors.

An infinite number of rape situations can be conceived, but some are more interesting and important because of public concern and reaction. Such are cross-race-line rape events, felony-rapes or group rapes. The situational aspects involved in these types of rape can be related to choice of victims, motivational elements, meeting places and interaction therein, as well as to victim-offender relationships. Studying these types and situations in depth, may shed more light on some aspects not touched on in the present study. I have avoided psychological and interpretational aspects of risk calculations by the offender and of victimological issues, such as victim responsibility in terms of vulnerable situation, seduction, and victim behavior before, during, and after the event.[264]

For reasons stated at the outset of the study I refrain from studying some basic issues related to rape. First, there is the influence which the offense may have on the apprehended offender due to his involvement in the process of criminal justice. Here, problems are of evidence of the differences between seduction and vulnerability and of false accusation, to mention only a few. The offense may have social psychological consequences for the victim, and different interpretations by her may ensue. Other crucial problems are the direct influences of the offenses,[265] or indirect, legal-process trauma because of police interrogation, court cross-examination, and the attitudes and reaction of "victim constituents" to the victim's sexual victimization.[266] All these aspects, including police[267] and court[268] disposition of rape cases, can be further related to types of victims, offenders, and rape situations. In short, we see the present study only as a beginning for a better understanding of what is seen in our culture as a special absorbing and revealing pattern of behavior.

263. On an "ideological" motivated rape see Cleaver, *Soul on Ice.*

264. For a review of the present field of victimology see: Fattah; Schafer. On Sex offenses see Amir.

265. See, for example: Friedman; Gagnon; Halleck, "Emotional Effects."

266. See: Amir; Libai.

267. See, e.g., "Comment: Police Discretion."

268. See, e.g., J. C. Howard.

18

Summary
and Conclusions

The primary purpose of this work has been to explore the nature and disclose the patterns of forcible rapes from among 646 cases that occurred in Philadelphia from 1 January 1958 to 31 December 1958, and from 1 January 1960 to 31 December 1960. The material presented is based on an empirical study of cases found in the files of the morals squad of the Philadelphia police department, where all complaints about rapes are recorded and centrally filed.

The emphasis in this study has not been on the psychological dynamics within the individual offender and victim but on their social characteristics, social relationships, and on the offensive act itself, that is, on the modus operandi of the crime and the situations in which rape is likely to occur. The patterns which emerged were derived from information about the 646 victims and 1,292 offenders who were involved in 370 cases of single rape, 105 of pair rape, and 171 of group rape. Patterns were sought regarding race, age, marital status, and employment differences, as well as seasonal and other temporal patterns, spatial patterns, the relationships between forcible rape, and the presence of alcohol and the previous arrest record of victims and offenders. In the analysis of modus operandi patterns were sought regarding: the initial interaction and meeting place of offender and victim, the place of the offense, the planning of the crime, the methods used to subdue the victim, the degree of violence in the rape event, the sexual humiliation to which the victim was subjected (other than forced intercourse), and the degree of the victim's resistance. Further questions were raised regarding: rape during the commission of another felony, the interpersonal relationship between victim and offender,

334

victim-precipitated rape, and unsolved cases of rape. Finally, all of these aspects were related to the phenomenon of group rape and to leadership functions in such situations.

The orientation toward these problems was strictly empirical and the method used was that of phenomenological inquiry. While the study was approached from a sociological viewpoint—that is, crimes as a socio-culturally learned behavior, committed within socioculturally defined situations— it was not guided by a specific theoretical system for explaining the offense studied. Nor was there an attempt to find causes of and specific explanations for the offense. Rather, the characteristics of the offense, the offender(s), and the victim(s) were sought. The suggested associations between them were tested primarily by the chi-square test of significance. A review of the existing reports and studies of forcible rape, most of which have been conducted in the United States, has been presented along with other works, believed to be relevant to the various aspects of the present research, in order to provide a perspective and a basis for comparison with the patterns found in the present study. No other study of forcible rape is known to us which deals with the number of variables included in the present study.[1] Some variables touched upon here are either new to research in sexual crimes in general, or to forcible rape in particular.[2]

Criticism has been made of previously published statistics which present crude rates of offenses and offenders and confuse data about the crime with data about the offenders, while telling us nothing about the victim. Finally, while most previous studies, although alluding to the necessity of examining both victim and offender, still treated them separately, the present work examined "victims and offenders, separately, as distinct units but also as mutually interacting participants"[3] in the various aspects and stages of the offense. Thus, this study's analysis yielded various patterns otherwise not discernible.

From the beginning of the present study it was maintained that an act, like criminal behavior, is a patterned and structured event. That does not mean that the present work is merely an exercise in serendipity. If some unexpected empirical uniformities appeared, the very choice of the general (sociological) approach to the study of crime and the selection

---

1. Mohr, Turner, and Jerry, *Pedophilia and Exhibitionism,* appeared while this study was being written and represents another, although more limited, example of this approach to the study of sexual offenses.

2. For the growing list of other phenomenological studies, not mentioned before, in which the offense is the prime target of analysis see: M. Cameron; Chein, et al.; McClintock; McClintock and Gibson; Martin; A. L. Wood.

3. Wolfgang, *Patterns,* p. 319. For other limitations of published crime statistics see Wolfgang, "Uniform Crime Reports."

of the variables could partly explain their emergence. Thus, the study was able to refute some of the misconceptions surrounding the crime of rape. Following is a list of some of these myths challenged and the findings of the study.[4]

It is commonly thought that: (1) Negro men are more likely to attack white women than Negro women. Rape was found to be an intraracial event, especially between Negro men and women. (2) Rape is symptomatic of a demographic structural strain due to sex–marital-status imbalance in the social structure. This theory was refuted, along with the derivative assumption about age-sex imbalance which might exist within the general populations. (3) Rape is a hot-season crime. Rape was found not to be particularly associated with the summer months, but spread over all seasons and months of the year. The "thermic law of delinquency" is not confirmed by the present study. (4) Rape usually occurs between total strangers. This assumption was challenged by the analysis of several variables. First, rape in a sizable proportion of cases is ecologically bound—that is, it occurs between males and females who live in the same area, a fact that allowed some knowledge of each other. The victim and offender, in more than one-third of the cases we studied, knew each other as close neighbors or acquaintances. Second, offenders and victims frequently met in the home or place of sojourn of either one of them, and the offense also occurred in that place. (5) Rape is associated with drinking. In two thirds of our cases alcohol was absent from the rape situation. (6) Rape victims are innocent persons. One-fifth of the victims had a police record, especially for sexual misconduct. Another 20 percent had "bad" reputations. (7) Rape is predominantly an explosive act. In almost three-quarters of the cases rape was found to be a planned event, and especially when the meeting place was in the residence of one of the participants or when the rape was a group affair. (8) Rape takes place in a dead-end street or dark alley. A *significant* association was found to occur between places where the victim and offender initially met each other (especially when the meeting was in one of the participants' residences) and the place of rape. (9) Rape is always a violent crime in which brutality is inflicted upon the victim. In a large number of cases (87 percent), only temptation and verbal coercion were used initially to subdue the victim; in 15 percent no physical force was used at all against the victim; and in almost 50 percent of the cases when force—in one degree or another—was used, the victim was only manhandled, beaten with brutality by her assailant(s). (10) The law is always justified in rigidly demanding the victim's resistance or some form of "genuine" nonconsent on her part in order to establish later that rape occurred. The folk and

4. For one good discussion of the problem with an attempt to disprove it by statistics see Falk, "The Public Image."

literary expressions which cast doubt on the prevalence of resistance, and hence on the assumption on which this demand is based, are found equally convincing. As it is commonly believed that almost no woman wants to be deprived of her sexual self-determination, it was surprising to find that over 50 percent of the victims failed to resist their attackers in any way. Race, age, and special circumstances were given as explanations for this result, but it seems that the law should give these factors more consideration. (11) Rape is a one-to-one forced sexual relationship. Among our cases, over two-fifths (43 percent) were found to be multiple-rape cases. The possibilities which are open for sociological and criminological studies are numerous, and it is hoped that someone will pursue these cases. (12) Victims are not responsible for their victimization either consciously or by default. The proportion of rape events precipitated by the victim and the characteristics of such rape events refute this claim and open the door for fruitful studies which might be made in the field of "victimology."

The following provide a summary of the major significant patterns emerging from the study. A *significant* association was found between forcible rape and the race of both victims and offenders. Negroes exceed whites both among victims and offenders, in absolute numbers as well as in terms of their proportion in the general population. Negroes have four times their expected number of victims, and the proportion of Negro offenders was four times greater than their proportion in the general population of Philadelphia. I have used Sellin's concept of "potential population"[5]—that is, the numbers of each race whose age and sex are such that they could be an offender or a victim, respectively, and from which the involvement of the participants can be presumed. When specific rates by age and sex were calculated on the basis of the "potential" population of each race, it was found that the rates for the Negro women who were rape victims (on the basis of total Negro female population) is almost twelve times higher than that of the white women who were victims (on the basis of white female population). Similarly, for offenders, when the rates were computed on the basis of male population in each racial group, the proportion of Negro offenders was twelve times greater than that of white offenders. Furthermore, when the rates were figured on the basis of the "potential" race population, the rates for Negro offenders turned out to be three times greater than that of Negro victims, a difference found to hold also for white offenders as compared to white victims. The data on racial differences reveals that forcible rape is mainly an intraracial event. In this sample, forcible rape occurred *significantly* more often between Negroes than between whites.

5. "The Significance of Records of Crime."

A *significant* association existed between age and forcible rape, the age group 15–19 years having the highest rates among offenders and among victims. In examining the relative ages of the offender(s) and the victims, we found that the higher the age of the offender, the more likely it was that the victim would be in a lower age group. When the differences were broken down further by race, it appeared that, regardless of the population basis, the top "risk" age group for Negro and white offenders is the same (15–19 and 20–25 years of age), but the rates for Negroes in these age levels is higher than for whites. For each age group, however, the rates show a greater proportion of Negro than of white males involved in forcible rape.

The age pattern for victims was found to be somewhat different from that of offenders. For victims there is a wider range of "critical" age groups. Both races had a high proportion of victims between the ages of 15 to 19 and 10 to 14 years, with the Negro-victim rates exceeding those of the white victims in these age groups, as well as in all other age groups. Examination of age differences according to race of victim and offender showed that offenders and victims were at the same age level, mainly in Negro and white interracial rape events. However, white victims tend to be younger than their white assailants by at least 10 years, while Negro offenders tend to be at least 10 years younger than their white victims. (The majority of cases of the latter description were felony-rape events.)

After examination of the marital status of both offenders and victims, it was found that both generally were unmarried. The highest rates for victims were in the "dependent" category, that is, below marriageable age and still unmarried. Offenders as a group—but Negroes more than whites—show the highest rate in the "single" group and the second highest rate in the "dependent" group. These results coincide with the age distribution of victims and offenders noted above. Victims are more spread out over the categories and, therefore, have higher rates than offenders in the "separated," "divorced," and "widowed" groups. Again, the results coincide with the greater spread of victims than of offenders over the age range. Negro victims showed a greater concentration in the "single" and "dependent" groups than did white victims who were, however, concentrated also in these groups. Negro offenders differ from their Negro victims in their marital status only in the "married" and "separated" categories, where Negro victims have higher rates than that of their Negro offenders. An attempt was made to check Von Hentig's[6] demographic explanation of forcible rape, which is that a disturbed sex ratio for unmarried persons aged 19–49 years resulting in a surplus of males, leads to rape as a solution to their problem of securing sexual

6. "The Sex Ratio."

partners. We found that the marital demographic structure of Philadelphia cannot explain the extent to which males, especially Negroes,
resort to forcible rape. The same applied to our attempt when marital
status, age, and sex ratio were analyzed together.

Examination of the occupational status of the offenders indicated that
90 percent of the offenders of both races belonged to the lower part of the
occupational scale: from skilled workers down to the retired and unemployed. The rate of Negro offenders in the unemployed category was
twice as high as the rate of unemployed Negroes in Philadelphia at that
time, and five times as high as that of white offenders when the semi-
skilled, unskilled and unemployed categories were combined.

Although the number of forcible rapes tended to increase during the
hot summer months, there was no significant association either with the
season or with the month of the year. While Negro intraracial rapes were
spread all over the year, white intraracial events showed a more consistent
increase during the summer, which was found also to be the season when
multiple rapes were most apt to occur.

Forcible rape was found to be *significantly* associated with days of the
week. The highest concentration of rapes (53 percent) was on weekends
(beginning Friday evening and ending Saturday night), with Saturday
being the peak day.

A study of the distribution of forcible rapes by hours of the day found
top "risk" hours to be between 8:00 P.M. and 2:00 A.M. Almost half of all
the rape events occurred during these hours. Finally, the highest number
of weekend rapes occurred on Fridays between 8:00 P.M. and midnight.

In the analysis of the ecology of forcible rape we found that in various
areas of Philadelphia, there was a correspondence between high rates of
crime against the person and the rates of forcible rape. Moreover, those
police districts where Negroes are concentrated were also the areas where
the rates of forcible rapes were highest. A check was made to determine
whether the offender(s) lived in the vicinity of the victim or of the offense. In the majority of cases (82 percent) offenders and victims lived
in the same area, while in 68 percent a neighborhood triangle was observed, that is, offenders lived in the vicinity of victim and offense. Also
observed are the patterns of residence mobility triangle, that is, instances
in which the site of the crime was in the area of the residence of the
offender but not of the victim. A new concept used in this study was that
of crime mobility triangle. In 4 percent of the cases the offenders lived in
the victims' vicinity, while the crime was committed outside the boundaries of their residential area. When correlating these ecological patterns
with the race and age factors, it was found that forcible rape was an
intraracial event between victims and offenders who were at the same age
level and who were ecologically bound, that is, victims and offenders

lived in the same area, which tended to be also the area of the offense. This was especially true for Negro intraracial rape.

Alcohol was found only in one-third of all the rape events. In 63 percent of the 217 cases in which alcohol was present, it was present in both the victim and the offender. The presence of alcohol in the rape situation appeared to be *significantly* associated with whites—both victims and offenders—and with the Negro victim when she had consumed alcohol alone before the offense. Alcohol was frequently found to be present in the victim, offender, or both in white intraracial rape events. Of the various combinations of drinking patterns, alcohol in the victim alone and in both victim and offender has stronger implications of causal relationships with the crime of rape than other drinking patterns.

Alcohol is a factor found to be strongly related to violence used in the rape situation, especially when present in the offender only. In terms of race, it was drinking Negro victims or the offenders who were involved most often in violent rapes. Also, alcohol was found to be *significantly* associated with sexual humiliation forced upon a drinking victim. Finally, weekend rapes were found to be *significantly* associated with the presence of alcohol in either the victim, the offender, or both. An explanation offered (as did Wolfgang in his homicide study)[7] is the fact that Friday brings payday and with it the greater purchase of alcohol and the more intense social and leisure activities.

A relatively high proportion of rapists in Philadelphia (50 percent) had previous arrest record. Contrary to past impressions, it was found that there are almost no differences between the races, for offenders or victims, in terms of police or arrest record, although Negro offenders had a *significantly* higher proportion of 2 or more offenses in their past than white offenders.

When cases of persistence in violating the law were examined, it was found that over 50 percent of those who had an arrest record as adults also had a record as juveniles.

Analysis of the type of previous offenses committed by the offenders revealed that only 20 percent of those who had a past arrest record, had previously committed a crime against the person, with Negro offenders outnumbering the whites in this respect. Among offenders with criminal records, 9 percent had committed rape in the past, and 4 percent had been arrested before for a sexual offense other than rape. When examining the continuity and persistence of offenses from juvenile to adult age, we found that the highest proportion in continuity was in offenses against the person. Thus, adults arrested for rape were found to be less-likely first offenders than adults arrested for other types of offenses.

7. *Patterns,* pp. 142–43.

The analysis of victims' criminal records revealed that 19 percent of victims had an arrest record, the highest proportion of these arrests being for sexual misconduct. We observed that 56 percent of the victims who had an arrest record had been charged with some sort of sexual offense. These offenses included juvenile misconduct, which often has a sexual connotation.

Another type of "record" was explored: the victim's "bad" reputation. It was found that 128 (or 20 percent) of the 646 victims had such reputations; with a *significantly* higher proportion of Negro victims having such a reputation. The assumption was made, and later confirmed, that a "bad" reputation, together with other factors such as ecological proximity, was a factor in what was termed "victim-precipitated" forcible rape.

The analysis of the modus operandi was made in terms of processes and characteristics of the rape situation, that is, sequences and conjunctures of events which enter into the perpetration of the offense. Five phases were distinguished according to offender's behavior, victim's reaction, and situational factors which finally set the stage for the rape event.

In phase one the concern was with the initial interaction between victim and offender, and the relevant problems of their place of meeting and the degree of planning of the offense. It was found that the most dangerous meeting places were the street, and the residence of the victims or offenders or place of sojourn. In one-third of the cases, the offender met the victim at, and committed the offense in the victim's home or place where she stayed. Such was especially the case in intraracial rape events.

On the basis of description of the event by the victim and offender, three degrees of planning were distinguished and analyzed for their relationship to some pertinent variables. Contrary to past impression, the analysis revealed that 71 percent of the rapes were planned. Most planned events were intraracial events when the meeting place was one of the participants' residences or when the rape was a group affair. Explosive rapes were characterized as being single interracial rapes, with the street as the meeting place.

The location of the offense is *significantly* associated with the place of initial meeting. Thus, when the meeting place was outside the participant's residence or place of sojourn, this is also where the offense took place. Movement of the crime scene was mainly from outdoors to inside. The automobile, which was already found as a vehicle of crime commission, was revealed to be the location of the offense in only 15 percent of the cases, and more often when white offenders were involved in the offense. A *significant* association was also found between the location of the rape in the participant's place and use of violence in the commission of the offense, as well as the subjection of the victim to sexually humiliating practices.

Next attention was turned to various aspects in the actual commission of the offense: nonphysical methods used to manipulate the victim into submission, the degrees of violence used against her, and the sexual humiliation and its content which she was forced to endure. Besides temptation, three forms of nonphysical methods were distinguished: verbal coercion, intimidation by physical gestures, and intimidation with a weapon or another physical object to force the victim into submission. Combined with verbal coercion, nonphysical aggression was used in the majority of cases (87 percent) with Negroes in *significant* proportion using both forms of intimidation against their Negro victims. The differences between intra- and interracial events in this respect were not found to be statistically significant.

Degrees of violence were classified into three main groups: roughness, beatings (brutal and nonbrutal), and choking. In 15 percent of the 646 rapes, no force was used. Of the cases in which force was used, 29 percent took the form of roughness, one-quarter were nonbrutal beatings, one-fifth were brutal beatings, and 12 percent involved choking the victim. Violence, especially in its extreme forms, was found to be *significantly* associated with Negro intraracial events and with cases in which the offender was Negro and the victim white. Also, a *significant* association was found between multiple rape and the use of force in the rape situation and between the latter and the outside as the place of rape. Multiple rape and the "outside" as the place of the offense were found to be *significantly* associated, too.

It was not merely to forced intercourse that the female was subjected in rape, but also to various forms of sexual practices usually defined as sexual deviations. It was found that sexual humiliation existed in 27 percent of all rape cases, especially in the forms of fellatio, cunnilingus, both, or in the form of repeated intercourse. Sexual humiliation was found to be *significantly* associated with white intraracial rapes, where the victims were subjected most frequently to fellatio and pederasty, and with Negro intraracial rapes where Negro victims were forced more often to repeated intercourse by their Negro assaulters. Sexual humiliation was found also to be *significantly* associated with multiplicity of offenders and with the presence of alcohol in the rape situation, especially when it had been consumed by the offender only or both by the offender and the victim. In these cases sexual humiliation appeared mainly in the form of fellatio.

The problematic issue of victim behavior was analyzed by dividing the varieties of victim behavior into three groups: submission, resistance, and fight. The analysis revealed that in over half of the rapes the victims displayed only submissive behavior; in 173 (or 27 percent) victims resisted the offender, and in 116 (or 18 percent) victims put up a strong fight against their attackers. In both intra- and interracial rapes Negro and white victims displayed the same proportion of either one of these forms of behavior. The highest proportion of the instances of submissive behavior were cases in which the victim was white and the offender Negro. These cases included almost all felony-rape events—in most of which the victim was older than her attacker. The younger the age, the more submissive was the victim; the most submissive victims were those aged 10–14 years. In the adult age (victims aged 30 and over), victims showed *significantly* more resistance. Victims who were 10 or more years younger or older than the offenders were more submissive, while those who were at the same age as their assailants (not more than ± 5 years) displayed the highest proportion of fighting behavior. Victims tended to fight more when they were more intimidated in the initial encounter with the offender, or when force was used against them by the offenders. As expected, the presence of alcohol in the victim diminished her capacity to resist, and her behavior was found to be mainly submissive in such cases.

The phenomenon of multiple rape has been given special attention in this study. A tentative theory which emphasizes the role of the leader, borrowing heavily from Redl's theory of the "central" person and his function as an "initiator" and/or "magical" seducer was suggested. The various aspects of the offense discussed before were then collated with the phenomena of MR, particularly with leadership functions. MR situations were divided into pair rape, in which 2 offenders rape 1 victim; and group rapes, in which 3 or more males rape 1 victim. Of the 646 cases of rape, 276 cases (or 43 percent) were multiple rapes. Of these cases, 105 were PR's and 171 were GR's. Of 1,292 offenders, 210 (or 16 percent) were involved in PR's, and 712 (or 55 percent) participated in GR's. Altogether, 912 offenders (or 71 percent) of the 1,292 offenders were involved in MR events.

The analysis of MR's revealed the following characteristics: more white than Negro offenders participated in PR and more Negro than white offenders were involved in GR. MR situations were found to be mainly an intraracial affair, with no differences in proportions between Negro and white intraracial events. The older the offender, the less likely he is to participate in GR; all of the offenders of ages 10–14 participated either in PR or GR. The highest proportion of PR or GR was perpetrated by offenders between the age 14 to 19. Like all other kinds of rape, GR's were found to be characterized by victims being in the same age level as the offenders. GR shows a tendency to occur more on weekends and to occur in the evening as well as late at night, and a tendency to be associated with the presence of alcohol. In GR alcohol was more likely to be present especially in the victim only, while in PR it was more often present only in the offender who was the leader.

A *significant* proportion of participants in MR than of SR offenders had a previous arrest record either for offenses against the person, for sex offenses other than rape, or for rape. This was true for PR leaders, as compared to their partners, but not for GR leaders vis-à-vis their followers. The homogeneity of the dyad is established for this as well as for other variables.

Turning to the modus operandi in MR situations, it was observed that MR offenders in such situations are most likely to attack victims who live in their area (neighborhood or delinquency triangles). The initial interaction between the victim and the offenders usually occurred first in the street; and there, also, the rape took place. There was little "mobility of crime scene" in multiple-rape situations.

MR's, especially GR's, were found to be planned events. PR's also tended to be planned, but in a lesser proportion. Compared to GR's, pair rapes showed a high proportion of cases of explosiveness or partial planning.

We found that MR situations, especially GR's, are characterized by temptation and coercion, while there was more use of intimidation in PR events. The leader was found to be the initiator of the manipulating acts, that is, he was the first to tempt or to intimidate the victim into submission.

A *significant* association existed between violence and MR's, especially GR's. GR and PR events are also characterized by the greater use of non-brutal beatings. Extreme violence and brutality characterize the SR events, since the lone offender most constantly subdue the victim and does not have the help of others. The leader in pair and group rapes was more violent than his followers, and he was also the one to initiate the beatings. GR's are also characterized by tormenting the victim with perverted sexual practices, especially in the form of repeated intercourse. Testing the theory of "magical seduction" it was found that only the PR leader inflicted sexual humiliation upon the victim, and especially in the forms of fellatio, cunnilingus, or both.

Is the leader responsible for both "magical seduction" and "initial action," or can he abstain from one of them and still be the leader of the group offense? When the association between these leadership functions was tested, it was found that both are *significantly* associated, that is, those who first attacked the victim were also the first to rape her. However, "magical seduction" was found to be the more important role of the leader. Introducing another leadership function, that of "commanding" and organizing the situation, we found that in group rape the "true" leader was the one who performed all three functions. However, if the three functions were not performed by the same person, the one who first raped the victim was also likely to be the one who commanded the event.

The futility of resistance and fight by the group-rape victim is revealed by the fact that in group-rape situations the victim was more submissive or resisted the offender but was less inclined to put up a strong fight. Pair-rape victims showed no definite pattern in this respect. For many variables pair rapes and group rapes show some variations from the cluster of patterns which distinguished the MR situations. It was mainly the PR which varied from the typical type of MR situations portrayed in our study. We found that in many instances PR resembled SR rape more than GR. Thus, it may be better to see PR's not as a form of group event but rather as a form of criminal "partnership."

In 76 cases (or 4 percent) of the 646 rape events, a felony in the form of burglary or robbery was committed in addition to the rape. These cases were mainly single rapes, and especially Negro intraracial rapes. A special trait of felony rape is the age disparity between victim and offender; in more than half of these cases the offender was at least ten years younger than the victims, and a higher proportion of the felony-rape cases in which the offender was Negro and the victim white, exhibited the age disparity. Examination of the previous record of felony-rapists showed them to be more often recidivists than the offenders in rape generally. Felony rapes also were characterized by a greater proportion of cases in which sexual humiliation was inflicted upon the victim. Because of the age differences between victim and offender, it was expected, and, indeed, found that victims of felony rapes were more inclined to be submissive than victims of rape generally.

Almost half (48 percent) of the identified victim-offender relationships conformed to our definition of "primary" relationships. When the types of primary contacts were further divided into "acquaintanceship" and more "intimate" contacts, the former constituted 34 percent and the latter contributed 14 percent of all types of victim-offender relationships. A detailed analysis of victim-offender relationships revealed that when primary relationships existed, a relatively large proportion of cases involved Negro victims whose assailants were their close neighbors, or victims who were drinking acquaintances of their white assaulters. As expected, Negro intraracial events involved mainly close neighbors. White intraracial events occurred mainly between acquaintances who established their relations just before the offense. Again, as expected, acquaintanceships were formed mainly between victims and offenders who were at the same age level. Neighbors met initially in one of the participants' residences, where the rape also took place. The automobile was the place of rape for those who were intimate. Although nonphysical means of coercion in its light forms were used between acquaintances, the closer the relationship was between victim and offender the greater was the use of physical force against the victim, and neighbors and ac-quaintances were found to be the most dangerous people so far as brutal rape was concerned.

As expected, a greater proportion of multiple than single rape was found to take place between strangers. In general, the analysis of the interpersonal relations between victim and offender lent support to those who reject the myth of the offender who attacks victims unknown to him. But, equally rejected is the notion that rape is generally an affair between, or a result of intimate relations between victims and offenders.

After discussing the psychological approach to victim-proneness and victim selection, I found it more fruitful to deal with vulnerable or risky situations rather than with psychological concepts like "victim prone-ness." It is probable that women entering these risk situations will more likely become victims of rape regardless of their own psychological char-acteristics. The following were the main features of vulnerable situations in which rape occurred: victims and offenders of single and multiple-rape events were either of the same race or age or both; victims of felony rape who tended to be at least 10 years older than her assailants; offenders, Negro and white, lived as neighbors or acquaintances in the same area as victims of their own race and age level, which was also the area where the crime was committed; offenders and victims who are of the same race and age level who met during the summer months, mainly on weekends and/or during the evening and night hours in places which allowed or encouraged the development of an acquaintanceship, or relations between neighbors; alcohol present in both white offender and white victim, or in white offender and Negro victim, or in the victim only, especially when her assailant was white; Negro victims having a "bad" reputation who lived in the neighborhood of their Negro attackers; groups of offenders who planned the rape of victims of their own race who lived in the same vicinity; victims and offenders who were neighbors of the same race and age, between whom primary relations existed; victims and offenders who established drinking relations just prior to the offense; or a drinking vic-tim who was accosted in the street by a stranger, usually of her own race.

The term "victim-precipitated," was introduced to refer to those rape cases in which the victims actually—or so it was interpreted by the offender—agreed to sexual relations but retracted before the actual act or did not resist strongly enough when the suggestion was made by the offender(s). The term applies also to cases in which the victim enters vulnerable situations charged with sexuality, especially when she uses what could be interpreted as indecent language and gestures or makes what could be taken as an invitation to sexual relations. After establish-ing the theoretical and legal basis, the Philadelphia data revealed several significant factors associated with the 122 victim-precipitated rapes, which comprised 19 percent of all rapes studied. These are: white victims; white intraracial rapes; alcohol in the rape situation, particularly in the victim or both in offenders and victims; victims with a bad reputation; victims who live in residential proximity to the offender(s) and/or to the area of offense; victims who meet their offenders in a bar, picnic, or party; victims who were raped outside their or the offenders' homes or places of sojourn; the subjection of victims to sexual humiliation; and victims who were in "primary" relationships with the offenders but who were not their relatives.

After discussing the problems involved in solved and unsolved crimes, two types of "unsolved" cases were distinguished: the "undetected," those cases in which the police could not attribute the recorded offense to any identifiable offender(s); and the "vanished," those cases about which the police have some information on suspected, identified, or alleged offenders but in which suspects are still at large. In 124 (or 19 percent) of the cases the offenders were classified as "undetected" and in 24 (or 4 percent) as "vanished." Together they represent 148 (or 23 percent) "unsolved" cases. Of 1,292 offenders, 405 (or 33 percent) were classified as undetected and 40 (or 34 percent) as unfounded offenders. In unsolved cases of rape in Philadelphia there was: a higher proportion of Negro offenders involved in Negro intraracial rape than in solved cases; a higher average age among the offenders than among offenders in general; a higher proportion of explosive types of rape; a higher proportion of cases in which alcohol was present in the victim only or in the offender only; a higher proportion of single-rape situations; and a higher proportion where there was delay by the victim or others in reporting the offense to the police, especially because of fear of the offender or an inability to adequately describe him. There can be little doubt that more studies are needed to give us more systematic and comparative knowledge of rapists' and victims' characteristics, and of social conditions which may explain more accurately the crime of rape.

References

![bars]

Abbott, G. "Sexual Problems of the Adolescent Girl." *Social Hygiene* 19 (1933): 251–62.

Abraham, K. "The Experiencing of Sexual Traumas as a Form of Sexual Activity" (1907). *Selected Papers*, pp. 47–63. London: The Hogarth Press, 1927.

——. "The Relationship between Sexuality and Alcoholism." *Selected Papers.* New York: Basic Books, 1950.

Abrahamsen, D. A. *The Mind and Death of a Genius.* New York: Columbia University Press, 1946.

——. "A Comment: The Spectral Epidemic of Sex Offenses: The Newspapers' View." *American Journal of Psychiatry* 108 (1951): 629–30.

——. *The Psychology of Crime.* New York: Columbia University Press, 1960.

——. "Rorschach Test of Wives of Sex Offenders." *Mental Disease and Disorder* 119 (1954): 167.

——. "Study of 102 Sex Offenders at Sing Sing." *Federal Probation* 14 (1956): 26–32.

——. *Who Are the Guilty?* New York: Evergreen, 1952.

Adler, H. "The Relation of Alcohol and Crime." In Emerson, *Alcohol and Man,* pp. 310–26.

Aichorn, A. *Wayward Youth.* New York: The Viking Press, 1935.

Alexander, F. *Fundamentals of Psychoanalysis.* New York: W. W. Norton, 1948.

——. "A Note on the Theory of Perversion." In Lorand and Balint, *Perversion: Psychodynamics and Therapy,* pp. 3–15.

Alexander, F., and Healy, W. *Roots of Crime.* New York: Alfred A. Knopf, 1935.

Alexander, F., and Staub, H. *The Criminal, the Judge, and the Public.* New York: The Macmillan Co., 1952.

Allen, C. *Sexual Perversions and Abnormalities*. London: Oxford University Press, 1940.

————. "The Treatment of Sexual Abnormality." *Medical Press and Circulation* 210 (1943): 23–25.

Allen, F. A. "Confinement of the Sexual Irresponsible." *Journal of Criminal Law and Criminology* 32 (1941): 196–99.

Alpert, H. "Emile Durkheim: Enemy of Fixed Psychological Elements." *The American Journal of Sociology* 63 (1958): 662–64.

American Psychiatric Association. *Diagnostic and Statistical Manual: Mental Disorders*. Washington, D.C.: Mental Hospital Service American Psychiatric Association, 1952.

Amir, M. "The Role of the Victim in Sex Offenses." In H.L.P. Resnik and M. E. Wolfgang, eds., *Sexual Offenses*. New York: John Wiley & Sons 1970 (forthcoming).

The Annual Philadelphia Police Report. Philadelphia, Penn., 1960, 1961, 1962.

Apfelberg, B. C., et al. "A Psychiatric Study of 205 Sex Offenders." *American Journal of Psychiatry* 100 (1944): 762–70.

Arada, C. C. "Coercion as a Defense to Rape." *Journal of Criminal Law and Criminology* 27 (1937): 645–66.

Archer, J., *Sexual Conduct of the Teenager*. New York: Spectrolux, 1954.

Arens, R., and Meadow, A. "Psycholinguistics on the Confession Dilemma." *Columbia Law Journal* 56 (1956): 19–46.

Argow, W. "Functional Classification of Criminal Behavior." *Journal of Criminal Psychodynamics* 3 (1942): 687–90.

Arlow, J. "Perversion: Theoretical and Therapeutic Aspects." *Journal of American Psychoanalytic Association* 2 (1954): 119–28.

Arnold, D. O., ed. *The Sociology of Subculture*. Berkeley, Calif.: The Glendessary Press, 1970.

Aschaffenburg, G. *Crime and Its Repression*. Boston: Little, Brown and Company, 1913.

"Assault with Intent to Rape: Subsequent Yielding." *Medical Law Journal* 36 (1947): 18–19.

Atckeson, T. D., and Williams, D. C. "A Study of Juvenile Sex Offenders." *American Journal of Psychiatry* 111 (1954): 366–70.

Bach, G. "Group Pathology." Paper presented at the meeting of the American Psychiatric Association, San Francisco, September 1955.

Bak, D. C. "Aggression and Perversion." In S. Lorand and M. Balint, eds., pp. 231–40.

Baker, H. M. "Sex Offenders in Massachusetts Court." *Journal of Social Psychiatry* 20 (1950): 102–7.

Bales, R. F. "The Equilibrium Problems in Small Groups." In Parsons et al., *Working Papers in the Theory of Action*, pp. 111–61.

————. *Interaction Process Analysis*. Reading, Mass.: Addison-Wesley, 1950.

————. "Task Roles and Social Roles in Problem-Solving Groups." In Maccoby, et al., *Readings in Social Psychology*, pp. 437–47.

Bales, R. F., and Borgatta, E. F. "Size of Group as a Factor in the Interaction Profile." In Hare, Borgatta, and Bales, *Small Groups: Studies in Social Interaction*, pp. 339–95.

Bales, R. F.; Hare, A. P.; and Borgatta, E. F. "Structure and Dynamics of Small Groups: A Review of Four Variables." In Gittler, *Review of Sociology: Analysis of Decade*, pp. 97–110.

Ball, S. C., and Logan, N. "Early Sexual Behavior of Lower-Class Delinquent Girls." *Journal of Criminal Law, Criminology, and Police Science* 51 (1960): 209–14.

Banay, R. S. "Alcohol and Crime." In *Alcohol, Crime and Society*, pp. 146–57. New Haven: Quarterly Journal Study of Alcohol, 1943.

————. "Cultural Influences in Alcoholism." *Journal of Mental Diseases* 102 (1945): 265–75.

————. "Physical Disfigurement as a Factor in Delinquency and Crime." *Federal Probation* 7 (1943): 21–26.

————. "Profile of a Sex Offender." *Journal of Social Therapy* 3 (1956): 85–96.

Bandura, A., and Walters, R. H. *Adolescent Aggression.* New York: The Roland Press, 1959.

————. "Dependency Conflict in Aggressive Delinquent." *The Journal of Social Issues* 14 (1958): 52–56.

Barnes, H. E., and Teeters, N. *New Horizons in Criminology,* 2d ed. Englewood Cliffs, New Jersey: Prentice-Hall, 1954.

Bartlett, F. C. *Remembering.* Cambridge: Cambridge University Press, 1932.

Bass, B. M. "Conformity, Deviation and General Theory of Interpersonal Behavior." In Berg and Bass, *Conformity and Deviation,* pp. 38–100.

Bates, F. R. "The Characteristics of the Population of Prisons and Reformatories in the U.S. in 1940." Master's Thesis, George Washington University, 1950.

Beacon, S. "Alcohol, Alcoholism and Crime." *Crime and Delinquency* 9 (1963): 1–15.

Beattie, R. H. "Problems of Criminal Statistics in the United States." *Journal of Criminal Law, Criminology, and Police Science* 46 (1955): 178–86.

Becker, H. S. "Becoming a Marijuana User." *The American Journal of Sociology* 59 (1953): 235–43.

————. *The Other Side.* New York: The Free Press of Glencoe, 1964.

————. *Outsiders.* New York: The Free Press of Glencoe, 1963.

Becker, H. S., and Useem, R. H. "Sociological Analysis of the Dyad." *The American Sociological Review* 7 (1942): 13–26.

Bell, D. "The Myth of Crime Wave." In D. Bell, *The End of Ideology.* Glencoe, Ill.: The Free Press, 1960.

Bell, Q. *On Human Finery.* London, 1947.

Bemmelen, J. M. "Crime in Europe Since World War II." In Grunhüt, *Sexual Crimes Today,* pp. 27–52.

Bender, L., and Blau, A. "The Reaction of Children to Sexual Relations with Adults." *American Journal of Orthopsychiatry* 7 (1937): 500–518.

Bender, L., and Curran, F. J. "Children and Adolescents Who Kill." *Journal of Criminal Psychopathology* 1 (1940): 297–316.

Bender, L., and Grugett, A., "A Follow-Up Study of Children who had Atypical Sexual Experience." *American Journal of Orthopsychiatry* 22 (1952) 825–37.

Bendix, R. *Max Weber: An Intellectual Portrait.* Garden City, N.Y.: Doubleday, 1960.

————. "Psychiatry in Prison." *Psychiatry* 14 (1951): 73–86.

Bensing, R. "A Study of Sex Law Enforcement in Louisville, Kentucky." *Kentucky Law Journal* 38 (1956): 392–412.

Bent, S. "Scarlet Journalism." *Scribner Magazine* 85 (1938): 509–33.

Benter, E. B. *The American Race Problem.* New York: Crimwell, 1927.

Berg, E. A., and Bass, B. M., eds. *Conformity and Deviation.* New York: Harper and Bros., 1961.

Berkowitz, L. *Aggression: A Social-psychological Analysis.* New York: McGraw-Hill Book Co., 1962.

Bettelheim, B. *Symbolic Wounds.* Glencoe, Ill.: The Free Press, 1954.

Bianchi, H. *Position and Subject Matter of Criminology.* Amsterdam: North Holland Publishing Co., 1956.

Biderman, A., et al., *Report of a Pilot Study in the District of Columbia on Victimization and Attitudes toward Law Enforcement.* Field Survey I of the President's Commission on Law Enforcement and the Administration of Justice, 1967.

Bion, W. R. "Experience in Groups." *Human Relations*. 1 (1948): 314–20, 487–96; 2 (1949): 13–27, 295–303; 3 (1950): 3–14, 395–402.

Blalock, H. M. *Social Statistics*. New York: McGraw-Hill, 1960.

Blanchard, W. H. "The Group Processes in Group Rape." *Journal of Social Psychology* 49 (1959): 750–66.

Bloch, D. A. "Sex Crimes and Criminals." *The American Journal of Nursing* 53 (1953): 440–43.

Bloch, H. A., and Flyn, F. T. *Juvenile Delinquency*. New York: Random House, 1956.

Bloch, H. A., and Geis, G. *Man, Crime, and Society*. New York: Random House, 1962.

Bloch, H. A., and Niederhoffer, A. *The Gang*. New York: Philosophical Library, 1958.

Bloch, I. *The Sexual Life of Our Times*. New York: Allied Books, 1925.

Blos, P. *The Adolescent Personality: A Study in Individual Behavior*. New York: Appleton-Century-Crofts, 1941.

Boggs, S. L. "Urban Crime Patterns." *American Sociological Review* 30 (1965): 899–908.

Bohannan, P., ed. *African Homicide and Suicide*. Princeton, N.J.: Princeton University Press, 1960.

Bonger, W. A. *Criminality and Economic Conditions*. Boston: Little, Brown and Company, 1916.

———. *Race and Crime*. New York: Columbia University Press, 1943.

Bordua, D. J. "Delinquent Subcultures: Sociological Interpretation of Gang Delinquency." *The Annals of the American Academy of Political and Social Science* 338 (1961): 119–37.

———., ed. *The Police: Six Essays*. New York: John Wiley & Sons, 1967.

———. *Sociological Theories and Their Implications for Juvenile Delinquency*, no. 2. Washington: Department of Health, Education and Welfare, 1960.

Bowling, R. W. "Note: Mental Deterioration among Sex Offenders." *Journal of Criminal Law, and Criminology* 34 (1941): 184–85.

———. "The Sex Offender and the Law" *Federal Probation* 14 (1950): 14–16.

Bowman, K. M. "The Challenge of Sex Offenders." *Mental Hygiene* 22 (1938): 10–20.

Bowman, K. M., and Engle, B. "Certain Aspects of Sex Psychopath Laws." *American Journal of Psychiatry* 14 (1954): 690–97.

———. "Sex Offenses: Legal and Medical Implications." *Law and Contemporary Problems* 35 (1960): 292–304.

Brancale, R., et al. "Psychiatric and Psychological Investigation of Convicted Sex Offenders." *American Journal of Psychiatry* 109 (1952): 17–21.

Branham, V. C., and Kutash, S. B., eds. *Encyclopedia of Criminology*. New York: Philosophical Library, 1949.

Breed, W. "Sex, Class and Socialization in Dating." *Marriage and Family Living* 18 (1956): 137–44.

Breman, M. "Urban Lower-class Negro Girls." *Psychiatry* 6 (1943): 307–24.

Bromberg, W. *Crime and the Mind*. Philadelphia: J. B. Lippincott, 1948.

———. "Emotional Immaturity and Anti-Social Behavior." *Journal of Criminal Psychopathology* 8 (1946): 423–453.

Broffenbrenner, U. "Socialization and Social Class through Time and Space." In Maccoby, et al., *Readings in Social Psychology*, pp. 400–25.

Bronson, F. R. "A Case of Rape of a Young Girl." *American Journal of Urology* 14 (1918): 490–94.

———. "False Accusation of Rape." *The American Journal of Sociology* 14 (1918): 539–59.

Brown, G. G. *Law Administration and Negro-White Relationships in Philadelphia*. Philadelphia Bureau of Municipal Research, 1947.

Brown, J. S. "Comparative Study of Deviations from Sexual Mores." *American Sociological Review* 17 (1957): 135–46.

Brown, R. W. "Mass Phenomena." In Lindzey, *Handbook of Social Psychology*, pp. 379–82.

Burke, K. "On Interpretation." In Burke, *Performance and Change,* New York: New Republic, Inc., 1935.

Burton, R. V., and Whiting, J. W. "The Absence of Father and Cross-sex Identity." *Merrill Palmer Quarterly* 7 (1961): 15–95.

Buss, A. H. *The Psychology of Aggression.* New York: John Wiley, 1961.

Caldwell, R. G., *Criminology,* 2d ed. New York: Ronald Press, 1964.

California Sexual Deviation Research (progress report, 1952; final report, 1954). Sacramento, Calif.: State Department of Mental Hygiene.

Cameron, D. E. *Remembering.* New York: Coolidge Foundation Publishers, 1947.

Cameron, M. *The Booster and the Snitch: Department Store Shoplifting.* New York: The Free Press, 1964.

Cameron, N. "The Paranoid Pseudo-Community." *American Journal of Sociology* 49 (1943): 32–38.

Camp, G. M. *Nothing to Lose: A Study of Bank Robbery in America.* Ph.D. dissertation, Yale University 1967.

Candy, H. G. "The Negro in Crime." In Branham and Kutash, *Encyclopedia of Criminology,* pp. 267–77.

Caplow, T. "Further Developments of a Theory of Coalitions in the Triad." *The American Journal of Sociology* 64 (1959): 488–93.

Carr, L. *Situational Analysis.* New York: Harper & Bros., Publishers, 1948.

Carter, L. F., et al. "The Behavior of Leaders and Other Group Members." *Journal of Abnormal and Social Psychology* 46 (1951): 585–95.

Cartwright, D., and Zander, A. *Group Dynamics: Research and Theory.* New York: Row, Peterson and Company, 1953.

Cassity, J. H. "Psychological Considerations of Pedophilia." *Psychoanalytic Review* 14 (1927): 689–99.

Chall, L. P. "Advances in Modern Sex Research." In Ellis and Abarbanel, *Encyclopedia of Sexual Behavior,* pp. 187–96.

Chamberlain, B. P. *The Negro and Crime in Virginia.* Publication of the University of Virginia, Phelps-Stokes Fellowship Papers, no. 15. Charlottesville: University of Virginia, 1936.

Chein, I., et al. *The Road to H.* New York: Basic Books, 1964.

Child, I. "Socialization." In Lindzey, *Handbook of Social Psychology,* pp. 450–589.

Childers, A. T. "Some Notes on Sex Mores among Negro Children." *American Journal of Orthopsychiatry* 6 (1936): 442–48.

City of Philadelphia. *Annual Report Bureau of Police, Department of Public Safety,* 1960.

Cleaver, E. *Soul on Ice.* New York: Dell Publishing Co., 1968.

Clinard, M. B., ed. *Anomie and Deviant Behavior: A Discussion and Critique.* New York: The Free Press of Glencoe, 1964.

————. "Criminology Research." In Merton et al., *Sociology Today,* pp. 509–36.

Clinard, M. B., and Quinney, R. *Criminal Behavior Systems.* New York: Holt, Rinehart & Winston, 1967.

Clinard, M. B., and Wade, A. L. "Toward the Delineation of Vandalism as a Sub-type of Juvenile Delinquency." *Journal of Criminal Law, Criminology, and Police Science* 48 (1958): 493–99.

Cloward, R. A., and Ohilin, L. E. *Delinquency and Opportunity.* Glencoe, Ill.: The Free Press, 1961.

Cohen, A. K. *Delinquent Boys: The Culture of the Gang.* Glencoe, Ill.: The Free Press, 1955.

————. *Deviance and Control.* Englewood Cliffs, N.J.: Prentice-Hall, 1966.

Cohen, A. K.; Lindesmith, A.; and Schuessler, K., eds. *The Sutherland Papers.* Bloomington, Ind.: Indiana University Press, 1956.

Cohen, A. K., and Short, J. F., Jr., "Juvenile Delinquency." In Merton and Nisbet, *Contemporary Social Problems,* pp. 77–126.

————. "Research in Delinquent Subcultures." *Journal of Social Issues* 24 (1958): 20–37.

Cohen, T. "Geography of Crime." In Roucek, *Sociology of Crime,* pp. 160–92.

Coleman, J. *"Social Structure and Social Climate in High School.* New York: The Free Press of Glencoe, 1961.

Collins, B. S., et al. "The Study of 132 Alleged Sex Offenders." Mimeographed. Minneapolis: State Department of Correction, September, 1962.

"Comment: Police Discretion and the Judgment That a Crime Has Been Committed—Rape in Philadelphia." *University of Pennsylvania Law Review* 117 (1968): 277–322.

"Commitment under the Criminal Sexual Psychopath Law in Cook County Illinois." *American Journal of Psychiatry* 105 (1948): 420–25.

Committee on Nomenclature and Statistics of the American Psychiatric Association. *Mental Disorder Diagnostic and Statistical Manual.* Washington, D.C.: Mental Hospital Service, American Psychiatric Association, 1952.

"Complaints about Rape." *West Virginia Law Review* 24 (1938): 335–41.

"Consent to Rape." *Illinois Law Review* 19 (1925): 410–26.

Cormier, B. M., et al. "The Latecomer to Crime," *Canada Journal of Correction* 3 (1961): 2–18.

————."Some Psychological Aspects of Criminal Partnerships." *Canada Journal of Correction* 3 (1961): 445–55.

"Corroborating Charges of Rape." *Columbia Law Review* 62 (1967): 1136–48.

Craig, R. *Sexual Psychopath Legislation: Task Force Report.* Submitted to the President's Commission on Law Enforcement and Administration of Justice. Washington, D.C., 1967.

Crawford, P. C. et al. "Working with Teenage Gangs." Welfare Council of New York City, New York, 1950.

Cressey, D. R. *Delinquency Crime and Differential Association.* The Hague: Mortimesnishoff, 1964.

————. "Epidemiology and Individual Conduct: A Case from Criminology." *Pacific Sociological Review* 3 (1960): 47–58.

————. *Other People's Money.* Glencoe, Ill.: The Free Press, 1953.

————. "Role Theory, Differential Associations, and Compulsive Crimes." In Rose, *Human Behavior and Social Processes,* pp. 443–67.

————. "The State of Criminal Statistics." *National Probation and Parole Association Journal* 3 (1957): 230–41.

Crime Records in Police Management. New York: The Institute of Public Administration, 1952.

Crook, E. B. "Cultural Marginality in Sexual Delinquency." *The American Journal of Sociology* 39 (1934): 493–97.

————. "Sexual Delinquency in Relation to Cultural Infiltration." *Sociology and Social Research* 19 (1934): 44–54.

Curant, V. W. "A Fetish Theory of Amorous Fixation." *Journal of Social Psychology* 30 (1949): 17–37.

Curran, F. J., et al. "Sex Perversion." *Practitioner* 172 (1954): 440–46.

Curran, F. J., and Schilder, P. "A Constructive Approach to the Problem of Childhood and Adolescence." *Journal of Criminal Psychopathology* 2 (1941): 305–20.

Curry, M. "The Relationship of Weather Conditions, Facial Characteristics and Crime." *Journal of Criminal Law and Criminology* 34 (1948): 253–61.

Cushing, J. G. N. "Psychopathology of Sexual Delinquency." *Journal of Criminal Psychopathology* 11 (1950): 49–56.

Cutton, C. J. "Can We End Sex Crimes?" *Christian Century* (22 December 1937), pp. 1594–95.

Dallas, Texas Annual Police Report. City of Dallas, Texas, January 1961.

The Dangerous Sex Offender. General Assembly of the Commonwealth of Pennsylvania, 1963.

Davidson, M. "Appraisal of Witnesses." *American Journal of Psychiatry* 110 (1954): 481–84.

————. *Forensic Psychiatry*. New York: The Ronald Press, 1957.

Davis, A. "Socialization and the Adolescent Personality." In *Adolescent Year-Book* vol. 43, pp. 168–96. Washington: National Council of Studies in Education, 1944.

Davis, A., and Havighurst, R. J. "Social Class and Color Differences in Child Rearing." *The American Sociological Review* 11 (1946): 698–710.

Davis, F. J. "Crime News in Colorado Newspapers." *The American Journal of Sociology* 57 (1951): 325–30.

Davis, H. *Homicide in American Fiction, 1798–1860*. Ithaca, N.Y.: Cornell University Press, 1957.

Davis, K. "Jealousy and Sexual Property." *Social Forces* 14 (1936): 345–405.

————. "The Sociology of Parent-Youth Conflict." *The American Sociological Review* 5 (1940): 523–34.

De Balzac, H. *The Physiology of Marriage*. New York: Liveright, 1932.

De May, J. A. "The Pennsylvania Sex Criminal Act." *University of Pittsburgh Law Review* 13 (1949): 739–49.

Denzin, N. K. "Symbolic Interactionism and Ethnomethodology." *American Sociological Review* 34 (1969): 922–35.

DePorte, J. V., and Parkurst, E. "Homicide in the New York State." *Human Biology* 7 (1935): 47–73.

De Quiros, B. *Modern Theories of Criminality*. Boston: Little, Brown and Co., 1911.

De River, D. *The Sexual Criminal*. Springfield, Ill.: Charles C. Thomas, 1956.

De Rougemount, D. *Love in the Western World*. New York: Harcourt and Brace Co., 1930.

Deutsch, A. "Sober Facts about Sex Crimes." *Colliers* (25 November 1950), pp. 15–17, 63–64.

Deutsch, H. *Psychology of Women*. New York: Grune & Stratton, 1944.

Devereaux, G. "The Awarding of the Penis as a Compensation for Rape," *International Journal of Psychoanalysis* 38 (1957): 398–401.

————. "Neurotic Crimes vs. Criminal Behavior." *Psychiatric Quarterly* 25 (1951): 73–80.

————. *Normal and Abnormal*. Washington: N.I.M.H., 1956.

Dexter, E. *Weather Influences: An Empirical Study of the Mental and Physiological Effects of Definite Meteorological Conditions*. New York: The Macmillan Co., 1904.

Dexter, L. A. "On the Politics and Sociology of Stupidity in our Society." In Becker, *The Other Side*, pp. 37–51.

Ditzion, S. *Marriage, Morals, and Sex in America*. New York: Bookman Assoc., 1953.

Dollard, J. *Caste and Class in a Southern Town*. New Haven, Conn.: Yale University Press, 1937.

Dollard, J., et al. *Frustration and Aggression*. New Haven, Conn.: Yale University Press, 1939.

Doshay, L. T. *The Boy Sex Offender and His Later Career*. New York: Grune & Stratton, 1943.

Douglass, J. H. "The Extent and Characteristics of Juvenile Delinquency among Negroes in the United States." *Journal of Negro Education* 28 (1959): 214–30.

Downs, D. *The Delinquent Solution: A Study in Subculture Theory.* London: Routledge, Kegan & Paul, 1966.

Drucker, A. J., and Christensen, H. Y. "Some Factors in Socio-sexual Modernism." *Marriage and Family Living* 14 (1952): 334–36.

Drzazga, T. *Sex Crimes.* Springfield, Ill.: Charles C. Thomas, 1960.

Dunham, H. W. *Crucial Issues in the Treatment and Control of Sex Deviation in the Community: A Report.* Michigan: State Department of Mental Health, 1951.

Durkheim, E. *Suicide.* Translated by J. A. Shoulding and G. Simpson. Glencoe, Ill.: The Free Press, 1951.

East, N. W. *Medical Aspects of Crime.* Philadelphia: Blakston Son & Company, 1936.

East, W. N. "Crime, Senescence and Senility." *Journal of Mental Science* 90 (1944): 835–50.

―――. "Sexual Offenders," *Medical Journal of Nervous and Mental Disease* 103 (1946): 636–67.

Eaton, J. W., and Polk, K. *Measuring Delinquency.* Pittsburgh: University of Pittsburgh Press, 1961.

"Editorial: Miscellaneous Cases of Rape." *American Journal of Urology* 15 (1919): 151–66.

"Editorial: Sex Offenses and the Public." *American Journal of Psychiatry* 6 (1952): 1–6.

Ehrmann, W. *Premarital Dating Behavior.* New York: Henry Holt, 1959.

―――. "Premarital Sex Relations." *Social Forces* 38 (1959): 158–64.

―――. "Some Knowns and Unknowns in Research into Human Sex Behavior." *Marriage and Family Laving* 19 (1957): 16–25.

Eidelberg, L. *The Dark Urge.* New York: Pyramid Books, 1961.

Einstader, W. J., "Armed Robbery: A Career Study in Perspective." Ph.D. dissertation, University of California, Berkeley, 1966.

Eissler, R. K., *Searchlight on Delinquency,* New York: International University Press, 1949.

Ellenberg, H., "Psychological Relationship between Criminal and Victim." *Archives of Criminal Psychodynamics* 1 (1955): 257–90.

Elliasberg, W. G. "The Acute Psychosexual Situation: Legal Meaning and Diagnosis." *Journal of Criminal Law and Criminology* 33 (1943): 443–56.

―――. "The Examination of Testimonial Capacity." *Journal of Criminal Law, Criminology, and Police Science* 45 (1954): 41–47.

Ellis, A. "Recent Studies on Sex and Love Relations of Young People." *International Journal of Sexology* 6 (1953): 161–63.

―――. *Sex Habits of the American Male.* New York: Prentice-Hall, 1948.

―――. *The American Sexual Tragedy.* New York: Charles Boni, 1951.

―――. *The Folklore of Sex.* New York: Charles Boni, 1951.

Ellis, A., and Abarbanel, A., eds. *Encyclopedia of Sexual Behavior.* New York: Hawthorn Books, 1961.

Ellis, A., and Brancale, R. *The Psychology of Sex Offenders.* Springfield, Ill.: Charles C. Thomas, 1956.

Emerson, H., ed. *Alcohol and Man.* New York: Macmillan, 1932.

Ennis, P. H., *Criminal Victimization in the U.S.: Report of a National Survey.* Field Survey II of the President's Commission on Law Enforcement and Administration of Justice, Washington, D.C., 1967.

Eralason, D. A. "The Scene of Sex Offenses." *Journal of Criminal Law and Criminology* 31 (1946): 339–40.

Erickson, M. C. "Child Rearing and Social Status." *The American Journal of Sociology* 53 (1946): 190–92.

Erickson, E. H. *Childhood and Society.* New York: W. W. Norton, 1956.

————. "Ego Development and Historical Change." In *The Psychoanalytic Study of the Child*. New York: International Universities Press, 1954.

————. "Youth: Fidelity and Diversity." *Daedalus,* 91 (1962) : 5–27.

Eynon, T. C., and Reckless, W. C. "Companionship at Delinquency Onset." *The British Journal of Criminology* 2 (1961) : 162–70.

Factor, M. "A Woman's Psychological Reaction to Attempted Rape." *Psychoanalytic Quarterly* 23 (1954) : 243–44.

Fairbairn, W. B. "The Psychological Factors in Sexual Delinquency." *Mental Hygiene* 23 (1939) : 51–58.

Falk, G. J. "The Influence of the Seasons on Crime Rates." *Journal of Criminal Law, Criminology, and Police Science* 43 (1952) : 199–213.

————. "The Public Image of the Sex Offenders." *Mental Hygiene* 48 (1964) : 612–20.

Fattah, E. A. "Quelques problèmes posés à la justice pénale par la victimologie." *International Annals of Criminology* 5 (1966) : 335–61.

Faulkes, S. H. "Group-Analytic Dynamics with Special Reference to Psychoanalytic Concepts." *International Journal of Group Psychotherapy* 7 (1957) : 40–53.

Feigel, H., and Brodbeck, M., eds. *Readings in the Philosophy of Science*. New York: Appleton-Century-Crofts, 1953.

Fenichel, O. *The Psychoanalytic Theory of Neuroses*. New York: W. W. Norton, 1945.

Ferdinand, T. N. *Typologies of Delinquency: A Critical Analysis*. Random House, 1966.

Ferenczi, S. "A Theory of Genitality." *Psychoanalytic Quarterly* 2 (1933) : 361–87.

————. "Confusion of Tongues between Adults and Child." *International Journal of Psychoanalysis* 30 (1949) : 225–30.

————. "Sex and Psychoanalysis." In Ferenczi *Collected Papers,* vol. 2. Boston: Badger Pub., 1916.

Ferracuti, F.; Hernandez, R. F.; and Wolfgang, M. E. "A Study of Police Errors and Crime Classification." *Journal of Criminal Law, Criminology, and Police Science* 53 (1962) : 113–19.

Ferracuti, F., and Wolfgang, M. E. "A Design for a Proposed Study of Violence." *The British Journal of Criminology* 3 (1963) : 377–88.

————. "The Prediction of Violent Behavior." *Corrective Psychiatry and Journal of Social Therapy* 10 (1964) : 289–301.

Ferri, E. *Criminal Sociology*. Boston: Little, Brown and Co., 1917.

Festinger, L., et al. "Some Consequences of Deindividualization in the Group." *Journal of Abnormal and Social Psychology* 47 (1952) : 382–89.

Fine, R. "Psychoanalytic Theory of Sexuality." In Slovenko, *Sexual Behavior and the Law,* pp. 147–71.

Fink, A. *Causes of Crime*. Philadelphia: University of Pennsylvania Press, 1938.

Fischer, P. H. "Analysis of the Primary Group." *Sociometry* 16 (1953) : 272–76.

Fitch, J. H. "Men Convicted of Sexual Offenses against Children." *The British Journal of Criminology* 3 (1962) : 18–31.

Flescher, H. "The Economy of Aggression and Anxiety in Group Formation." *International Journal of Group Psychotherapy* 7 (1957) : 31–39.

Foote, N. N. "Sex As Fun." *Social Problems* 1 (1954) : 59–63.

"Forcible and Statutory Rape: Exploration on the Consent Standard." *Yale Law Review* 62 (1952) : 55–83.

Ford, C., and Beach, F. *Patterns of Sexual Behavior*. New York: Harper, 1951.

Fox, A. N. "Crime and Advantage." *Archives of Criminal Psychodynamics* 1 (1955) : 247–56.

Fox, V. "Emotional Dynamics in Group Violence." *Archives of Criminal Psychodynamics* 16 (1955) : 255–77.

————. "Intelligence, Race and Age as Selective Factors in Crime." *Journal of Criminal Law and Criminology* 37 (1946): 141–52.

Fox, V., and Volakakis, J. "The Negro Offender in a Northern Industrial Area." *Journal of Criminal Law, Criminology, and Police Science* 46 (1956): 641–48.

Foxe, A. *Crime and Sexual Development.* New York: The Monogram Editions 1936.

Frankel, E. E. "Lady Killer." *Cosmopolitan* 143 (1957): 68–83.

Fraz, M., *The Romantic Agony,* 2d ed. New York: Meridian, 1950.

Frazier, E. F. *The Negro Family in the United States.* Chicago: University of Chicago Press, 1934.

————. "Negro Sexuality." In Ellis and Abarbanel, *Encyclopedia of Sexual Behavior,* vol. II, pp. 769–75.

————. "Sex Morality among Negroes." *Journal of Religious Education* 23 (1928): 447–50.

Freud, A. *The Ego and the Mechanisms of Defense.* New York: International Universities Press, 1946.

Freud, S. "Beyond the Pleasure Principle." In *Collected Papers.* London: The Hogarth Press, vol. II, 1933.

————. "A Child is Being Beaten." *Collected Papers.* London: The Hogarth Press, 1933.

————. *Group Psychology and the Analysis of the Ego.* London: The Hogarth Press, 1933.

————. *New Introductory Lectures in Psychoanalysis.* London: The Hogarth Press, 1933.

————. "Paranoia and Homosexuality." In *Collected Papers.* London: The Hogarth Press, vol. II, 1933.

————. "Thoughts for the Time on War and Death." In *Collected Papers.* London: The Hogarth Press, 1933.

————. "Three Essays on the Theory of Sexuality." In *Collected Papers.* London: Imago, 1949.

Freund, B. *The Ego in Love and Sexuality.* New York: Grune and Stratton, 1960.

Friedlander, K. *The Psychoanalytic Approach to Juvenile Delinquency.* New York: International Universities Press, 1947.

Friedman, A. "Late Consequences (Damage) in Children and Adolescents." *Excerpta Criminologica* 30 (1965): 722–33.

Fromm, E., *The Art of Loving.* New York: Harper, 1956.

Frosch, J., and Bromberg, W. "The Sex Offender: A Psychiatric Study." *American Journal of Orthopsychiatry* 9 (1939): 761–76.

Frumkin, R. M. "Race of Men Serving Life Sentences in the Ohio Penitentiary." *Journal of Negro Education* 24 (1955): 506–8.

Fyvel, F. R. *Trouble Makers: Rebellious Youth in an Affluent Society.* New York: Schocken Books, 1961.

Gagnon, J. "Female Child Victims of Sex Offenses." *Social Problems* 13 (1956): 176–92.

Gans, H. J. *The Urban Villagers,* Glencoe, Ill.: The Free Press, 1962.

Gardner, G. E. "The Aggressive Destructive Impulse in the Sex Offender." *Mental Hygiene* 34 (1950): 45–63.

————. "The Community and the Aggressive Child." *Mental Hygiene* 34 (1950): 44–48.

Garner, J. R. "Detailed Examination Required to Determine Whether Rape has been Committed." *American Journal of Jurisprudence* 1 (1938): 29–31.

Garofalo, R. B. *Criminology.* Boston: Little, Brown and Company, 1914.

Garrel, J. "The Sexual Psychopath Laws: Validity and Construction." *Baylor Law Review* 14 (1962): 93–107.

Gebhard, P. H., et al. *Sex Offenders.* New York: Harper & Row, 1965.

Gemert, P. J. *A Comparison of Release and Recidivist From June 1, 1946 to May 31, 1961.* Harrisburg, 1962.

Gerrard, N. C. "The Core Member of the Gang." *The British Journal of Criminology* 4 (1964): 361–71.

Gibbens, J. C. H. "Sexual Behavior of Young Criminals." *Journal of Mental Science* 103 (1957): 527–40.

Gibbons, D. C. *Changing the Law Breaker.* Englewood Cliffs, N.J.: Prentice-Hall, 1965.

Gibbons, D. C., and Garrity, D. "Some Suggestions for the Definition of Etiology and Treatment Theory." *Social Forces* 38 (1959): 51–57.

Gibbs, C. A. "Leadership." In Lindzey, *Handbook of Social Psychology,* pp. 877–920.

———. "The Principles and Traits of Leadership." *Journal of Abnormal and Social Psychology* 44 (1947): 54–79.

Gilbert, C. C. "Rape and Sexual Perversion." In Peterson, et al., *Legal Medicine and Toxology,* vol. 1.

Gilchrist, J. S. "The Formation of Groups under Conditions of Success and Failure." *Journal of Abnormal and Social Psychology* 47 (1952): 178–87.

Gillespie, W. H. "Notes in the Analysis of Sexual Perversions." *International Journal of Psychoanalysis* 33 (1952): 397–402.

———. "The Structure and Etiology of Sexual Perversions." In Lorand and Balint, *Perversion: Psychodynamics and Therapy,* pp. 231–43.

Gillin, J. *Criminology and Penology,* 3d ed. New York: Appleton-Century Co., 1945.

———. "Social Background of Sex Offenders." *Social Forces* 14 (1935): 237–39.

———. *The Wisconsin Prisoner.* Wisconsin: Wisconsin University Press, 1946.

Ginsberg, E., ed. *The Nation's Children.* New York: Columbia University Press, 1960.

Ginzberg, E. *Sex and Class Behavior.* New York: New American Library of World Literature, 1948.

Gittler, J. B., ed. *Review of Sociology: Analysis of a Decade.* New York: John Wiley and Sons, 1957.

Glaser, D. "The Differential-Association Theory of Crime." In Rose, *Human Behavior and Social Processes,* pp. 425–43.

———. "Victim Survey Research: Theoretical Implications." In Guenther, *Criminal Behavior and Social Systems,* pp. 136–48.

Glazer, N. "Why Jews Stay Sober." *Commentary* 13 (1952): 181–86.

Glover, E. "The Relation of Perversion Formation to the Development of Reality Sense." *International Journal of Psychoanalysis* 14 (1933): 486–504.

———. "The Social and Legal Aspects of Sexual Abnormalities." *Medical Legal Journal* 13 (1945): 133–48.

Glueck, B. C., Jr. *New York Final Report on Deviated Sex Offenders.* Albany, New York: Department of Mental Hygiene, 1956.

———. "Psychodynamic Patterns in Sex Offender." *Psychiatric Quarterly* 28 (1954): 1–21.

Glueck, S., and Glueck, E. *Delinquents in the Making.* New York: Harper & Bros., 1952.

———. *Unraveling Juvenile Delinquency.* New York: The Commonwealth Fund, 1950.

Goffman, E. *The Presentation of Self in Everyday Life.* New York: Doubleday and Co., 1959.

Goldberg, J. *Girls on the City Streets.* New York: Foundation Books, 1935.

Goldstein, J. "Police Discretion Not to Involve the Criminal Process." *Yale Law Journal* 7 (1960): 543–91.

Gomzan, W. A. "A Theory of Coalition Formations." *The American Sociological Review* 26 (1961): 373–82.

Gonzales, J. P., et al. "Virginity, Rape and Sexual Assault: Examination of Semen." In Gonzales's *Legal Medicine, Pathology and Toxology.* New York: Appleton-Century Co., 1937.

Gordon, R. H., et al., "Values and Gang Delinquency: A Study of Street Corner Groups." *American Journal of Sociology* 67 (1963): 109–28.

Gouldner, A. W., ed. *Studies in Leadership.* New York: Harper & Bros., 1950.

Grant, V. "Preface to a Psychology of Sexual Attachment." *Journal of Social Psychology* 33 (1954): 187–230.

Graves, L. R. "Clinical and Laboratory Evidence of Rape." *Tennessee Medical Journal* 55 (1926): 389–91.

———. "Detailed Examination Is Required To Determine Whether Rape Was Committed." *American Journal of Medical Jurisprudence* 1 (1938): 28–31.

Gray, K. "Amnesia in Criminal Trial." *Journal of Social Therapy* 1 (1955): 100–107.

Green, A. "The 'Cult of Personality' and Sexual Relations." *Psychiatry* 4 (1941): 344–48.

———. "Middle Class Male Child and Neurosis." *The American Sociological Review* 11 (1946): 31–41.

Greenley, A., and Casey, J. "An Upper and Middle Class Deviant Gang." *The American Catholic Sociological Review* 24 (1963): 33–42.

Griffith, E. F. "Alcohol and Sex." *The British Journal on Inebriety* 36 (1938): 57–63.

———. "Sex Problems of Adolescents." *Practitioner* 172 (1954): 420–26.

Grisbey, S. E. "The Raiford Study: Alcohol and Crime." *Journal of Criminal Law, Criminology, and Police Science* 54 (1963): 296–306.

Grossberg, R. "The Problem of Sex Offenses." *Health Education Journal* 8 (1950): 158–61.

Grosser, G. "Juvenile Delinquency and Contemporary American Sex Roles." Ph.D. dissertation, Harvard University, 1952.

Group for the Advancement of Psychiatry. *Psychiatrically Deviated Sex Offenders.* Report no. 9, May 1949; Revised February, 1953. Topeka, Kansas, 1953.

Grunbaum, A. "Causality and the Science of Human Behavior." In Feigel and Brodbeck, *Readings in the Philosophy of Science,* pp. 216–48.

Grunhüt, M. *Sexual Crime Today: A Symposium.* The Hague: University of Leiden, 1960.

———. "Statistics in Criminology." *Journal of the Royal Statistical Society* 64 (1951): 149–56.

Guenther, A. L., ed. *Criminal Behavior and Social Systems.* Chicago: Rand, McNally & Co., 1970.

Guttmacher, M. S. *Sex Offenses.* New York: W. W. Norton, 1951.

Guttmacher, M. S., and Weihofen, H. *Psychiatry and the Law.* New York: W. W. Norton, 1952.

———. "Sex Offenses." *Journal of Criminal Law, Criminology, and Police Science* 43 (1952): 153–75.

Gyon, R. *The Ethics of the Sexual Act.* New York: Alfred A. Knopf, 1948.

Hacker, H. M. "The New Burden of Masculinity." *Marriage and Family Living* 9 (1957): 227–33.

Hacker, J., and Fryn, M. "The Sexual Psychopath Act in Practice." *Columbia Law Review* 43 (1955): 776–82.

Hadly, E. E. "Comment on Pedophilia." *Medical Journal and Records* 124 (1946): 157–62.

Hagood, M. T. *Statistics for Sociologists.* New York: Henry Holt, 1947.

Haines, W., et al. "Commitment under the Criminal Sexual Psychopath Law

in Cook County, Illinois." *American Journal of Psychiatry* 105 (1948):
420–25.

Hakeem, M. "A Critique of the Psychiatric Approach to Crime and Correction." *Law and Contemporary Problems* 23 (1958): 650–82.

Hall, J. *General Principles of Criminal Law.* Indianapolis: Bobbs-Merrill Co., 1947.

———. "Intoxication and Criminal Responsibility." *Howard Law Journal* 57 (1944): 1045–1984.

Halleck, S. L. "The Physician's Role in Management of Victims of Sex Offenders." *Journal of American Medical Association* 180 (1962): 273–78.

———. "Emotional Effects of Victimization." In Slovenko, *Sexual Behavior and the Law,* pp. 673–86.

Hammer, E. G. "A Comparison of H. T. P's of Rapists and Pedophiliacs." *Journal of Projective Techniques* 18 (1954): 346–54.

———. "Psychoanalytical Hypothesis Concerning Sex Offenders." *Journal of Clinical and Experimental Psychopathology* 18 (1957): 177–264.

———. "The Relationships between Psychosexual Pathology and the Sex of the First Drawn Person." *Journal of Clinical Psychology* 10 (1954): 168–70.

Hammer, E. G., and Glueck, B. C., Jr. "Psychodynamic Patterns in Sex Offender: A Four Factor Theory." *Psychiatric Quarterly* 31 (1957): 235–45.

Hanson, K. *Rebels in the Streets: The Story of New York's Girl Gangs.* Englewood Cliffs, N.J.: Prentice-Hall, 1964.

Hare, A. P. *Handbook of Small Group Research.* New York: The Free Press of Glencoe, 1962.

———. "Interaction and Consensus in Different Size Groups." *The American Sociological Review* 17 (1952): 261–67.

Hare, A. P.; Borgatta, E. F.; and Bales, R. F. *Small Groups: Studies in Social Interaction.* New York: A. Knopf, 1955.

Harris, C. "Sex Crimes: Their Causes and Cure." *Coronet* (August 1946) pp. 23–25.

Hartman, A., and Schroeder, B. C. "Criminality and the Age Factor." *Journal of Criminal Psychopathology* 5 (1942): 351–67.

Hartog, R. "Discipline in Early Life of Sex Delinquents." *The Nervous Child* 9 (1951): 167–74.

Hartung, F. E. *Crime, Law and Society.* Detroit: Wayne University Press, 1965.

Hartwell, S. W. *A Citizen's Handbook of Sexual Abnormalities.* State of Michigan, Lansing, 1950.

Hayner, N. S. "Crimogenic Zones in Mexico City." *American Sociological Review* 11 (1946): 428–38.

Healy, W. *The Individual Delinquent.* Boston: Little, Brown and Co., 1915.

Healy, W., and Bronner, A. F. *Delinquents and Criminals.* New York: The Macmillan Co., 1928.

Hecksler, H. "On the Culpability and Crime." *The Annals of the American Academy of Political and Social Science* 339 (1962): 33–34.

Heider, F. *The Psychology of Interpersonal Relations.* New York: John Wiley and Sons, 1958.

Hemphill, J. K. "Situational Factors in Leadership." *Ohio State University: Educational Research Monographs,* no. 32, 1949.

Henninger, J. M. "The Senile Sex Offender." *Mental Hygiene* 23 (1939): 436–44.

Henry, A. F., and Short, J. F., Jr. *Suicide and Homicide.* Glencoe, Ill.: The Free Press, 1954.

Henry, G. W., and Gross, A. A. "The Sex Offender: A Consideration of Therapeutic Principles." *National Probation and Parole Association* (1940), 114–37.

Herman, M. "Aberrant Sex Behavior." *Annals of New York Academy of Science* 47 (1947): 639–45.

Herren, R. "The Evidence of Children and Adolescents Concerning Sexual Offenses." *International Criminal Police Review* 96 (1956): 385–95.

Hewitt, H. "Investigation of Rape." *Tennessee State Medical Association Journal* 30 (1937): 286–91.

Hewitt, L. E., and Jenkins, R. L. *Fundamental Patterns of Maladjustment.* Springfield, Ill.: Charles C. Thomas, 1947.

Himelhoch, J., and Fava, S., eds. *Sexual Behavior in American Society.* New York: W. W. Norton, 1955.

Hinkle, R. C., and Hinkle, G. *The Development of Modern Sociology.* New York: Random House, 1954.

Hirning, L. C. "The Sex Offender in Custody." In Lindner and Seliger, *Handbook of Correctional Psychology,* pp. 233–56.

Hirschfield, M. *Sexual Abnormality.* New York: Emerson Books, 1948.

Hoch, P., and Zubin, J. *Anxiety.* New York: Grune & Stratton, 1950.

———. *Psychosexual Development in Health and Disease.* New York: Grune & Stratton, 1949.

Hoffer, F. W. *The Jails of Virginia.* New York: Appleton-Century-Crofts, 1933.

Hoffman, W. F. *Pennsylvania Criminal Law and Criminal Procedure.* Hershey, Penn.: State Public Civic Association, 1958.

Hohman, L. B., and Schoffner, L. B. "The Sex Life of Unmarried Men." *The American Journal of Sociology* 52 (1946): 501–7.

Hollander, F. P., ed. *Leaders, Groups, and Influence.* New York: Oxford University Press, 1964.

Hollingshead, A. B. *Elmtown's Youth.* New York: Science Editions, 1961.

Hollingsworth, H. L. *Psychology and Ethics: A Study of the Sense of Obligation.* New York: Roland Press, 1949.

Homans, G. C. *The Human Group.* New York: Harcourt, Brace & Co., 1950.

Hook, S., ed. *Determinism and Freedom.* New York: New York University Press, 1958.

———. *Psychoanalysis: Scientific Method and Philosophy.* New York: Grove Press, 1960.

Hoover, J. E. "How Safe is Your Daughter?" *American Magazine* 144 (1947): 32–33.

Howard, E. G. "Alcohol and Crime." *The American Journal of Sociology* 24 (1918): 61–68.

Howard, J. C. *Administration of Rape Cases in the City of Baltimore and the State of Maryland.* Baltimore, Maryland: Monumental Bar Association, 1967.

Hsu, F.L.K. "Sex Crime and Personality: A Study in Comparative Cultural Patterns." *American Scholar* 21 (1951): 68–75.

Huhmer, M. "Rape and Satyriasis." *American Journal of Urology* 14 (1918): 362–70.

Hughes, J. H. "The Minnesota Sexual Irresponsible Law." *Mental Hygiene* 25 (1941): 76–80.

Hukner, M. "Is Rape Always a Crime?" *Medical Times* 96 (1918): 33–35.

Hulbert, H. S. "Post Sex Crime Amnesia." *Journal of Criminal Law and Criminology* 37 (1946): 191–92.

Hull, C. C. *A Behavioral System.* New Haven, Conn.: Yale University Press, 1957.

Hurwitz, S. *Criminology.* London: George Allen and Unwin, 1942.

Hyde, H. M. *The Trial of Oscar Wilde.* Edinburgh: William Hodge Co., 1948.

Ichheiser, G. "Misunderstanding of Human Relations." *The American Journal of Sociology* 55 (1949) no. 2.

Illinois Commission Report on Sex Offenders. Springfield, Ill., 1953.

Inkeles, A. "Personality and Social Structure." In Merton, et al., *Sociology Today,* pp. 249–77.

James, J. "The Distribution of Free-forming Small Group Size." *The American Sociological Review* 18 (1953): 570–79.

Jansyn, L. R., Jr. "I—Formal Characteristics" and "II—Leadership Structure and Behavior." *The Structure and Dynamics of the Street Corner Group.* Springfield, Ill.: Illinois Department of Public Welfare, Institute for Juvenile Research, 1962.

Jenkins, R. L. H. "The Making of Sex Offenders." *Focus* 30 (1951): 129–31.

Jenkins, R. L. H., and L. F. Hewitt. *Fundamental Patterns of Maladjustment.* Springfield, Ill.: State of Illinois, 1947.

Jennings, H. H. *Leadership and Isolation.* New York: Longmans, Green, Pale, 1943.

Johnson, A. M. "Parental Influences in Unusual Sexual Behavior in Children." *Psychoanalytic Quarterly* 25 (1956): 37–55.

———. "Permissiveness in Child Rearing and Their Relationships to Juvenile Delinquency." *Proceedings of Staff Meeting of Mayo Clinic* 30 (1955): 557–65.

———. "Sanction for Super-Ego Lacunae of Adolescents." In Eissler, *Searchlight on Delinquency,* pp. 225–45.

Johnson, A. M., and Szurek, S. A. "Genesis of Anti-Social Acting out in Children and Adults." *Psychoanalytic Quarterly* 21 (1952): 323–43.

Johnson, G. B. "The Negro and Crime." *Journal of Criminal Law and Criminology* 30 (1940): 622–30.

———. "The Negro in Crime." *The Annals of the American Academy of Political and Social Science* 217 (1941): 93–105.

Jonassen, C. T. "A Re-evaluation and Critique of the Logic and Some Methods of Shaw and McKay." *American Sociological Review* 14 (1949): 608–15.

Kanin, E. J. "Male Aggressions in Dating Relations." *The American Journal of Sociology* 63 (1957): 197–204.

Kanin, E. J., and Kirkpatrick, C. "Male Sex Aggression in University Campuses." *American Sociological Review* 22 (1953): 52–58.

Kaplan, S. J. "The Geography of Crime." In Roucek, *Sociology of Crime,* pp. 169–93.

Kardiner, A. *Sex and Morality.* London: Routledge and Kegan, Paul, 1955.

Kardiner, A., and Ovesey, S. C. *The Mark of Oppression.* New York: W. W. Norton, 1951.

Karpman, B. "A Case of Pedophilia (legally rape) Cured by Psychoanalysis." *Psychoanalytic Review* 37 (1950): 235–76.

———. "Crime and Adolescence." *Mental Hygiene* 21 (1937): 384–96.

———. "Criminality as an Expression of Psychosexual Development." *Journal of Criminal Psychopathology* 3 (1942): 382–424.

———. "Felonious Assault Revealed as a Symptom of Abnormal Sexuality." *Journal of Criminal Law and Criminology* 37 (1946): 193–215.

———. "The Obsessive Paraphilias." *Archives of Neurology and Psychiatry* 32 (1934), 577–626.

———. "The Principles and Aims of Criminal Psychopathology." *Journal of Abnormal and Criminal Psychopathology* 1 (1940): 187–218.

———. *The Sexual Offender and His Offenses.* New York: The Julian Press, 1954.

Kaufman, M. *The Admissibility of Confession in Criminal Cases.* Toronto: The Carswell Co., 1960.

Kelznechz, T., ed. *The Drinking Problem.* London: P. S. King & Son, 1910.

Kephart, W. M. *Racial Factors in Urban Law Enforcement.* Philadelphia: University of Pennsylvania Press, 1957.

Kinberg, O. "Alcohol and Criminality." *Journal of Criminal Law and Criminology* 11 (1944): 114–18.

Kinsey, A. C., et al. "Concepts of Normality and Abnormality in Sexual Behavior." In Hoch and Zubin, *Psychosexual Development in Health and Disease,* pp. 11–32.

Kinsey, A. C.; Pomeroy, W. B.; and Martin, C. E. *Sexual Behavior in the Human Male.* Philadelphia: Saunders, 1948.

Kinsie, P. M. "Sex Crimes and the Prostitution Racket." *Journal of Social Hygiene* 36 (1950): 250–52.

Klein, M. W. "Factors Related to Juvenile Gang Membership." *Sociology and Social Research* 51 (1968): 49–62.

Klien, M. "Notes on Some Schizoid Mechanisms." *International Journal of Psychoanalysis* 27 (1946): 99–110.

―――. *The Psychoanalysis of Children.* New York: W. W. Norton, 1935.

Kluckhohn, C. "Sexual Behavior in Cross-Cultural Perspective." In Himelhoch and Fava, *Sexual Behavior in American Society,* pp. 332–45.

Kobrin, S. "The Conflict of Values in Delinquency Areas." *The American Sociological Review* 16 (1951): 653–61.

Kohler, W. *Dynamics in Psychology.* New York: Liveright, 1940.

Korn, R. R., and McCorkle, L. W. *Criminology and Penology.* New York: Holt, Rinehart and Winston, 1959.

Kramer, D., and Karr, M. *Teen-age Gangs.* New York: Henry Holt & Co., 1953.

Krinsky, C. M., and Michaele, J. "A Survey of 100 Offenders Admitted to Boston Psychiatric Hospital." *Journal of Criminal Psychopathology* 2 (1940): 199–201.

Kupperstein, L. *An Analysis of Sex Offenses Committed in Philadelphia during 1962.* Philadelphia: Pennsylvania Prison Society, 1963.

Kvaraceus, W., and Miller, W. B. *Delinquent Behavior: Culture and the Individual.* Washington: National Education Association of the U.S., 1959.

La Mare, T. E., and Lubeck, S. G. "Conformity and Deviance in the Situation of Company." *American Sociological Review* 33 (1968): 760–73.

Lander, B. *Toward An Understanding of Juvenile Delinquency.* New York: Columbia University Press, 1954.

Landis, J. T. "Experience of 500 Children with Adult's Sexual Relations." *Psychiatric Quarterly* 30 (1956): 91–109.

Lanzer, I. A., "Review of Von Hentig book, The Criminal and his Victim," *Journal of Criminal Law, Criminology and Police Science* 10 (1950): 384–85.

Laughlin, L. B. "The Disposition of Sex Complaints on the Level of Police Investigation." Master's Thesis, Wayne University, 1956.

Laurenson, H. "The Cool Cat Era." *Park East* (January 1953), pp. 33–34.

Lawton, S. V., and Archer, J. *Sexual Conduct of the Teenager.* New York: Spectrolux Corporation, 1954.

Lemert, E. M. "An Isolation and Closure Theory of Naive Check Forgery." *Journal of Criminal Law, Criminology, and Police Science* 44 (1953): 296–307.

Lenox, W. G. "Amnesia: Real or Feigned." *American Journal of Psychiatry* 99 (1942): 737–41.

Leonard, V. A. "Sexual Psychopath Laws Upheld." *Journal of Criminal Law and Criminology* 40 (1949): 186–87.

Leppman, F. "Essential Differences between Sex Offenders." *Journal of Criminal Law, Criminology, and Police Science* 32 (1941): 360–80.

Lerner, M. *America As a Civilization.* New York: Simon and Schuster, 1957.

Levy, D. "The Interaction of Institutions and Policy Groups: The Origin of Sex Crime Legislation." *The Lawyer's Legal Notes* 5 (1951): 3–12.

Lewin, K. *Field Theory in Social Science.* D. Cartwright, ed. New York: Harper, 1951.

————. "Some Social and Psychological Differences between the United States and Germany." *Character and Personality* 4 (1936): 265–93.

Lewis, H. "The Changing Negro Family." In Ginsberg, *The Nation's Children,* pp. 108–37.

Lewinson, R. *History of Sexual Customs.* New York: Harpers, 1958.

Libai, D. *The Protection of the Child Victim of Sexual Offenses in the Justice System.* Ph.D. dissertation, University of Chicago, 1968.

Liebowitz, S. S. "New Facts About Sex Crimes." *Coronet* 36 (1954): 65–76.

Lind, A. W. "Some Ecological Patterns of Community Disorganization in Honolulu." *American Journal of Sociology* 36 (1930): 206–20.

Lindesmith, A. R. *Opiate Addiction.* Bloomington, Ind.: Principia Press, 1957.

Lindesmith, A. R., and Dunham, H. W. "Some Principles of Criminal Typology." *Social Forces* 19 (1941): 307–14.

Lindner, R. M., and Seliger, R. V., eds. *Handbook of Correctional Psychology.* New York: Philosophical Library, 1947.

Lindsey, B. B., and Evans, W. *The Revolt of Modern Youth.* New York: Liveright, 1925.

Lindzey, G., ed. *Handbook of Social Psychology.* Reading, Mass.: Addison-Wesley, 1954.

Lippit, R. "An Experimental Study of the Effect of Democratic and Authoritarian Group Atmospheres." *University of Iowa Studies in Child Welfare* 16 (1940): 143–45.

Lofan, R., et al. "Victimology and Criminology of Debauchery of Youth. *Experta Criminologica* 1 (1961): 454.

Lombroso, C. *Crime: Its Causes and Remedies.* Boston: Little, Brown, and Company, 1911.

London, L. S., and Capiro, P. S. *Sexual Deviations: Psychodynamic Approach.* Washington: Linacre Press, 1950.

Lorand, S., and Balint, M. *Perversion: Psychodynamics and Therapy.* New York: Random House, 1956.

Lottier, S. "The Distribution of Criminal Offenses in Metropolitan Regions." *Journal of Criminal Law and Criminology* 29 (1938): 37–50.

Luckman, M. *On the Validity of the Testimony of Female Children and Adolescents as Regard Sexual Offenses.* Stuttgart: E. Emke, 1959.

Lukas, E. J. "Alcohol and Crime." *Journal of American Medical Association* 127 (1957): 1010–11.

————. "What are the Common Beliefs Concerning the Role of the Negro in Delinquency and Crime?" *Journal of Criminal Law and Criminology* 36 (1945): 272–74.

Maccoby, E., et al., eds. *Readings in Social Psychology,* 3d ed. New York: Holt, Rinehart and Winston, 1958.

MacDonald, M. W. "Criminally Aggressive Behavior in Passive Effeminate Boys." *American Journal of Orthopsychiatry* 8 (1938): 70–78.

Machtinger, S. J. "Psychiatric Testimony for the Impeachment of Witnesses in Sex Crime." *Journal of Criminal Law and Criminology* 39 (1949): 34–45.

Magnus, A. R. "Sexual Deviation and the Family." *Marriage and Family Living* 15 (1953): 325–31.

————. "Sexual Deviation Research in California." *Sociology and Social Research* 37 (1953): 175–81.

Malinowski, B. "Individual and Society in Functional Analysis." *The American Journal of Sociology* 44 (1939): 939–46.

Mann, T. *Introduction to the Short Novels of Dostoyevsky.* New York: Dial Press, 1951.

Mannix, D. P. *The Beast.* New York: Ballantine Books, 1959.

Mapes, C. C. "Sexual Assault." *Urology and Cutaneous Review* 21 (1917): 430–35.

Marces, B. "A Dimensional Study of Prison Population." *The British Journal of Criminology* 1 (1960–61): 130–53.

Markey, O. S. "A Study of Aggressive Sex Misbehavior in Adolescents Brought to the Juvenile Court." *American Journal of Orthopsychiatry* 20 (1950): 719–31.

Martin, J. M. *Juvenile Vandalism*. Springfield, Ill.: Charles C. Thomas, 1961.

Martin, J. M., and Fitzpatrick, J. P. *Delinquent Behavior: A Redefinition of the Problem*. New York: Random House, 1965.

Massachusetts Report of the Commission for the Investigation on the Prevalence of Sex Crimes, nos. 1169, 2169. Boston: House Dept., 1948.

Maslow, A. W., et al. "Some Parallels between Sexual and Dominant Behavior of Infra-Human Primates and the Fantasies of Patients in Psychotherapy." *Journal of Mental and Nervous Disorders* 4 (1960): 202–12.

Matza, D. *Becoming Deviant*. Englewood Cliffs, New Jersey: Prentice-Hall, 1969.

―――. *Delinquency and Drift*. New York: John Wiley and Sons, 1964.

Matza, D., and Sykes, G. H. "Juvenile Delinquency and Subterrean Values." *The American Sociological Review* 26 (1961): 716–19.

Maurer, D. *Whiz Mob*. New Haven: College and University Press, 1964.

Mawrer, H. R. "A Psychocultural Analysis of Alcoholism." *The American Sociological Review* 11 (1948): 546–57.

Mayer, E. E. "The Sex Deviate." *Pennsylvania Medical Journal* 53 (1950): 23–27.

Mayo-Smith, R. S. *Statistics and Sociology*. Cambridge: Cambridge University Press, 1907.

Mays, J. B. "Delinquency Areas—A Reassessment." *British Journal of Criminology* 13 (1963): 216–30.

McClintock, F. H. *Crimes of Violence*. London: Macmillan, 1963.

McClintock, F. H., and Gibson, E. *Robbery in London*. London: Macmillan, 1961.

McCord, W., and McCord, P. V. "Family Relationships and Sexual Deviance in Lower-Class Adolescents." *The International Journal of Social Psychiatry* 8 (1962): 165–80.

McEntire, D., and Weckler, J. E. "The Role of the Police." *The Annals of the American Academy of Political and Social Science* 244 (1946): 82–89.

McKeown, J. T. "Poverty, Race and Crime." *Journal of Criminal Law and Criminology* 39 (1948): 480–83.

Mead, M. *Male and Female*. New York: William Morrow, 1949.

―――. *Sex and Temperament in Three Primitive Societies*. New York: New American Library, 1950.

Mead, M., and Wolfstein, M., eds. *Childhood and Contemporary Culture*. Chicago: University of Chicago Press, 1956.

Mendelson, B. "The Origin of the Doctrine of Victimology." *Exerpta Criminologica* 3 (1963): 229–40.

Menninger, K. *Man against Himself*. New York: Harcourt and Brace, 1938.

Merton, R. K. "Self Fulfilling Prophecy." *Antioch Review* 8 (1948): 193–210.

Merton, R. K., and Nisbet, R. A., eds. *Contemporary Social Problems*. New York: Harcourt, Brace and World, 1961.

Meyers, E. "Girls Involved in Sexual Offenses." In Meyers, ed., *Studies in Children,* pp. 157–66. New York: King Crown Press, 1948.

"Michigan Commission: New Light on Sex Offenders." *Journal of Social Hygiene* 38 (1952): 29–36.

Mihim, F. P. "Sex Psychopath Statutes in the Light of Recent Appeals." *Journal of Criminal Law, Criminology, and Police Science* 44 (1953): 716–36.

Miller, D. R., and Swanson, G. E. *Inner Conflict and Defense*. New York: Holt, Rinehart and Winston, 1960.

Miller, W. B. "Aggression in a Boys' Street Corner Group." *Psychiatry* 24 (1961): 283–89.

———. "Female Sexual and Mating Behavior." Dittoed.

———. "Implication of Lower Class Culture for Social Work." *Social Service Review* 33 (1959): 219–36.

———. "Lower Class Culture as a Generating Milieu of Gang Delinquency." *The Journal of Social Issues* 14 (1958): 5–19.

Miller, S. M., and Riessman, F. "The Working Class Subculture: A New View." *Social Problems* 9 (1961) 86–97.

Mills, C. W. "Situated Actions and Vocabularies of Motive." *The American Sociological Review* 5 (1950): 904–13.

Mills, T. M. "The Coalition Patterns in Three Person Groups." *The American Sociological Review* 19 (1954): 657–67.

Minow, N. "The Illinois Proposal to Confine Sexually Dangerous Persons." *Journal of Criminal Law, and Criminology* 40 (1949): 186–97.

Moberg, D. O. "Old Age and Crime." *Journal of Criminal Law, Criminology and Police Science* 44 (1953): 764–76.

Model Penal Code (tentative draft no. 4). American Law Institute, 1955.

Mohr, J. W. "A Follow-up Study of Sexual Offenders." *Forensic Clinic,* Clarke Institute, Ottawa: 1960–61.

———. "A Short Survey of Sexual Offenders in Ontario Reformatory, Millbrook." *Canada Journal of Correction* 5 (1963): 229–35.

———. "Rape and Attempted Rape." Mimeographed. Toronto: Toronto Psychiatric Hospital, October 1965.

Mohr, J. W.; Turner, R. E.; and Jerry, M. B. *Pedophilia and Exhibitionism.* Toronto: University of Toronto Press, 1965.

Monahan, A. J. "Rape: Evidence and Corroboration." *Cornell Law Quarterly* 9 (1924): 465–67.

Montegaza, P. *The Sexual Relations of Mankind.* New York: Eugenic Publishing Co., 1935.

Moore, E. H. The Accuracy of Testimony Relative to Time Interval." *Journal of Criminal Law and Criminology* 26 (1935): 210–15.

Mores, R. *The Sexual Revolution.* New York: Monarch, 1962.

Morris, T. *The Criminal Area.* London: Routledge & Kegan Paul, 1958.

Moses, E. R. "Differentials in Crime Rates between Negroes and Whites, Based on Comparison of Four Socio-economically Equated Areas." *American Sociological Review* 12 (1947): 411–20.

Murdock, G. P. *Social Structure.* New Haven: Yale University Press, 1949.

Murphy, G. *Personality: A Biosocial Approach to Origin and Structure.* New York: Harper & Bros., 1947.

Murray, H. *Explorations in Personality.* New York: Oxford University Press, 1938.

Nagel, W. H. "The Notion of 'Victimology' in Criminology." *Experta Criminologica* 3 (1963): 245–7.

Neiman, L. J. "Peer Groups and Attitudes toward the Female Role." *Social Problems* 2 (1959): 104–10.

The Negro in Detroit. Detroit Bureau of Governmental Research, 1936.

The Negro in New Jersey. A Report of the Survey of the Interracial Committee of the N. J. Conference of Social Work, Newark, 1932.

Nettler, G. "Good Men, Bad Men, and the Perception of Reality." *Sociometry* 24 (1961): 279–94.

Neumann, Von J., and Morgenstern, O. *Theory of Games and Economics Behavior.* Princeton, N.J.: Princeton University Press, 1947.

Newcomb, T. M., and Hartly, E., eds. *Readings in Social Psychology.* New York: Holt, Rinehart and Winston, 1958.

New Hampshire Report of the Interim Commission to Study the Causes and Prevention of Serious Sex Crimes. Concord, 1949.

Newman, D. J. "The Effect of Accommodation in Justice Administration on Criminal Statistics." *Sociology and Social Research* 46 (1962): 144–55.

———. "Pleading Guilty for Consideration: A Study of Bargain in Justice." *Journal of Criminal Law, Criminology, and Police Science* 46 (1956): 780–90.

Normandeau, A. *Trends and Patterns in Crime of Robbery: Philadelphia, Pa. 1960–66.* Ph.D. dissertation, University of Pennsylvania, 1967.

Noskitz, J. D. "The Meaning of the Car." In Solvenko, *Sexual Behavior and the Law,* pp. 204–9.

"Note: Legal Disposition of Sexual Psychopaths." *University of Pennsylvania Law Journal* 96 (1948): 872–77.

"Note: Mental Deterioration among Sex Offenders." *Journal of Criminal Law, Criminology* 34 (1941): 184–85.

Nye, F. I., et al. "Socio-economic Status and Delinquent Behavior." *The American Journal of Sociology* 63 (1958): 381–89.

Oltman, J. E., and Freedman, S. "Acute Heterosexual Inadequacy." *Psychiatric Quarterly* 12 (1938): 664–68.

Palsley, N. "The Hustler." *Social Problem,* vol. 12. 1964.

Pamelee, M. *Criminology.* New York: The Macmillan Co., 1919.

Parsons, T. "Age and Sex in the Social Structure of the United States." *The American Sociological Review* 7 (1942): 604–12.

———. "Youth in the Context of American Society." *Daedalus* 91 (1962): 97–123.

Parsons, T., et al. *Theories of Society.* New York: The Free Press of Glencoe, 1961.

———. *Working Papers in the Theory of Action.* Glencoe, Ill.: The Free Press, 1953.

Parsons, T., and Bales, R. F. "The Dimension of Action Space." In Parsons, *Working Papers in Theory of Action,* pp. 63–109.

Parsons, T., and Shils, R., eds. *Toward a General Theory of Action.* Cambridge, Mass. Harvard University Press, 1951.

Partridge, B. *The History of Orgies.* New York: Crown Publishers, 1960.

Pasco, H. "Deviate Sexual Behavior and the Sex Criminal." *Canadian Medical Association Journal* 84 (1961): 206–11.

Pearson, H. J. *Emotional Disorders in Children.* New York: W. W. Norton, 1944.

Pennsylvania Criminal Law and Criminal Procedure, section 721, "Rape." Hershey, Penn.: State Public Civic Association, 1958.

Pennsylvania Law Encyclopedia. Philadelphia: G. T. Bisel Co., 1960.

Pennsylvania Sex Offenders: A Report of the Joint State Commission to the General Assembly. Harrisburg, 1951.

Perkins, R. N. "The Law of Homicide." *Journal of Criminal Law and Criminology* 36 (1946): 401–8.

Peto, P. O. "The Taking of Statements from Victims and Witnesses of Sexual Offenses." *The Criminal Law Review* (1960): pp. 86–88.

Petterson, M., et al. *Legal Medicine and Toxology,* Philadelphia: W. B. Saunders, 1948.

Pettigrew, T. *A Profile of the Negro American.* Princeton, N.J.: Van Nostrand, 1964.

Pfoutz, H. W. "Near Group Theory and Collective Behavior: A Critical Reformulation." *Social Problems* 9 (1961): 167–71.

Philadelphia City Planning Commission. *Philadelphia Population by Race, 1960–1961.* City of Philadelphia, January 1967.

Piatrowsky, A. Z., and Abrahamsen, D. "Sexual Crime, Alcohol, and the Rorschach Test." *The Psychiatric Quarterly* (suppl.) 26 (1952): 248–60.

Piker, P. "The Psychiatrist Looks at Sex Offenders." *Journal of Social Hygiene* 33 (1947): 392–97.

Pitt, J. R. "The Definition of the Situation and the Internalization of Object." In Parsons, et al., *Theories of Society,* vol. 2, pp. 719–43.

Pittman, D. J., and Gordon, C. W., *The Revolving Door.* Glencoe, Ill.: The Free Press, 1958.

Plant, J. S., *The Envelope: A Study of the Impact of the World upon the Child.* New York: The Commonwealth Fund, 1950.

———. "Understanding Sex Delinquency." *National Probation and Parole Association Journal* (1932–33), pp. 203–11.

Ploscowe, M. *Crime and Criminology.* New York: Collier, 1939.

———. *Sex and the Law.* New York: Prentice Hall, 1951.

———. "Sex Offenses: The American Legal Context." *Law and Contemporary Problems* 25 (1960): 225–71.

Pollak, J. "Postmortem Examination in Cases of Suspected Rape." *American Journal of Clinical Pathology* 13 (1943): 309–14.

Pollens, B. *The Sexual Criminal.* New York: McCall, 1938.

Polsby, N. "The Hustler," *Social Problems* 12 (1964): 3–15.

Porterfield, A. L. "Sexual Psychopaths, Psychiatrists, and the Court." *Journal of Criminal Law and Criminology* 38 (1947): 55–66.

Porterfield, A. L., and Salley, E. H. "Current Folkways of Sexual Behavior." *American Journal of Sociology* 52 (1946): 209–16.

The President's Commission on Law Enforcement and the Administration of Justice. Washington: Government Printing Office, 1967.

The Problem of the Sex Offender: A Symposium. Montgomery County Mental Health Clinics, 1962.

Purdon's Pennsylvania Statutes Annotated. Philadelphia: George T. Bisel Co., 1963.

Puttkammer, R. W. "Consent in Rape." *Illinois Law Review* 19 (1925): 410–28.

Quetelet, A. *Lettres à S. A. R. Le Duc Régnant de Saxe-Cobourg et Gotha. Sur la théorie des probabilités aux Science Morales et politiques.* Brussels, 1846.

Rabban, M. "Sex Identification in Young Children in Two Diverse Social Groups." *Genetic Psychological Monographs* 42 (1952): 91–158.

Rabinovitch, R. D. "Sexual Psychopath." *American Journal of Orthopsychiatry* 43 (1953): 610–21.

Rado, S. "Emergency Behavior." In P. C. Hoch and J. Zubin, *Anxiety.* New York: Grune and Stratton, 1950, pp. 150–79.

Radzinowicz, L., ed. "English Criminal Statistics: A Criminal Analysis." In *Modern Approach to Criminal Law.* London, 1948.

———. *In Search of Criminology.* Cambridge, Mass.: Harvard University Press, 1962.

———. *Sexual Offenses.* London: Macmillan, 1957.

Rainwater, L. *And the Poor Get Children.* Chicago: Quadrangle Books, 1960.

"Rape Allegations of Force." *Michigan Law Review* 21 (1923): 801–7.

"Rape: Physical Examination." *Columbia Law Review* 20 (1920): 674–75.

Ravenscraft, D. R. "Examination of Nebraska Statutes of the Sexual Criminal." *Nebraska Law Review* 29 (1950): 506–51.

"Recent Legislation: Pennsylvania New Sex Crime Act." *University of Pennsylvania Law Review* 100 (1952): 827–56.

Reckless, W. C. *The Crime Problem.* New York: Appleton-Century-Crofts, 1950.

———. "A New Theory of Delinquency and Crime." *Federal Probation* 25 (1961): 42–46.

Reckless, W. C.; Dinitz, S.; and Murray, E. "The Good Boy in a High Delinquency Area." *Journal of Criminal Law, Criminology, and Police Science* 48 (1957): 18–25.

——. "Self Concept as an Insulator against Delinquency." *American Sociological Review* 21 (1956): 744–46.

Redl, F. "Group Emotion and Leadership." *Psychiatry* 4 (1942): 573–96.

——. "The Psychology of Gang Formation and the Treatment of Juvenile Delinquents." *Psychoanalytic Study of the Child,* vol. 1, pp. 367–77. New York: International Universities Press, 1945.

——. "The Phenomenon of Group Contagion and Shock Effect in Group Therapy." In Eissler, *Searchlight on Delinquency,* pp. 315–28.

Redl, F., and Wineman, D. *The Aggressive Child.* Glencoe, Ill.: The Free Press, 1957.

——. *Children Who Hate: The Disorganization and Breakdown of Behavior Control.* Glencoe, Ill.: The Free Press, 1951.

Reid, I. D. A. "A Study of 200 Negro Prisoners in the Western Penitentiary of Pennsylvania." *Opportunity* 3 (1925): 168–74.

Reiff, F. *Freud: The Mind of the Moralist.* New York: Rinehart, 1943.

Reik, T. *The Psychology of Sex Relations.* New York: Rinehart, 1943.

Reinhardt, J. M. "The Gentle Sex Murderer." *Police* 1 (March and April 1957): 12–14.

——. *Sex Perversions and Sex Crimes.* Springfield, Ill.: Charles C. Thomas, 1957.

——. "The Sex Killer." *Police* 5 (1961): 1–3.

Reinhardt, J. M., and Fisher, E. C. "The Sexual Psychopath and the Law." *Journal of Criminal Law and Criminology* 39 (1949): 734–42.

Reiss, A. J. "Delinquency and the Failure of Personal and Social Control." *The American Sociological Review* 26 (1951): 196–207.

——. "Sex Offenses: The Marginal Status of the Adolescent." *Law and Contemporary Problems* 25 (1960): 309–34.

——. "Sexual Code in a Teen-Age Culture." *The Annals of the American Academy of Political and Social Science* 388 (1961): 53–63.

Reiss, I. L. *Premarital Sexual Standards in America.* Glencoe, Ill.: The Free Press, 1960.

——. "Sociological Studies of Sexual Standards." In Winakur, *Determinants of Human Sexual Behavior,* pp. 101–42.

Report of the Mayor's Committee for the Study of Sex Offenses. New York, 1940.

Report on the Study of 102 Sex Offenders at Sing-Sing Prison. Albany, N.Y.: New York State Hospital Press, 1950.

Reuter, E. B. *The American Race Problem.* New York: Crimwell, 1927.

Revitch, E., and Weiss, R., "The Pedophilia Offender." *Disease and Nervous System* 23 (1962): 73–78.

Riesman, D.; Denney, R.; and Glazer, N. *The Lonely Crowd.* New Haven: Yale University Press, 1950.

Rife, D. W. "Scientific Evidence in Rape Cases." *Journal of Criminal Law and Criminology* 31 (1940): 232–35.

Robin, G. D. "Patterns of Department Store Shoplifting." *Crime and Delinquency* 9 (1963): 163–73.

Robinson, W. S. "Biological Correlates and Behavior of Individuals." *The American Sociological Review* 15 (1950): 351–57.

Robison, S. M. *Can Delinquency be Measured?* New York: Columbia University Press, 1936.

Roche, P. Q. "Sexual Deviation." *Federal Probation* 14 (1950): 3–11.

Rodman, H. "Controversies over Lower-Class Culture: Delinquency and Illegitimacy." *Canadian Review of Sociology and Anthropology* 5 (1967): 254–62.

Roebuck, J. B. "The Negro Numbers Man As a Criminal Type: The Construction and Application of a Typology." *Journal of Criminal Law, Criminology, and Police Science* 54 (1963): 48–60.

Roeburt, J. *Sex Life and the Criminal Law.* New York: Belmont Books, 1963.

Rofer, W. F. "Survey of Wakefield Prison Population, 1948–1949." *The British Journal of Delinquency* 5 (1950): 245–53.

Rosaneff, A. J. "Human Sexuality: Normal and Abnormal from Psychiatric Standpoint." *Urology and Cutaneous Review* 33 (1929): 523–30.

Rose, A. M., ed. *Human Behavior and Social Processes.* New York: Houghton Mifflin, 1966.

Rosen, L. "Matriarchy and Lower-Class Negro Male Delinquency." *Social Problems* 17 (1969): 175–89.

Roth, N. "Factors in the Motivation of Sexual Offenders." *Journal of Criminal Law, Criminology and Police Science* 42 (1952): 631–35.

Rottman, D. R. "Alcoholism and Crime." *Federal Probation* 11 (1947): 31–33.

Roucek, J. S., ed. *Sociology of Crime.* New York: Philosophical Library, 1961.

Rowe, M. J. "Alcohol and Crime." *Journal of Delinquency* 4 (1919): 135–51.

Rubinstein, L. H. "Sexual Motivation in Ordinary Offenses." In Slovenko, *Sexual Behavior and the Law,* pp. 604–27.

Ruskin, S. H. "Analysis of Sex Offenders among Male Psychiatric Patients." *American Journal of Psychiatry* 97 (1941): 955–68.

Salisbury, H. E. *The Shook-up Generation.* New York: Harper and Bros., 1958.

Sanger, W. W. *The History of Prostitution: Its Extent, Causes and Effects throughout the World.* New York: Eugenics Pub. Co., 1937.

Saul, L. J. *Emotional Maturity.* Philadelphia: J. B. Lippincott, 1947.

Savitz, L. D. "Crime and the Negro: A Critical Review of the Literature." Hectograph. Philadelphia Department of Sociology, Temple University, 1962.

Savitz, L. D., and Lief, H. I. "Negro and White Sex Crime Rates." In Slovenko, *Sexual Behavior and the Law,* pp. 210–20.

Schacter, S. *The Psychology of Affiliation: Experimental Studies of the Sources of Gregariousness.* Stanford: Stanford University Press, 1959.

Schafer, S. *The Victim and His Criminal: A Study in Functional Responsibility.* New York: Random House, 1968.

Schafer, S., and Geis, G. "Forcible Rape: A Comparative Study of Offenses Known to the Police in Boston and Los Angeles, 1967." A paper presented at the Annual Meeting of the American Sociological Association, September, 1969.

Schapper, B. "The Best Defense against Sex Perverts." *Today's Health* 36 (1958): 28–29.

Scheidlinger, S. "Freudian Concepts of Group Relations." In Cartwright and Zander, *Group Dynamics: Research and Theory,* pp. 52–61.

———. *Psychoanalysis and Group Behavior.* New York: W. W. Norton & Co., 1952.

Schmid, C. F. *Social Saga of Two Cities: An Ecological Statistical Study of the Social Trends in Minneapolis and St. Paul.* Minneapolis: Minneapolis Council of Social Agencies, 1937.

———. "Urban Crime Areas: Part I." *American Sociological Review* 25 (1960): 527–42.

Schmolhausen, S. M. "Freud and the Sexual Revolution." *Journal of Abnormal and Social Psychology* 25 (1930): 299–306.

Schor, E. M. *Crimes without Victims.* Englewood Cliffs, N.J.: Prentice-Hall, 1965.

Schorr, J. K. "Violence in Juvenile Gangs." *American Journal of Orthopsychiatry* 33 (1963): 29–37.

Schroeder, B. C. "Criminal Behavior in the Later Period of Life." *American Journal of Psychiatry* 92 (1936): 915–24.

Schuessler, K. F., and Cressey, D. R. "Personality Characteristics of Criminals." *The American Journal of Sociology* 55 (1950): 476–84.

Schultz, L. G. "Interviewing the Sex Offender's Victim." *Journal of Criminal Law, Criminology, and Police Science* 50 (1960): 448–52.

Schutz, A. "The Problem of Social Reality." In *Collected Papers,* vol. 1. The Hague: Martinus Nijhoff, 1962.

Schwartz, B., and Post, R. S., "The Effect in Philadelphia, Pennsylvania's Increased Penalties for Rape and Attempted Rape." *Journal of Criminal Law and Criminology and Police Sciences* 59 (1968): 509–15.

Scrapitti, F. R., et al. "The Good Boy in a High Delinquency Area: Four Years Later." *The American Sociological Review* 25 (1960): 255–68.

Sears, R. R., et al. *Patterns of Child Rearing.* Evanston, Ill.: Row Peterson and Co., 1957.

Seeman, M., and Morris, R. T., "The Problem of Leadership." *Social Forces* 56 (1950): 149–55.

Segal, J. "Notes on Symbolic Formation." *International Journal of Psychoanalysis* 30 (1958): 391.

Seliger, R. V. "Alcohol and Crime." *Journal of Criminal Law, Criminology, and Police Science* 44 (1953): 438–41.

Sellin, T. "Crime and Delinquency in the U.S.: An Overall View." *The Annals of the American Academy of Political and Social Science* 339 (1962): 11–24.

———. "Culture Conflict and Crime." *Social Science Research Council Bulletin,* 1938.

———. "The Basis of Crime Index." *Journal of Criminal Law and Criminology* 22 (1931): 335–56.

———. "The Negro Criminal: A Statistical Note." *The Annals of the American Academy of Political and Social Science* 140 (1928): 52–64.

———. "The Significance of Records of Crime." *Law Quarterly Review* 47 (1951): 489–504.

———. "The Sociological Study of Criminality." *Journal of Criminal Law and Criminology* 41 (1950): 406–22.

———. "Race Prejudice and the Administration of Justice." *The American Journal of Sociology* 41 (1935): 212–17.

———. *Research Memorandum on Crime in the Depression.* New York: Social Science Research Council, 1937.

Sellin, T., and Wolfgang, M. E. *The Measurement of Delinquency.* New York: John Wiley and Sons, 1964.

Selling, L. S. "Results of Therapy of Cases of Sex Deviates." *Journal of Criminal Psychopathology* 3 (1949): 477–93.

———. "Significant Factors in the Study and Treatment of Sex Offenders." *Medical Records and Circulation* 149 (1934): 173–75.

Selvin, H. C. "Durkheim's Suicide and Problems of Empirical Research." *The American Journal of Sociology* 63 (1958): 607–19.

Selznick, P. *Leadership in Administration.* Evanston, Ill.: Row, Peterson and Co., 1957.

Seward, G. H. *Sex and the Social Order.* New York: McGraw-Hill, 1946.

Shaw, C. *Brothers in Crime.* Chicago: University of Chicago Press, 1938.

Shaw, C. R., and McKay, H. D. *Delinquency Area.* Chicago: University of Chicago Press, 1929.

Sheldon, H. D. "A Comparative Study of the Non-Whites and White Institutional Population in the U.S." *Journal of Negro Education* 22 (1933): 355–62.

Sherif, M., and Cantril, H. *The Psychology of Ego-involvement.* New York: John Wiley and Sons, 1947.

Sherif, M., and Sherif, C. W. *Reference Groups.* New York: Harper and Row, 1964.

Shiver, J. "Negro Crime." *Comparative Psychological Monographs* 16 (1940): no. 81.

Shoenfield, A. "The Sex Criminal: A Report of 16 Articles Representing the Consensus of Authorities Relative to the Development of Deviate Sex Behavior." Detroit News, 1950.

Short, J. F., Jr. "The Sociological Context of Delinquency." *Crime and Delinquency* 6 (1960): 365–75.

———. "Gang Delinquency and Anomie." In Clinard, *Anomie and Deviant Behavior: A Discussion and Critique,* pp. 98–128. New York: The Free Press of Glencoe, 1964.

———. "Research in Delinquent Subcultures." *The Journal of Social Issues* 24 (1958): 20–37.

———. "Street Corner Groups and Patterns of Delinquency: A Progress Report." *American Catholic Sociological Review* 24 (1963): 12–32.

Short, J. F., Jr., and Nye, F. I., "Extent of Unrecorded Criminality." *Journal of Criminal Law, Criminology and Police Science* 49 (1958): 296–302.

Short, J. F., Jr., and Strodtbeck, F. L. "Responses of Gang Leaders to Status Threats." *American Journal of Sociology* 68 (1963): 517–79.

Short, J. F., Jr., et al. "Perceived Opportunities, Gang Membership and Delinquency." *The American Sociological Review* 30 (1965): 56–68.

———. "Values and Gang Delinquency." *The American Journal of Sociology* 69 (1963): 109–28.

Short, J. F., Jr.; Strodtbeck, F. L.; and Cartwright, D. C. "A Strategy for Utilizing Research Dilemmas: A Case from the Study of Parenthood in Street-Corner Gangs." *Sociological Inquiry* 32 (1962): 185–202.

"Should Sexual Psychopaths Be Subjected to Bail?" *Chicago-Kent Law Review* 30 (1952): 160–63.

Shupe, L. M. "Alcohol and Crime." *Journal of Criminal Law, Criminology, and Police Science* 44 (1954): 660–65.

Sievert, R. "The Evolution of Sexual Criminality in Germany." In Grunhüt, *Sexual Crime Today.* The Hague: The University of Lieden, 1960.

Simmel, G. "The Number of Members as Determining the Sociological Form of the Group." *The American Journal of Sociology* 8 (1902–3): 1–46, 158–96.

———. *The Sociology of George Simmel.* Translated by K. H. Wolff. Glencoe, Ill.: The Free Press, 1950.

Simpson, J. "Medical Legal Aspects of Rape." In *Reference Handbook of the Medical Sciences,* New York, 1917.

Simpson, J. E., and Van Arsdol, M. D. "Residential History and Educational States of Delinquents and Nondelinquents." *Social Problems* 15 (1967): 25–40.

Skolnick, J. H., and Woodworth, J. R. "Bureaucracy Information and Social Control: A Study of a Morals Detail." In Bordua, *The Police,* pp. 99–137.

Slavson, S. R. *Analytic Group Psychotherapy.* New York: Columbia University Press, 1956.

Slovenko, R., ed. *Sexual Behavior and the Law.* Springfield, Ill.: Charles C. Thomas, 1965.

Slovenko, R., and Philips, C. "Psychosexuality and the Criminal Law." *Vanderbilt Law Review* 15 (1961–62): 797–878.

Smelser, N. J. *Theory of Collective Behavior.* New York: The Free Press of Glencoe, 1963.

Smith, M. "Leadership: The Management of Social Differentials." *Journal of Abnormal and Social Psychology* 31 (1936): 348.

Sorokin, P. *The American Sexual Revolution.* Boston, Mass.: Porter Sargent Pub., 1956.

"The Spectral Epidemic of Sex Offenses: A Comment." *The American Journal of Psychiatry* 108 (1951): 629–30.

Spencer, J. C. "Contribution to the Symposium on Sexual Deviation." *Canada Journal of Correction* 3 (1961): 481–85.

Spergel, I. *Racketville, Slumtown, Haulburg.* Chicago: University of Chicago Press, 1964.

Sperling, O. E. "Psychodynamics of Group Perversion." *Psychoanalytic Quarterly* 25 (1956): 56–65.

Spirer, F. "Negro Crimes." *Comparative Psychological Monographs,* vol. 16, no. 8, 1940.

Stein, H. S., and Cloward, R. S. *Social Perspectives on Behavior.* Glencoe, Ill.: The Free Press, 1958.

Stekel, W. *Sexual Aberration,* vols. 1 and 2. New York: Liveright Pub. Co., 1930.

Stern, M. "Facts of Sex Offenses against Children." *Parents Magazine* 29 (1954): 42–43.

Stern, R. S. "Components and Stereotypes in Ecological Analysis of Social Problems." *Urban Affairs Quarterly* 3 (1967): 3–22.

Strodtbeck, F. L., and Short, J. F., Jr. "Aleatory Risks vs. Short-run Hedonism in Explaining Gang Actions." *Social Problems* 12 (1964): 127–41.

Stogdill, R. M. *Individual Behavior and Group Achievement.* New York: Oxford University Press, 1959.

————. "Leadership, Membership and Organization." *Psychological Bulletin* 47 (1950): 1–14.

Stott, D. H. "Spotting the Delinquency-Prone Child." *Howard Journal* 10 (1959): 87–95.

Stürup, G. K. "Sexual Offenders and Their Treatment in Denmark and Other Scandinavian Countries." *International Review of Criminal Policy.* U. N. Social Welfare, 1953.

Sudnow, D. "Normal Crimes: Sociological Measures of the Penal Code in a Public Defender Office." *Social Problems* 3 (1946): 255–76.

Sullivan, W. C. "The Criminality of Alcoholism." In Ketznechz *The Drinking Problem,* pp. 189–98.

Sutherland, D. E. "Medical Evidence of Rape." *Canadian Medical Association Journal* 81 (1959): 407–8.

Sutherland, E. H. "The Diffusion of Sexual Psychopath Laws." *The American Journal of Sociology* 56 (1950): 142–48.

————. *The Professional Thief.* Chicago: University of Chicago Press, 1937.

————. "The Sexual Psychopath Laws." *Journal of Criminal Law and Criminology,* 40 (1950): 443–53.

————. *White Collar Crime.* New York: Dryden Press, 1949.

Sutherland, E. H., and Cressey, D. R. *Criminology,* 4th ed. Philadelphia: J. B. Lippincott, 1947.

————. *Criminology,* 5th ed. Philadelphia: J. B. Lippincott, 1955.

Svalastoga, K. "Rape and Social Structure." *Pacific Sociological Review* 5 (1962): 48–53.

Sykes, G. M., and Matza, D. "Techniques of Neutralization: A Theory of Delinquency." *The American Sociological Review* 22 (1957): 664–70.

Symonds, J. *The Great Beast.* New York: Roy Publishers, 1952.

Syvrud, G. A. "The Victim of Robbery." Ph.D. dissertation, University of Washington, Seattle, 1967.

Szasz, T. S. *Law, Liberty and Psychiatry.* New York: Basic Books, 1964.

————. *The Myth of Mental Illness.* New York: Harper, 1961.

Taft, D. R. *Criminology,* 3d ed. New York: The Macmillan Press, 1956.

————. "Testing the Selective Influences of Areas of Delinquency." *American Journal of Sociology* 48 (1942): 202–312.

Tappan, P. W. *The Habitual Sex Offender.* New Jersey, 1950.

————. "The Sexual Psychopath—Civic Social Responsibility." *Journal of Social Hygiene* 35 (1949): 354–73.

———. "Sentences for Sex Criminals." *Journal of Criminal Law, Criminology*, 42 (1951): 332–37.

———. "Some Myths about Sex Offenders." *Federal Probation* 19 (1955): 7–12.

———. "Who is the Criminal?" *The American Sociological Review* 12 (1947): 96–102.

———. *Crime, Justice and Correction*. New York: McGraw-Hill, 1965.

Tarde, G. *Penal Philosophy*, 3d ed. Boston: Little, Brown and Company, 1912.

Thibout, J. W., and Riecken, H. W. "Authoritarianism, Status and Communication of Aggression." *Human Relations* 8 (1955): 95–120.

Thomas, W. I. *The Unadjusted Girl*. Boston: Little, Brown and Company, 1923.

Thompson, G. N. "Electroshock and Other Therapeutic Considerations in Sexual Psychopathology." *Journal of Nervous and Mental Diseases* 109 (1949): 531–34.

———. "Legal Aspects of Pathological Intoxication." *Journal of Social Therapy* 2 (1956): 82–87.

Thrasher, F. M. *The Gang*. Chicago: University of Chicago Press, 1927.

Toobert, S.; Bartelmea, K.; and Jones, E. "Some Factors Related to Pedophilia." *International Journal of Psychiatry* 4 (1958): 272–79.

Trankel, F. M. "Was Lars Sexually Assaulted: The Reliability of Witnesses and Experts." *Journal of Abnormal and Social Psychology* 56 (1956): 385–95.

Trasler, G. *The Explanation of Criminality*. London: Routledge and Kegan Paul, 1962.

———. "Strategic Problems in the Study of Criminal Behavior." *The British Journal of Criminology* 4 (1964): 422–42.

Turk, A. T. "Prospects for Theories of Criminal Behavior." *Journal of Criminal Law, Criminology and Police Science* 55 (1965): 454–561.

Turner, J. D. "Differential Punishment in a Bi-racial Community." Master's thesis, Indiana University, 1948.

Turner, R. H. "Role Taking: Process versus Conformity." In Rose, *Human Behavior and Social Processes*, pp. 20–41.

Tyler, A. S. *Principles and Practice of Medical Jurisprudence*, 10th ed. London: J. A. Churchill, 1948.

Tylor, G. R. *Sex in History*. New York: Ballantine Books, 1954.

Uniform Crime Reports. Washington: United States Department of Justice, 1958, 1960, 1961.

United States Bureau of the Census. *United States Census of Population*, "I: Number of Inhabitants, United States Summary." 1950.

———. *United States Census of Population*, "III: Census Tract Statistics, chapter 42." 1960.

Van Doren, J. A. "Sociology and the Problem of Power." *Sociologio Neerlandica* 1 (1962): 1–46.

Van Vechten, C. C. "Differential Criminal Case Mortality in Selected Jurisdictions." *The American Sociological Review* 7 (1942): 833–39.

Verkko, V. *Homicide and Suicide in Finland and their Dependence on National Character*. Copenhagen. G. E. C. Gad Forlag, 1951.

Vincent, C. "Ego-Involvement in Sexual Relations." *The American Journal of Sociology* 65 (1959): 287–96.

———. *Unmarried Mothers*. Glencoe, Ill.: The Free Press, 1961.

Volberg, L. R. *Techniques of Psychotherapy*. New York: Grune and Stratton, 1954.

Vold, G. B. "Extent and Trends of Capital Crime in the United States." *The Annals of the American Academy of Political and Social Science* 284 (1952): 1–8.

———. *Theoretical Criminology*. New York: Oxford University Press, 1958.

Von Hentig, H. *Crime: Causes and Conditions*. New York: McGraw-Hill Publications, 1947.
──────. *The Criminal and His Victim*. New Haven: Yale University Press, 1948.
──────. "The Criminality of the Negro." *Journal of Criminal Law and Criminology* 39 (1948): 480–83.
──────. "Remarks on the Interaction of Perpetrator and Victim." *Journal of Criminal Law and Criminology* 31 (1940–41): 303–9.
──────. "The Sex Ratio." *Social Forces* 30 (1951): 443–49.
Von Kraft-Ebing, R. *Psychopathia Sexualis*. New York: Pioneer Publications, 1941.
Von Neumann, J., and Morgenstern, D. *Theory of Games and Economic Behavior*. Princeton, N.J.: Princeton University Press, 1947.
Voss, H. L. "Insulation and Vulnerability to Delinquency: A Comparison of the Hawaiians and Japanese." Ph.D. dissertation, University of Wisconsin, Madison, 1961.
Waggoner, W. R., and Bond, D. A. "Juvenile Aberrant Sexual Behavior." *American Journal of Orthopsychiatry* 11 (1941): 275–92.
Walbarst, A. L. "Sexual Perversion." *Medical Journal and Record* 134 (1931): 5–9, 62–65.
Walker, K., and Straus, E. R. *Sexual Disorder in the Male*. Baltimore: The Williams Company, 1939.
Waller, W. "Dating and Rating Complex." *The American Sociological Review* 2 (1937): 724–34.
Wallerstein, J. S., and Wyle, C. J. "Our Law-abiding Law Breakers." *Federal Probation* 25 (1947): 107–12.
Weber, M. *Theory of Social and Economic Organization*. Glencoe, Ill.: Free Press, 1947.
──────. "Three Types of Legitimate Rule." In Weber, *The Theory of Social and Economic Organization,* pp. 328–30.
Wecksler, H. "On the Culpability and Crime." *The Annals of the American Academy of Political and Social Science,* vol. 339 (1962).
Weihofen, H. *Mental Disorder As a Criminal Defense*. Buffalo, New York: Dennis and Company, 1954.
Weinstein, J. B. "The Law's Attempt to Obtain Useful Testimony." *The Journal of Social Issues* 13 (1957): 6–12.
Weisse, J. "The Study of Girls' Sex Victims." *Psychiatric Quarterly* 29 (1955): 87–96.
Wenger, P. A. "A Comparative Study of 800 Temperate and Intemperate Inmates of a Penal Institution." *New York State Medical Journal* 45 (1945): 1531–36.
Wertham, F. "Psychiatry and Sex Crimes." *Journal of Criminal Law and Criminology* 38 (1938): 847–53.
Westley, W. "Violence and the Police." *American Journal of Sociology* 59 (1953): 39–41.
Wheeler, S. "Criminal Statistics: The Reformulation of the Problem." *Journal of Criminal Law, Criminology and Police Science* 58 (1967): 317–24.
Wheeler, S. "Sex Offenses: A Sociological Critique." *Law and Contemporary Problems* 25 (1960): 258–79.
White, C. "The Relation of Felonies to Environmental Factors in Indianapolis." *Social Forces* 10 (1932): 408–513.
Whitman, H. *The Sex Age*. New York: Doubleday, 1962.
Whiting, W., and Child, I. L. *Child Training and Personality*. New Haven: Yale University Press, 1953.
Whyte, W. F. "A Slum Sex Code." *The American Journal of Sociology* 49 (1943): 24–31.
──────. *Street Corner Society*. Chicago: University of Chicago Press, 1955.

Wichsler, H. "On the Culpability and Crime." *The Annals of the American Academy of Political and Social Science* 339 (1962): 33–34.

Wile, I. S. "The Sexual Conduct of Adolescents." *Social Hygiene* 20 (1934): 429–41.

———. "The Sexual Problems of Adolescents." *Social Hygiene* 20 (1934): 429–41.

———. "Sex Offenders and Sex Offenses, Classification and Treatment." *Journal of Criminal Psychopathology* 3 (1941): 11–31.

———. "Sex Offenses against Young Victims." *Journal of Mental Hygiene* 3 (1941): 11–31.

Wile, W. F. "Case Study of a Rapist: An Analysis of the Causation of Criminal Behavior." *Journal of Social Therapy* 7 (1961): 10–21.

Williams, A. H. "A Psychoanalytic Approach to the Treatment of the Murderer." *International Journal of Psychoanalysis* 41 (1960): 532–39.

Williams, J. B. "Where is the Reign of Terror?" United States Congress House of Representatives, 84th Congress, 2d Session, Washington, D.C., March 27, 1932.

Wilson, H. C. "Juvenile Delinquency in Problem Families in Cardiff." *British Journal of Delinquency* 99 (1958): 94–105.

Wilson, J. B., and Pescore, M. J. *Problems of Prison Psychiatry.* Idaho: Caxton Printing, 1932.

Winakur, G. *Determinants of Human Sexual Behavior.* Springfield, Ill.: Charles C. Thomas, 1963.

Winkler, E. G., et al. "Alcoholism and Anti-social Behavior: Statistical Analysis." *Psychiatric Quarterly* (suppl.) 28 (1954): 242–54.

Wisconsin's Experience with Its Sex Deviation Law: A Statistical Picture, 1951–56. State of Wisconsin, Department of Public Welfare, Statistical Bulletin C-17, Mimeo, 1957.

Witman, H. *The Sex Age.* New York: Doubleday, 1962.

Witteles, D. G. "What Can We Do about Sex Crimes?" *Saturday Evening Post* (11 December 1948), p. 104.

Wolfgang, M. E. *Patterns in Criminal Homicide.* Philadelphia: University of Pennsylvania Press, 1958.

———. "Uniform Crime Reports: A Critical Appraisal." *University of Pennsylvania Law Review* 111 (1963): 711–38.

———. "Victim-precipitated Criminal Homicide." *Journal of Criminal Law, Criminology and Police Science* 48 (1957): 1–11.

———. "Volume of Sexual Offenses." In *Symposium on the Sexual Criminal at the College of Physicians, April, 1960.* Pennsylvania Mental Health, 1960.

Wolfgang, M. E., et al. *The Sociology of Crime and Delinquency.* New York: John Wiley and Sons, 1962.

———. *Crime and Race: Conceptions and Misconceptions.* New York: American Jewish Congress, Institute of Human Relations Press, 1964.

Wolfgang, M. E., and Ferracuti, F. "Subculture of Violence: An Introductive Analysis of Homicide." Paper presented at the 1960 Annual Meeting of American Sociological Association (New York: 29–31, August, 1960).

———. "Violent Aggressive Behavior as a Socio-Psychological Phenomenon," Paper presented at the Annual Meeting of the American Society of Criminology, Cleveland, Ohio, December 29, 1963.

Wolfstein, M. "Fun Morality." In Mead and Wolfstein, *Childhood and Contemporary Culture,* pp. 168–78.

Wood, A. C. *Crime and Aggression in Changing Ceylon.* Transaction of the American Philosophical Society, no. 8:51, part 8, Dec. 1961.

Wood, A. L. "Minority Group Criminality and Cultural Integration." *Journal of Criminal Law and Criminology* 37 (1946–47): 498–510.

Wood, F. J. *Cultural Values of American Ethnic Groups.* New York: Harpers, 1956.

Wooton, B. *Crime and the Criminal Law*. London: Stevens and Sons, 1963.
——. *Social Science and Social Pathology*. London: George Allen and Unwin, 1959.
Work, N. N. "Negro Criminality in the South." *The Annals of the American Academy of Political and Social Science* 49 (1913): 74–81.
Wortis, J. "Sex Taboos, Sex Offenders and the Law." *American Journal of Orthopsychiatry* 9 (1939): 554–64.
Wyeheart, M. K. "Newspapers and Criminal Justice." In *Criminal Justice, in Cleveland*, Cleveland Foundation (1927), pp. 544–46.
Yablonsky, L. "The Delinquent Gang as a Near-Group." *Social Problems* 7 (1959): 108–13.
——. *The Violent Gang*. New York: The Macmillan Co., 1962.
Yinger, J. H., Jr. "Contra-culture and Sub-culture." *The American Sociological Review* 25 (1960): 624–35.
Zilboorg, G. *The Psychology of the Criminal Act and Its Punishment*. New York: Harcourt and Brace, 1954.

Name Index

Subject Index

temporal patterns, 14; victim behavior, 164; victim-offender relationships, 16–17, 234, 238, 240, 242–43,
245–46, 248; victim-precipitated rape,
17, 264; violence, 14. *See also*
Significant associations

Ideological rapist, 328
Illegitimate opportunity, 186
Incest, 8, 31, 33, 230, 307
Indecent assault, 37
Interpersonal relationships: acquaintance, 233, 234, 235, 236, 238, 239,
240, 242, 243, 245, 246, 248, 249, 250;
close friend, 233, 235, 236, 238, 239,
245; close neighbor, 233, 235, 236, 238,
239, 245; family friend, 233, 235, 236,
239; friend or boyfriend, 233, 235, 236,
237, 239; intimate relations, 235, 236,
238, 239, 240, 242, 243, 248; primary
contact, 234; primary relation, 234,
235, 236, 237, 238, 242, 243, 245,
246, 248; relative, 233, 235, 237, 239;
secondary relations, 234; stranger,
233, 235, 236, 238, 239, 245, 246,
248, 250, 251. *See also* Significant
associations; Victim-offender
relationships
Initial interaction. *See* Initial meeting
place; Place of rape, and group rape
Initial meeting place: classification of,
138–39, 141–42; in group rape, 212–
13; noted in other studies, 138–39;
by race, 139–40; and victim-offender
relations, 240–41; in victim-precipitated cases, 269, 272–73
Initiatory acts. *See* Group rape;
Leadership in group rape
Insanity, 262–63
Insulation theory, 263
Intellectual rapist (libertine), 317, 318
Interracial rapes. *See* Race, forcible
rape by
Investigation. *See* Police
Irresistible impulse, 262
Italy, 79

Juvenile delinquency, and group rape,
185–91
Juvenile rape, and previous record,
113–17

Kansas City, 36

Labelling, 4
Law of forcible rape: and age of offender, 17, 18; and alcohol, 97; and

consent, 18, 161–65, 230; and evidence, 18–19, 163–64; and the concept
of force, 19; and felony rape, 178–79;
and situational elements, 18, 25, 130–
31, 133–35, 140–41, 264–66; and
victim-precipitated rape, 264–66
Leadership in group rape: and alcohol,
208–9; characteristics of, 195–99;
definitions of, 195–99; and initiatory
acts, 197–99, 220–23; and magical
seduction, 197–99, 220–23; and nonphysical force, 220–22; and physical
force, 220–22; and sexual humiliation,
222–25; and theoretical considerations, 183–84, 186–87, 191, 195–99;
type of, 197–99; and victim-offender
relationships, 248–49. *See also* Group
rape; Significant associations
Legal procedure, tempo of, 333
Literary fiction, 7–8
Los Angeles, 36
Love relations vs. forcible rape, 256–57.
See also Vulnerable rape situations
Louisville, 30

Magical seduction, 197–99, 220–23. *See
also* Leadership in group rape
Marital status: by age, 62; noted in
other studies, 69; in Philadelphia,
61–63; by race, 61–63; and theory of
sex ratio, 63–68, 338
Maryland, 49
Masculinity, 190
Masochism, 172, 254, 295–96
Means and methods used. *See*
Nonphysical force; Physical force
(violence); Sexual humiliation;
Significant associations; Victim
behavior; Victim-offender relationships
Measurement, problems of, 8, 9, 26–39,
279–81; suggestions for research in,
332. *See also* Previous record;
Unsolved forcible rape
Medical report, 163–64, 176–77
Mens rea, 131, 140
Miami, 36
Minneapolis, 59
Mobility triangle. *See* Spatial patterns
Modus operandi: alcohol related to,
102–4; definition of, 135, 136–37;
phases of, 14, 135–37; suggestions
for research in, 331–33; theoretical
and legal basis for analysis, 14, 28–
29, 135–37; in victim-offender relationships, 242–45; and victim-
precipitated cases, 273–74. *See also*